Brian Koma

SAMS
Teach Yourself
TCP/IP Network
Administration
in 21 Days

SAMS

A Division of Macmillan Computer Publishing
201 West 103rd St., Indianapolis, Indiana, 46290 USA

Sams Teach Yourself TCP/IP Network Administration in 21 Days

Copyright© 1998 by Sams Publishing

International Standard Book Number: 0-672-31250-6

Library of Congress Catalog Card Number: 98-85199

Printed in the United States of America

First Printing: July, 1998

00 99 98   4   3   2   1

Trademarks

Dedication

To my family

EXECUTIVE EDITOR
Laurie Petrycki

ACQUISITIONS EDITOR
Sean Angus

DEVELOPMENT EDITOR
Jim Chalex

MANAGING EDITOR
Sarah Kearns

PROJECT EDITOR
Christopher Morris

COPY EDITOR
Amy Lepore

INDEXER
Joy Dean Lee

TECHNICAL EDITOR
Ron Scrimger

PRODUCTION
Terri Edwards
Brad Lenser
Donna Martin

Contents at a Glance

Contents

About the Author

BRIAN KOMAR is a trainer and consultant with Online Business Systems, a consulting firm developing complete, practical computer solutions. Brian holds a Bachelor of Commerce (Honours) degree and several professional designations, including Microsoft Certified Trainer (MCT), Fellow Life Management Institute (FLMI), and Microsoft Certified Systems Engineer (MCSE). Recently, he has added MCSE + Internet to his growing list of certifications.

Brian is active in leading-edge consulting work in network security, TCP/IP implementations, and firewall solutions. He has years of IT experience and business expertise in accounting and actuarial services. He continues to author technical books using real-life experience gathered from ongoing consulting projects.

Away from work, Brian enjoys spending time with his wife Krista and tries not to think about computers.

Acknowledgements

There are several people that I would like to thank who were directly or indirectly involved with the creation of this book.

Firstly, I would like to thank Laurie Petrycki, Jim Chalex, and Rob Scrimger for all of their assistance in the development of the book. Without their help, this book would not exist.

I would also like to thank Nancy Maragioglio, Sean Angus, and Stephanie Layton for bringing me onboard the Macmillan Computer Publishing team. It has been a great year working with the people at Macmillan.

I would also like to acknowledge three people who played a part in the development of my skills: Greg Matthew, Pat Gowryluk, and Malcolm Crooks. Greg taught me the fundamentals of computer science that have taken me to where I am today; Pat gave me my start in the IS industry; and it was Malcolm who saw my potential as a consultant when he hired me at Online Business Systems.

All of my students over the years deserve some credit for this book as well. It was through my attempts to find better ways to teach TCP/IP that they assisted in developing the material you see before you. On many occasions they were the "guinea pigs" as I tried new methods of teaching these topics.

Lastly, I would like to thank my wife Krista who put up with the endless hours of my writing this book.

Tell Us What You Think!

As the reader of this book, *you* are our most important critic and commentator. We value your opinion and want to know what we're doing right, what we could do better, what areas you'd like to see us publish in, and any other words of wisdom you're willing to pass our way.

As the Executive Editor for the Networking team at Macmillan Computer Publishing, I welcome your comments. You can fax, email, or write me directly to let me know what you did or didn't like about this book—as well as what we can do to make our books stronger.

Please note that I cannot help you with technical problems related to the topic of this book, and that due to the high volume of mail I receive, I might not be able to reply to every message.

When you write, please be sure to include this book's title and author as well as your name and phone or fax number. I will carefully review your comments and share them with the author and editors who worked on the book.

Fax: 317-581-4663

E-mail: networking@mcp.com

Mail: Executive Editor
         Networking
         Macmillan Computer Publishing
         201 West 103rd Street
         Indianapolis, IN 46290 USA

Introduction

Welcome to Teach Yourself TCP/IP Network Administration in 21 Days. This book will introduce you to many of the tasks and concepts that you will require administering a TCP/IP network. Much of the material in this book is based on the material that I have presented in classroom training and consulting engagements over the last few years.

This book is intended for a wide audience. The material ranges from an introductory level, covering the history of the Internet and basic network concepts, and then progresses into advanced topics such as DNS configuration and SNMP management. Each chapter includes information on the functionality of a protocol and how to implement the protocol in a networking environment. The end of the chapter looks at implementing the theory by deploying a solution.

I have organized the book into loose "sections." In the first section, the topics are more of an introductory nature. They can help build a solid foundation of how the TCP/IP protocol suite has evolved. Included in this material is an introduction to networks and the protocols involved in the TCP/IP protocol suite. These first few chapters can be skipped by a more experienced reader.

The next section takes a more in-depth look at some of the more commonly implemented protocols in the TCP/IP suite. This includes a look at how IP addresses are assigned in a network and how to segment a network using subnet masking. Other topics discussed in this section include TCP and UDP, name resolution methods, DNS configuration, routing concepts, and the automatic assignment of IP addresses to your clients.

The next section switches gears and starts to look at the types of network applications that are implemented in TCP/IP networks. Topics included in this section include Remote Command Applications, File Transfer protocols, electronic mail programs, network management, and dial-up networking. Each section looks at the various protocols that are involved with each of these network applications.

Following the discussion on network applications, specific technologies that are implemented in a TCP/IP environment are discussed. Topics include firewalls, the Network File System, Network Information System, and NetBIOS over TCP/IP. This section closes with the issues of running IP over an ATM network.

The final section looks at configuring various servers and clients to operate in a TCP/IP environment. This includes detailed configuration information. This section closes with a discussion on some of the future issues that you will face in a TCP/IP environment. If you are interested in what changes IPv6 will bring to the TCP/IP environment, check this information out.

At the end of each chapter you will find questions that will review the material covered in each day. Detailed answers to these questions can be found in Appendix B at the back of the book. I have tried to provide several pen and paper exercises that will require you to create configuration files or solve subnet masking problems.

The examples in this book come primarily from the Windows NT Server 4.0 environment. Detailed instructions on setting up TCP/IP services in a Windows NT environment can be found at the end of most days. This is not to say that UNIX and IntranetWare environments have been disregarded. Throughout the book, references and UNIX-specific examples are discussed. Configuring TCP/IP in an IntranetWare environment is covered in detail in Day 19, "Configuring Network Servers to Use TCP/IP."

The following conventions are used throughout the book:

- Commands that you would type in at a command prompt are displayed in the following font:

  `netstat -a`

- TCP/IP Configuration files and their paths are also referred to in the same typeface (e.g., `/etc/services`).

RFC 1234
- If there is a specific RFC that is related to the topic being discussed, the symbol you see to the left will appear beside the text referring to the specific RFC number.

- Keywords in the text are *italicized* to draw attention to them. Definitions for these keywords can be found in the glossary in Appendix C.

- Throughout the book, you will find several "sidenotes," as shown here.

WHY USE SIDENOTES?

These aside comments address common issues, problems and additional information that supplement the day's material. Each sidenote is titled to help you determine if the note is relevant to your situation.

If you have any questions in regards to the material discussed in this book, please drop me a line at my email address bkomar@online-can.com.

DAY 1

The History of the Internet

This first day of your 21-day exploration of TCP/IP discusses where it all started. It discusses the evolution of the Internet and the driving force behind the TCP/IP protocol suite. The first section provides an overview of the Internet's development and its growth over the years.

The second section examines the governing bodies of the Internet and the roles they play in its continued growth in size and technology.

Finally, you will learn about the defining documents of the TCP/IP protocol suite—Requests for Comment (RFCs). This section discusses the process of creating RFCs and the maturity cycle of a Request for Comment.

This Day can be skimmed or skipped by more experienced readers. It is provided to help inexperienced users learn about the development of the Internet, the makeup of its governing bodies, and the role of TCP/IP in its growth.

How Did the Internet Begin?

Understanding the evolution of the Internet you know today helps to explain how the TCP/IP protocol has evolved. The evolution has been driven by different forces through the years, beginning with the 1957 launching of Sputnik by the USSR. The United States formed the Advanced Research Projects Agency (ARPA), within the Department of Defense, to lead the U.S. in science and technology applicable to the military.

In 1962, Paul Baran was commissioned by the U.S. Air Force to develop a method that would enable the U.S. to maintain control over its military even after a nuclear attack. Baran had to develop a decentralized solution so that if a major U.S. city were to be destroyed, the military could still counterattack. The final proposal was to implement a packet-switched network.

Packet switching breaks down data into datagrams (or packets) that are labeled to include source and destination addresses. These packets are forwarded from network to network until they reach the intended destination computer. If an initial connection is unavailable, the packets should be able to find an alternate route to the destination. The destination also can request that packets lost during transmission be re-sent by the source computer when the data is reassembled at the destination (see Figure 1.1).

FIGURE 1.1.

Requesting that a lost packet be re-sent.

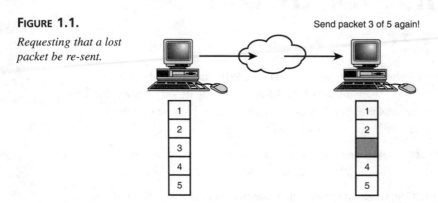

Send packet 3 of 5 again!

Stage I—The ARPAnet

In 1968, Bolt, Beranak, and Newman (BBN) was contracted by ARPA to build this packet-switching network known as the ARPAnet. The following were the initial four sites connected:

1

- University of California at Los Angeles—Network Measurements Center using a Xerox DSS 7:SEX
- Stanford Research Institute—Network Information Center using an SDS940/Genie
- University of California at Santa Barbara—Culler-Fried Interactive Mathematics using an IBM 360/75:OS/MVT
- University of Utah—Graphics using a DEC DPD-10/Tenex

The network was wired together using 50Kbps circuits and was managed by information message processors (IMP) that ran on Honeywell 516 minicomputers. The protocol used to communicate between hosts was the network control protocol (NCP), which enabled hosts running on the same network to transfer data.

PROTOCOLS IN A NETWORK

A *protocol* is a language used for communication between two networked hosts. The protocol defines how data should be packaged for transmission on the network so the receiving host can unpackage it when upon reception. For two hosts to communicate on a network, they must be running a common protocol.

By 1972, the ARPAnet had increased to 32 nodes. Ray Tomlinson created an email program that enabled a user to send personal messages across the network. This application started moving the network away from its military roots. Academics using the ARPAnet began to use it to communicate with remote colleagues. Mailing lists also started evolving at this time. The Advanced Research Projects Agency was renamed the Defense Advanced Research Projects Agency (DARPA).

In 1973, development began on the protocol suite now known as the Transmission Control Protocol/Internet Protocol (TCP/IP) protocol suite. Vinton Cerf headed this development from Stanford along with Bob Kahn from the DARPA. The major goal of this protocol was to enable separate computer networks to interconnect and communicate with one another.

In 1976, two major networking developments occurred. Dr. Robert J. Metcalfe of Xerox developed Ethernet, which allowed for the development of local area networks (LANs). The other major development was the implementation of SATNET, the Atlantic packet satellite network that linked the United States with Europe.

> **INTERNET VERSUS INTERNET**
>
> In 1982, the term *internet* was defined as a connected set of networks using the TCP/IP protocol suite. The *Internet* was defined as connected TCP/IP internets. This book will continue this distinction, using the term *Internet* to refer to the global network.

By 1983, the ARPAnet had been split into the ARPAnet and the MILNET (Military Network). This separated the public portion of the ARPAnet from the military component. The year 1983 also was the cut-off for use of NCP on the ARPANET. All participating networks had to switch to TCP/IP. With the splitting of the ARPAnet, the Internet Activities Board (IAB) was established to promote continued use of the ARPAnet.

As a result of the increase in participants on the ARPAnet and the MILNET, the University of Wisconsin introduced a better name-resolution method. The domain name space (DNS) provided a distributed database of hostname-to-IP-address resolution. This database replaced the static host files that had to be maintained at each host on the ARPAnet. Domain name servers maintain the domain name space. These DNS servers each contain a portion of the entire domain name space. If a query is issued to resolve a hostname to an IP address, the query ultimately is resolved by the authoritative DNS server.

Stage II—NSFNET

In 1985, the National Science Foundation began deploying new T1 lines at 1.544Mbps for the next generation of the ARPAnet, known as the NSFNET.

With the movement toward the NSFNET, the National Science Foundation introduced two enhancements to the TCP/IP protocol. The Network News Transfer Protocol (NNTP) was introduced to increase Usenet News performance, and Mail Exchanger (MX) records were developed for use with DNS servers.

By the time the NSFNET T1 backbone was completed, traffic had increased greatly, revealing the need for more bandwidth. Advanced Network Systems (ANS) was assigned the task of researching a high-speed networking solution. This started the migration to a T3, 45Mbps, backbone on NFSNET. While the migration was still taking place, the Department of Defense officially took the ARPAnet out of service.

The Internet continued to grow. The National Science Foundation created InterNIC to monitor the following Internet services:

- Directory and database services provided by AT&T.
- Registration services provided by Network Solutions, Inc.
- Information services provided by General Atomics.

Internet traffic continued to increase, resulting in a movement to an Asynchronous Transmission Mode (ATM) network backbone running at 145Mbps. This backbone privatized on April 30, 1996, when the National Science Foundation contracted four companies to take over providing Internet access.

The Internet Today

Today, the backbone networks of independent Internet service providers carry most Internet traffic. Providers include MCI, AT&T, Sprint, UUnet, ANS, and many others. The Internet Society is searching for a method of host and network addressing to meet the growth patterns of the Internet. IPv6 (discussed in Day 21) appears to be the new standard to lead the Internet into the next century. A major issue facing Internet users is to work together during the transition period.

IPv6 IMPLEMENTATIONS TO DATE

IPv6 already is being implemented on some networks in the United States. Its usage should continue to grow in the next few years as more hardware and software implementations are created.

Who Is in Charge of the TCP/IP Protocol?

The Internet Society was established in 1992 to oversee the internetworking technologies and applications of the Internet. Its primary function is to promote and encourage the growth and availability of the Internet. This includes the development of future protocols for use on the Internet.

Within the Internet Society, additional advisory groups are responsible for the development of the Internet. These groups include the Internet Architecture Board, the Internet Engineering Task Force, and the Internet Research Task Force.

The Internet Architecture Board (IAB)

The Internet Architecture Board (IAB) is the technical advisory group within the Internet Society. Its jurisdiction includes the following:

- Setting Internet standards
- Managing the Request for Comment publication process
- Reviewing the operation of the Internet Engineering Task Force (IETF) and the Internet Research Task Force (IRTF)

- Performing strategic planning for the Internet to identify long-range problems and opportunities
- Acting as an international technical-policy representative for the Internet
- Resolving technical issues outside the mandates of the IETF and the IRTF

When first established, the IAB was known as the Internet Activities Board. Every member of the IAB was responsible for investigating an area of concern. Each member chaired a task force that investigated a pressing issue facing the Internet.

In the summer of 1989, the continuing growth of the Internet led to the restructuring of the IAB. The existing structure was too flat and needed to be organized into separate task forces—the Internet Research Task Force (IRTF) and the Internet Engineering Task Force (IETF) (see Figure 1.2).

FIGURE 1.2.
The Internet Architecture Board architecture.

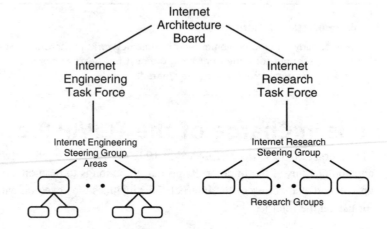

The Internet Engineering Task Force (IETF)

The Internet Engineering Task Force primarily is concerned with short- to medium-length projects. Any technical problems and needs that arise as the Internet develops also fall within the mandate of the IETF. The IETF existed even before the Internet Architecture Board reorganization. Before the reorganization, the IETF included more than 20 working groups, each of which investigated a specific problem. The entire IETF met regularly to hear from the working groups and to discuss the proposed standards of the TCP/IP protocol suite.

Due to its growth, IETF meetings became too large for a single person to chair. With the reorganization of the Internet Architecture Board, the IETF split into separate areas. Each area was assigned to research specific issues, and each was assigned a manager. These managers and the chairman of the IETF make up the Internet Engineering Steering Group (IESG).

Technical areas investigated by the IETF include the following:

- Applications
- Internet services
- Operations
- Network management

- Host and user services
- Routing
- Security
- OSI integration

The Internet Research Task Force (IRTF)

The Internet Research Task Force heads all research activities related to TCP/IP protocols, including any proposed changes to the Internet architecture in general. Many projects, after being researched by the IRTF, are passed on to the IETF for further development.

Within the IRTF, the Internet Research Steering Group (IRSG) functions as an advisory board. The IRSG sets priorities and coordinates all research projects.

Requests for Comment (RFCs)

All the standards of the TCP/IP protocol are published by the Internet Architecture Board in the form of Requests for Comment, better known as RFCs. The problem with RFCs is that, although all TCP/IP standards are published as RFCs, not all RFCs specify standards.

When looking through the list of RFCs, you might notice some numbers are missing. These RFC numbers were assigned for proposed RFCs that never made it to print. Among the published RFCs that definitely do not describe Internet standards, you can examine RFC 968 titled "Twas the night before start-up" by V.G. Cerf. This RFC is a comical look at the problems a network administrator can face when installing a network. Another humorous RFC is RFC 0527 titled "ARPAWOCKY" by D.L. Covill. This RFC brings home the point that network administrators have their own language when discussing technology.

THE HITCHHIKER'S GUIDE TO THE INTERNET

RFC 1118 is titled "The Hitchhiker's Guide to the Internet." It is an excellent document that provides help to new Internet users. It supplies information about how the direction of the Internet is determined. It also defines many common terms used when discussing the Internet and discusses how to acquire information from the Internet.

Requests for Comment do not use a prescribed format. Anyone can submit a proposal for publication as an RFC. Incoming documents are reviewed by a technical expert, the IETF or IRTF, or the RFC editor and then are assigned a classification. This classification determines whether the contents of the RFC are considered a standard of the TCP/IP protocol suite.

The following are standard classifications of RFCs:

- *Required.* All required RFCs must be implemented on all TCP/IP hosts and gateways.
- *Recommended.* Although they are not required, recommended RFCs generally are implemented by all TCP/IP hosts and gateways.
- *Elective.* An elective RFC does not have to be implemented. If it is implemented, however, its configuration has been defined fully in an elective RFC.
- *Limited use.* A limited-use RFC is not intended for general use.
- *Not recommended.* These RFCs are not recommended for implementation.

The Maturation Process of an RFC

Requests for Comment go through a maturation process before they are accepted as an Internet standard. The six maturity levels of an Internet standard are shown in Table 1.1.

TABLE 1.1. INTERNET STANDARD MATURITY LEVELS.

Maturity level	Description
Internet Standard	This specification is granted after the RFC has reached a high degree of technical maturity. The IESG has established this RFC as an official standard protocol and has assigned the protocol an STD number. It sometimes is easier to find the Internet Standard for a protocol by viewing the STD documents rather than RFCs. When an RFC has been deemed to be an Internet Standard, it also is assigned a standard number (as well as its original RFC number).
Draft Standard	This specification is well understood and is known to be stable. It can be used as a basis for developing the final implementation. At this stage, substantial testing and comment on the RFC is desired. There is still a possibility that the protocol might change before it becomes a standard protocol.
Proposed Standard	This specification has gone through an intensive review process. Implementing and testing by several groups is desired. You should expect changes to be published before it becomes an Internet Standard.

Maturity level	Description
Experimental Protocol	This designation generally is applied to protocols that are not recommended for implementation unless your network is participating in the experimentation process. It is not intended for operational use.
Informational Protocol	These are protocols developed by vendors or other standard organizations outside the scope of the IESG. They are published to provide information about their specifications to the Internet community.
Historic Protocol	These protocols are unlikely to become standards. They have been phased out, replaced by newer protocols, or dropped due to a lack of interest.

Keep in mind that, when a document is published, it is assigned an RFC number. If in time the RFC needs to be updated, a new RFC is published with a new RFC number. Unfortunately, RFCs are not designated as obsolete. You must make sure you have the most recent RFC for a specific topic.

FINDING THE CURRENT RFC FOR A SPECIFIC PROTOCOL

Two common methods are used to find the most current RFC relating to a specific protocol. The Internet Architecture Board publishes a quarterly memo called the IAB Official Protocol Standard; it contains a list of the most recent RFCs related to each protocol. You also have the option to view the Standard One (STD0001) This first standards document contains up-to-date lists of all Internet standard protocols. The document also contains lists of RFCs that have attained the following maturity levels: draft standard protocols, proposed standard protocols, experimental protocols, informational protocols, and historical protocols.

The maturity process of a protocol becoming an Internet standard is shown in Figure 1.3.

The following is the maturity process of an RFC:

1. A protocol is brought forward as a standard to the IESG. Only the IESG can recommend that a protocol enter the standards track. Likewise, a protocol moves from one state to another along the standards track based only on the recommendations of the IESG.

2. The transition from a proposed standard to a draft standard can take place only after the protocol has been a proposed standard for at least six months.

FIGURE 1.3.

The maturity process of a Request For Comment.

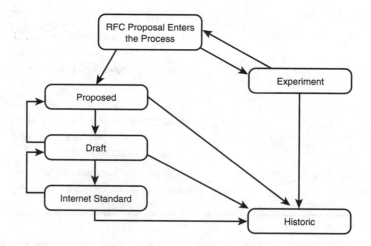

3. The transition from a draft standard to an Internet standard can take place only after the protocol has been a draft standard for at least four months.

4. Occasionally, it might be determined that a protocol is not ready for standardization. It then is assigned to an experimental state. To be placed back in the standards track, the protocol must be resubmitted by the IESG after being reworked.

5. Sometimes a protocol is replaced by another protocol. It then is moved to the historic state. This can occur at any part of the process.

Obtaining RFCs

Requests for Comment can be obtained from the Internet using FTP, email, or Web methods. The following sections show you how to retrieve RFCs using different techniques. No matter which method you use, one of the first documents you retrieve should be rfc-index.txt. This document contains an up-to-date list of all RFCs released until that point in time. This list includes descriptions of each RFC and is stored in reverse chronological order. It also states whether an RFC has become obsolete and been replaced by a new RFC.

Retrieving RFCs Using FTP

RFCs can be retrieved from `ftp://ds.internic.net/rfc`. Anonymous users can access this site using the account `anonymous` and their email account as the password.

A specific RFC can be retrieved using the following command:

```
Get rfcxxxx.txt
```

In this command, *xxxx* is the RFC number.

The following example shows a connection to the FTP site at dn.internic.net using the native FTP client that ships with Windows NT 4.0:

```
C:\users\default>ftp
ftp> open ds.internic.net
Connected to ds.internic.net.
220-              InterNIC Directory and Database Services
220-
220-
220 ds1 FTP server (Version 4.105 Fri Jan 5 14:34:54 EST 1996) ready.
User (ds.internic.net:(none)): anonymous
331 Guest login ok, send your email address as password.
Password:
230- Guest login ok, access restrictions apply.
230- Local time is: Fri Feb  6 15:38:47 1998
230
ftp> cd /rfc
250 CWD command successful.
ftp> get rfc1918.txt
200 PORT command successful.
150 Opening ASCII mode data connection for rfc1918.txt (22271 bytes).
226 Transfer complete.
22778 bytes received in 18.30 seconds (1.24 Kbytes/sec)
ftp> bye
221 Goodbye.
```

Remember to set the default directory to the location where you want to store the RFC document. In this example, the RFC1918.txt file will be stored in the c:\users\default directory.

Obtaining RFCs Through Email

You also can receive the text of specific RFCs by emailing a specific mail server on the Internet. This mail server responds to specific message body text and returns the desired RFC file.

You can send an email request for an RFC to mailserv@ds.internic.net.

The message body should contain the following text:

```
Send RFCxxxx.txt
```

In the preceding, *xxxx* is the desired RFC number. In addition to the Send command, the following commands also are valid:

- help
- person *name, organization[, country]*

- institution *name, country[, keyword, ...]*
- ls/dir *path[, path, ...]*
- file *path[, path, ...]*
- send/document-by-name *name[, name ...]*
- document-by-keyword *keyword[, keyword, ...]*
- resource-by-name *name[, name, ...]*
- resource-by-keyword *keyword[, keyword, ...]*
- whois *name*
- limit *value_of_max_msg_unit_size*
- encoding type*(default, mime, uuencode or btoa)[, mandatory]*
- return-to/path *return_address_or_route*
- begin
- end/exit

When sending the message to the mail server, you need to keep some restrictions in mind. The mail server ignores the subject field entirely. All commands and their parameters are not case sensitive, and there can be only one command per line. The mail server itself limits a user to 15 queries per request, does not return more than 500KB of information, and limits message processing to 15 seconds. If you exceed these parameters when performing a request, all information to that point is returned to the requestor.

Obtaining RFCs Through the World Wide Web

Requests for Comment also can be retrieved using the World Wide Web. As of April 1, 1998, InterNIC has ceased providing access to RFCs from its Web site. If you attempt to connect to RFCs from the InterNIC site, you are redirected to the Information Sciences Institute Web site. This following is the address of this site:

http://www.isi.edu/rfc-editor/rfc.html

RFCs can be retrieved from this site using searches based on keywords or by RFC number.

Appendix A, "RFC Reference," includes a list of all released RFCs to date of publication of this book. These RFCs are listed by category.

Applying What You Have Learned

Today's material helps you understand how the Internet has evolved since its inception in the late 1960s. The Internet has been the primary driving force in the evolution of the TCP/IP protocol suite. Knowing how the TCP/IP suite has evolved over the years can help you appreciate the development of the protocol.

Spend some time reviewing Appendix A and the list of RFCs. You don't need to read every single RFC. Instead, pick an area of technology that interests you and read its definition in the appropriate RFC. The following questions test your ability to find the appropriate RFC based on Appendix A.

Test Your Knowledge

1. What type of network is the Internet based on?
2. Which RFCs are related to the Telnet protocol?
3. What group within the Internet Society is in charge of researching short- to medium-term projects?
4. When an RFC is categorized as obsolete, is it removed from the list of RFCs?
5. Can an RFC be updated after it has been released?
6. What methods can be used to retrieve the text of a specific RFC?
7. Are any RFC numbers missing? Why would they not exist?

ANSWERS TO TEST YOUR KNOWLEDGE QUESTIONS

The answers to the Test Your Knowledge questions can be found in Appendix B, "Answers to End of Day Test Your Knowledge Questions."

Preview of the Next Day

Day 2 covers types of networks. The discussion includes local area networks (LANs) and wide area networks (WANs). If you understand how networks are installed and how communication occurs in each class of network, you will better understand how TCP/IP is able to transmit information between hosts on remote networks.

After discussing types of networks, Day 2 then discusses the OSI Reference model. The OSI model provides a design standard for network systems. If you understand how a network model can be implemented in a layered format, you will better understand what happens to data when one application connects to another.

DAY 2

Network Types and Open Systems Architecture

The goal for today's material is to gain a better understanding of some of the common local and wide area network topologies. You also will learn about the Open System Interconnect (OSI) Reference model and its implications for network design.

This section covers the following topics:

- Local area networks
- Wide area networks
- The need for open systems
- The OSI reference model

If you are already familiar with the concepts of local and wide area networks, you might want to skip ahead in this chapter to the section, "What Are Open Systems?"

Defining Network Types

Before you learn how to implement TCP/IP in your network, you first need to understand the common types of network topologies you can implement. Understanding how information travels in specific LAN and WAN environments can help you determine which topology to implement in your organization.

Local Area Networks (LANs)

Local area networks (LANs) are the most common networks in smaller offices. A local area network has the following characteristics:

- The network operates in a contained area. This could be a single floor in a building or simply within a single building.

- The hosts within the LAN are interconnected with high-bandwidth network connections such as ethernet or token ring.

- All facets of the local area network often are privately managed. No third parties are required for connectivity solutions.

- Local area network services are available on a 7-day, 24-hour basis.

When looking at network operating systems, you will find two basic types of local area networks: peer-to-peer networks and server-based networks.

Peer-to-peer networks operate with no dedicated servers on the network. Each host functions as both a client and a server. The user at each host determines what information or peripherals he is willing to share with the other members of the network. Peer-to-peer networks generally are relegated to smaller organizations; they do not scale well to larger ones. They have several security issues as a result of each host's capability to control its own security.

In *server-based networks*, at least one host is dedicated to server functionality. Client computers do not share any information with other computers. All data is stored on the central server. Most corporate networks are based on this methodology. Within a server-based network, servers can play several roles. These roles include the following:

- *File and print servers.* These provide a secure repository for all data. They also can manage print queues that provide access to network-sharable print resources.

- *Application servers.* These provide the server side of client/server applications. In a client/server environment, the client runs a small version of the program (the stub) that allows connectivity to the server. The server side of the application is used to perform processor-intensive queries on behalf of the client. Examples of application servers include Web servers and database servers.

- *Mail servers.* These provide electronic-message capabilities for the clients of the network. With the use of gateways, mail transport can take place between heterogeneous mail systems.

- *Fax servers.* These provide incoming and outgoing fax services to network users.

- *Security servers.* These provide security to the local area network if it is connected to any larger networks such as the Internet. Security servers include firewalls and proxy servers. Security servers are discussed on Day 16.

- *Communication servers.* These enable external data flow to occur between the network and remote clients. A remote client can use a modem to dial in to the local area network. The system dialed in to is the communication server. A communication server can be configured with one or more modems to allow external access to the network. After the client has dialed in to the network, he can function as if he were directly connected to the network using a network card.

When implementing a local area network, several facets of the network must be considered. These include the location of the computers, the location of the cables, and the connectivity hardware required. The term used to define these network design issues is *network topology*. The following four local area network topologies are commonly in use today:

- Bus networks
- Star networks
- Ring networks
- Dual-ring networks

Bus Networks

A bus network is the simplest method used to network computers. A bus network consists of a single cable that connects all computers, servers, and network peripherals in a single network segment (see Figure 2.1).

Hosts on a bus network communicate with each other by putting information on the cable addressed to the physical address of the network card used to connect the destination computer to the segment. This physical address is called the Media Access Control (MAC) address.

FIGURE 2.1.

A bus topology network.

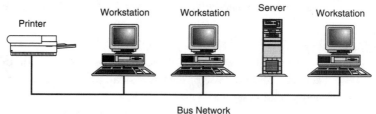

Bus Network

NETWORK CARDS AND MAC ADDRESSES

Each network card is assigned a unique MAC address. MAC addresses commonly are 12-digit hexadecimal addresses. Each network card manufacturer is assigned a prefix to be used for its network cards. It is the responsibility of the network card manufacturer to make sure no two of its cards have the same MAC address.

When data is put on the network, it actually is sent to all the computers in the network. Each computer investigates the data to see whether the destination address of the information matches its MAC address. If it matches, the computer reads the information. If it doesn't match, the computer discards the information.

Ethernet networks are the most common implementations of bus networks. Ethernet networks use a method called Carrier Sense Multiple Access with Collision Detection (CSMA/CD). This means only one computer at a time can send data on the bus network. If a host wants to transmit data and detects there is already data on the network, it waits for the network to clear before transmitting its information. If two hosts simultaneously start to transmit data on the network, a *collision* occurs. The hosts can detect that a collision has occurred. One of the transmitting hosts transmits a jam signal. This causes the collision to last long enough for all other hosts to recognize it. Each transmitting host waits a random amount of time before trying to retransmit the data. This time interval is randomized to prevent two hosts from repeatedly sending collision packets on the network.

Wiring Standards in a Bus Network   Networked computers commonly are linked together using network cabling. The following are two wiring standards for communications on a bus network:

- *10Base2*. Also known as thin ethernet, it allows network segments up to 185 meters on coaxial cable.

- *10Base5*. Also known as thick ethernet, it allows network segments up to 500 meters on coaxial cable.

Another common wiring standard implemented in local area networks is the 10Base-T standard. This standard is discussed in the section about star networks.

Hardware Utilized in a Bus Topology Network   Both thin ethernet and thick ethernet require the following additional network hardware to link the hosts together:

- BNC connectors

- Terminators

- AUI connectors

British Naval Connector (BNC) connectors enable the various thinnet coaxial cable segments to interconnect. Each host has a T-connector that is used to link the cable segment to a host computer (see Figure 2.2).

FIGURE 2.2.

BNC connector types.

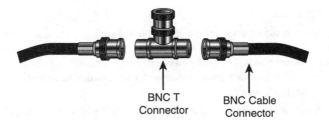

BNC T
Connector

BNC Cable
Connector

A *terminator* is placed at each end of the coaxial cable to absorb any free signals. Because data is sent to every host on the network segment, it is possible for data to continue to travel on the network even after it has reached the destination host. Terminators absorb these free signals to prevent the electronic signal from bouncing back on the segment, which prevents other hosts from transmitting data. In a bus network, all open cable ends must be terminated. If they are not, it can lead to the network being down.

TROUBLES WITH TERMINATORS

I have faced troubles with terminators on a few occasions. I was teaching at a remote site, for example, and a technician was reinstalling systems in the room next to me. During the reinstall, he unplugged the coaxial cable from a T-connector. My classroom was connected to the same network segment. None of my students were able to connect to my computer. We terminated our network segment before it reached the other classroom, and all network communication resumed normally.

AUI connectors commonly are used with thick ethernet cabling. These devices use a DB15 connector to link to the network card (see Figure 2.3).

FIGURE 2.3.

An AUI connector.

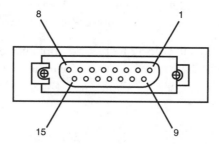

The AUI connector plugs its male pronged DB15 connector into the female pronged DB15 connector on the network card.

MIXING MEDIA

At times, you might encounter a situation in which the computers in your office are networked using one type of cable medium, but the network cards do not support that cable medium. In this situation, it sometimes is easier to purchase *transceivers* to convert the network cards instead of purchasing new network cards.

Transceivers have two interfaces. One interface is a BNC connector and the other is an AUI connector. This enables a network card with an AUI interface to be used on a bus network utilizing BNC connectors. The transceiver passes information between the two connectors so the AUI-type network card can still participate in the network.

Star Networks

In a star network, cable segments to a central connection unit, or *hub*, connect all computers (see Figure 2.4). In some cases, the hub also might be referred to as a *concentrator*.

The hub topology is the most prevalent network topology implemented in networks today. The chief advantage of the hub topology over the bus topology is that, if a cable segment is broken, only the host connected to the hub on that cable segment is affected. The following are other benefits of using a star topology:

- It is easy to stack hubs to increase the number of ports that a host can link into the hub stack. This helps star-based networks to grow in size.

FIGURE 2.4.

A star topology network.

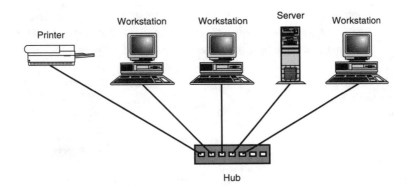

- Different cable types can be used to connect to the hubs.
- If an active hub is used, network activity and traffic can be centrally monitored using network management protocols such as the Simple Network Management Protocol (SNMP).

When implementing a star network, you use different cabling types than in a bus network. The most common wiring standard used with star-based networks is 10Base-T wiring, which carries ethernet signals on inexpensive twisted-pair wiring. The following five categories of unshielded twisted pair (UTP) cables can be used:

- *Category 1.* Used in traditional UTP telephone cable. It can carry only voice traffic, not data.
- *Category 2.* Certified for data transmissions of up to 4Mbps (early token ring).
- *Category 3.* Certified for data transmissions of up to 10Mbps (ethernet).
- *Category 4.* Certified for data transmissions of up to 16Mbps (token ring).
- *Category 5.* Certified for data transmissions of up to 100Mbps (fast ethernet).

Depending on the type of wiring you implement, different cable connectors are used to interface the wiring segments with the network cards. *RJ45 connectors* commonly are used with UTP wiring. RJ45 connectors look much like phone connectors, but they are about twice as big. In some cases, especially with older token-ring network cards, *DB9 connectors* are used to interface the network cabling with the network cards. DB9 connectors look like AUI connectors, except there are nine pins rather than 15 pins on the connector.

Ring Network

In a ring network, all the computers are joined together in a logical circle. Data travels around the circle and passes through each computer. In a physical layout, a ring network appears to be the same layout as a star network. The key difference is the connection unit known as a Multi-Station Access Unit (MAU). Within the MAU, data signals are passed in a ring from one host to the next (see Figure 2.5).

FIGURE 2.5.

A ring topology network.

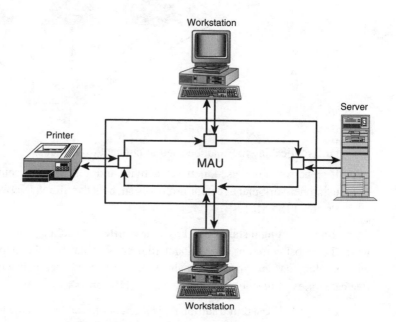

Data is transmitted around the ring using a method called *token passing*. When a host needs to transmit data, it modifies the token with the data it wants to send and configures the token with the MAC address of the destination host. The data passes by each computer until it reaches the destination host. The destination host modifies the token to indicate the data was received successfully. After the sending host verifies that the data was received, the frame is removed from the network. The token is released so another host on the network can transmit data.

Only a single token exists in a ring topology network. If a client wants to transmit data and the token is in use, he must wait. Although this sounds inefficient, the token travels at roughly the speed of light. If the total cable length for a network is 400 meters, a token can circle this ring around 5,000 times per second.

> **COMPARING THE TOKEN TO A CAMPFIRE STICK**
>
> The best analogy for a token-ring network is a campfire stick. Anyone sitting around a campfire can speak only when holding the campfire stick. After a person has spoken, he passes the campfire stick to the person sitting at his left. If a person forgets to say something, he must wait until everyone else has had a turn using the campfire stick.

Dual Ring Networks

Dual ring networks commonly run the Fiber Distributed Data Interface (FDDI). FDDI can be used to link local area networks to metropolitan area networks (MANs). FDDI is limited to a maximum ring length of 62 miles and operates at 100Mbps.

There are differences between token ring and FDDI when it comes to token passing. A computer on an FDDI network can transmit as many frames as it can produce in a preset time interval before letting the token go. In addition, several frames can circulate the ring at once. This leads to an overall edge in speed to FDDI over token ring.

Traffic in a dual ring network consists of two similar streams flowing in opposite directions (see Figure 2.6).

FIGURE 2.6.

A dual ring topology network.

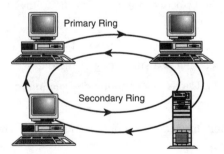

One ring is called the primary ring; the other ring is the secondary ring. Under normal operation, all data flows on the primary ring, and the secondary ring remains idle. The secondary ring is used only if a break occurs in the primary ring. The ring automatically reconfigures itself to use the secondary ring when necessary and continues to transmit.

Workstations generally are connected only to the primary ring. These single-attachment hosts connect to the ring using a dual-attached concentrator (DAC). These clients only have a connection to the primary ring. The DAC and dual-homed stations have connections to both the primary and secondary rings. When the primary ring is broken, only stations with dual connections are involved in calculating an alternative route.

The primary medium for an FDDI network is fiber-optic cable. This means the following:

- An FDDI network is more secure because it does not emit electromagnetic-field signals that can be tapped.
- An FDDI network can transmit over longer distances without the use of repeaters to strengthen the signal.
- An FDDI network is immune to electromagnetic noise.

Wide Area Networks (WANs)

Local area network implementations have physical and geographic limitations. As the future unfolds, the need increases for networking that requires connectivity over larger distances.

Most wide area networks (WANs) are simply combinations of local area networks and additional communications links between the LANs. The following terms are used to describe the scope or size of a WAN:

- *Metropolitan area networks.* MANs are WANs in a small geographic area. Generally, they are localized to a single city or region.
- *Campus area networks.* CANs is a common designation for WANs that link faculties at a university campus.

For practical implementation, these are no different from a wide area network except for the area they physically cover.

Communications over a wide area network use one of the following transmission technologies:

- Analog
- Digital
- Packet switching

Analog and digital technologies commonly are implemented as point-to-point technologies. In other words, they are configured between two distinct hosts. Packet switching, on

the other hand, links several hosts using a MESH or cloud technology. Any host participating in the cloud can establish a session to another host in the cloud.

The following sections discuss these technologies in more detail.

Analog Wide Area Network Connectivity

Analog phone lines can be used to connect networks despite the poor line quality and
slower speeds. The public-switched telephone network (PSTN) was primarily designed
for voice traffic; it also can be used for data traffic. Remote users connecting to the home
network from the road generally use PSTN access. Although it is possible to purchase a
dedicated analog line to connect networks, the cost of a conditioned line generally is pro-
hibitive, and other networking solutions are investigated.

Digital Wide Area Network Connectivity

A more common method of linking a WAN is to use digital data service (DDS) lines.
DDS provides a point-to-point synchronous connection. A company can lease dedicated
circuits that provide full-duplex bandwidth by setting up a permanent link from each
endpoint of the network.

Digital lines are preferable to analog lines due to increased speed and lack of transmission errors. Digital traffic does not require a modem. Instead, data is sent from a router
on a network to a channel service unit/data service unit (CSU/DSU) (see Figure 2.7).

FIGURE 2.7.

Communication over a
digital network.

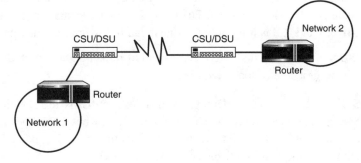

The CSU/DSU converts network data into digital bipolar signals that can traverse the
synchronous communications environment.

The following are common digital connectivity methods:

- T1
- T3

- ISDN
- Switched 56

T1   T1 service is the most widely used digital service at higher data speeds. T1 can transmit a full-duplex signal at a rate of 1.544Mbps. T1 can be used to transmit voice, data, and video signals.

Because of the high cost of a T1 line, many subscribers opt for fractional-T1 service. Instead of using a T1's full bandwidth, the subscriber uses one or more T1 channels. Each T1 channel is a 64Kbps increment.

T3   T3 service can provide voice and data-grade service at speeds up to 45Mbps. This is the highest-capacity service available to the consumer today. As with T1 service, Fractional-T3 service is available as an alternative to multiple T1 lines.

Integrated Services Digital Network (ISDN)   ISDN is an interLAN connectivity method that can carry data, voice, and imaging signals. Two flavors of ISDN are available: basic rate ISDN and primary rate ISDN.

Basic rate ISDN provides two bearer channels (known as B channels) that communicate at 56Kbps, an 8Kbps link-management channel, and one data channel (known as a D channel) that carries signal and link management data at a rate of 16Kbps. A network using both B channels can provide a 128Kbps data stream.

Primary rate ISDN can provide the entire bandwidth of a T1 link by providing 23 B channels and one D channel. The D channel under Primary rate ISDN communicates at 64Kbps and still is used only for signal and link-management data.

ISDN is a demand-dial interface. Instead of remaining active at all hours, it demand-dials whenever a connection is required.

Switched 56   Many telephone companies offer LAN-to-LAN digital dial-up services. Switched 56 is a circuit-switched version of a 56Kbps DDS line. The key advantage of a switched 56 line over a dedicated line is that it can be enabled on demand. This eliminates the cost of a dedicated WAN connection.

Packet-Switching Networks

Packet-switching networks enable you to transmit data over an any-to-any connection. Sometimes a packet-switched network is described as a mesh network. When information is transmitted over the network, it is not known what path the information will take between the sender and the recipient of the data (see Figure 2.8).

FIGURE 2.8

A packet-switching network.

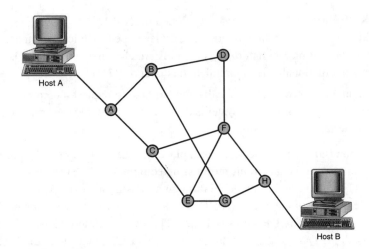

The original data is broken into smaller *packets*. Each packet is tagged with the destination address and a sequence number. As the packet traverses the network between the source and destination hosts, it travels on the *best current path*. Each packet travels along its own unique best current path. This way, if a network link goes down during the transmission of a stream of packets, not all the packets have to be re-sent. Some of the packets will have found an alternate route when the link went down.

Figure 2.8 shows one path that can be taken from Host A to Host B. In the diagram, a packet has been routed from Host A to Host B by crossing the networks located at A, C, F, and H. If the network located at F goes down, packets that have arrived at network C need to find an alternate route to network H. One possible alternative is to traverse networks E and G to arrive at network H.

At the destination host, the packets might arrive at different times or out of sequence. Because each packet has a sequence number, however, the original message can be rebuilt. The destination host also can request that missing packets be re-sent based on the missing sequence numbers.

Packet-switching networks are fast and efficient. They have their own method of managing routing traffic. For consumers, they offer high-speed network links that are affordable. Charges are implemented on a per-transaction basis rather than a flat-rate fee.

The following are three common implementations of packet-switching networks:

- X.25
- Frame Relay
- Asynchronous Transfer Mode (ATM)

X.25 Networks X.25 was developed in the 1970s to provide users with WAN capabilities over public data networks. It was developed by phone companies, and its attributes are international in nature. It is administered by an agency of the United Nations called the International Telecommunications Union (ITU).

In an X.25 network, a host calls another host to request a communications session. If the call is accepted, the two systems can begin a full-duplex information transfer. Either host can terminate the session.

A point-to-point connection takes place between data terminal equipment (DTE) at the client site and data circuit-terminating equipment (DCE) at the carrier's facilities. The DTE is connected to the DCE through a translation device known as a packet assembler/disassembler (PAD). The DCE connects to packet switching exchanges (PSEs), more commonly known as switches. The switches interconnect with each other until they reach the DCE of the destination host. This DCE connects to the DTE of the host to complete the communications session (see Figure 2.9).

FIGURE 2.9.

The X.25 network.

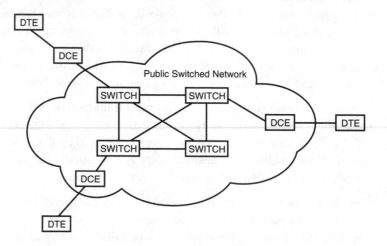

The end-to-end communication between the two DTEs is accomplished by an association known as a virtual circuit. *Virtual circuits* enable communication between two defined endpoints to take place through any number of intermediate nodes. These nodes do not have to be a dedicated portion of the network. The circuit is not a physical data link; it is bandwidth that can be allocated on demand. The following are the two types of virtual circuits:

- *Permanent virtual circuits.* PVCs are used for common data transfers known to occur on a regular basis. Although the route is permanent, the client pays only for the time the line is in use.

- *Switched virtual circuits.* SVCs are used for data transfers that are sporadic in nature. The connection uses a specified route across the network. The route is maintained until the connection ceases.

The X.25 protocol contains many error-correcting algorithms. They exist because X.25 first was implemented across PSTNs that required this feature.

Frame Relay Network communications have moved toward digital and fiber-optic environments. There is less need for the error checking found in the X.25 protocol. Frame Relay provides fast, variable-length packet-switching over digital networks. Frame Relay includes a cyclic redundancy check (CRC) algorithm that can detect whether a packet is corrupted and can discard it. It does not, however, ask for retransmission of the data. It leaves that up to the higher levels of the protocol.

Frame Relay uses permanent virtual circuits (PVCs) so the entire path between two hosts is known from end to end. This creates an optimal network environment in which the path between two hosts is predetermined. Instead of always having to calculate the best path to a remote host, the PVC has predetermined that route. In addition, because the hosts are connected using a common frame relay network, packets do not have to be fragmented due to differing Maximum Transmission Units (MTUs). The MTU is the largest packet size that can be used on a network segment.

Frame Relay also includes the following Local Management Interface (LMI) extensions:

- *Virtual circuit status messages* provide information about PVC integrity. They report the addition of any new PVCs and the deletion of existing PVCs. These status messages prevent hosts from sending messages to a PVC that has ceased to exist.

- *Multicasting* is an optional LMI extension that enables a host to send a single frame destined for multiple recipients. This reduces overall network traffic because a single frame can be sent to multiple hosts instead of one message per host.

- *Global addressing* provides globally significant connection identifiers. Frame Relay uses data link connection identifiers (DLCIs) to identify a circuit ID. When global addressing is implemented, each connection has a globally unique ID. This ID is known to all other connections (see Figure 2.10).

FIGURE 2.10.

Global addressing under Frame Relay.

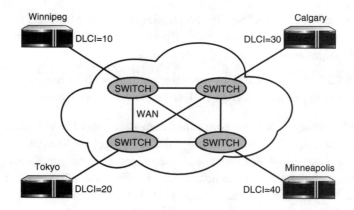

If Winnipeg must send a frame to Minneapolis, Winnipeg places a value of 40 in the DLCI field and sends the frame into the Frame Relay network. When the frame arrives in Minneapolis, the network changes the DLCI field contents to 10. This shows that the frame came from the Winnipeg network. This addressing scheme enables the WAN to function using the same methods as a LAN.

- *Simple flow control* provides an XON/XOFF flow-control mechanism. Frame Relay includes simple congestion-notification messages that enable the network to inform user devices when network resources are approaching a congested state. The simple flow control LMI extension is provided for devices that cannot use these notification messages and that need some level of flow control.

Asynchronous Transfer Mode (ATM)   Asynchronous Transfer Mode (ATM) uses advanced technology to segment data into cells at high speeds. Each cell is a fixed length, consisting of 5 bytes of header information and 48 bytes of payload data. The use of a fixed-length packet results in higher transfer speeds because the network spends less time processing incoming data. It also helps in planning application bandwidth. Cells cross the ATM network by passing through devices known as ATM switches. These switches analyze header information to switch the cell to the next ATM switch that ultimately leads to the destination network. ATM enables more than one computer to transmit at the same time through the use of multiplexers. The topic of TCP/IP over ATM is discussed more fully on Day 18.

When an ATM device wants to establish a connection with another ATM device, it sends a signaling request packet to the ATM switch on its network (see Figure 2.11).

FIGURE 2.11.

A signaling request transits the network.

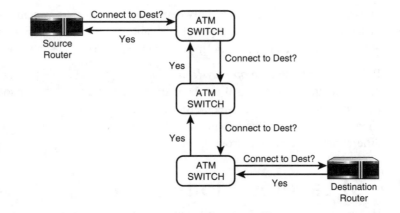

The request includes the ATM address of the target ATM device as well as Quality of Service (QOS) parameters. The QOS parameters essentially set minimum guidelines that must be met for transmission. They include values for peak bandwidth, average sustained bandwidth, and burst size. If the actual traffic flow does not meet the QOS specifications, the cell can be marked as *discard eligible*. This means any ATM switch that handles the cell can drop the cell in periods of congestion. At each switch, the signaling request is reassembled and examined. If the switch table has an entry of the destination ATM device and the ATM switch can accommodate the QOS requested for the connection, it forwards the cell to the next ATM switch. When the cell signaling request reaches the destination endpoint, it responds with an accept message.

What Are Open Systems?

The concept of open systems is derived from a need for standardization. Many people have encountered a situation in which they must choose between competing products. The major problem is that if you buy BigCorp's XYZ product, you are tied to that product as your networking solution.

The goal of open systems is to reduce vendor-specific solutions. You should be able to choose between vendors to provide the actual products used when you implement your solution. You should be able to change your mind down the road and change to a different vendor's solution without having to redesign your entire network. The solution should be able to plug in to the place held by the former product.

TCP/IP is a good example of an open system for a protocol suite. Through the use of RFCs, all TCP/IP standards are fully documented. They have been designated as required or elective components to be included in a vendor's implementation of TCP/IP. The goal of TCP/IP is to provide connectivity between heterogeneous systems. You might have to make some choices about how you implement the connectivity. By using TCP/IP, however, you know you have an underlying framework that is available on most platforms.

Be careful with the term *open systems*. Many times it is bandied about as the end-all and be-all. Competing products drive the market to come up with better solutions. If there is absolutely no difference between Product A and Product B, why would you not always choose the cheaper of the two products? People need a reason to buy a product. What differentiates one product from the next?

Use of Layered Models

In networking, layered models often are used to represent the various networking functions that must be performed. The following are reasons for using layered models:

- They divide all the functions of a network's operation into less-complex elements.
- They enable vendors to focus design and development on specific areas.
- They make it possible for layers to remain unaffected by changes in other layers of the network—as long as each layer presents an interface with which the layers above and below it can communicate.
- They provide a framework for network development.
- They divide the complexity of networking into easy-to-learn subsets of network operations.

When working in a layered model, each layer only should be concerned with the layers immediately above and below it. Many times, the adjacent layers are referred to as the $n + 1$ and the $n - 1$ layers, in reference to the currently observed layer (see Figure 2.12).

FIGURE 2.12.

The interaction between network layers.

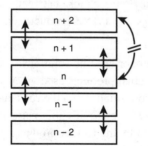

The *n + 1* and *n – 1* layers only can communicate with the *n* layer of the network. It is not possible for the *n* layer to communicate with the *n + 2* layer without transferring information through the *n + 1* layer.

The Open System Interconnection (OSI) Reference Model

2

In the early 1980s, the International Standards Organization (ISO) saw the need to develop a network model to help vendors create interoperable network solutions. They developed what is now known as the Open System Interconnection (OSI) reference model. Even though other networking models have been created, they often are related back to the OSI reference model when vendors want to provide education about their products.

The OSI reference model is made up of the following seven distinct layers:

- Application layer
- Presentation layer
- Session layer
- Transport layer
- Network layer
- Data link layer
- Physical layer

The OSI reference model describes how information makes its way from an application on one host system to an application on another host system. As information descends through the network layers on the sending host, it changes its format through each layer. The data from higher layers is encapsulated within header information from the layer directly below it (see Figure 2.13).

This diagram shows that, as data descends through the left-side host, the previous layer's header and data combination is encapsulated within the next layer's header layer; for example, the original data of an email message is encapsulated within a segment header. The segment header ensures that the message hosts are able to reliably communicate with each other.

FIGURE 2.13.

Data encapsulation in the OSI reference model.

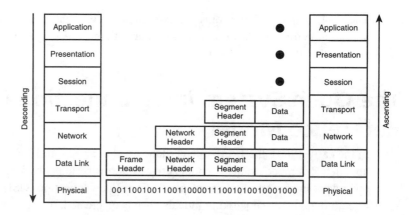

At the network layer, the data (which now comprises the segment header and the original data passed from the higher layers) is placed within a packet that contains a network header. This network header includes the source and destination logical addresses. In a TCP/IP internetwork, these are the IP addresses of the source and destination hosts. These addresses assist in packet routing between the two hosts over the internetwork.

At the data link layer, the network header and its data are encapsulated within a frame header. The frame header defines how the information will be transported through the network interface onto the physical network. Each device on the network requires framing to connect to the next device in the network. The frame header also includes the physical addresses of the source and destination hosts.

Finally, at the physical layer, the frame header and its data are converted into a format that enables the information to be transmitted on a network medium such as network cabling.

When the data is received at the destination host, the bits are converted back to a frame header and its data. As the information moves up through the network layers, each header is used to determine how to move the data up through the layers. At each layer, the previous layer's header information is stripped off so that the data is back in the same format it was in when transmitted by the matching layer on the source host.

Now that the basic features of the OSI reference model have been reviewed, the following sections briefly examine each specific layer of the model. Each layer has a preset function it must perform. As data descends through the layers, the upper layer's header and data become the data section of the next lower layer. Data cannot skip a layer as it descends through the OSI model. This simplifies the process of data transmission. It also enables new protocols to be developed because they must simply interact with the layers above and below the layer in which they are implemented.

The Physical Layer

The physical layer defines the electrical currents, physical pulses, or optical pulses that are involved in transporting data from the Network Interface Card (NIC) of a host to the communications system. This layer includes the connection to the communications system. The requirements and characteristics for transmission generally are documented in standards such as the V.35 or RS-232 standards. The physical layer is responsible for transmitting bits from one computer to another.

The Data Link Layer

The data link layer sends data frames from the network layer to the physical layer. When the data link layer receives bits from the physical layer, it translates these bits into data frames. A data frame commonly includes the following components:

- *Destination ID*. This ID usually is the MAC address of the destination host or the default gateway.
- *Sender ID*. This ID usually is the MAC address of the source host.
- *Control information*. This includes information such as the actual frame type, routing, and segmentation information.
- *Cyclic redundancy check (CRC)*. CRC provides error correction and verifies that the data frame is received intact by the destination reference host.

The data link layer is subdivided into two sublayers—the logical link control (LLC) and media access control (MAC) sublayers. The LLC sublayer provides error control and works primarily with the network layer to support connectionless or connection-oriented services. The MAC sublayer provides access to the actual LAN medium. It primarily functions with the physical layer.

The Network Layer

The network layer determines the best way to move data from one host to another. It manages the addressing of messages and the translation of logical addresses (such as IP addresses) to physical addresses (MAC addresses).

The network layer also determines the route data traverses between source and destination host. If the packets being transmitted are too large for a destination host's topology, the network layer compensates by breaking the data into smaller packets. These packets are then reassembled at the destination.

2

The Transport Layer

The transport layer segments and reassembles data into a data stream. It provides an end-to-end connection between source and destination hosts. When data is transmitted from a source to a destination host, the data is segmented into smaller collections of information. The segments are numbered sequentially and are sent to the destination host. When the destination host receives the segments, it sends an acknowledgment of their receipt. If a segment is not received, the destination host can request that a specific segment be resent. This provides error control for data transport.

The Session Layer

The session layer enables two applications on separate hosts to establish a communication connection called a *session*. These sessions ensure that messages are sent and received with a high degree of reliability.

The session layer performs security functions to make sure two hosts are allowed to communicate across a network. The session layer coordinates the service requests and responses that occur when applications communicate between hosts.

The following are common protocols and interfaces that function at the session layer:

- *Winsock.* Many protocols use the Winsock programming interface. This interface defines the ports, protocols, and addresses of two hosts that are going to communicate on a network.

- *Remote Procedure Calls (RPCs).* An RPC is a redirection mechanism that enables a request to be built on a client and then executed on a server at the security level of the client.

- *X Window systems.* These permit intelligent terminals to communicate with UNIX computers as if they were directly attached.

The Presentation Layer

The presentation layer determines how data is formatted when exchanged between network computers. The data received from the application layer is translated into a commonly recognized, intermediary format.

The presentation Layer also is responsible for all translation of data, encryption of data, character set conversions, and protocol conversions. The presentation layer is responsible for syntax conversion between two communicating hosts, for example, if one of the hosts used the ASCII standard for its text and data representation and the other host used EBCDIC.

The following are common presentation formats handled by the presentation layer:

- *ASCII.* The *American Standard Code for Information Interchange* is an 8-bit character set used to define all alphanumeric characters. It is the most common implementation of text transmissions on computers.

- *EBCDIC.* The *Extended Binary Coded Decimal Interchange Code* is a text representation method used extensively on IBM mainframe and mini computers.

- *External data representation (XDR).* XDR is used by applications such as NFS and NIS to provide a universal format for text transmission between two hosts. It facilitates text transmissions between two hosts using different text representations (such as EBCDIC and ASCII).

- *Binary files.* Most sound, graphics, and executable files are converted into a binary format at the presentation level. When the data is received at a destination host, the extension of the file relates the presentation format to an associated application.

The Application Layer

The application layer enables programs to access network services. It does not deal with programs that require only local resources. To use the application layer, a program must have a communications component that requires network resources.

The following are types of programs currently in use that use the application layer:

- *Electronic mail.* The application layer provides network communication services. Common implementations include products such as Microsoft Exchange Server and Lotus Notes.

- *Electronic Data Interchange* (EDI). The application layer provides improved business flow for ordering, shipments, inventory, and accounting between associated businesses.

- *Conferencing applications.* The application layer enables users in remote locations to use conferencing applications such as video, voice data, and fax exchange. A common program that uses this technology is Microsoft Net Meeting.

- *World Wide Web.* Through the use of browsers, users can view information in formats such as text, graphics, sound, and video from remote network locations. The most common Web servers in use today include Apache Web Server, Netscape SuiteSpot, and Microsoft Internet Information Server.

Applying What You Have Learned

Test Your Knowledge

1. What are the primary differences between a Frame Relay network and an X.25 network?

2. What is the primary difference between ATM and Frame Relay networks?

3. What advantages does an FDDI network have over a token-ring network?

4. Describe the major differences between a peer-to-peer network and a server-based network.

5. What element does Quality of Service (QOS) add to ATM transmissions?

Match the OSI reference model layers to their functionality.

6.	Application	a. Determines the best route from source to destination
7.	Presentation	b. Enables programs to access network resources
8.	Session	c. Performs a binary transmission
9.	Transport	d. Provides an end-to-end connection between a source and destination hosts
10.	Network	e. Responsible for translation of all data
11.	Data link	f. Divided into two sublayers
12.	Physical	g. Coordinates service requests and responses between two hosts

Preview of the Next Day

Tomorrow, you begin to look specifically at the TCP/IP protocol suite. You start with a look at the TCP/IP protocol layered model and then compare the TCP/IP layered model to the OSI reference model. You then look at the core protocols of the TCP/IP suite and their function in the TCP/IP layered model.

This leads you into the next week, during which you investigate configuring TCP/IP on a host system.

DAY **3**

The TCP/IP Layer Model and the Core Protocols of the TCP/IP Suite

Today's material can be split into two separate sections: the TCP/IP layer model and the core protocols of the TCP/IP protocol suite. First you will compare the TCP/IP layer model to the OSI model so you can determine how TCP/IP varies from the OSI layer model. You then will examine the protocols used at each IP layer. The following protocols are discussed:

- Address Resolution Protocol (ARP)
- Internet Protocol (IP)
- Internet Control Message Protocol (ICMP)
- Internet Gateway Message Protocol (IGMP)
- Transmission Control Protocol (TCP)
- Universal Datagram Protocol (UDP)

The discussion of these protocols provides more in-depth information about the functionality provided by each layer of the TCP/IP layer model. It also clarifies how each layer interacts with the layers above and below it.

The TCP/IP Layer Model

The TCP/IP layer model is based on a four-layered network (see Figure 3.1).

FIGURE 3.1.

The TCP/IP four-layer model.

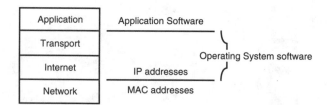

Within the four layers, specific boundaries are observed. In the Network Interface layer, only physical MAC addresses are used for address resolution. Even when an interface does not have a physical address—as is the case with a modem—a logical physical address is used. Modems are commonly used to connect to networks, yet they do not have a physical MAC address. When a modem connects to the network, a logical address is assigned to the modem so communication can take place.

In the Internet layer, logical IP addresses are mapped to the physical MAC addresses. Each host in a TCP/IP internetwork is assigned a unique IP address. This address identifies hosts and identifies the subnetwork on which a host resides.

All protocols used in the transport and Internet layers are provided by the operating system. Applications do not have to provide their own transport or internetworking protocols. This makes it easier for applications to be deployed on different operating systems. The application only has to interface with either TCP or UDP as a transport protocol.

All protocols and software used in the application layer are application dependent. You can switch the underlying protocols, and many of the applications will continue to operate. You can, for example, use the Microsoft TCP/IP stack on your Windows 95 client and use an FTP client. You can just as easily replace the TCP/IP stack with the Net Chameleon IP stack. Your application will still operate in this environment because the FTP software functions beyond the operating system. It interfaces with whatever TCP/IP protocol stack is used. This concept is known as *boundary layers*. A new protocol at any of the four layers of the TCP/IP model only needs to interact with the layer immediately above or below the level in which it functions.

The following sections go into more detail about the processes completed in each layer of the TCP/IP layer model.

The Network Interface Layer

The network layer merges outgoing frames on the wire and pulls incoming frames off the wire. The format used by these frames depends on the network topology implemented.

The network layer adds a preamble at the beginning of the frame and adds a cyclical redundancy check (CRC) to ensure that the data is not corrupted in transit. When the frame arrives at the destination, the CRC value is recalculated to determine whether the data has been corrupted in transit. If the frame arrives intact, it is passed up the network layer model. If the frame is corrupted, it is discarded at this point.

> **ISSUES WITH FRAME TYPES**
>
> On a single network segment, all hosts must use the same frame type for communication to occur. Multiple frame types can be run on a single network segment, but only hosts with same frame types can actually communicate.

The Internet Layer

The Internet layer provides three primary functions: addressing, packaging, and routing. The Internet Protocol (IP) resides in this layer of the TCP/IP protocol layer suite. IP provides connectionless, non-guaranteed delivery of information. This means the IP protocol does not perform any checks or measures to make sure the information has been received successfully by the destination host. Packets could be lost or could arrive out of order.

When information arrives from the transport layer, the IP protocol adds a header to the information. The header includes the following information:

- *Source IP address.* This is the IP address assigned to the sending host.
- *Destination IP address.* This is the IP address assigned to the target host.
- *Transport protocol.* The protocol used by the transport layer is stored within the IP header. This way, when the datagram arrives at the host system, the Internet layer knows whether to transfer the datagram using the TCP or UDP protocols.
- *Checksum.* This ensures that the data arriving at this layer has not been corrupted in transit.

- *Time-to-live (TTL)*. Each time the datagram crosses a router, the TTL is decreased by a value of at least one. When the TTL reaches a value of zero, the datagram is dropped from the network.

The Internet Layer also determines how to route a datagram to a destination host. If it is determined that the destination IP host is on the same network segment, the datagram is sent directly to the target host. If IP determines that the destination host is located on a remote network segment, IP uses the source host's routing table to determine the best route to reach the network on which the remote host is located. If there is not an explicit route in the routing table, the source host uses its default gateway to send the datagram to the remote host.

DEFAULT GATEWAYS

The *default gateway* is the preferred router a host uses to route traffic to remote network segments.

Other processes that occur in the Internet layer are *fragmentation* and *reassembly*. Sometimes, when information is transferred between network segments, the network segments might not use the same network topology. The recipient's network topology cannot work with the same datagram size as the sending host's network. In this case, IP breaks data into smaller pieces. When the data is received at the destination host, the smaller pieces are re-assembled into the original data packet. When the data is broken up, the following information is appended in each separate packet:

- *Flag*. The fragment flag bit in the IP header of each packet fragment is set to designate that the data has been fragmented. On the last packet fragment, the flag bit is not set because no more fragments follow.

- *Fragment ID*. When a datagram is broken into smaller pieces, the fragment ID identifies all the pieces of the original datagram. This information is used by the client to reassemble the datagram.

- *Fragment offset*. When the smaller pieces are reassembled into a single datagram, the fragment offset determines the order in which the fragments should be reassembled.

The Transport Layer

The transport layer provides end-to-end communication between hosts using *ports*. The following two protocols are provided in the TCP/IP layer model to transport data:

- Transmission Control Protocol (TCP)
- Universal Datagram Protocol (UDP)

TCP provides connection-oriented communication on a TCP/IP network. When two hosts communicate using the TCP protocol, a session must be established between the two hosts. This is so each host can determine the next sequence number the other host will be using. A TCP connection provides a level of reliability. Transmissions use sequence numbers and acknowledgments to make sure the destination host successfully receives the data. If a destination host does not receive a specific segment, it can request that the source host resend the packet (see Figure 3.2).

FIGURE 3.2.

TCP uses sequence numbers to ensure delivery.

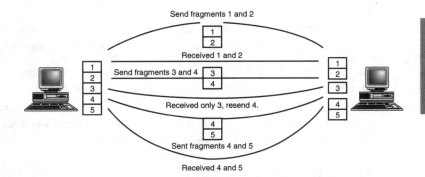

In Figure 3.2, the host on the left has segmented a data package into five segments. It sends segments 1 and 2 to the host on the right. When the host on the right receives the fragments, it acknowledges their receipt. The host on the left then sends the next two fragments (fragments 3 and 4). For whatever reason, the host on the right receives only the third fragment. When it sends the acknowledgment, it only acknowledges the receipt of fragment 3. The host on the left resends fragment 4 and also sends fragment 5. Upon receipt, the receiving host acknowledges both fragments. Now it can reassemble the data into its original format. The TCP protocol is covered in depth on Day 5. Topics discussed include the TCP three-way handshake and the use of sliding windows in TCP data transmissions.

A UDP protocol provides connection-less service. It is not guaranteed that the destination host will receive the information. Applications that use UDP are on their own to make sure data is successfully delivered to the recipient host. The only protection you have in a UDP packet is that there is a checksum value within its header. The checksum makes sure the data was not corrupted in transit.

A common analogy used when comparing the TCP and UDP protocols is the post office versus a courier service. The post office is much like the UDP protocol. When you place a letter to your friend in the mailbox, it is not guaranteed that the mail will get to them. Most of the time it reaches them successfully. When you must make sure that a business associate receives a package, however, you are not going to use a typical mail service. Instead, you use a courier service to make sure the business associate receives the package in a predetermined amount of time. Along the way, you can check the progress of the package. When the business associate receives the package, he acknowledges its receipt by signing for the package.

Just as it costs more to use a courier service rather than the post office, there is additional cost on the network when using the TCP protocol. Periodically, the recipient host must send an acknowledgment that it has received the last transmissions successfully. The sending host often waits for an acknowledgment before it continues to send data.

You, as a network administrator, do not have a choice which transport protocol to implement. This is determined by the higher-level application using the transport protocol. Many applications use TCP so they do not have to provide reliable data transport. The TCP protocol can handle reliable transmission of data using sequence numbers and acknowledgments. An application that uses UDP has to ensure reliability on its own.

The Application Layer

Network-based applications function on the application layer in the TCP/IP layer model. *Network-based applications* refers to applications that connect to or communicate with remote network hosts. Network applications that run on a TCP/IP network generally fit into one of two categories:

- Winsock applications
- NetBIOS applications

Winsock applications use the Windows Sockets service application-programming interface (API). These include utilities such as FTP, Telnet, SNMP, and IRC.

NetBIOS applications use NetBIOS names and messaging services over a TCP/IP network. The Windows NT 4.0 network operating system still uses NetBIOS names for its networking name resolution.

Comparing the OSI Model to the TCP/IP Model

The following comparisons can be made between the seven-layer OSI reference model and the four-layer TCP/IP model (see Figure 3.3):

- The TCP/IP layer model combines both the physical and data link layers of the OSI Model into the TCP/IP model's network layer. It does not differentiate between the physical network cards and their drivers. This enables TCP/IP to be implemented in any network topology.

- The Internet layer of the TCP/IP model corresponds the network layer of the OSI Reference model. Both layers provide addressing and routing services.

- The transport layer in each model enables end-to-end communication sessions to occur between two hosts.

- The application layer in the TCP/IP model combines the session, presentation, and application layers of the OSI model. The TCP/IP model includes all issues of how data is represented and how sessions are maintained within the definitions of an application.

3

FIGURE 3.3.

Comparing the OSI and TCP/IP layer models.

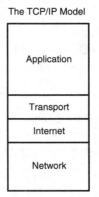

Defining the Core Protocols in the IP Layer Model

Now that you are familiar with the logical layout of the TCP/IP layer model, the following sections discuss the specific protocols involved in the TCP/IP layer model. This provides more details into the specific functionality provided by protocols in each layer of the TCP/IP model.

Protocols in the Internet Layer

As previously discussed, the Internet layer provides all addressing, packaging, and routing in the TCP/IP protocol suite. The protocols in this layer either interact with the physical network components in the network interface layer or provide logical addressing information to the transport layer. The following are the actual protocols located in the Internet layer:

- Address Resolution Protocol (ARP)
- Internet Can Message Protocol (ICMP)
- Internet Protocol (IP)
- Internet Group Messaging Protocol (IGMP)

Address Resolution Protocol (ARP)

RFC 826 For two hosts to communicate successfully on a network segment, they must resolve each other's hardware addresses. This is accomplished in the TCP/IP protocol suite using the Address Resolution Protocol (ARP). ARP resolves a destination host's IP address to a MAC address. It also makes sure the destination host is able to resolve the sender's IP address to a MAC address.

Frequently on a network, a client computer communicates with a central server. Instead of querying each time for the server's MAC address, the ARP protocol makes use of the *ARP cache*. The ARP cache stores a list of IP addresses recently resolved to MAC addresses. If the target IP address' MAC address is found in the ARP cache, this MAC address is used as the target address for communication.

The following rules must be followed when maintaining the ARP cache:

- Each new entry is configured with a *time-to-live (TTL)* value. The actual value depends on the operating system in use. When the time-to-live value reaches zero, the entry is removed from the ARP cache.

- If a new entry is not reused in the first two minutes of its life, it is removed from the ARP cache.

- In some TCP/IP implementations, the time-to-live value is reset to its initial value every time an entry is reused in the ARP cache.

- Each implementation of TCP/IP sets a maximum number of entries in the ARP cache. If the ARP cache fills up and a new entry must be added, the oldest entry in the ARP cache is removed to make room for the new entry.

The ARP Process   When a host needs to communicate with another host on a local network segment, the following process is used (see Figure 3.4):

1. The calling host checks its ARP cache to determine whether there is an entry for the IP address of the destination host.

2. If an entry cannot be found, the calling host creates an ARP packet that asks the destination host to reply with its MAC address. Included in the ARP packet are the IP address and MAC address of the calling host so the destination host can add this information to its ARP cache. This ARP packet is sent to the ethernet broadcast address FF-FF-FF-FF-FF-FF. This means every host on the segment investigates the packet.

3. Each host investigates the ARP packet to see whether the destination host IP address in the ARP packet matches its IP address. If it does not, the packet is ignored. If it matches, the destination host adds the IP address and MAC address information of the sending host to its ARP cache.

4. The destination host creates an ARP reply containing its IP address and MAC address information. This reply is returned to the calling host.

5. The calling host adds the IP address and MAC address information to its ARP cache. Communication now can begin between the two hosts.

FIGURE 3.4.

The ARP process when communicating with a local host.

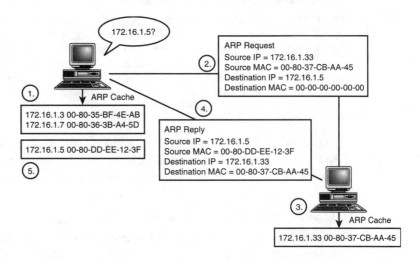

The process differs when the target host is located on a remote network (see Figure 3.5). This can be determined by comparing the target host's IP address to the sending host's IP address/subnet mask combination. This is discussed on Day 4 in the section "The ANDing Process."

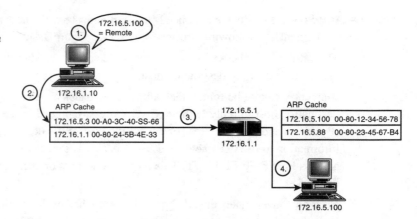

FIGURE 3.5.

The ARP process when communicating with a remote host.

1. The sending host determines whether the destination host is located on a remote network. The sending host inspects its TCP/IP configuration and finds the address for its default gateway. The *default gateway* is the router on the host's network segment where all outbound network traffic is directed.

> **THE IMPLEMENTATION OF DEFAULT GATEWAYS**
>
> Not all TCP/IP implementations use default gateways. If they are not used, explicit routes are configured for each remote network. If the remote network is not defined in the routing table, traffic cannot be sent to that remote network. In these implementations, the sending host determines which router to send the data to reach the remote network and uses ARP to find that router's MAC address.

2. The sending host inspects its ARP cache to see whether it has recently resolved the MAC address of the default gateway. If it hasn't, the host sends an ARP packet to determine the MAC address using the same local ARP resolution method previously discussed.

3. The data is transferred to the default gateway.

4. The default gateway now inspects the destination host's IP address. If the default gateway has an interface on the network segment on which the host is located, it inspects its ARP cache for an entry for the destination host. If the default gateway does not have an interface on the network segment on which the destination host is located, it uses its routing table to determine which router to pass the information to. It inspects its ARP cache for the MAC address of the target router's interface. If

it does not have an entry in the ARP cache, it uses ARP to determine the MAC address.

ARP CACHES WHEN A HOST HAS MORE THAN ONE NETWORK CARD

For multihomed (multiple interfaced) hosts, a separate ARP cache is maintained for each interface.

The ARP Packet   The ARP packet is shown in Figure 3.6. This packet format is used for both the ARP protocol and the Reverse Address Resolution Protocol (RARP). The RARP protocol is discussed in Day 10 with the topic of automatic configuration.

FIGURE 3.6.

The ARP packet structure.

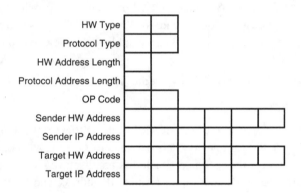

Table 3.1 describes each field in an ARP packet.

TABLE 3.1. THE ARP PACKET FIELDS.

Field	Definition
Hardware Type	Designates the type of hardware used in the network layer.
Protocol Type	The field indicates the protocol address type in the protocol address fields. For an IP address, this value is set to 08-00.
Hardware Address Length	The length in bytes of the hardware address. For ethernet and token-ring networks, this is 6 bytes.
Protocol Address Length	The length of the protocol address. For IPv4, this is 4 bytes.

continues

TABLE 3.1. CONTINUED

Field	Definition
Op Code	Determines whether the packet is an ARP request or an ARP reply. Possible values include: (1) ARP request, (2) RARP request, (3) ARP reply, or (4) RARP reply.
Sender's hardware address	The hardware address of the sending host.
Sender's protocol Address	The IP address of the sending host.
Target's hardware address	The hardware address of the target host. This is set to 00-00-00-00-00-00 in an ARP request.
Target's protocol address	The IP address of the target host.

Using the ARP Command   Each TCP/IP protocol suite provides an ARP command for viewing and modifying the ARP cache. In Windows NT, the ARP command can be used for three purposes: viewing the ARP cache, adding a static entry to the ARP cache, and removing an ARP cache entry.

The following command is used to view the ARP cache:

```
ARP -a [IP address]
```

This command displays all the current ARP cache entries. You can use [IP Address] to optionally provide the parameters. This parameter filters the ARP command so only the physical addresses for the specified IP address are displayed. Use this when you are trying to determine the MAC address for a single IP address, and there are several entries in the ARP cache. In Windows NT, you also can use the ARP -g command with the same results.

To add a static entry to the ARP cache that will not expire according to normal ARP cache rules, use the following command:

```
ARP -s "IP Address" "Physical Address"
```

If you want to add a static entry for the host 172.16.2.16 with MAC address 0080D7225FBF, for example, type the following command:

```
ARP –s 172.16.2.16 00-80-D7-22-5F-BF
```

Note that the MAC address uses a hyphen to separate each pair of hexadecimal characters. It generally is not recommended that you add static entries to the ARP cache. If a network card failed or was replaced on host 172.16.2.16, you would not be able to communicate with this host because you would have the incorrect MAC address.

> **STATIC ARP ENTRIES REALLY ARE NOT THAT STATIC**
>
> Static ARP entries remain in the ARP cache until the host is restarted. When
> this occurs, the ARP cache is flushed and static entries are not re-created. If
> an IP address has been assigned a static entry in the ARP cache, and if an
> ARP broadcast sent on the network suggests a different physical address, the
> new address replaces the old address in the ARP cache.

If you want to remove an incorrect entry from the ARP cache (such as an incorrectly
entered static entry), use the following command:

```
ARP -d "IP address"
```

If you want to remove your previous entry for the host at 172.16.2.16, type the
following:

```
ARP -d 172.16.2.16
```

3

> **HOSTS CAN UPDATE ARP PACKETS**
>
> Although the ARP packet is sent with a specific host's IP address, other
> hosts still inspect the ARP packet to see whether it is intended for them. If a
> host notices that the ARP packet contains an IP address/MAC address combi-
> nation that does not match an entry in its ARP cache, it updates its cache
> with the information in the ARP packet. This information is more timely and
> should be trusted over an entry in the ARP cache.

Internet Control Message Protocol (ICMP)

RFC 792 The Internet Control Message Protocol provides an error-reporting mechanism
and controls messages to the TCP/IP protocol suite. This protocol was created
primarily to report routing failures to the sending host.

The following functions can be performed by the ICMP protocol:

- Provide echo and reply messages to test the reliability of a connection between
  two hosts. This usually is accomplished with the PING (Packet Internet Groper)
  command.

- Redirect traffic to provide more efficient routing when a router becomes congested
  due to excess traffic.

- Send out a time-exceeded message when a source datagram has exceeded its allocated time-to-live and has been discarded.

- Send out router advertisements to determine the address of all routers on a network segment.

- Provide a source-quench message to tell a host to slow down its communications when the communications are saturating a router or a network WAN link.

- Determine what subnet mask is in use on a network segment.

ROUTING PROTOCOLS

Routing is discussed on Day 9, "Gateway and Routing Protocols." See this chapter when reviewing the concept of routing and the functionality provided by routing protocols.

The ICMP Packet Format   The ICMP packet format is shown in Figure 3.7, with fields described in Table 3.2.

FIGURE 3.7.

The ICMP packet structure.

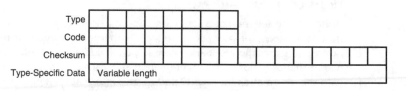

TABLE 3.2. THE ICMP PACKET FIELDS.

Field	Definition
Type	This 8-bit field indicates the type of ICMP packet being transmitted. The following are possible types:

- 0—Network unreachable

- 1—Host unreachable

- 2—Protocol unreachable

- 3—Port unreachable

- 4—Fragmentation needed

- 5—Source route failed

- 6—Destination network unknown

- 7—Destination host unknown

- 8—Source host isolated

Field	Definition
	• 9—Communication with destination network administratively prohibited
	• 10—Communication with destination host administratively prohibited
	• 11—Network unreachable for type of service
	• 12—Host unreachable for type of service
Code	This field provides additional information not provided in the Type field for the destination host.
Checksum	This field provides error detection for the ICMP portion of the packet.
Type Specific Data	This data depends on the type of functionality ICMP is providing. If it's Echo Request/Echo Reply (the most common), this information includes an identifier and a sequence number that are used to identify each echo request sent and each reply.

Using the ICMP Protocol to Troubleshoot Connectivity   One of the most common problems a network administrator faces is determining why a specific computer cannot communicate with the rest of the network. Many times, it is the result of an incorrect TCP/IP protocol configuration. The ICMP protocol can help determine which configuration parameter potentially is incorrect.

Figure 3.8 shows a test network on which you could test the TCP/IP configuration for a host with IP address 172.16.2.200.

FIGURE 3.8.

Testing a host's IP configuration.

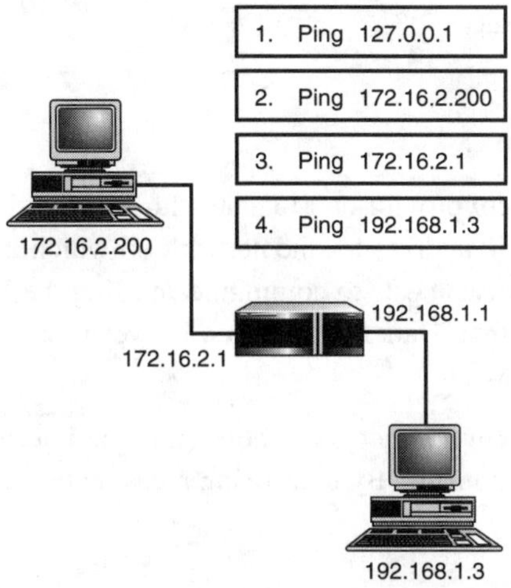

1. Start by pinging a reserved IP address. This address (known as the *loopback address*) is 127.0.0.1. If you ping this successfully, the TCP/IP protocol suite has been installed correctly.

2. Next ping the IP address assigned to your host (in this example, 172.16.2.200). If you can ping this IP address, the IP address has been configured correctly on your host. This also indicates that TCP/IP has been bound to the correct network interface card (NIC).

3. Next ping the IP address of the configured default gateway. Pinging this address proves you can communicate with another host on the same network segment. If you cannot do this, try pinging a different host on the same network segment. If neither ping works, you probably have an incorrect subnet mask configured. If you can ping one host but not the other, make sure you have the correct addresses and that both hosts are running. In this example, you would ping 172.16.2.1.

4. Finally, ping an IP address for a host on a remote network segment. This proves all routing functions are working correctly. If this does not work, double-check your subnet mask. If it is incorrect, TCP/IP might assume the remote host actually is a local host and won't be able to communicate properly with it. All packets destined for the remote host won't be properly directed to the default gateway on the network segment. In this example, 192.168.1.3 could be pinged to test this step.

A SHORTCUT FOR HOST TESTING

When testing a host's configuration, you actually could just perform step 4. Here's why: If you can ping the host at 192.168.1.3, you successfully used your default gateway. Because the response returned to your computer, you have configured your IP address correctly. For all this to occur, you must be running the TCP/IP protocol.

Internet Protocol (IP)

RFC 791   The Internet Protocol provides all logical addressing of hosts. Each host is assigned a unique IP address for the network on which it is running. The IP protocol is connectionless. For two hosts to communicate using the IP protocol, they do not have to establish a session first. Data is exchanged between the systems using a best-effort delivery system.

As with any protocol that provides network addressing, the Internet Protocol comprises both network and host components. By comparing a destination computer's IP address with its own source IP address, IP can determine whether the packet must be routed to the destination host or can be sent directly to it.

UNDERSTANDING IP ADDRESSES

Tomorrow you will learn the specifics of IP addressing. Today, it is important to understand that the IP address assigned to a host not only represents the host, it also indicates on which logical subnetwork the host is located.

The format of an IP packet is shown in Figure 3.9.

FIGURE 3.9.

The IP packet format.

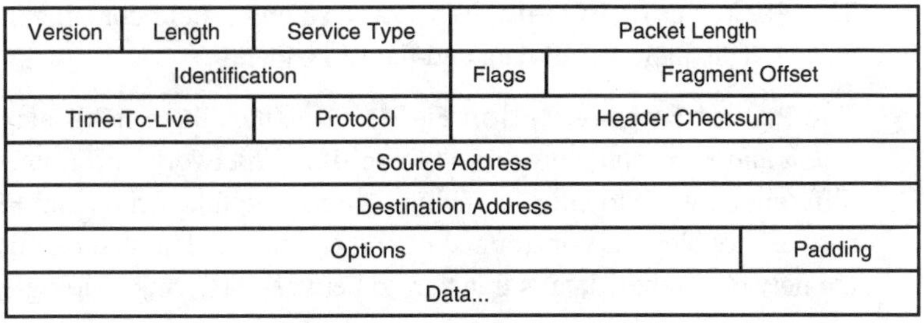

Version	Length	Service Type	Packet Length	
Identification			Flags	Fragment Offset
Time-To-Live		Protocol	Header Checksum	
Source Address				
Destination Address				
Options				Padding
Data...				

The following sections describe each field in an IP packet.

The Version Field   The Version field indicates which version of the IP protocol is used for formatting the IP datagram. The current version of the IP protocol is version 4, but work is continuing on the IPv6 protocol. If the receiving computer cannot handle the IP protocol version, it simply drops the packet. The length of the Version field is 4 bits.

The Length Field   The Length field indicates the IP header's length. All fields in an IP packet are of fixed length except the IP Options and Padding fields. This field determines the dividing line between the header and data portions of the packet. The Length field is subtracted from the Packet Length field to determine where the data starts.

The Service Type Field   The Service Type field tells IP how to handle the IP packet. It includes the five subfields in Figure 3.10.

FIGURE 3.10.

The Service Type subfields.

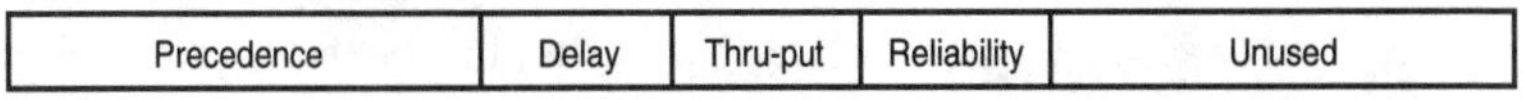

Precedence	Delay	Thru-put	Reliability	Unused

The Precedence subfield sets the importance of a datagram. This 3-bit subfield can range from a value of 0 (normal) to a value of 7 (network control). The higher the number, the more important the packet. Theoretically, higher precedence packets should be routed to the destination address faster than lower precedence packets.

The Delay, Throughput, and Reliability subfields all specify the desired transport of the packet. These three subfields usually are all set to 0. If they are set to 1, they indicate that low delay, high throughput, and high reliability are desired. When multiple routes are available to a remote network, these subfields can be used to determine which route to take.

The last two bits of the Server Type field currently are unused in IP version 4.

The Packet Length Field   The Packet Length field contains the total length of the IP packet. This includes all data and the IP header.

The Packet Fragmentation Fields   The next three fields play a part in the *fragmentation* and *reassembly* processes. In an IP internetwork, information can travel between different network topologies including ethernet, token ring, and FDDI networks. Each network topology is constrained by the amount of data that can fit into a single frame on the network. When data is transferred between differing topologies, it sometimes must be broken into smaller fragments that can be transported across the other network topology.

The size of these fragments is based on the maximum size that can be handled by the network topology across which the datagram is traveling. When a packet is fragmented, a mechanism also must be provided that enables the original packet to be reassembled at the destination host.

The Identification field contains a unique identifier that marks the original datagram. If an original packet is broken into three fragments, each of the three fragments has the same Identification field.

The Flags field, which is 3 bits, controls fragmentation. The first bit currently is unused. The second bit is the Don't Fragment (DF) bit, and the third bit is the More Fragments (MF) bit. If the DF bit is set to 1, the datagram cannot be fragmented. If the data is transferred to a network that cannot handle frames of this size, the datagram is dropped (because it cannot be fragmented). This often is used for circumstances in which packet size is being tested and the packet should not be fragmented into smaller fragments. The MF bit is set to 1 when an original packet has been fragmented. The MF bit indicates that the current packet is followed by more packets. In the last packet of a fragment, the MF bit is set to 0. This indicates that no more packets follow.

The Fragment Offset field is used in conjunction with the MF bit when reassembling the fragmented packet. Many times, the destination host receives the fragmented packets out of order. The MF bit, Identification field, and Fragment Offset field help determine how to rebuild these fragmented packets into the original packet. The offset value always is based on the beginning of the message.

If a 1500-byte packet must be broken into fragments not larger than 700 bytes, for example, the following would occur: The first fragment would be assigned the same ID as the original 1500-byte packet. The MF bit would be set to 1, and the Fragment Offset would be set to 0. The second fragment would have the same ID as the original packet and also would have the MF bit set to 1. The Fragment Offset for the second fragment would be set to 700. The final fragment would have the same ID as the original packet. This would be the final packet, so the MF bit would be set to zero because no more fragments follow. The fragment offset would be set to 1400 for this packet.

The Time-to-Live Field   The time-to-live (TTL) field indicates how long a datagram can exist on a network. Each time the packet crosses a router, its value decreases by at least one second. When the TTL field reaches a value of zero, the datagram is discarded at the current router. A message is sent to the source host stating that the packet was dropped using the ICMP protocol so the source host could resend the packet.

The Protocol Field   The Protocol field indicates which high-level protocol was used to create the information stored in the data portion of the packet. This field assists in moving the packet up to the correct protocol in the TCP/IP layer model. It also defines the format of the data portion of the packet. A protocol identification number (PIN) assigned by the Network Information Center (NIC) represents each protocol. ICMP, for example, is protocol number 1; TCP is protocol number 6.

The Header Checksum Field   The Header Checksum field makes sure the header information has not been corrupted in transit. This checksum is only for the header portion of the packet. It results in reduced processing at each router because the checksum is not calculated on the entire packet. The Header Checksum must be recalculated at every router the packet traverses. This is because the TTL field decrements at each router, necessitating that a new checksum be calculated.

The Source and Destination IP Address Fields   The Source IP Address and Destination IP Address fields contain the 32-bit IP addresses of the source and destination hosts. These values are not changed in transit.

The Options Field   The Options field can be composed of several codes of variable length. More than one option can be used in an IP packet. If more than one is used, the fields appear consecutively in the IP header. Each option is 8 bits long and consists of three subfields.

The first bit represents the *copy flag*. It determines how this option should be treated when an original packet is fragmented. If the copy flag is set to 0, the option only should be copied to the first fragment. If the copy flag is set to 1, the option should be copied to all fragments of the original packet.

The *option class* is represented by 2 bits. The option class can have one of four values assigned to it. A value of 0 means the option has to do with a datagram or a network control. A value of 2 means the option is used for debugging or measurement purposes. Values of 1 and 3 are reserved for future use and have not been defined yet.

The *option number* is represented by the final 5 bits. Each combination of option class and option number is shown in Table 3.3.

TABLE 3.3. VALID IP OPTION CLASSES AND OPTION NUMBERS.

Option Class	Option Number	Description
0	0	End of option list.
0	1	Used for padding. Indicates that no option has been set.
0	2	Security options for military applications.
0	3	Loose source routing. This option indicates a sequence of IP addresses that should be used as the route to a destination host. Loose source routing enables multiple network hops to exist between designated source addresses.
0	7	Used to trace routes to a destination. Useful for determining which exact route was traversed between a source and destination host. Each router that handles the IP packet adds its IP address to the options list.
0	9	Strict source routing. As with loose source routing, strict source routing specifies a routing path to a destination host. The difference is that, if the designated route cannot be followed, the packet is discarded.
2	4	Internet timestamp that enables timestamps to be recorded along a route. Each router records its IP address and a timestamp, indicating the time the router handled the packet. This time is based on milliseconds since midnight Greenwich Mean Time (or Universal Time). Due to non-synchronization of clocks, these times only should be considered estimates of the exact time.

The Padding Field   The Padding field's contents are based on the options selected for an IP packet. The padding ensures that the datagram's header is rounded to an even number of bytes.

Internet Group Management Protocol (IGMP)

RFC 1112   At times, instead of sending information from a source host to a single destination host, you will need to send information to multiple destination hosts. One method is to use *broadcasting*. There are two major issues with broadcasting. First, all hosts on the network must examine the packet to determine whether it is intended for them. Second, many routers are configured not to forward broadcasts to other network segments. Both these issues can cause congestion on the network.

An alternative to broadcasting is *multicasting*. Instead of an IP packet's destination being all machines on the network, the destination can be a specific group of computers. Multicast packets are delivered using UDP. Therefore, they might be lost or delayed in transit.

The following are some facts about IP multicast groups:

- All multicast addressing is based on Class D IP addresses, which range from 224.0.0.1 through 239.255.255.255. TCP/IP address classes are discussed on Day 4.

- The address 224.0.0.1 is reserved. It represents the *all hosts* group. This group includes all IP hosts and routers participating in IP multicasting on a network segment.

- An IP host can dynamically join or exit an IP multicast group at any time.

- IP multicast addresses should appear only as destination addresses. They rarely appear as source addresses because multicast addresses are not usually bound to network interface cards. Some forms of UNIX do allow this capability. In these cases, a multicast address can appear as the source address.

The fields in an IGMP packet are shown in Figure 3.11.

FIGURE 3.11.

The Service Type subfields.

Version	Type	Unused	Checksum
Group Address			

- *Version.* This field indicates the protocol version in use. For IGMP packets, this is set to a value of 1.

- *Type.* This field indicates whether the IGMP message is a query sent by a multicast router (a value of 1) or a response sent by an IP host (a value of 2).

- *Checksum.* This field is a checksum for the entire IGMP message. It makes sure the information has not been corrupted in transit. The same algorithm used for calculating IP header checksums also is used for IGMP checksums.
- *Group Address.* This field contains the IP multicast of the group in which a host is reporting membership. In the case of a multicast group query, this field is set to all zeroes.

Applying What You Have Learned

Today's material covered a lot of information. You started with a comparison of the TCP/IP and OSI layer models. Be sure you know what functionality is provided by each layer. This can help you determine which layer each protocol in the TCP/IP protocol suite exists.

The following questions will further your knowledge of the protocols that exist in each of the TCP/IP layers.

Test Your Knowledge

1. What are the four layers of the TCP/IP layer model?
2. What is meant by the term *boundary layer*?
3. What layers of the OSI model can be matched to the network interface layer of the TCP/IP layer model?
4. What functionality is provided by the transport layer in the TCP/IP layer model?
5. What physical address is obtained by the ARP protocol when the destination host is located on the same network segment?
6. What physical address is obtained by the ARP protocol when the destination host is located on a remote network segment?
7. What services are provided by the ICMP protocol?
8. Does the IP protocol provide connection-oriented or connectionless service?
9. Why is multicasting preferred over broadcasting when sending data to multiple hosts?

Preview of the Next Day

Tomorrow's material digs into the Internet Protocol. Topics discussed include the basic formatting of an IP address, the various classes of IP addresses, and general information about the use of subnet masks.

The end of the day overviews some features of IPv6. If you are interested in a more detailed description of IPv6, see Day 21, "Future Applications of TCP/IP."

DAY 4

Internet Protocol (IP) Addresses

Today you will learn about the assignment of IP addresses to hosts. This chapter discusses the rules for assigning IP addresses. Also, we'll look into how subnet masks are used to determine what portion of a 32-bit address is used to represent the network and what portion is used to identify a host on that network. The following topics are covered in this chapter:

- The assignment of IP addresses
- A comparison of dotted-decimal notation versus binary representation
- The classes of IP addresses
- The role of a subnet mask in routing decisions
- The ANDing process, which is used when routing is determined
- The role of Private Address Ranges
- The future of IP addressing

Internet Protocol Address Basics

IP addresses uniquely identify each host on a TCP/IP internetwork. A *host* can be a computer, a terminal, a router, or even a hub. You can think of it like this: A host is any physical device on your network that fits one of the following properties:

- You use this device to access other devices on the network.
- You connect to this device as a shared network component.
- You need to manage this device to make sure it is functioning correctly.

Every host in a TCP/IP internetwork requires a unique IP address. This IP address must be unique across the entire internetwork. With a large worldwide network such as the Internet, a number-assigning authority is required. For the Internet, the Internet Assigned Number Authority (IANA) sets policies regarding how IP addresses are assigned and is in charge of these assignments. If you need to obtain network IP addresses to join the Internet, they can be obtained on the Internet at the site http://rs.internic.net.

ACQUIRING AN IP ADDRESS

Although IP addressing ultimately is the domain of the Internet Assigned Number Authority (IANA), you usually will acquire your network's pool of IP addresses from a local Internet service provider. Most ISPs have pools of IP addresses available to assign to their clientele.

What happens if a host uses the same IP address as another host on the network? It depends on your implementation of TCP/IP. In most implementations, the second host with the duplicate IP address has its IP stack disabled. Most often, a warning message is issued to both hosts, making them aware that a duplicate IP address has been found on the network. In other scenarios, both systems continue to try to use the same IP address. This is a difficult scenario to troubleshoot. The only way to find the culprit is to use ARP commands to determine the MAC addresses of the hosts using the duplicate IP addresses.

How Do You Write an Address?

Each IP address is a stream of 32 1s and 0s. This is why the current version of IP addressing is known as 32-bit addressing. It would be confusing if addresses were referred to in this manner. Therefore, *dotted-decimal representation* is used for IP addresses. Before dotted-decimal representation is discussed, however, you should briefly review the binary number system.

Binary Representation

The binary numbering system consists of only two digits: 0 and 1. All numbers are represented as streams of 0s and 1s. Figure 4.1 shows the representation of numbers 0 through 15 in the binary system.

FIGURE 4.1.

Binary representation of numbers 0 through 15.

	128's	64's	32's	16's	8's	4's	2's	1's	
0	0	0	0	0	0	0	0	0	=0
1	0	0	0	0	0	0	0	1	=1
2	0	0	0	0	0	0	1	0	=2
3	0	0	0	0	0	0	1	1	=2+1
4	0	0	0	0	0	1	0	0	=4
5	0	0	0	0	0	1	0	1	=4+1
6	0	0	0	0	0	1	1	0	=4+2
7	0	0	0	0	0	1	1	1	=4+2+1
8	0	0	0	0	1	0	0	0	=8
9	0	0	0	0	1	0	0	1	=8+1
10	0	0	0	0	1	0	1	0	=8+2
11	0	0	0	0	1	0	1	1	=8+2+1
12	0	0	0	0	1	1	0	0	=8+4
13	0	0	0	0	1	1	0	1	=8+4+1
14	0	0	0	0	1	1	1	0	=8+4+2
15	0	0	0	0	1	1	1	1	=8+4+2+1

You can think of the binary digits as place holders that can be added together. If a 1 is entered in a column, that column should be included in the total when converting the binary number to decimal representation.

The column values of 128, 64, 32, 16, 6, 4, 2, and 1 are all *powers of 2*. In other words, the 1s column actually is the value 2^0. The 2s column is the value 2^1. Figure 4.2 shows the translations for the eight columns. This collection of eight bits is referred to as an *octet* of information. Remember that 8 bits also is referred to as a *byte* of information.

As you can see, each column is a power of 2. As you move left through the columns, each column is two times the number in the previous column.

FIGURE 4.2.

Calculating each of the binary columns for an octet.

2^n		Dec	Actual
2^0	=	1	1
2^1	=	2	2
2^2	=	4	2 x 2
2^3	=	8	2 x 2 x 2
2^4	=	16	2 x 2 x 2 x 2
2^5	=	32	2 x 2 x 2 x 2 x 2
2^6	=	64	2 x 2 x 2 x 2 x 2 x 2
2^7	=	128	2 x 2 x 2 x 2 x 2 x 2 x 2

WHY DISCUSS BINARY NUMBERING?

Although it might seem trivial to review the binary numbering system, it is a good idea to practice translating numbers between 0 and 255 to binary numbers. When working with advanced IP addressing issues, such as calculating pools of IP addresses for use in subnet masking, this knowledge can greatly reduce the amount of time spent at this task.

The number 131, for example, would be represented as 128 + 2 + 1. In binary, this is 10000011. The number 63 would be represented as 32 + 16 + 8 + 4 + 2 + 1, which is 00111111 in binary.

The good news is you only work with up to eight digits, or an octet, when working with binary and IP addresses. The 32-bit address is represented in dotted-decimal format using four octets of information. These four 8-bit collections form the 32-bit IP address for a host.

What is the highest decimal digit allowed for an octet? If you convert 11111111 to decimal, you have 128 + 64 + 32 + 16 + 8 + 4+ 2 + 1 = 255. Therefore, the largest value allowed for any of the decimals in dotted-decimal format is 255. The lowest is 00000000, or simply 0.

Dotted-Decimal Notation

It is difficult and tiresome to write addresses in binary. Instead of using binary, therefore, dotted-decimal notation is more commonly used for addresses.

An IP address (as previously mentioned) comprises four octets of information to make up the 32-bit address. Each octet is more commonly written in decimal notation.

For example, the IP address

01111111 00000000 00000000 00000001

is more commonly written as 127.0.0.1.

Each octet of information is translated into its decimal equivalent. The octets are then separated using a period between each octet.

IP Address Classes

On a single network segment, all IP hosts share the same network address. Each host on that segment must have a unique host portion of the address. Five pools of IP addresses have been designated as classes of IP addresses. Only the first three can be assigned to hosts on a network.

Each of the first three classes of IP addresses is composed of a network and host portion of those IDs. Figure 4.3 shows the details of the address classes.

FIGURE 4.3.

The five classes of IP addresses.

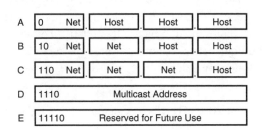

Class A Addresses

A Class A address allocates 8 bits to the network portion of the address and 24 bits to the host portion of the address. A Class A address has a first octet value between 1 and 126. These numbers are represented in binary by patterns that resemble 0#######. This allows for 126 distinct networks of 16,774,214 hosts per network. These numbers are determined using the following calculations:

- The first digit of the first octet in a Class A address is 0; this leaves 7 bits to create each unique network ID. The value of 2^7 is 128. Two addresses cannot be used, however. The value 0 cannot be used as a network ID. The value 127 also cannot be used because it is reserved for loopback functions. This leaves 126 unique network IDs.

- There are 24 bits left for the host ID. The value of 2^{24} is 16,777,216. A host ID cannot be all 0s or all 1s. This eliminates two host IDs from the pool, resulting in 16,777,214 unique hosts per network.

Class B Addresses

A Class B address allocates 16 bits to the network portion of the address and 16 bits to the host portion of the address. A Class B address has a first octet value between 128 and 191. These numbers are represented in binary by patterns that resemble 10######. This allows for 16,384 unique networks with 65,534 host per network. These numbers are determined using the following calculations:

- The first two digits of the first octet of a Class B address are 1 and 0; this leaves 14 bits to represent each unique network ID. If you calculate 2^{14}, you determine the total number of Class B network IDs to be 16,384.

- There are 16 bits left for the host ID. The value of 2^{16} is 65,536. A host ID cannot be all 0s or all 1s. This removes two host IDs from the pool, resulting in 65,534 unique hosts per network.

Class C Addresses

A Class C address allocates 24 bits to the network portion of the address and 8 bits to the host portion of the address. A Class C address has a first octet value between 192 and 223. These numbers are represented in binary by patterns that resemble 110#####. This allows for 2,097,152 unique networks with 254 hosts per network. These numbers are determined using the following calculations:

- The first three digits of a Class C address are 1, 1, and 0; this leaves 21 bits to represent each unique network ID. If you calculate 2^{21}, you determine the total number of Class C network IDs to be 2,097,152.

- There are 8 bits left for the host ID. The value of 2^{8} is 256. A host ID cannot be all 0s or all 1s. This removes two host IDs from the pool, resulting in 254 unique hosts per network.

Class D Addresses

Class D addresses are reserved for multicast group usage and cannot be assigned to individual hosts on a network. Remember from Day 3 that IP hosts can dynamically register into multicast groups using the IGMP protocol.

A Class D address has a first octet value between 224 and 239 and is represented in binary with a pattern matching 1110####. The remaining 28 bits represent the multicast group to which the host belongs.

Class E Addresses

Class E addresses are experimental addresses that are not available to the public. They have been reserved for future use. A Class E address has a first octet value between 240 and 255. This is represented in binary with values that match the pattern 1111####.

General Guidelines for IP Addressing

The following are general guidelines that can be applied when assigning network and host IDs:

- All hosts on the same physical network segment should have the same network ID.
- Each host on a network segment must have a unique host portion of the IP address.
- A network ID can never be 127. This value has been reserved for loopback functions.
- A network ID cannot be all 1s. This represents a broadcast address.
- A host ID cannot be all 1s. This also represents a broadcast address for the network.
- A network ID cannot be all 0s. This represents the local network.
- A host ID cannot be all 0s. It is customary to represent a network using the network portion of the ID with a host ID set to all 0s. This cannot be allocated to an individual host.

Special IP Addresses

Some IP addresses have been reserved and cannot be assigned to individual hosts or be used as network IDs. These reserved addresses include the following:

- Each network address is represented by the network ID with the host ID set to all 0s. Table 4.1 shows the format for each IP address class's network address.

TABLE 4.1. NETWORK ADDRESSES BY CLASS.

Class	Network ID
A	w.0.0.0
B	w.x.0.0
C	w.x.y.0

- A network ID with the host ID set to all 1s represents a network's broadcast address. Table 4.2 shows the format for each IP address class's broadcast address.

TABLE 4.2. BROADCAST ADDRESSES BY CLASS.

Class	Network ID
A	w.255.255.255
B	w.x.255.255
C	w.x.y.255

- The IP address 255.255.255.255 is reserved as the *limited broadcast address*. This address can be used at any time when the network ID is not yet known by a host. Routers generally are configured not to forward this broadcast beyond the local network segment.

- The network address 127 is reserved for loopback functions. It cannot be assigned to a network segment.

- The IP address 0.0.0.0 is reserved to mean *this host*. This only is an option when a host such as a DHCP client is starting up and has not yet received an IP address. This topic is discussed on Day 10.

The Role of Subnet Masks

Subnet masks designate which bits of an IP address represent the network portion and which bits represent the host portion. Default subnet masks are used with Class A, Class B, and Class C IP addresses, as follows:

- Class A—255.0.0.0
- Class B—255.255.0.0
- Class C—255.255.255.0

The Class A subnet mask tells you the first 8 bits of the IP address represent the network portion of the address. The remaining 24 bits represent the host portion of the address. Let's say a host has the IP address 11.25.65.32. Using the default subnet mask, the network address would be 11.0.0.0. The host component of the address would be 25.65.32.

The Class B subnet mask tells you the first 16 bits of the IP address represent the network portion of the address. The remaining 16 bits represent the host address within the network. If a host has the IP address 172.16.33.33, the network portion of the address would be 172.16.0.0. The host component would be 33.33.

The Class C subnet mask tells you the first 24 bits of the IP address represent the network portion of the address. The remaining 8 bits represent the host address within the network. If a host has the IP address 192.168.2.3, the network portion of the address would be 192.168.2.0. The host component would be 3.

The ANDing Process

When a source host attempts to communicate with a destination host, the source host uses its subnet mask to determine whether the destination host is on the local network or a remote network. This is known as the ANDing process.

The AND function has the following properties:

- If the two compared values are both 1, the result is 1.
- If one of the values is 0 and the other is 1, the result is 0.
- If both of the compared values are 0, the result is 0.

The source and destination IP addresses are compared to the source's subnet mask using the ANDing process. An AND result is created for each of the addresses. If the result is the same, the hosts are on the same network. If the result is different, the destination host is on a remote network. All traffic destined for that remote host should be directed to the router indicated in the source host's routing table. If no explicit route is defined in the routing table, the traffic is directed to the source host's default gateway.

Figure 4.4 shows two hosts that want to communicate. Host A (with IP address 172.16.2.4) wants to communicate with Host B (with IP address 172.16.3.5). If the subnet mask for Host A is 255.255.0.0, will the hosts communicate using local transmissions or will they send information to the default gateway?

FIGURE 4.4.

Using the ANDing process.

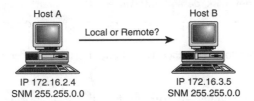

Host A   Local or Remote?   Host B

IP 172.16.2.4   IP 172.16.3.5
SNM 255.255.0.0   SNM 255.255.0.0

4

When converted to binary, the address 172.16.2.4 is as follows:

`10101100 00010000 00000010 00000100`

When converted to binary, the address 172.16.3.5 is as follows:

`10101100 00010000 00000011 00000101`

If the ANDing process is performed, the result for Host A using its subnet mask of 255.255.0.0 is as follows:

```
HOST A's IP Address    10101100 00010000 00000010 00000100
Host A's Subnet Mask   11111111 11111111 00000000 00000000
ANDING Result          10101100 00010000 00000000 00000000
```

The result for Host B is as follows:

```
HOST B's IP Address    10101100 00010000 00000011 00000101
Host A's Subnet Mask   11111111 11111111 00000000 00000000
ANDing Result          10101100 00010000 00000000 00000000
```

As you can see, the two results match. This indicates that, as far as Host A is concerned, the two hosts are on the same physical network. Communication can occur directly between the two hosts.

Day 6 further examines the art of subnet masking. It also examines the use of nonstandard subnet masking to further segment a group of IP addresses into smaller segments.

Common Subnet Mask Problems

As previously discussed, the subnet mask determines whether a destination host is on the local network or a remote network. Most troubleshooting of subnet masking is performed using the IPCONFIG and PING utilities.

THE IPCONFIG UTILITY

In some TCP/IP implementations, the IPCONFIG utility is called IFCONFIG. Whatever the name, this utility reveals the current TCP/IP configuration for the host on which the command is run. This includes the configuration of the IP address, subnet mask, default gateway and DNS server.

The following are symptoms that incorrect subnet masks have been implemented on your network:

- You are able to communicate with hosts on the local network, but you are unable to communicate with remote hosts.

- You are able to communicate with all hosts on the remote network except one specific host. When you try to communicate with that host, you receive messages such as Timed out warnings.

- You are unable to communicate with a host on the local network because your host believes it is located on a remote network.

Local Network Addresses

RFC 1918   Three pools of IP addresses have been reserved for use on local networks behind firewalls and proxy servers. The following are the reserved address pools:

- 10.0.0.0 through 10.255.255.255
- 172.16.0.0 through 172.31.255.255
- 192.168.0.0 through 192.168.255.255

These addresses were created to provide networks not attached to the Internet with a pool of IP addresses that do not conflict with any addresses currently in use on the Internet. If networks using these reserved addresses link to the Internet in the future, they do not have to worry about an address conflict with any other network on the Internet.

The network in Figure 4.5 uses the network address 192.168.3.0 for the internal network. In this example, the firewall has a component known as the Local Address Table (LAT). The Local Address Table designates that the internal interface of the firewall is on the 192.168.3.0 network. Any hosts using an IP addresses that belong on the 192.168.3.0 network *must* be located on the internal side of the firewall. A host trying to connect from the Internet side of the firewall will be stopped by the firewall for security reasons.

FIGURE 4.5.

Use of reserved local network addresses.

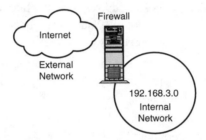

When I first started to set up firewalls, I was not aware of the reserved local address tables. I used the network address 131.107.0.0 with the subnet mask 255.255.0.0 for my internal network.

I thought I correctly configured this network range into the firewall's LAT and communications function—until someone attempted to send email to a recipient at `microsoft.com`. The mail server for the domain `microsoft.com` was located at 131.107.3.42. When the email was forwarded to our firewall, it resolved the Mail Exchanger (MX) record for `microsoft.com` and determined that it needed to forward the mail to 131.107.3.42. Using its LAT table, the firewall determined that this server must be located somewhere on our local network. The mail was not successfully delivered—ever!

Using the IP ranges prescribed in RFC 1918, you can protect yourself from this situation. These IP addresses are not in use on the Internet. They only can be used behind firewalls and proxy servers that obscure or hide their local addressing schemes from the Internet.

4

The Future of IP Addressing (IPv6)

With the growth of the Internet, the current IP addressing scheme is quickly running out of available addresses. The IETF, recognizing this, has been commissioned to create the next generation of the IP address.

Several published RFCs lay out the needs for the new protocol. This new release of the IP protocol, now known as IPv6, should begin to replace the current IPv4 as the year 2000 rolls out.

The following are major changes in the next release of IPv6:

- *Expanded addressing capabilities.* The address size for IPv6 will be 128 bits, which will provide a larger pool of IP addresses for the Internet. This pool will provide each Internet user with a pool of IP addresses equal to the total number of IP addresses available on the Internet today.

- *Simplification of the IP header.* Much of the IPv4 header information has been made optional or has been dropped entirely. This will speed up processing of the IP header information by receiving hosts.

- *Improved extensibility of the IP header.* The IP header has been formatted to provide more efficient forwarding, more flexibility on the length of option fields, and easier inclusion of new options in the future. This will enable the IP header to change as the protocol evolves over the next few years, without having to redesign the entire header format.

- *Improved flow control.* IP datagrams will be able to request better quality of service. This will include time-specific delivery of information and the capability to request a minimum bandwidth availability or real-time service.

- *Increase security.* The IP header will include extensions to support authentication of source and destination hosts, and better assurance of noncorruption of data. This also will provide the option of encrypting data as it is transported over the network.

These IP protocol enhancements should help the Internet continue to grow. They also should help continue the increase in functionality provided to applications using TCP/IP as their base protocol suite. Specific information about IPv6 is discussed on Day 21, "Future Applications of TCP/IP."

Applying What You Have Learned

The material covered today is the starting point for understanding how to configure TCP/IP on a network. Today you learned about the notation used to represent IP addresses, the five classes of IP addresses, and the function of the subnet mask. This chapter also provided a brief overview of what IPv6 will provide for future use of the TCP/IP protocol suite.

Test Your Knowledge

1. Convert the decimal numbers in Table 4.3 to binary representation.

TABLE 4.3. CONVERTING FROM DECIMAL TO BINARY.

Decimal	Binary
127	
0	
76	
248	
224	
57	
135.56.204.253	

2. Convert the binary numbers in Table 4.4 to decimal format.

TABLE 4.4. CONVERTING FROM BINARY TO DECIMAL.

Binary	Decimal
11100110	
00011100	
01010101	
11001100	
11001010 00001100 10100011 11110010	
00011011 10001001 01111111 10000101	

3. Identify the address class of the IP addresses in Table 4.5.

TABLE 4.5. IDENTIFYING ADDRESS CLASSES.

IP Address	IP Address Class
131.107.2.8	
127.0.0.1	

continues

TABLE 4.5. CONTINUED

IP Address	IP Address Class
225.34.56.7	
129.33.55.6	
10.2.4.5	
223.223.223.223	

4. What is the broadcast address for a host with IP address 172.30.45.67, assuming the default subnet mask is implemented on the network?

5. What is the network address for a host with IP address 201.200.200.15, assuming the default subnet mask is implemented on the network?

6. Based on the network in Figure 4.6, will the host named SUSAN be able to communicate with the host named KELLY?

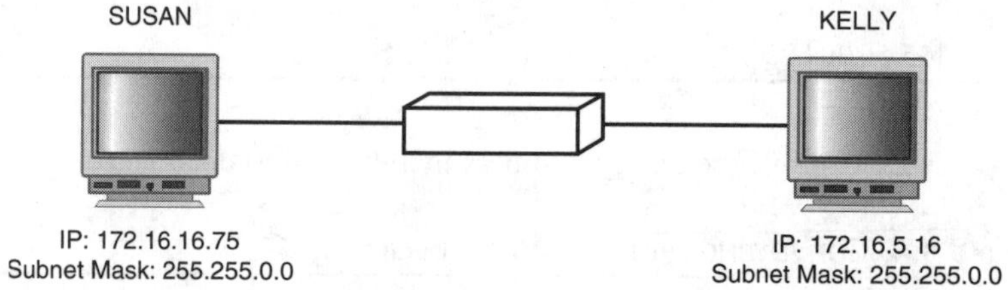

FIGURE 4.6.

A sample network.

SUSAN

IP: 172.16.16.75
Subnet Mask: 255.255.0.0

KELLY

IP: 172.16.5.16
Subnet Mask: 255.255.0.0

7. What subnet mask could be used to enable SUSAN and KELLY to communicate correctly?

8. What pools of IP addresses have been reserved for use on local area networks by the Internet Assigned Number Authority?

9. What advantages does IPv6 have over IPv4?

Preview of the Next Day

Tomorrow you will examine the transport layer of the TCP/IP layered model. The TCP and UDP protocols also are examined in-depth. The following topics are covered:

- The TCP protocol header
- The TCP three-way handshake process
- TCP sliding windows performance enhancements
- TCP port usage
- The UDP protocol header
- UDP port usage

DAY 5

Transport Control Protocol (TCP) and User Datagram Protocol (UDP)

Today, you investigate the two protocols located in the transport layer of the TCP/IP layered model. Transmission Control Protocol (TCP) and User Datagram Protocol (UDP) transport application data over the network. TCP is used for guaranteed delivery, and UDP is used for nonguaranteed delivery.

This chapter covers the following:

- The situations in which a guaranteed delivery is preferred over a nonguaranteed delivery
- Which applications are designed for use with which protocol
- The TCP and UDP header formats
- How TCP establishes and terminates a session
- How sliding windows improve transmission performance when using TCP
- The well-known TCP and UDP ports

Connection Versus Connectionless Traffic

The two protocols in the transport layer of the TCP/IP layered model provide transport mechanisms for applications over a TCP/IP network. The TCP protocol delivers guaranteed or reliable delivery of information. UDP delivers information using a nonreliable or nonguaranteed method.

At first glance, you might write off the UDP protocol. If delivery is not guaranteed, why would you use this transport protocol? The answer is in the overhead involved with a guaranteed protocol such as TCP. Two hosts exchanging data using TCP must exchange status information in addition to the actual exchange of data. This status includes acknowledgment messages that indicate whether previous segments were received successfully.

Transmission Control Protocol (TCP)

In its simplest implementation, a guaranteed protocol waits to make sure the recipient host receives a segment of information before it transmits the next available segment (see Figure 5.1).

FIGURE 5.1.

The guaranteed delivery process.

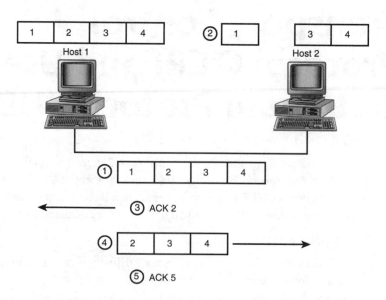

The recipient machine sends an acknowledgment packet that indicates the next segment it expects to receive. If every segment is acknowledged by the recipient host, the traffic involved with the file transfer doubles.

> **WHAT TRANSPORT DO MULTICASTS USE?**
>
> By definition, multicasts are transmitted from a single host to multiple hosts that are members of the target multicast group. The goal of a multicast is to send a single transmission of data that multiple hosts can read. The sending host cannot wait for acknowledgments from every recipient before it sends the next packet of data. As a result, all multicast applications use UDP as the underlying transport protocol.

User Datagram Protocol (UDP)

In some circumstances, guaranteed delivery is not required. UDP delivers a best-effort attempt to transfer data between two hosts. Error detection can be performed when using the UDP protocol, but it is the responsibility of the higher-level application using UDP as its transport protocol. UDP can send information to a destination host without first establishing a session with that host. When timely delivery is important, UDP delivers information to a host faster than TCP. An example of this is Simple Network Management Protocol (SNMP).

SNMP monitors a network and is alerted to problems in the physical topology of the network. This is accomplished using traps. A *trap* is a triggered event based on a rule. Let's say, for example, a host is configured to issue a trap when its hard disk space is less than 100MB. The trap is sent immediately after the condition exists. If TCP were used instead, the host first would have to establish a session with the SNMP management system before it could send the SNMP trap. UDP enables the SNMP trap to be sent as soon as the trap event occurs.

Another common example is RealAudio. A host sending a RealAudio feed does not want every packet of data to be acknowledged by the recipient host. The playback quality would be greatly reduced if each packet were acknowledged.

The Use of Ports and Sockets

Both TCP and UDP act as an intermediary between applications and the Internet Protocol (IP) to provide transport over an internetwork. So far, you have learned that individual hosts are assigned IP addresses (made up of the network and host IDs) to uniquely identify themselves on an internetwork.

An issue that needs to be resolved—in addition to which host information must be sent to—is which application running on the host should receive the information. This can be resolved using ports.

5

Ports provide an application endpoint on a host and can be any number between 0 and 65,535. Ports numbered between 0 and 1,023 are *well-known ports* that have been pre-assigned an associated application by the Internet Assigned Number Authority (IANA). Lists of specific TCP and UDP ports can be found later in this chapter.

Port numbers on the client side are generated dynamically by the operating system when the client attempts to connect to the remote host. The random port numbers are generated with a minimum value of 1,024 (because the ports between 0 and 1,023 are reserved for the well-known ports).

When a source host wants to communicate with a Winsock-based application running on another host, it connects to the server's application port number. The actual address connected to is the server's IP address and port number. The combination of IP address, transport protocol, and port number is called the *socket address.*

When a TCP session is established, both hosts participating in the session must agree to participate. The following two distinct functions take place:

- The host functioning as the server performs a passive open. The *passive open* indicates to the operating system on which port the application is willing to accept connections. This port is said to be in a *listening state.*

- The host functioning as the client contacts its operating system for a port assignment when it requests to connect to the server's application. This is an *active open* because the session actually is established at this point between the client and server hosts.

It is possible for a single port on a host to have multiple sessions connected to it. Let's say, for example, two clients are connecting to a mail server using SMTP to send mail (see Figure 5.2).

FIGURE 5.2.

Multiplexing a TCP port.

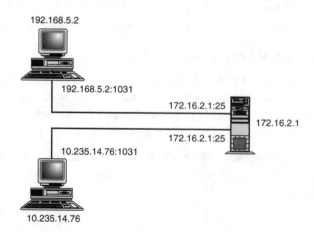

192.168.5.2

192.168.5.2:1031

172.16.2.1:25

172.16.2.1

172.16.2.1:25

10.235.14.76:1031

10.235.14.76

The client with IP address 192.168.5.2 is using TCP to send mail to the mail server at IP address 172.16.2.1. At the same time, the client with IP address 10.235.14.76 also is connected to the mail server for the purpose of sending mail. Both clients dynamically use port 1031 at the client side. How does the server know which client sent which message? This is handled using the full-socket information. The client at the top socket address is 192.168.5.2:1031. This is one endpoint for communication and 172.16.2.1:25 is the other. The bottom host's socket address is 10.235.14.76:1031. This is one endpoint and the other is 172.16.2.1:25. End-to-end communication sessions often are referred to as *virtual circuits.*

Messages are not intermixed because TCP uses both endpoints when identifying a communication stream. Even though both communication streams use port 1031 on the client side and communicate with 172.16.2.1:25, they also have unique socket addresses at the client side. This distinguishes the two mail sessions.

CLIENT SIDE PORT ASSIGNMENTS

Figure 5.2 displays an unlikely scenario. Because client hosts are randomly assigned a port over 1,024 when they connect to a server, the chance of two client systems connecting to a server using the same client port is highly unlikely.

Transmission Control Protocol

RFC 793

As previously mentioned, the TCP protocol provides reliable, connection-oriented delivery in the TCP/IP protocol suite. The TCP protocol provides the following features to the TCP/IP protocol suite:

- A mechanism for reliable communication between two hosts using an unreliable base protocol (IP).
- A start-up sequence to establish an end-to-end communication session.
- A mechanism to reassemble data that arrives out of order (based on its sequence numbers).
- The capability for a source host to distinguish between different applications running on a destination host (based on their port numbers).
- Timers that enable retransmission of lost packets to occur in a timely manner.
- Simplified application development. Because TCP handles acknowledgments and retransmission of lost or corrupted data, the applications do not have to provide this service.

5

The following are some well-known Winsock applications that use TCP as their transport protocol:

- FTP
- Telnet
- SMTP mail servers
- Web servers

As discussed on Day 3, a good analogy for the TCP protocol is a guaranteed message-delivery service such as UPS. When you send a package using UPS, you can track its delivery. You also can make sure your desired recipient receives the package because they must sign to acknowledge receipt.

The TCP Header Format

TCP segments are sent within an Internet datagram. The format of a TCP header is shown in Figure 5.3.

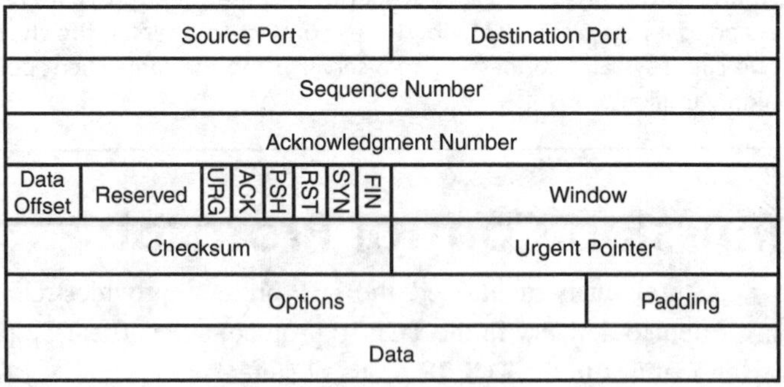

FIGURE 5.3.

The TCP header format.

- *Source Port.* This 16-bit field contains the TCP port used by the local host for the TCP connection.
- *Destination Port.* This 16-bit field contains the TCP port used by the remote host for the TCP connection.
- *Sequence Number.* This 32-bit field indicates the order in which segments should be reassembled at the destination host. This field also is used during the TCP/IP three-way handshake to synchronize sequence numbers.
- *Acknowledgment Number.* This 32-bit field indicates which sequence number the sending host expects to receive next from the destination host.
- *Data Offset.* This 4-bit field indicates the size of the TCP header in 32-bit words. Using the Data Offset field, you can determine where the data begins in the TCP segment.

- *Reserved.* This 6-bit field is reserved for future use. It should be set to all zeros.

- *Urgent Control Bit.* If this 1-bit field is set to 1, the Urgent Pointer field is significant and should be read.

- *Acknowledgment Control Bit.* If this 1-bit field is set to 1, the Acknowledgment field is significant and should be read.

- *Push Control Bit.* If this 1-bit field is set to 1, the segment is requesting that a push function take place. This occurs when an application wants to send its data stream immediately instead of waiting for the transmission buffer to be full before delivery takes place.

- *Reset Control Bit.* If this 1-bit field is set to 1, this TCP packet is requesting that the connection be reset.

- *Synchronize Control Bit.* This 1-bit field indicates that sequence numbers should be synchronized. This occurs during the establishment of a TCP session.

- *Finish Control Bit.* If this 1-bit field is set to 1, the sending host has no more data to send.

- *Window Size.* This 16-bit field indicates how many octets of data the sending host is willing to accept at a time. This establishes the sending and receiving window size in TCP Sliding Windows.

- *Checksum.* The checksum makes sure the TCP header and payload have not been corrupted in transit. It also covers some of the fields found in the IP header. These fields are known as the *pseudo-header*. The fields included are shown in Figure 5.4.

The checksum is calculated using a mathematical technique called the *one's complement.*

5

FIGURE 5.4.

The TCP pseudo-header.

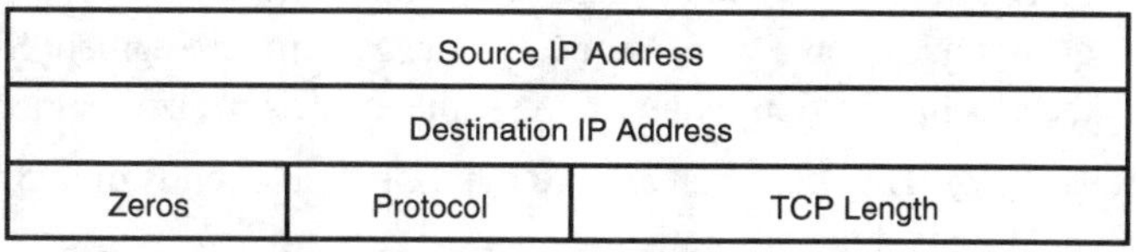

Source IP Address		
Destination IP Address		
Zeros	Protocol	TCP Length

EXPLANATION OF ONE'S COMPLEMENT

The one's complement is a common checksum technique. Let's say, for example, you want to calculate the one's complement of the following value:

`0000100010101111`

If the number has a 0 as a placeholder, the one's complement of a 0 is a 1. Similarly, the one's complement of a 1 is a 0. Therefore, the following is the one's complement of the preceding number:

1111011101010000

In binary arithmetic, the one's complement is one way to represent a negative number. The only problem with using the one's complement for negative numbers is that it results in two values for zero.

Take, for example, the number 1 (or 00000001 in binary). If you calculate the one's complement of this number, you get 11111110. Adding these two numbers should produce a value of 0. Instead, it adds up to 11111111 in binary, as follows:

```
  00000001
  11111110
  _____
  11111111
```

Therefore, when using the one's complement, both 00000000 and 11111111 can represent zero. UDP itself uses 11111111 when a checksum is calculated to have a value of zero.

- *Urgent Pointer.* If the Urgent Control Bit field is set to 1, this field is then interpreted. It designates which portion of the data is urgent by giving an offset from the sequence number in this segment. It points to the sequence number that follows the urgent data.

- *Options.* This variable-length field can contain one or more of three possible options: (0) End of Option List, (1) No-Operation, or (2) Maximum Segment Size. The End of Option List option is used at the end of all options in the TCP segment, not after each individual option. The No-Operation option is used between options to align subsequent options on a word boundary. The Maximum Segment Size option is used during the synchronization sequence to set the maximum size segment a host can receive.

- *Padding.* This field makes sure the TCP header ends on a 32-bit boundary. The padding is done with all zeros.

- *Data.* The actual data included in the TCP segment.

The Establishment of a TCP Session (TCP Three-Way Handshake)

When a host wants to communicate with a destination host using TCP, the destination host must agree to communicate. If the destination host does not agree to communicate, a TCP session cannot be established. This session establishment is called the *TCP three-way handshake* (see Figure 5.5).

FIGURE 5.5.

The TCP three-way handshake.

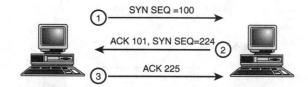

1. In the first step of a three-way handshake, the computer that wants to establish a session sends a TCP packet with the SYN (synchronize) flag set to 1. This indicates that the sending host wants to synchronize sequence numbers with the destination host. It also sends its current sequence number to the destination host.

2. The destination host, if it wants to establish the communication session, responds with an acknowledgment. (Setting the ACK flag to 1 indicates that the response is an acknowledgment.) The acknowledgment references the next sequence number it expects to receive. This establishes the TCP connection in one direction. To establish the connection in the return direction, the destination host also sets the SYN flag to 1 and sends its current sequence number.

3. The original source host responds to the destination host's TCP packet with an acknowledgment that includes the sequence number it expects to receive next. This establishes a full-duplex connection.

The actual sequence numbers are chosen randomly at the sending host. After a sequence number has been established, it continues to increment by one for each segment of data transmitted. By attaching a sequence number to every segment of data transmitted, the TCP protocol can keep track of all transmitted information, even though the underlying protocol might be unreliable in nature (such as IP). The sending host keeps a copy of the data it has transmitted in a send buffer until it receives an acknowledgment that the data has been received successfully at the destination. This way, if an acknowledgment is not received, it can resend the same segment.

Closing a TCP Session

A modified three-way handshake is used to close a TCP session. The closing must occur in both directions for the TCP session to cease to exist. It is possible, however, for one direction to terminate before the other direction has completed transmitting.

Figure 5.6 shows the steps involved in closing a TCP session.

1. After communicating over a TCP session for a while, an application might determine that it no longer needs the session. It will indicate that it wants to end the session. This closing results in TCP sending a segment with the FIN flag turned on.

5

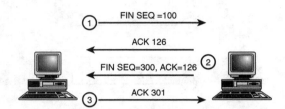

FIGURE 5.6.

Closing a TCP session.

2. TCP sends an acknowledgment segment containing the next expected sequence number. This is sent independently because the application software at the receiving end must be informed that the connection has been closed. This can take some time, and the sending host should be informed that the segment with the FIN flag set has been received. After the application completes its shutdown, it uses TCP to send a segment with the FIN flag set to indicate that it also has completed the session. It still contains an acknowledgment for the original FIN segment.

3. The original host sends an acknowledgment containing the sequence number expected next by the right-side host.

Message Flow Using TCP

After the full-duplex connection has been established, communication can begin between the two hosts.

An application in the upper layers of the TCP/IP layer model passes a stream of data to TCP. TCP receives the stream of bytes and assembles them into segments. If the stream of data does not fit into a single segment, each separate segment is given a sequence number. This sequence reorders the segments into the original data stream at the recipient host.

During the TCP/IP three-way handshake, the hosts have the option to exchange their maximum segment size during the synchronization process. This is the size used for each segment to be transmitted. The window size is exchanged in every TCP segment. This enables the window size to be adjusted during a transmission if necessary.

Figure 5.7 shows how a transmission between two hosts can occur.

In the figure, Host 1's TCP protocol has received a data stream that needs to be transmitted to Host 2. Based on the segment size negotiated during the TCP three-way handshake, the data stream must be broken into four segments.

Host 1 sends all four segments to Host 2 using a sliding window (discussed in the next section). This is shown in step 1. Unfortunately, only segments 1, 2, and 4 arrive successfully at Host 2 (see 2).

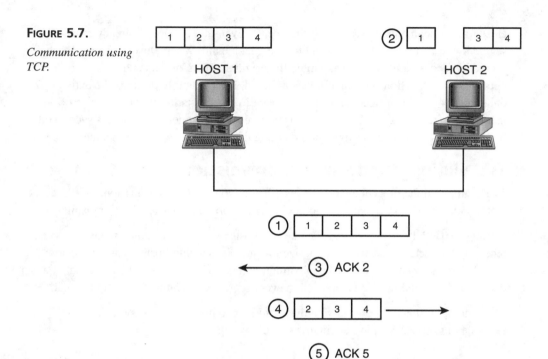

FIGURE 5.7.

Communication using TCP.

When Host 1 sent the four segments, it also set retransmission timers for each segment. *Retransmission timers* indicate when a segment should be re-sent if no acknowledgment is received. There is no *nack* (not-acknowledged) feature in TCP. If the retransmission time reaches zero, Host 1 resends that segment.

RETRANSMISSION TIMERS

When the sending host's retransmission timer reaches zero and the segments in the send window are re-sent, the retransmission timer is reset to double the previous amount of time. This acknowledges that the previous segments were not received successfully and provides a longer time frame for the delivery of the next attempt.

Host 2 received segments 1, 2, and 4 successfully. Because segments 1 and 2 are contiguous, however, Host 2 returns an acknowledgment to Host 1 indicating it received only the first segment successfully (see 3). As with all acknowledgments, Host 2 acknowledges using the next segment number it expects to receive.

Host 1 sends segments 2, 3, and 4 again (see 4). Even though Host 2 already received segment 4, it is not a problem to send this segment again. When Host 2 receives these segments successfully, it can reassemble the original stream of data and pass it up to the upper-layer application for which it was destined. Host 2 simply discards the extra copy of segment 4. An error does not need to be sent to Host 1 stating that two copies of segment 4 were received. To show that it has now received segments 2, 3, and 4 successfully, Host 2 sends an acknowledgment indicating that it expects to receive segment 5 next.

TCP Sliding Windows in Transmission

The example in the preceding section described a typical TCP transmission. TCP uses a method known as *sliding windows* to get better performance out of a TCP transmission.

During the TCP three-way handshake, the two hosts exchange transmit window sizes. The receiving host sets its receive window size to equal the sending host's transmit window size. The window size indicates the maximum number of segments that can be sent at any one time. This window size is included in every segment transmitted to the other host.

The sending host creates a send window set to its maximum transmission size. The example in Figure 5.8 shows a window size of six segments.

FIGURE 5.8.

The sending host using a sliding windows size of six segments.

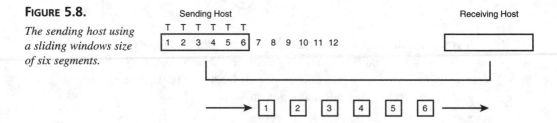

The sending host is able to send segments 1 through 6 to the receiving host. When the sending host sends the six segments, an individual retransmission timer is set on each individual segment. If only segments 1, 2, and 5 are received, the receiving host sends back an acknowledgment containing the segment number 3. This indicates that it received segments 1 and 2. Even though it also received segment 5, it only can indicate that it received the first two contiguous segments.

The sliding window at the sending host slides to the right past the two acknowledged segments. Segments 7 and 8 now can be transmitted to the receiving host (see Figure 5.9).

If no acknowledgment is received for segments 3 through 6 sent in the original window, their retransmission timers eventually reach zero. When this occurs, the segments are resent and the retransmission timer is reset to twice the initial value (see Figure 5.10).

FIGURE 5.9.

The sliding window now enables segments 7 and 8 to be sent.

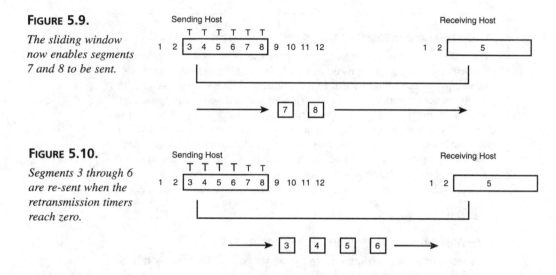

FIGURE 5.10.

Segments 3 through 6 are re-sent when the retransmission timers reach zero.

When the receiving host has received all segments up to and including segment 7, it sends an acknowledgment indicating that the next segment it expects is segment 8. The send window slides past segments 3 through 7 now that they have been acknowledged. Segments 8 through 12 are now sent to the receiving host. Retransmission timers are set on each of the segments, and the process begins again (see Figure 5.11).

FIGURE 5.11.

The final segments are delivered.

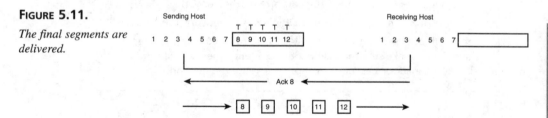

5

As you can see, using a sliding window can increase the performance of a TCP data transfer. Instead of having to send acknowledgments for every segment received, the receiving host can send a single acknowledgment indicating that multiple segments have been received.

A TCP window can be too big, however. If you manually configured the window size too large, too many segments could be lost during transmission. This causes more data resends due to the retransmission timers expiring.

DELAYED ACKNOWLEDGMENT TIMERS ON THE RECIPIENT

The receiving host does not have to wait for the entire receive window to fill before it sends an acknowledgment to the sending host. An acknowledgment also can be sent when two contiguous segments are received. This is why an acknowledgment was sent to acknowledge segments 1 and 2. In some implementations of TCP, the recipient host starts a timer known as the *delayed acknowledgment timer* when it receives a segment. When the delayed acknowledgment time reaches zero, it also sends an acknowledgment to the sending host. This enables an acknowledgment to be sent, even if two contiguous segments were not received.

CONFIGURING SLIDING WINDOW SIZE IN WINDOWS NT

The setting for sliding windows size can be set only in the Registry. It is set in the following location of the Registry:

```
HKEY_LOCAL_MACHINE\System\CurrentControlSet\Services\
Tcpip\Parameters
```

In this key, you can create a value named TCPWindowSize. The datatype is REG_DWORD. This entry does not exist by default. Its default value is the smaller of the following:

- Four times the maximum TCP data size on the network
- 8,192 rounded up to an even multiple of the network TCP data size

For an ethernet segment, the default is tuned to 8,760 bytes. To keep the defaults, make sure the TCPWindowSize value does not exist. It already is tuned for best performance on an ethernet network.

The States of a TCP Connection

During its lifetime, a TCP connection goes through a series of state changes. A TCP connection moves from one state to the next due to various events, including user calls such as OPEN, SEND, RECEIVE, CLOSE, ABORT, and STATUS. The following are states of a TCP connection:

- LISTEN. In the LISTEN state, a host is waiting for a connection request from any remote HOST.
- SYN-SENT. In the SYN-SENT state, a host has sent a connection request and is waiting for a return request to complete the full-duplex connection.

- SYN-RECEIVED. In the SYN-RECEIVED state, the host is waiting for an acknowledgment of its connection request. It already has received and sent a confirmation request.

- ESTABLISHED. The ESTABLISHED state is the normal state used for data transfer between two hosts. It represents an open connection between the two hosts.

- FIN-WAIT1. The FIN-WAIT1 state occurs when the host is waiting for either a connection termination request from the remote host or an acknowledgment of the connection termination request it sent earlier.

- FIN-WAIT2. The FIN-WAIT2 state occurs when the host is waiting for a connection termination request from the remote host.

- CLOSE-WAIT. The CLOSE-WAIT state represents the time when the TCP connection waits for the connection termination request from the upper-level application.

- CLOSING. The CLOSING state occurs when the host is waiting for a connection termination request acknowledgment from the remote host.

- LAST-ACK. The LAST-ACK state occurs when the host is waiting for acknowledgment of the connection termination request it already sent to the remote host.

- TIME-WAIT. The TIME-WAIT state occurs when the host is waiting a sufficient amount of time to make sure the remote host has received the acknowledgment of its connection termination request.

- CLOSED. The CLOSED state is not a state at all. It refers to the fact that no connection exists between the two hosts.

VIEWING TCP CONNECTION STATES

When you have established a session to another host using TCP, you can examine the connection states for your session using the command NETSTAT. This command is discussed at the end of today's material in the section "Determining What Ports Are in Use."

5

Well-Known TCP Ports

The Internet Assigned Number Authority has designated several default port numbers for use with the TCP protocol. If these ports also can be accessed by the UDP protocol, the UDP protocol strives to use the same port numbers.

WHEN MIGHT YOU CHANGE PORTS?

TCP/IP hosts can use their own port numbers rather than the reserved port numbers. This often occurs when an organization wants to provide a common TCP/IP application server but wants to hide its existence. Instead, the application server can be configured to respond to a nonstandard port number. An organization might, for example, want to provide telnet access to a server. Instead of using the standard port address of 23 for communication, the address 2323 could be assigned. If telnet clients attempt to connect to this telnet server, they have to configure their client software to connect to port 2323.

Port numbers also can be changed when an application server has two forms of the same application software loaded. A Windows NT server, for example, might have both Internet Information Server and Netscape Suitespot Server. It is not possible for both Web servers to respond to requests on port 80. You could configure one server to respond to requests on port 8000 while the other continues to use port 80.

Some of the more common TCP ports are shown in Table 5.1. They are stored in the Services file located in the /etc directory.

TABLE 5.1. TCP PORT NUMBER EXAMPLES.

Port	Service Name	Aliases	Description
0			Reserved
1	TCPMUX		TCP port service multiplexer
5	RJE		Remote job entry
7	ECHO		Echo service
9	DISCARD	SINK NULL	Discard service
11	SYSTAT	USERS	Active users
13	DAYTIME		Returns date and time
17	QOTD	QUOTE	Quote of the day
19	CHARGEN	TTYTST SOURCE	Character generator
20	FTP-DATA		File Transfer Protocol—data
21	FTP		File Transfer Protocol—control
23	TELNET		Telnet
25	SMTP	MAIL	Simple Mail Transfer Protocol
37	TIME	TIMESERVER	Time

Port	Service Name	Aliases	Description
42	NAME	NAMESERVER	Host name server
43	WHOIS	NICNAME	Who is service
53	DOMAIN	NAMESERVER	Domain name server
67	BOOTPS		Bootstrap protocol server
68	BOOTPC		Bootstrap protocol client
77	RJE	NETRJS	Any private RJE service
79	FINGER		Finger
80	HTTP	WWW	WWW's Hypertext Transmission Protocol
101	HOSTNAMES	HOSTNAME	NIC hostname server
102	ISO-TSAP		ISO TSAP
103	X400		X.400
104	X400-SND		X.400 SND
105	CSNET-NS		CSNET mailbox name server
110	POP3	POSTOFFICE	Post Office Protocol 3
111	SUNRPC		Sun RPC Portmap
113	AUTH	AUTHENTICATION	Authentication service
117	UUCP-PATH		UUCP path service
119	NNTP	USENET	Network News Transfer Protocol
139	NBSESSION	NETBIOS-SSN	NetBIOS Session Service
143	IMAP		Internet Mail Access Protocol
389	LDAP		Lightweight Directory Access Protocol
540	UUCP	UUCPD	uucp daemon
543	KLOGIN		Kerberos authenticated rlogin
544	KSHELL	CMD	Kerberos remote shell
666	DOOM		Doom from ID software
749	KERBEROS-ADM		Kerberos administration
750	KERBEROS	KDC	Kerberos authentication—tcp
751	KERBEROS_MASTER		Kerberos authentication
754	KRB_PROP		Kerberos slave propagation
1723	PPTP		Point-to-Point Tunneling Protocol

5

User Datagram Protocol

RFC 768 The User Datagram Protocol provides nonguaranteed delivery of information at the transport layer. UDP delivers information to a remote host with little overhead. No mechanisms exist to make sure the destination host successfully receives the package. Any application using UDP for its transport mechanism needs to include the following services:

- Retransmission of lost data
- Fragmentation and reassembly of large data streams
- Flow control
- Congestion avoidance

UDP only provides a basic checksum to make sure the UDP datagram has not been corrupted during transport. In spite of its shortcomings, UDP does have some benefits. It provides services such as multicasts and broadcasts that are not available using TCP.

In local area networks, which generally do not have delivery problems, data transfer over UDP generates less network traffic than TCP. This is because acknowledgment packets are not sent whenever data is received.

The User Datagram Protocol Header Format

The User Datagram Protocol header uses the format in Figure 5.12.

FIGURE 5.12.

Guaranteed delivery process.

Source Port	Destination Port
Length	Checksum
Data...	

- *Source Port.* This 16-bit field is optional for UDP. It contains the port used if a reply needs to be sent to the sending system. If not used, this field is padded with zeros.
- *Destination Port.* This 16-bit field contains the destination port address on the recipient host. This provides an endpoint for communication.
- *Length.* This 16-bit field contains the length in octets of the UDP header and its data payload.
- *Checksum.* This 16-bit field makes sure the UDP packet has not been corrupted in transit. It is calculated much like the TCP header's checksum. The calculation of the checksum requires some information from the IP header. This information, known as the *pseudo-header*, contains the fields in Figure 5.13.

FIGURE 5.13.

The UDP pseudo-header.

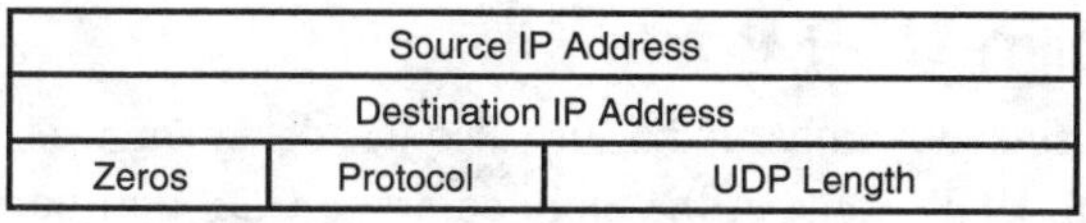

Source IP Address		
Destination IP Address		
Zeros	Protocol	UDP Length

To calculate the checksum, use the mathematical one's complement calculation (discussed previously in this chapter) on the pseudo-header, the UDP header, and the data within the header. This information can be padded with zeros at the end (if necessary) to make the total a multiple of two octets.

- *Data.* This variable-length field contains the upper-level application data to be transported using UDP.

The following are some well-known applications that use UDP:

- Trivial File Transfer Protocol (TFTP)
- Simple Network Management Protocol (SNMP)
- Domain name server (DNS)

Communication Using UDP

When a source host wants to communicate with a destination host using UDP, a session does not need to be established (unlike with TCP). The source host's application knows which port it needs to communicate with on the destination host. If the source application needs replies, it also includes its port address in the UDP header.

The UDP datagram is encapsulated as data in an IP datagram (see Figure 5.14).

FIGURE 5.14.

A UDP header and data is encapsulated in the IP data payload.

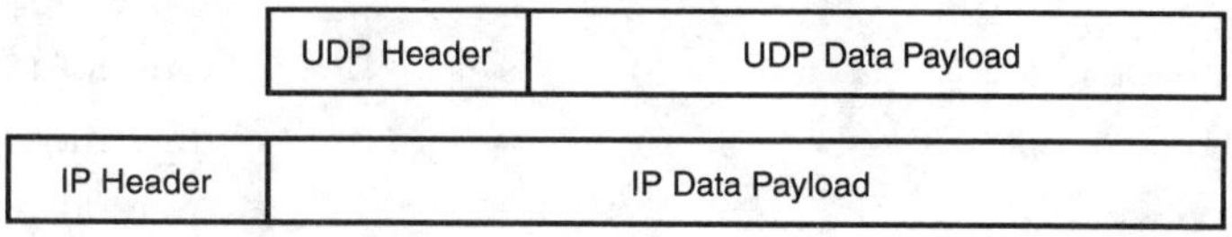

UDP Header	UDP Data Payload

IP Header	IP Data Payload

When the IP datagram arrives at the destination host, the IP header is stripped away revealing the original UDP header and data payload. The destination port number is determined from the UDP header, and UDP transfers the data to that designated port number.

If the designated port number is not available on the destination host, an ICMP error message is sent back to the host. The error message states that the port was unreachable, and the datagram is discarded.

5

Well-Known UDP Ports

The Internet Assigned Number Authority also has designated several default port numbers for use with UDP. Some of the more common UDP port numbers are shown in Table 5.2. If you compare Table 5.1 with Table 5.2, you can see that several ports are available in both TCP and UDP. The two protocols always will strive to use the same port number.

TABLE 5.2. UDP PORT NUMBER EXAMPLES.

Port	Service Name	Aliases	Description
0			Reserved
7	ECHO		Echo service
9	DISCARD	SINK NULL	Discard service
11	SYSTAT	USERS	Active users
13	DAYTIME		Returns date and time
17	QOTD	QUOTE	Quote of the day
19	CHARGEN	TTYTST SOURCE	Character generator
37	TIME	TIMSERVER	Time
39	RLP	RESOURCE	Resource location
42	NAME	NAMESERVER	Host name server
43	WHOIS	NICNAME	Who is service
53	NAMESERVER	DOMAIN	Domain name server
67	BOOTPS		Bootstrap protocol server
68	BOOTPC		Bootstrap protocol client
69	TFTP		Trivial FTP
111	SUNRPC		Sun Microsystems RPC
123	NTP	NTPD NTP	Network time protocol
137	NBNAME		NetBIOS name service
138	NBDATAGRAM		NetBIOS datagram service
161	SNMP	SNMP	Simple Network Management Protocol network monitor
162	SNMP-TRAP	SNMP	Simple Network Management Protocol traps
512	BIFF	COMSAT	UNIX Comsat
513	WHO	WHOD	UNIX Remote Who daemon
514	SYSLOG		System log
525	TIMED	TIMESERVER	Time daemon
2049	NFS		sun nfs

> **LISTS OF COMMONLY DEFINED PORTS**
>
> A list of commonly defined ports is available in all TCP/IP implementations. It is stored in a configuration file named Services. In Windows NT, this file is located in the directory *%SystemRoot%\System32\Drivers\Etc* in which *%SystemRoot%* is the directory in which Windows NT is installed.

Determining What Ports Are in Use

Users learning TCP/IP often want to determine what ports actually are in use. Day 16 shows how these ports can be configured to allow desired traffic to pass through a security server called a *firewall*.

Windows NT provides the NETSTAT command to reveal which ports are in use. A similar command can be found in all implementations of TCP/IP.

The following is the syntax of the NETSTAT command:

```
NETSTAT [-a] [-e] [-n] [-s] [-p protocol] [-r] [interval]
```

- -a. This option shows all current connections and all ports currently in a listening state.
- -e. This option shows ethernet statistics.
- -n. This option shows all addresses and ports in numerical format. The NETSTAT command usually resolves IP addresses to host names using host-name resolution and resolves port numbers to service names using the Services file.
- -s. This option shows the statistics by protocol. It can be combined with the –p option to show statistics only for a specific protocol.
- -p protocol. This option shows only the connections for the specified protocol. Possible protocols include TCP, UDP, and IP.
- -r. This option first displays the routing table and then displays the actual connection table.
- interval. This option sets the update interval for showing active connections.

The following code shows a portion of the results displayed when the computer named INSTRUCTOR connects to a computer named SIDESHOWBRI. Currently connected applications include FTP and WWW.

5

```
ftp> !netstat

Active Connections

   Proto  Local Address           Foreign Address          State

   TCP    instructor:1168         SIDESHOWBRI.online-can.com:ftp
   ➥ESTABLISHED
   TCP    instructor:1249         SIDESHOWBRI.online-can.com:80   ESTABLISHED
   TCP    instructor:1250         SIDESHOWBRI.online-can.com:80   ESTABLISHED
   TCP    instructor:1251         SIDESHOWBRI.online-can.com:80   ESTABLISHED
   TCP    instructor:1252         SIDESHOWBRI.online-can.com:80   ESTABLISHED
   TCP    instructor:1253         SIDESHOWBRI.online-can.com:80   ESTABLISHED
   TCP    instructor:1254         SIDESHOWBRI.online-can.com:80   ESTABLISHED
   TCP    instructor:1255         SIDESHOWBRI.online-can.com:80   ESTABLISHED
   TCP    instructor:1256         SIDESHOWBRI.online-can.com:80   ESTABLISHED
```

From this listing, you can see that the INSTRUCTOR computer is using port 1168 when communicating with the FTP server on SIDESHOWBRI. The port used on SIDESHOWBRI is port 21, the ftp port.

You also can see that the INSTRUCTOR computer has eight separate TCP sessions connected to port 80 on SIDESHOWBRI. When a Web page is downloaded, each individual graphic or object on the page is transferred with a unique TCP session. On INSTRUCTOR, the port numbers were assigned in ascending numeric order as they were established.

The following code shows the results of issuing the NETSTAT command on SIDESHOWBRI during these sessions.

```
   Proto  Local Address           Foreign Address          State

   TCP    sideshowbri:ftp       INSTRUCTOR.online-can.com:1168   ESTABLISHED
   TCP    sideshowbri:ftp-data  INSTRUCTOR.online-can.com:1169   TIME_WAIT
   TCP    sideshowbri:80        INSTRUCTOR.online-can.com:1249   ESTABLISHED
   TCP    sideshowbri:80        INSTRUCTOR.online-can.com:1250   ESTABLISHED
   TCP    sideshowbri:80        INSTRUCTOR.online-can.com:1251   ESTABLISHED
   TCP    sideshowbri:80        INSTRUCTOR.online-can.com:1252   ESTABLISHED
   TCP    sideshowbri:80        INSTRUCTOR.online-can.com:1253   ESTABLISHED
   TCP    sideshowbri:80        INSTRUCTOR.online-can.com:1254   ESTABLISHED
   TCP    sideshowbri:80        INSTRUCTOR.online-can.com:1255   ESTABLISHED
   TCP    sideshowbri:80        INSTRUCTOR.online-can.com:1256   ESTABLISHED
```

Note that all the entries in the NETSTAT results are now reversed. This is because you are now viewing the TCP end-to-end communication session from the point of view of SIDESHOWBRI.

The NETSTAT command also can determines which UDP services are in a listening state on a computer. The following code shows the results of a NETSTAT -a -p UDP command:

```
U:\>netstat -a -p UDP

Active Connections

    Proto   Local Address          Foreign Address        State
    UDP     sideshowbri:echo       *:*
    UDP     sideshowbri:discard    *:*
    UDP     sideshowbri:daytime    *:*
    UDP     sideshowbri:qotd       *:*
    UDP     sideshowbri:chargen    *:*
    UDP     sideshowbri:name       *:*
    UDP     sideshowbri:tftp       *:*
    UDP     sideshowbri:135        *:*
    UDP     sideshowbri:snmp       *:*
    UDP     sideshowbri:1027       *:*
    UDP     sideshowbri:1038       *:*
    UDP     sideshowbri:1046       *:*
    UDP     sideshowbri:1073       *:*
    UDP     sideshowbri:1074       *:*
    UDP     sideshowbri:1083       *:*
    UDP     sideshowbri:1084       *:*
    UDP     sideshowbri:1268       *:*
    UDP     sideshowbri:domain     *:*
    UDP     sideshowbri:bootp      *:*
    UDP     sideshowbri:nbname     *:*
    UDP     sideshowbri:nbdatagram *:*
```

In this list, you can see the following UDP-transport-based applications running on SIDESHOWBRI:

- A DHCP server (sideshowbri:bootp)
- A trivial FTP server (sideshowbri:tftp)
- A domain name server (sideshowbri:domain)
- A SNMP agent (sideshowbri:snmp)
- A NetBIOS Nname server or WINS server (sideshowbri:nbname)

The NETSTAT command can help troubleshoot the ports in use between a client host and a server host.

Applying What You Have Learned

Test Your Knowledge

1. What is the difference between the TCP and UDP protocols?
2. How does TCP provide reliable transport?

5

3. What is a delayed acknowledgment timer?

4. Describe the TCP three-way handshake process.

5. Can a sliding window be configured too large?

6. If the TCP window size of the sending host is smaller than the receive window of the destination host, which computer adjusts its TCP window size?

7. What fault tolerance is provided in a UDP header?

8. What is a TCP pseudo-header?

9. Connect to a Web site using a Web browser. After you have connected, start a command prompt and type the following command:

```
netstat -a
```

What port are you connected to on the Web server? What port(s) are you using on your host system?

Preview of the Next Day

Tomorrow's material provides detailed information about a methodology for calculating nondefault subnet masks. The following topics are covered:

- Determining which subnet mask is required based on the number of subnets required on the network
- Determining the maximum number of hosts that can exist on a network segment given a specific subnet mask
- Determining the pools of IP addresses used for each network segment based on the network IP address and the selected subnet mask

The method described revolves around using a subnet shortcut table that makes the calculations easier to perform.

DAY 6

The Art of Subnet Masking

Today you will learn what to do when the default subnet mask associated with an IP address requires modification. Today's material covers the following aspects of modified subnet masking:

- Determining when a customized subnet mask is required
- Deciding how many unique subnets are required
- Deciding whether the subnet mask chosen provides enough host IP addresses for each subnet
- Determining the network address, broadcast address, and pool of IP addresses for a specific network address/subnet mask combination
- Determining the need for variable-length subnet masking
- Understanding the concept of Classless Internet Domain Routing (CIDR)

The Need for Customized Subnets

Many times, when working with an assigned network address from the InterNIC, situations arise that require you to segment the network using a subnet mask that is not the default subnet mask for the network address. An IP address, as discussed on Day 4, "Internet Protocol (IP) Addresses," is logically broken into network and host portions. In a subnetting scenario, the host portion of the address is further broken into a subnet portion and a host portion. Figure 6.1 shows the default subnet mask assigned to Class A addresses. If 8 more bits are taken from the host portion of the address, these additional bits represent the subnetwork that this network address represents. The combined network and subnet portions of the subnet mask are known as the *extended network prefix*.

FIGURE 6.1.

Extending the network prefix for a Class A Address.

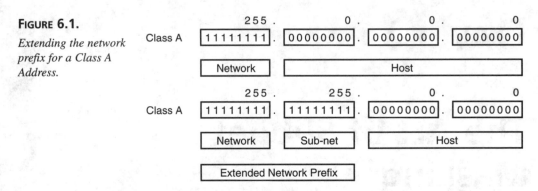

The most commonly asked question is "Why would I want or have to do this?" The following circumstances require you to consider subnetting a network:

- If your network uses mixed topologies, such as ethernet and token ring, you need to segment the network based on topology. Each of these segments requires its own unique network address.

- Redirecting network traffic to isolate bandwidth-intensive applications or hosts to their own segment of the network.

- Reducing the number of addresses you might need for the InterNIC for your network.

- Distributing IP addresses more efficiently on your network. If you have two network segments joined by a serial connection, you only need two addresses for that segment. It is wasteful to allocate an entire Class C address range (254 addresses) to this segment.

The process of subnetting an assigned network address is based on the following questions that must be answered:

- How many network segments does the network need addresses for today? A *network segment* is a physical section of the network separated from all other areas by a routing device.
- How many network segments will the network need in the future?
- How many hosts will be needed on the largest segment of the network today?
- What will the future needs be for hosts on any one segment of the network?

The correct subnet masking decision is the one that correctly answers all these questions.

Determining a Subnetting Solution

The next three subsections guide you through a step-by-step solution for determining which subnet mask meets a network's subnetting needs. This solution helps you determine the number of subnets required, the number of hosts provided for each subnet, and the pool of IP addresses for each subnet.

The goal of this section is to determine a new separation point between the network and host portions of the IP address instead of using the default subnet mask based on the IP address class. Remember that when a host attempts to communicate with a second host, it performs the ANDing process. It uses the ANDing function against both its own IP address and the target host's IP address. If the ANDing function's results are the same, the hosts are on the same network segment. If the results are different, the destination host is on a remote network.

REVIEWING THE ANDING PROCESS

If you need to refresh your memory, the ANDing process was discussed in detail on Day 4 in the section "The ANDing Process."

6

As a result of this process, the subnet mask takes a specific amount of host bits from the address and makes them part of the network portion of the address. The ANDing process then is performed on the modified subnet mask.

Determining the Number of Subnets

The first step in choosing a modified subnet mask is to determine how many subnets a network requires. Each individual network segment requires a unique network ID. The network in Figure 6.2, for example, requires eight unique network IDs.

FIGURE 6.2.

A sample network.

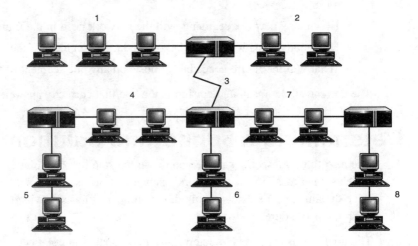

Some people might initially question why network 3 requires network IDs because there are no hosts on this segment. You must keep in mind, however, that each router on these segments has a network interface that requires an IP address.

Assume this network can use the Class B address 156.32.0.0. Using the default Class B subnet mask 255.255.0.0, this allocates the first 16 bits, or 156.32, to represent the network address. The remaining 16 bits represent the host component of the address.

You need to use some of the 16 host bits to segment this network address into the required eight segments. The process used determines how many bits are needed from the host portion of the address to accomplish this. Because you require eight networks, the bits taken from the host portion of the address need to provide at least eight different combinations.

The first step is to convert the number 8 into its binary representation, which is 1000.

WHAT IF THE BITS ARE ALL ONES?

A special case exists in which this method does not work. If the number of networks required converts to all ones in binary, you must take an additional bit to represent the number of networks required. If the number of

> networks is seven, for example, this converts to 111 in binary. In this case, 4
> bits are required to make up seven subnetworks. This is because subnetwork
> addresses of all zeros or all ones are not allowed in many networking imple-
> mentations.

The number 8 is represented using 4 bits. These four bits must be taken from the host
portion of the address to represent the network portion of the address (see Figure 6.3).

FIGURE 6.3.

Taking 4 bits from the host portion of the address.

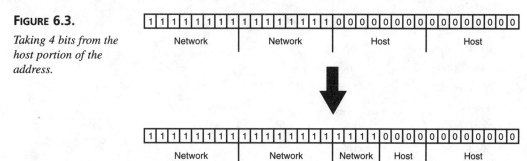

In this case, the host portion of the address includes the third and fourth octets of the
32-bit address. The 4 bits are taken from the left-most bits. This results in the new subnet
mask represented in Figure 6.3.

The third octet is now represented as 11110000, which translates to 240 in the decimal
system. This means you can use the subnet mask 255.255.240.0 to segment this network
into at least eight subnetworks.

ALTERNATE NOTATION

It often is difficult to work with decimal-represented subnet masks. Another
common method represents the number of bits required for the network
portion of the address as a decimal number following the network address
in dotted decimal format. The network ID 156.32.0.0 with the subnet mask
255.255.240.0, for example, is represented as 156.32.0.0/20 in this notation.
This shows that the first 20 bits of this network address represent the network. This shorthand method can be less clumsy to use than the standard
representation of a subnet mask.

```
Network ID/network bits
```

6

How many unique network addresses can be allocated using this subnet mask? Table 6.1 shows all the possible combinations that can be created using these four bits.

TABLE 6.1. DETERMINING ALL POSSIBLE NETWORK COMBINATIONS FOR A **240** SUBNET MASK.

Binary	Decimal
00000000	0
00010000	16
00100000	32
00110000	48
01000000	64
01010000	80
01100000	96
01110000	112
10000000	128
10010000	144
10100000	160
10110000	176
11000000	192
11010000	208
11100000	224
11110000	240

Sixteen possible combinations can be created using unique patterns for the first 4 bits of an octet. This does not always provide 16 separate subnets for addressing. Some routing protocols do not advertise both the network address and the subnet mask. In these cases, you cannot use a subnet ID that is all zeros. This is because the network ID for the network 156.32.0.0/16 is equivalent to the subnetwork address 156.32.0.0/20. Unless the routing protocol advertises the subnetwork mask, both network addresses simply appear as 156.32.0.0, and you cannot tell the difference between them. The broadcast address for the network ID 156.32.240.0/20 is 156.32.255.255. This is the same as the broadcast address for the network ID 156.32.0.0/16. Again, without the subnet mask included, you do not know which network's broadcast address is represented by 156.32.255.255. This leaves you with 14 valid subnetwork addresses.

The following equation can be used as a shortcut for determining the number of networks:

$$2^n - 2$$

In this equation, n represents the number of bits required for the subnet mask. Table 6.2 shows how many subnets are available if you use up to one octet of bits from the host portion of an address.

TABLE 6.2. NUMBER OF SUBNETS PROVIDED BY *N* BITS OF THE HOST ADDRESS.

n Bits	Formula	# of Subnets
1	$2^1 - 2$	-
2	$2^2 - 2$	2
3	$2^3 - 2$	6
4	$2^4 - 2$	14
5	$2^5 - 2$	30
6	$2^6 - 2$	62
7	$2^7 - 2$	126
8	$2^8 - 2$	254*

If you use additional bits from the host portion of the address, the number of subnetworks provided continues to grow using this formula.

6

Does this handle your future network growth needs? It depends. You have to look at expected expansion within the organization. If you require 14 subnets today, this number is probably insufficient for future growth.

Determining the Number of Available Hosts

The next step in subnet masking is to determine the number of hosts available on each segment of the network. This is calculated by first determining the number of bits left to represent the host portion of the address. In the example, this is 12 bits.

The number of hosts provided by each segment of this network addressing scheme is calculated using the same formula:

$$2^n - 2$$

In this equation, n is the number of bits left to represent the host portion of the address. The number 2 is subtracted from this number because a host address cannot be all zeros or all ones. Remember that a host address of all zeros represents this network, and a host address of all ones is the broadcast address for that host.

The subnet mask 255.255.240.0 against the Class B address 156.32.0.0 gives you $2^{12} - 2 = 4,094$ hosts per segment.

This probably is a sufficient number of hosts for future growth of the network.

Establishing the Available Pools of IP Addresses for a Subnet Mask

The final step in determining a subnetting solution is to identify the actual addresses that would be used for the network segments.

The first addresses to be determined are the actual network addresses that would represent each of the individual subnetworks. Table 6.1 showed the actual decimal representations of the 16 different network addresses for a 240 subnetwork mask. Using these values, you would come up with the network addresses in Table 6.3.

TABLE 6.3. NETWORK ADDRESSES FOR A 255.255.240.0 SUBNET MASK.

Binary Network Address	Dotted Decimal Notation
~~10011100 00100000 00000000 00000000~~	~~156.32.0.0~~
10011100 00100000 00010000 00000000	156.32.16.0
10011100 00100000 00100000 00000000	156.32.32.0
10011100 00100000 00110000 00000000	156.32.48.0
10011100 00100000 01000000 00000000	156.32.64.0
10011100 00100000 01010000 00000000	156.32.80.0
10011100 00100000 01100000 00000000	156.32.96.0
10011100 00100000 01110000 00000000	156.32.112.0
10011100 00100000 10000000 00000000	156.32.128.0
10011100 00100000 10010000 00000000	156.32.144.0
10011100 00100000 10100000 00000000	156.32.160.0
10011100 00100000 10110000 00000000	156.32.176.0

Binary Network Address	Dotted Decimal Notation
10011100 00100000 11000000 00000000	156.32.192.0
10011100 00100000 11010000 00000000	156.32.208.0
10011100 00100000 11100000 00000000	156.32.224.0
10011100 00100000 11110000 00000000	~~156.32.240.0~~

As previously discussed, the network addresses 156.32.0.0 and 156.32.240.0 often are not used if routing protocols that do not transmit subnet masks are used.

The second addresses to be determined are the broadcast addresses for each network. The broadcast address is represented by a host address of all ones. Table 6.4 shows the broadcast addresses for each of these segments.

TABLE 6.4. BROADCAST ADDRESSES USING A 255.255.240.0 SUBNET MASK.

Binary Network Address	Dotted Decimal Notation
10011100 00100000 00011111 11111111	156.32.31.255
10011100 00100000 00101111 11111111	156.32.47.255
10011100 00100000 00111111 11111111	156.32.63.255
10011100 00100000 01001111 11111111	156.32.79.255
10011100 00100000 01011111 11111111	156.32.95.255
10011100 00100000 01101111 11111111	156.32.111.255
10011100 00100000 01111111 11111111	156.32.127.255
10011100 00100000 10001111 11111111	156.32.143.255
10011100 00100000 10011111 11111111	156.32.159.255
10011100 00100000 10101111 11111111	156.32.175.255
10011100 00100000 10111111 11111111	156.32.191.255
10011100 00100000 11001111 11111111	156.32.207.255
10011100 00100000 11011111 11111111	156.32.223.255
10011100 00100000 11101111 11111111	156.32.239.255

6

The final step is to create a pool of addresses for each of the networks. The pool begins with the address immediately following the network address and ends with the address before the broadcast address. Table 6.5 summarizes all the information for each network address.

TABLE 6.5. ADDRESS POOLS FOR THE 156.32.0.0/20 NETWORK.

Network Address	Beginning Address	Ending Address	Broadcast Address
156.32.16.0	156.32.16.1	156.32.31.254	156.32.31.255
156.32.32.0	156.32.32.1	156.32.47.254	156.32.47.255
156.32.48.0	156.32.48.1	156.32.63.254	156.32.63.255
156.32.64.0	156.32.64.1	156.32.79.254	156.32.79.255
156.32.80.0	156.32.80.1	156.32.95.254	156.32.95.255
156.32.96.0	156.32.96.1	156.32.111.254	156.32.111.255
156.32.112.0	156.32.112.1	156.32.127.254	156.32.127.255
156.32.128.0	156.32.128.1	156.32.143.254	156.32.143.255
156.32.144.0	156.32.144.1	156.32.159.254	156.32.159.255
156.32.160.0	156.32.160.1	156.32.175.254	156.32.175.255
156.32.176.0	156.32.176.1	156.32.191.254	156.32.191.255
156.32.192.0	156.32.192.1	156.32.207.254	156.32.207.255
156.32.208.0	156.32.208.1	156.32.223.254	156.32.223.255
156.32.224.0	156.32.224.1	156.32.239.254	156.32.239.255

Building a Subnet Shortcut Table

The steps to determine the correct subnet mask and the associated pools of addresses can take several calculations. This section shows you some shortcuts that can be taken to determine the network addresses, the pools of IP addresses, and broadcast addresses for each subnet.

To determine subnet calculations, you can use a table consisting of three rows of information (see Figure 6.4).

FIGURE 6.4.

Building a subnet shortcut table.

# of Bits		1	2	3	4	5	6	7	8
Incrementing Value									
Subnet Mask									
# of Networks									

In this table, you must calculate the increment value for each column, the subnet mask values to be used, and the number of subnetworks each subnet mask provides.

The first row to be calculated is the increment value row. This is based on the actual binary value each column represents. In the "Binary Representation" section of Day 4, you learned that octet values can be represented as a string of eight binary bits. These bits have the values shown in Figure 6.5.

FIGURE 6.5.

Calculating the incrementing value row.

# of Bits	1	2	3	4	5	6	7	8
Incrementing Value	128	64	32	16	8	4	2	1
Subnet Mask								
# of Networks								

A TRICK FOR CALCULATING THE INCREMENTING VALUES

If you cannot remember each binary bit place value, you can calculate them by entering a value of 1 in the rightmost column. As you move left, each column is double the value of the previous column. The second column from the right, for example, has a value of 2. This continues until you reached the final column, which has a value of 128.

These increment values determine the starting addresses of each pool of addresses provided by a specific subnet mask.

The second row of the table determines the subnet mask value based on the number of bits taken from the host portion of the address. These values are calculated by totaling the binary bit place values up to that column. The first column has a bit value of 128, so the subnet mask for that column also is 128. If you use two bits to represent the subnet mask, the subnet mask value is 128 + 64 = 192. If you use three bits to represent the subnet mask, the subnet mask value is 128 + 64 + 32 = 224. When you calculate the subnet mask value for all eight columns, the results look like Figure 6.6.

6

FIGURE 6.6.

Determining the subnet mask values.

# of Bits	1	2	3	4	5	6	7	8
Incrementing Value	128	64	32	16	8	4	2	1
Subnet Mask	128	192	224	240	248	252	254	255
# of Networks								

AN ALTERNATIVE CALCULATION TO FIND THE SUBNET MASK VALUES

Because you already have calculated the binary bit place value for each column, you also can use the following formula:

256 - Binary Bit Place

This results in the same values for the subnet mask. The first method, however, does provide a better rationale of how the subnet values actually are determined.

The final step in building the table is to calculate the number of subnets provided by each subnet mask. The following is the formula for calculating the number of subnets provided:

$2^n - 2$

In this formula, n is the number of bits used to represent the subnet mask. If three bits are used to represent the subnet mask, for example, this provides $2^3 - 2 = 6$ pools of IP addresses. Figure 6.7 shows the table after all # of Networks values have been calculated.

FIGURE 6.7.

The completed subnet shortcut table.

# of Bits	1	2	3	4	5	6	7	8
Incrementing Value	128	64	32	16	8	4	2	1
Subnet Mask	128	192	224	240	248	252	254	255
# of Networks	0	2	6	14	30	62	126	254

WHAT IF I NEED MORE THAN 8 BITS?

There are a few catches when you need to grab more than 8 bits to represent the subnet mask. For the incrementing value, just continue again from the leftmost column. If you require 9 bits, for example, this is represented using an increment value of 128. The subnet mask is made up of 9 bits. The first 8 bits are represented by 255, and the last bit is represented by 128. Finally, the number of networks provided by 9 bits is $2^9 - 2 = 510$ networks.

The following examples use this table.

Using the Subnet Shortcut Table for a Class A Address

This section walks you through an example of using the subnet shortcut table to determine an optimal subnet mask for a scenario.

A network has been assigned the 65.0.0.0 network address by InterNIC. You want to segment the network into four subnetworks. The largest segment of this network requires addressing for 8,000 hosts, but this number could grow to 10,000 hosts in the next two years. What subnet mask can be used uniformly across the network to provide this subnetworking?

Using Figure 6.7, you can see that if you want to provide at least four subnetworks, you need to look at the third column, which provides six subnetworks. This provides growth for two additional networks in the future.

The associated subnet mask in this column is 224. For a Class A address, this is a subnet mask of 255.224.0.0. This also can represented in shorthand notation as 65.0.0.0/11, representing the 11 bits that now represent the network portion of the address.

This leave you with 21 bits to represent the host portion of the address. If you calculate $2^{21} - 2$, the number of hosts per subnetwork is 2,097,150. This is more than enough hosts per segment.

Finally, using the chart, you can see that the incrementing value for a 224 subnet mask is 32. Table 6.6 shows how all network addresses can be determined using this incrementing value. The left column is created by continually adding the incrementing value to itself until the actual subnet mask value is reached.

TABLE 6.6. USING THE INCREMENT VALUE OF 32.

Increment Value	Network Address	Beginning Address	Ending Address	Broadcast Address
n	65.n.0.0	65.n.0.1	65.n_{next}−1.255.254	65.n_{next}−1.255.255
0	n/a	n/a	n/a	n/a
32	65.32.0.0	65.32.0.1	65.63.255.254	65.63.255.255
64	65.64.0.0	65.64.0.1	65.95.255.254	65.95.255.255
96	65.96.0.0	65.96.0.1	65.127.255.254	65.127.255.255
128	65.128.0.0	65.128.0.1	65.159.255.254	65.159.255.255
160	65.160.0.0	65.160.0.1	65.191.255.254	65.191.255.255
192	65.192.0.0	65.192.0.1	65.223.255.254	65.223.255.255
224	n/a	n/a	n/a	n/a

6

Note that the values of 0 and 224 are used in this example. They can be used if the network uses a routing protocol that advertises the subnet mask in addition to the network address.

The broadcast addresses and pools of IP addresses can easily be calculated by completing Table 6.6 using the calculations in each row header.

Using the Subnet Shortcut Table for a Class B Address

This next example uses the subnet shortcut table to calculate subnets for a Class B address.

In this example, the network has acquired from InterNIC the Class B address of 190.158.0.0. You want to segment the network into 18 different subnets. The largest network segment requires 1,800 host addresses.

Using the subnet shortcut table in Figure 6.7, you notice that providing 18 subnetworks requires 5 bits of the host address. This provides a maximum of 30 subnets. A total of 21 bits is used to represent the network ID. This leaves a total of 11 bits to represent the host address. Eleven host bits provide $2^{11} - 2 = 2,046$ hosts per network segment.

This appears to meet the requirement of 18 subnetworks of 1,800 hosts. This solution provides for up to 30 networks of growth and enables each subnet to have up to 2,046 hosts. Therefore, the network ID 190.58.0.0 with subnet mask 255.255.248.0 can be used for this subnetworking example.

The actual calculation of network address, beginning addresses, ending address, and broadcast address is performed as shown in Table 6.7. The increment value used for the calculation of all addresses is 8 (as indicated in Figure 6.7) when you use 5 bits for the network mask.

TABLE 6.7. SUBNETWORK ADDRESSES FOR 190.58.0.0/21.

Increment Value	Network Address	Beginning Address	Ending Address	Broadcast Address
n	190.58.n.0	190.58.n.1	$190.58.n_{next}-1.254$	$190.58.n_{next}-1.255$
8	190.58.8.0	190.58.8.1	190.58.16.254	190.58.16.255
16	190.58.16.0	190.58.16.1	190.58.24.254	190.58.24.255
24	190.58.24.0	190.58.24.1	190.58.32.254	190.58.32.255
32	190.58.32.0	190.58.32.1	190.58.40.254	190.58.40.255
40	190.58.40.0	190.58.40.1	190.58.48.254	190.58.48.255
48	190.58.48.0	190.58.48.1	190.58.64.254	190.58.64.255

Increment Value	Network Address	Beginning Address	Ending Address	Broadcast Address
64	190.58.64.0	190.58.64.1	190.58.72.254	190.58.72.255
72	190.58.72.0	190.58.72.1	190.58.80.254	190.58.80.255
80	190.58.80.0	190.58.80.1	190.58.88.254	190.58.88.255
88	190.58.88.0	190.58.88.1	190.58.96.254	190.58.96.255
96	190.58.96.0	190.58.96.1	190.58.104.254	190.58.104.255
104	190.58.104.0	190.58.104.1	190.58.112.254	190.58.112.255
112	190.58.112.0	190.58.112.1	190.58.120.254	190.58.120.255
120	190.58.120.0	190.58.120.1	190.58.128.254	190.58.128.255
128	190.58.128.0	190.58.128.1	190.58.136.254	190.58.136.255
136	190.58.136.0	190.58.136.1	190.58.144.254	190.58.144.255
144	190.58.144.0	190.58.144.1	190.58.152.254	190.58.152.255
152	190.58.152.0	190.58.152.1	190.58.160.254	190.58.160.255
160	190.58.160.0	190.58.160.1	190.58.168.254	190.58.168.255
168	190.58.168.0	190.58.168.1	190.58.176.254	190.58.176.255
176	190.58.176.0	190.58.176.1	190.58.184.254	190.58.184.255
184	190.58.184.0	190.58.184.1	190.58.192.254	190.58.192.255
192	190.58.192.0	190.58.192.1	190.58.200.254	190.58.200.255
200	190.58.200.0	190.58.200.1	190.58.208.254	190.58.208.255
208	190.58.208.0	190.58.208.1	190.58.216.254	190.58.216.255
216	190.58.216.0	190.58.216.1	190.58.224.254	190.58.224.255
224	190.58.224.0	190.58.224.1	190.58.232.254	190.58.232.255
232	190.58.232.0	190.58.232.1	190.58.240.254	190.58.240.255
240	190.58.240.0	190.58.240.1	190.58.248.254	190.58.248.255

6

Using the Subnet Shortcut Table for a Class C Address

This final example works through Class C subnetting. Class C subnetting sometimes is more confusing, but the same methodology can be used to calculate the correct subnet mask for a given subnetting situation.

In this example, a network has acquired the address 195.5.6.0 from InterNIC. You need to segment the network into seven different subnets, with each subnet providing a maximum of nine hosts.

Using the subnet shortcut table, you see that four bits must be used to provide seven sub-networks. Using four bits means using a 240 subnet mask. For a Class C address, this is represented as 255.255.255.240 (or in shorthand notation, 195.5.6.0/28).

This leaves four bits to represent the host address. The calculation of $2^4 - 2$ shows that you have provided for 14 hosts per segment.

This solution meets all your business needs. All that is left is to create a table of network addresses (see Table 6.8). As with Class A and Class B addresses, start with the first column containing your increment values. For a 240 subnet mask, these values are incremented by 16s. Note that for a Class C address, the actual calculations for the columns change a bit.

TABLE 6.8. NETWORK ADDRESSING FOR **195.5.6.0/28.**

Increment Value	Network Address	Beginning Address	Ending Address	Broadcast Address
n	195.5.6.n	199.5.6.n+1	$199.5.6.n_{next}-2$	$199.5.6.n_{next}-1$
0	n/a	n/a	n/a	n/a
16	199.5.6.16	199.5.6.17	199.5.6.30	199.5.6.31
32	199.5.6.32	199.5.6.33	199.5.6.46	199.5.6.47
48	199.5.6.48	199.5.6.49	199.5.6.62	199.5.6.63
64	199.5.6.64	199.5.6.65	199.5.6.78	199.5.6.79
80	199.5.6.80	199.5.6.81	199.5.6.94	199.5.6.95
96	199.5.6.96	199.5.6.97	199.5.6.110	199.5.6.111
112	199.5.6.112	199.5.6.113	199.5.6.126	199.5.6.127
128	199.5.6.128	199.5.6.129	199.5.6.142	199.5.6.143
144	199.5.6.144	199.5.6.145	199.5.6.158	199.5.6.159
160	199.5.6.160	199.5.6.161	199.5.6.174	199.5.6.175
176	199.5.6.176	199.5.6.177	199.5.6.190	199.5.6.191
192	199.5.6.192	199.5.6.193	199.5.6.206	199.5.6.207
208	199.5.6.208	199.5.6.209	199.5.6.222	199.5.6.223
224	199.5.6.224	199.5.6.225	199.5.6.238	199.5.6.239
240	n/a	n/a	n/a	n/a

Variable-Length Subnet Masking

RFC 1009 Even using the subnetting methods already discussed, the potential to waste IP addresses still exists. If you review the solution in the first example, you'll notice several thousand IP addresses are wasted. Because the solution had to use the same subnet mask for all segments, you were bottlenecked into an inefficient solution. *Variable-length subnet masking (VLSM)* enables each subnet to have its own unique subnet mask. This means a network is not locked into a fixed number of networks with a fixed number of hosts. This leads to more efficient use of an organization's IP address space.

The use of VLSM depends on a routing protocol that contains information about the subnet mask for each route. If the subnet mask is not included in the routing protocol, you must use the same subnet mask for each network segment.

A VLSM Routing Example

VLSM is a better method of subnetting for most networking solutions. Let's say, for example, that a company with offices in Toronto, Minneapolis, and Seattle has been assigned the 175.50.0.0 Class B address. In each city, there are four offices. The largest office on each segment will have no more than 1,500 hosts. Within each office, several departments need to maintain separate pools of IP addresses (see Figure 6.8).

FIGURE 6.8.

Another sample network.

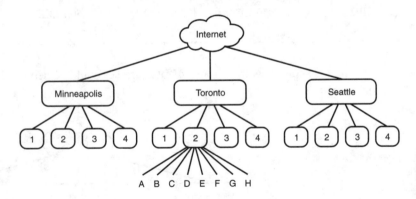

With VLSM, the initial four questions for determining which subnet mask to use become the following:

- How many total subnets does this level need today?
- How many total subnets will this level need in the future?
- How many hosts are on this level's largest subnet today?
- How many hosts will there be on this level's largest subnet in the future?

These questions must be answered at each level of the network design. Using Figure 6.8, you can see that the top hierarchy level currently requires three subnetworks, one for each of the three cities. If you use a 255.255.224.0 subnet mask at this level, it provides six networks of 8,190 hosts. This initial network mask leaves some room for growth. You have three additional networks available, and even if all four offices in a city grew to the maximum of 1,500 hosts, you still have an additional 2,190 host IP addresses available.

The pools of IP addresses for this solution are shown in Table 6.9.

TABLE 6.9. NETWORK ADDRESSING FOR **175.50.0.0/19.**

Increment Value	Network Address	Beginning Address	Ending Address	Broadcast Address
n	175.50.n.0	175.50.n.1	$175.50.n_{next}.254$	$175.50.n_{next}.255$
0	n/a	n/a	n/a	n/a
32	175.50.32.0	175.50.32.1	175.50.63.254	175.50.63.255
64	175.50.64.0	175.50.64.1	175.50.95.254	175.50.95.255
96	175.50.96.0	175.50.96.1	175.50.127.254	175.50.127.255
128	175.50.128.0	175.50.128.1	175.50.159.254	175.50.159.255
160	175.50.160.0	175.50.160.1	175.50.191.254	175.50.191.255
192	175.50.192.0	175.50.192.1	175.50.223.254	175.50.223.255
224	n/a	n/a	n/a	n/a

Figure 6.9 shows how these pools of IP addresses could be deployed to each of the three networks.

FIGURE 6.9.

Assigning network addresses to the three cities.

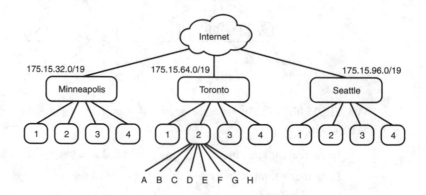

Looking specifically at Toronto, you know you need to provide four network segments within this city. Again, you can use two bits for the subnet mask. The issue now, however, is that this is an additional two bits from the host portion of the address. This leads to using a subnet mask of 255.255.248.0 for each of these four network segments.

USING SUBNET IDS THAT ARE ALL ZEROS OR ONES

When working with variable-length subnet masks, you now can use the all-zero and all-one subnets. This is because VLSM requires that the subnet mask be advertised with each route in the routing table.

The pools of IP addresses for each of these segments are shown in Table 6.10.

TABLE 6.10. NETWORK ADDRESSING FOR 175.15.64.0/21.

Increment Value	Network Address	Beginning Address	Ending Address	Broadcast Address
n	175.50.n.0	175.50.n.1	175.50.n_{next}-1.254	175.50.n_{next}-1.255
64	175.50.64.0	175.50.64.1	175.50.63.254	175.50.63.255
72	175.50.72.0	175.50.72.1	175.50.95.254	175.50.95.255
80	175.50.80.0	175.50.80.1	175.50.127.254	175.50.127.255
88	175.50.88.0	175.50.88.1	175.50.159.254	175.50.159.255

If the pool of IP addresses assigned to the downtown office is 175.50.64.0/21, the final step is to determine how to allocate a pool of addresses to each department. If you have eight separate departments that require a separate pool of IP addresses, you need to grab another 3 bits of the host portion of the address. Table 6.11 shows the pools of IP addresses you can create using an additional three bits.

TABLE 6.11. NETWORK ADDRESSING FOR 175.15.64.0/24.

Increment Value	Network Address	Beginning Address	Ending Address	Broadcast Address
n	175.50.n.0	175.50.n.1	175.50.n.254	175.50.n.255
64	175.50.64.0	175.50.64.1	175.50.64.254	175.50.64.255
65	175.50.65.0	175.50.65.1	175.50.65.254	175.50.65.255

6

continues

TABLE 6.11. CONTINUED

Increment Value	Network Address	Beginning Address	Ending Address	Broadcast Address
66	175.50.66.0	175.50.66.1	175.50.66.254	175.50.66.255
67	175.50.67.0	175.50.67.1	175.50.67.254	175.50.67.255
68	175.50.68.0	175.50.68.1	175.50.68.254	175.50.68.255
69	175.50.69.0	175.50.69.1	175.50.69.254	175.50.69.255
70	175.50.70.0	175.50.70.1	175.50.70.254	175.50.70.255
71	175.50.71.0	175.50.71.1	175.50.71.254	175.50.71.255

This provides eight pools of 254 addresses. As long as each subnet requires no more than 254 host addresses, this is a potential network solution at each office.

Conditions that Must Exist for VLSM to Occur

If you are considering implementing VLSM for your network, the following conditions must exist for a successful implementation:

- The routing protocol must support advertising of a route's subnet mask. (Routing protocols are discussed in tomorrow's material.)

- The routing algorithm must be based on the *longest match route*. In the preceding example, the following routes could have been used to describe a department in the Toronto downtown office (see Figure 6.10).

FIGURE 6.10.

Choosing the longest match route to 175.60.65.17.

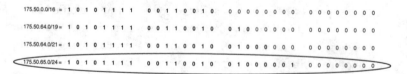

If you are looking for the host 175.50.65.17, all four routes can be used to refer to the host. The final route, however, is the longest match for this address. The *longest match route* is much more specific and should be selected over all other routes when a routing algorithm is determining the path to that network.

- For efficient routing tables, address pools must be assigned to match the physical topology. The preceding example illustrated that if someone from the Internet wants to reach the Toronto downtown office, the initial route for the 175.50.0.0 network reaches the boundary router for the organization. The routing table on this router recognizes that the route is for a client in the Toronto office and routes it to the 175.50.64.0/19 network. From there, it further distinguishes that it is from the downtown office and routes it to the 175.50.64.0/21 network. Finally, it is distributed to the third floor network at 175.50.66.0/24.

Each of the preceding prerequisites must be met for VLSM to be implemented on the network. Of these prerequisites, the last one requires the most thought and planning when you design your network.

Classless Inter-Domain Routing

RFC 1517–1520 The exponential growth of the Internet has raised concerns about the availability of IP addresses and the capability of the Internet to handle the associated routing tables. In response to these concerns, the concept of *Classless Inter-Domain Routing (CIDR)* was developed. The following are features of CIDR:

- CIDR removes the concept of Class A, Class B, and Class C addresses. Every address is simply an address that contains network and host portions. There is a not predefined subnet mask based on the first bits of the address.

- CIDR supports *route aggregation*. A single route can represent the address space of thousands of actual routes. Using a single routing entry to represent several networks can help keep the Internet backbone routing tables smaller and more efficient.

AN ALTERNATIVE SOLUTION

IPv6 is another solution that has evolved as a result of Internet growth. IPv6 solves the problem by increasing the address length from 32 bits to 128 bits. The IPv6 addressing scheme is discussed in detail on Day 21, "Future Applications of TCP/IP."

By removing the limitations of Class A, B, and C addresses, a pool of addresses can be formed using any contiguous pool of IP addresses. Any arbitrary-sized network can be created to fit an organization's networking needs.

For CIDR to be implemented, all routers must be able to advertise both the network address and the subnet mask for the network. This network mask determines what bits represent the network.

6

> **WHAT ABOUT SUPERNETTING?**
>
> In some journals, CIDR is referred to as *supernetting*. The basic concept is still that you can create collections of addresses that usually are separate networks.

Table 6.12 shows some common CIDR address blocks that can be created.

TABLE 6.12. COMMON CIDR BLOCK RANGES.

Network Prefix Length	Dotted Decimal Representation	Hosts per Segment	Class B Network Complement	Class C Network Complement
/13	255.248.0.0	524,286	8 B's	2048 C's
/14	255.252.0.0	262,142	4 B's	1024 C's
/15	255.254.0.0	131,070	2 B's	512 C's
/16	255.255.0.0	65,534	n/a	256 C's
/17	255.255.128.0	32,766	n/a	128 C's
/18	255.255.192.0	16,382	n/a	64 C's
/19	255.255.224.0	8,190	n/a	32 C's
/20	255.255.240.0	4094	n/a	16 C's
/21	255.255.248.0	2046	n/a	8 C's
/22	255.255.252.0	1022	n/a	4 C's
/23	255.255.254.0	510	n/a	2 C's

The biggest concern a network administrator should have with CIDR addressing is that several TCP/IP implementations do not allow a subnet mask to be assigned if it is shorter than the default subnet mask. If *every* host in the network does not support this, you cannot deploy a CIDR-based network.

The same methods are used to calculate CIDR addressing as to calculate VLSM addressing. The most important attribute used when choosing a CIDR addressing pool, however, is the number of hosts required per segment. If the number of hosts required per segment is greater than 254, a network can be assigned a supernet of Class C addresses rather than a Class B address. This generally results in a more efficient deployment of IP addresses.

Applying What You Have Learned

The best way to master subnet masking is to work through several subnetting examples. The questions for this chapter review subnetting examples for Class A, Class B, and Class C addresses.

Test Your Knowledge

1. Assuming you own the 10.0.0.0/8 network, how many bits do you need to use from the host portion of the address to create 115 subnets?

2. What extended network prefix must be used for the subnetwork example?

3. What are the network address, broadcast address, and pool of IP addresses for the third subnet?

   Network address =

   Broadcast address =

   Beginning Address =

   Ending Address =

4. Assuming you own the 172.30.0.0/16 network address, how many bits do you need to use from the host portion of the address to create 14 subnets?

5. What extended network prefix must be used for the subnetwork example?

6. What are the network address, broadcast address, and pool of IP addresses for the third subnet?

   Network address =

   Broadcast address =

   Beginning Address =

   Ending Address =

7. Assuming you own the 192.168.23.0/24 network address, how many bits do you need to use from the host portion of the address to provide for 10 subnets?

8. How many hosts does this provide for each subnet?

6

9. Complete the following table of addresses:

Network Address	Beginning Address	Ending Address	Broadcast Address

10. For the following host IP addresses, determine the network address and broadcast address for the network they participate in:

172.16.67.16 with subnet mask 255.255.240.0

192.168.54.76 with subnet mask 255.255.255.224

157.76.2.198 with subnet mask 255.255.255.128

Figure 6.11 shows a network that requires a variable-length subnet mask solution. You want to create a solution that does not waste IP addresses and that provides a routing solution that matches the topology.

REMEMBER VLSM ROUTERS AND SUBNET MASKS

When designing your network layout, remember that the routers used for a VLSM solution can support all zeros as a network address.

FIGURE 6.11.

*Design a VLSM solu-
tion for this network.*

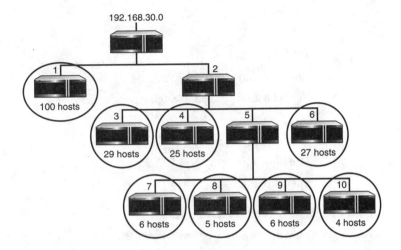

Answer the following questions about this network:

11. What network address can be used for the subnetwork #1?

     _____.____.____.____/____

12. Identify the network addresses that can be used for subnetwork #3, subnetwork #4,
     and subnetwork #6.

13. What are the broadcast addresses for subnetworks 7, 8, 9, and 10?

The following questions review Classless Inter-Domain Routing. Remember that the key
to performing CIDR is to not apply the default subnet mask to the IP address. You are
now taking bits from the network address rather than from the host portion of the
address.

14. What network address can be used to aggregate the following pool of network
     addresses?

     198.163.32.0/24   198.163.33.0/24
     198.163.34.0/24   198.163.35.0/24
     198.163.36.0/24   198.163.37.0/24
     198.163.38.0/24   198.163.39.0/24

15. For the following CIDR networks, complete the missing information for each net-
     work address.

     Beginning Address:200.200.64.1
     Ending Address: _____.____.____.____

6

Subnet Mask: 255.255.252.0

Beginning Address:____.____.____.____
Ending Address: 172.39.255.254
Subnet Mask: 255.248.0.0

Beginning Address:198.16.0.1
Ending Address: 198.31.255.254
Subnet Mask: ____.____.____.____

Preview of the Next Day

Tomorrow you will learn how networks can determine paths between themselves using routing protocols. You also will investigate how to create your own static routes for smaller networks and how routers can use dynamic routing to update their routes automatically.

DAY 7

Resolution of IP Addresses and Logical Names

In the preceding chapters, you examined the actual addressing scheme used in a TCP/IP network. Today's material reviews two of the primary methods used to apply logical names to these IP addresses: *hostnames* and *NetBIOS names*.

These two methods make it easier for users to access resources on a TCP/IP network. In your network system, you can apply one or both of these resolution methods.

This chapter also examines the future of name resolution on the Internet. Dynamic domain name servers currently are being developed. They will provide automated registration of hostnames to a DNS server.

Today's material also will look at some of the key text files that can be configured in a TCP/IP environment. You will learn the specific parameters that can be set and the syntax within each file.

Resolving IP Addresses to MAC Addresses

For communication to take place between two computers, the computers' network cards must be able to locate each other. In a TCP/IP network, each host is assigned an IP address to represent that host on the network. As you saw in Day 3, ARP is the protocol used to resolve an IP address to the MAC address of the network card. Remember, even though you are now considering assigning logical names to a host, this step *must* occur for actual communications to take place.

Resolving Logical Names to IP Addresses

Instead of working with IP addresses to locate hostnames, it is preferable to use human names. The following name-resolution methods can be performed on a TCP/IP network:

- Hostname resolution
- NetBIOS name Resolution

Actual use of these logical names takes place in the application level of the TCP/IP layer model (see Figure 7.1).

FIGURE 7.1.

Resolving logical names to MAC addresses.

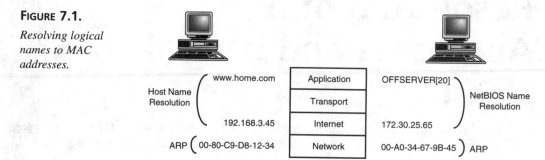

	www.home.com	Application	OFFSERVER[20]	
Host Name Resolution		Transport		NetBIOS Name Resolution
	192.168.3.45	Internet	172.30.25.65	
ARP	00-80-C9-D8-12-34	Network	00-A0-34-67-9B-45	ARP

As you can see, either hostname resolution or NetBIOS name resolution is used to resolve the logical name to an IP address. The resolution method used depends entirely on the application that needs to resolve the name. NetBIOS applications use NetBIOS name resolution; Winsock applications use hostname resolution.

After the IP address has been determined for the logical name, ARP is used to determine the actual MAC address. Remember from Day 3 that the MAC address ARP resolves depends on whether the destination host is on a local or remote network. If the destination is on the same network as the source, ARP resolves the actual MAC address of the destination host. If the destination host is on a remote network, ARP finds the MAC address of the router used to send the data to the remote network. The frame is transmitted to the default gateway, which forwards it to the destination host's network.

The following sections examine the specific actions taken in both hostname resolution and in NetBIOS name resolution.

Hostname Resolution

Hostname resolution has been used since the beginning of the Internet. Originally, all information was stored in a centralized HOSTS.TXT file. Any new hosts on the Internet registered their hostname and IP address into this central file maintained by the Network Information Center.

All participating hosts on the Internet downloaded this centralized file to their own systems. As the Internet grew, the need to move away from this centralized file became evident. The following problems were noticed:

- Updates occurred on a daily basis because of the increased size of the Internet.
- The Stanford Research Institute's network—where the HOSTS.TXT file existed—became a bottleneck for the Internet.
- A hostname could not be duplicated *anywhere* on the Internet because of the flat nature of the name space.
- Name updates took a few days to become visible to the Internet as a whole.

The suggested solutions all advised that the new name-resolution method be hierarchical in design. The other key suggestion was that the database be distributed in nature rather than centralized. This way, each organization could maintain its own hostnames.

The Domain Name Space

The *domain name space* is a tree-like structure representing all the domains that make up the name space for the Internet. The *root domain* is at the top of the tree (see Figure 7.2).

The root domain does not have an actual text label; it is expressed using a period (.).

Below the root domain are the *top-level domains*. There are two variations of top-level domains. In the first variation, the top-level domains represent types of businesses. The second variation uses a two-digit code to represent the country in which an organization is located. Table 7.1 shows the current top-level domains.

7

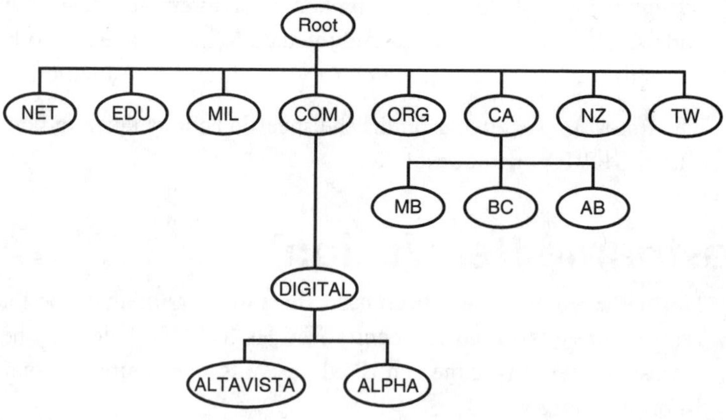

Figure 7.2.

The domain name space.

Table 7.1. Top-level domain names.

Name	Description
com	Commercial organizations
edu	Educational institutions and universities
org	Not-for-profit organizations
net	Network facilities
gov	Non-military government organizations
mil	Military government organizations
num	Phone numbers
arpa	Reverse lookups domains
xx	Two-digit country codes (such as CA for Canada, NZ for New Zealand, and TW for Taiwan)
firm*	Businesses and firms
shop*	For businesses offering goods to purchase
web*	Entities emphasizing activities related to the World Wide Web
arts*	Entities emphasizing cultural and entertainment activities
rec*	Entities emphasizing recreation/entertainment activities
info*	Entities providing information services
nom*	Provides nonenclature (such as a personal nom de plume)

These generic top-level domains have been added because of the need to expand the domain name space. Most organizations desire a COM top-level domain name and find that their first few choices are already taken. This should provide additional expansion.

Second-level domains, which contain hosts and other subdomains, exist below the top-level domains. Figure 7.2 shows four second-level domains. Digital is an example of an organization that has registered a second-level domain in the COM top-level domain. MB, BC, and AB represent a common separation technique within a country domain; in this case, they represent individual provinces within Canada. MB stands for Manitoba, BC stands for British Columbia, and AB stands for Alberta. This provides a complete geographic breakdown within a country's top-level domain.

ALTAVISTA and ALPHA represent subdomains below the DIGITAL.COM second-level domain. If you want to view the Web pages of a Web server in the ALTAVISTA domain, type www.altavista.digital.com—the *uniform resource locator (URL)* for the site—in a browser. A hostname that includes its full domain name path is called a *fully qualified domain name (FQDN)*. If you are sitting at another host in the altavista.digital.com domain, you can refer to the server using just its hostname, www. The FQDN makes sure the application knows that the full path to the host is specified in the URL.

ACQUIRING A SECOND-LEVEL DOMAIN
You cannot use just any second-level domain name on the Internet. You must register your domain name with InterNIC. Visit http://rs.internic.net/ and configure the name you want to use. The name you want might already be taken. Be prepared to perform some searches to determine whether the name you want is already taken.

Hostname Resolution Process

The process used when a computer needs to resolve a hostname to an IP address is shown in Figure 7.3.

1. Is the name you are trying to resolve the name of the host you are working on?
2. Is the name you are trying to query located in the HOSTS file? (The HOSTS file is discussed in detail later today.)
3. Does the DNS server have an entry for this host?

7

FIGURE 7.3.

*The hostname
resolution process.*

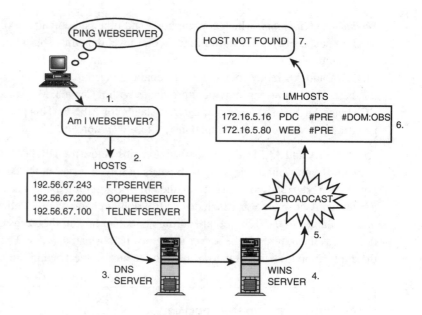

RESOLVING HOSTNAMES FOR MICROSOFT CLIENTS

Microsoft clients have access to additional methods for resolving hostnames
because of their dependence on NetBIOS names. Some NetBIOS name-
resolution methods also can be used to resolve a hostname. These additional
resolution steps start at step 4. Non-Microsoft clients deliver a name-not-
resolved message if the name is not resolved in the first three steps.

---

4. Is the hostname registered with the WINS server?

5. Can the hostname be resolved using a local network broadcast?

6. Is the hostname included in the LMHOSTS file? (The LMHOST file is discussed
   in detail later today.)

If none of these resolution methods find an IP address for the target hostname, the application returns an error message stating that the hostname could not be found. This is
step 7 in Figure 7.3.

Roles in the Domain Name Space (DNS) System

Within the domain name space system, the following key components are involved in the name-resolution process:

- The domain name space
- Resolvers
- Name servers

The *domain name space* (as previously discussed) is the distributed, hierarchical database that contains all hostnames to IP addresses on the Internet. This database resolves the requested hostname to an IP address.

Resolvers are the actual clients attempting to resolve a hostname to an IP address. The resolver functionality either is built into the calling application or is running on the host computer as part of the TCP/IP protocol stack.

Name servers are the physical hosts that accept the requests from the DNS resolvers and that return the IP address for the requested hostname. Depending on the resolution method configured, the name server returns the IP address corresponding to a hostname, the hostname corresponding to an IP address, a response stating that the hostname is unknown, or a referral to another name server that can resolve the request.

The following roles can be played by each name server:

- Primary name server
- Secondary name server
- Master name server
- Caching-only name server

Primary Name Server

A *primary name server* manages a zone of information. A *zone* encompasses the part of the domain name space for which the particular name server is responsible. The zone files are stored locally on the primary name server, and all modifications to these zone files should be performed only at this server. A primary name server's zone of authority can encompass more than one domain. It can manage subdomains below a specific domain, or it can host the zone files for several different second-level domains (see Figure 7.4).

7

FIGURE 7.4.

Name server's zones of authority.

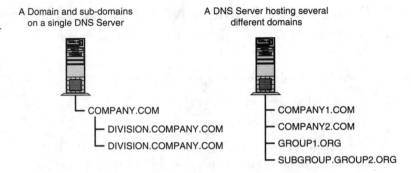

A Domain and sub-domains on a single DNS Server

A DNS Server hosting several different domains

COMPANY.COM
— DIVISION.COMPANY.COM
— DIVISION.COMPANY.COM

— COMPANY1.COM
— COMPANY2.COM
— GROUP1.ORG
— SUBGROUP.GROUP2.ORG

THE RELATIONSHIP BETWEEN ZONES AND DOMAINS

Many people assume a zone file always matches a domain. This is not necessarily true. The company XYZ.com, for example, registers the subdomains Research, Marketing, and Sales. Although it is possible for the zone to include XYZ.com and the three subdomains, it also is possible for one or more of the subdomains to be managed in its own separate zone of authority (see Figure 7.5).

FIGURE 7.5.

A domain that includes three zone files.

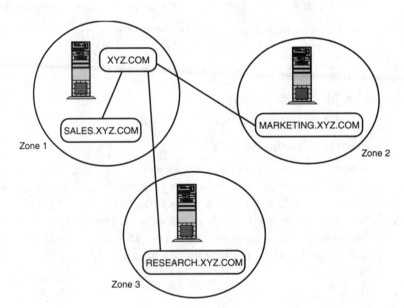

XYZ.COM

SALES.XYZ.COM

Zone 1

MARKETING.XYZ.COM

Zone 2

RESEARCH.XYZ.COM

Zone 3

Secondary Name Server

A *secondary name server* obtains its zone information from another name server that has a copy of the zone file. The other name server could be another secondary name server, or it could be a primary name server. The actual transmission of the zone information is called a *zone transfer*.

The following are some reasons that secondary name servers are implemented:

- An additional name server with the same zone data can help balance traffic between the two servers.

- An additional name server can be located at a remote site to increase the speed of hostname resolution for the resolvers at that remote site.

- An additional name server for a zone can provide fault tolerance in case one of the name servers is down.

- A secondary name server is required if you are registering your domain with InterNIC.

Secondary name servers are sometimes referred to as *slave name servers* because they only store copies of the original zone data files. No updates are performed on the zone files stored on a secondary name server.

Master Name Server

A *master name server* is a name server that transfers its zone files to a secondary name server. Although you might assume that only primary name servers function as master servers, it also is possible for a secondary name server to function as a master server. This generally occurs when network links dictate the flow of traffic. Figure 7.6 shows a network in which it might be better for a secondary name server to function as a master name server.

FIGURE 7.6.

Scenario in which a secondary name server should function as a master name server.

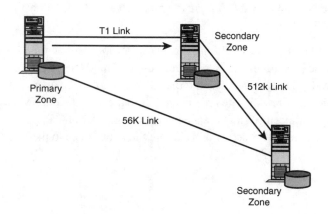

T1 Link

Secondary Zone

Primary Zone

512k Link

56K Link

Secondary Zone

7

A secondary name server must be configured with the IP address of its master name server. When the secondary name server boots, it communicates with its configured master name server and initiates a zone transfer of the DNS data.

Caching-Only Name Server

A *caching-only name server* does not store any zone data file information locally. Whenever a host queries a caching-only server, it makes the request on behalf of the resolver, caches the result, and returns the IP address for the requested host to the resolver. If another host makes the same request, the caching-only server uses its cached information to fulfill the request.

This implementation of DNS is useful for a slow WAN link. Instead of having a secondary name server that requires that an entire zone transfer be sent to it regularly, a caching-only server can be located at the remote location. Only actual requests and responses are sent to the caching-only server. Frequently visited locations are stored in cache and do not require WAN traffic for resolution.

Query Types Under DNS

The following types of queries can be requested by a resolver when it queries a name server:

- Recursive queries
- Iterative queries
- Inverse queries

Recursive Queries

In a *recursive query*, the designated name server must either respond with the requested hostname's IP address or return an error. Many times, the name server changes its role to be a resolver and asks its configured name server to find the hostname's IP address (see Figure 7.7).

This configuration is useful for a local network located behind a firewall on the Internet. In this case, it is necessary to configure the internal DNS to perform recursive queries to the firewall's DNS server. The internal DNS cannot make queries to any computers located beyond the firewall. The only computer that can make queries on the exterior network is the firewall itself. Using a recursive query, the firewall can pass the resolver's request to its configured DNS server and can provide a response to the IP address of the desired host.

FIGURE 7.7.

Performing a recursive query through a firewall.

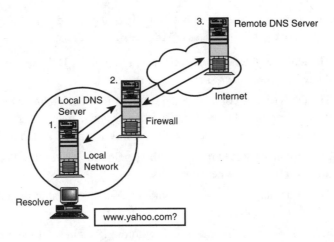

Iterative Queries

In an *iterative query*, the queried name server only has to provide its best answer to the DNS resolver. The response could be the actual IP address of the requested host, a name-could-not-be-resolved error, or a referral to a different DNS server that might provide the IP address for the requested hostname (see Figure 7.8).

FIGURE 7.8.

An iterative DNS query.

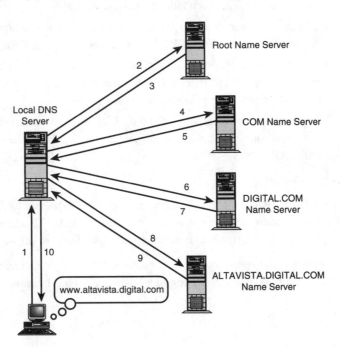

7

Figure 7.8 actually shows a combination of recursive and iterative queries. Follow these steps to resolve the name www.altavista.digital.com:

1. The DNS resolver makes a recursive query to its DNS server, requesting the IP address for www.altavista.digital.com.

2. The DNS server, not having the result in its DNS cache, does not have another forwarder configured to perform another recursive query. Instead, it sends an iterative name query to a root name server for www.altavista.digital.com.

3. The root name server returns to the local name server the IP address of a COM top-level domain server to try next.

4. The local name server sends another iterative request to the COM name server, asking it to resolve www.altavista.digital.com.

5. The COM name server responds with the IP address of the digital.com authoritative name server.

6. The local name server sends another iterative query to the digital.com name server, asking it for the IP address of www.altavista.digital.com.

7. Assuming that the altavista.ditital.com subdomain is stored in a separate zone file on another name server, the digital.com name server responds with the IP address of the altavista.digital.com authoritative name server.

8. The local name server sends another iterative query to the altavista.digital.com name server, requesting the IP address of www.altavista.digital.com.

9. The altavista.digital.com name server responds with the IP address www.altavista.digital.com. If the name does not exist in this domain, it returns an invalid hostname response at this point.

10. The local name server first caches the IP address for www.altavista.digital.com. After it has added the hostname and corresponding IP address to cache, it returns the IP address to the calling DNS resolver.

Inverse Queries

An *inverse query* occurs when you attempt to find the associated fully qualified domain name for an IP address. Rather than trying to determine the IP address for a given hostname, you are trying to find the hostname for a specific IP address.

This common task is performed by network security analysts when they try to resolve the IP address of a host in a security log to a hostname on the Internet.

This also is commonly used when setting rules on a firewall to restrict access to specific sites. If a rule has been established that network users should not be granted access to www.badstuff.com, the firewall also can be configured to perform reverse lookups. This prevents users from typing in the address 192.168.5.67 and circumventing the rule to block access.

Performance Tuning for DNS

A key performance factor for a DNS server is the capability to cache recently resolved hostnames. When a DNS server resolves a hostname for a resolver, it places the resolved hostname into its cache. The next time that hostname is queried, instead of going through the process of resolving that same name, the IP address can be returned from the cache.

This capability is based on the Time-To-Live (TTL) field in a DNS reply message. The TTL field designates when the DNS record should be removed from the cache of a DNS name server.

The TTL field is honored when a record is resolved from another name server's cache. Figure 7.9 shows how the TTL field is honored during a DNS resolution process.

FIGURE 7.9.

DNS servers honor the TTL field when resolving a hostname.

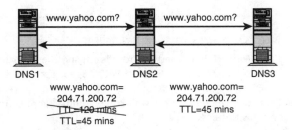

DNS1 has forwarded a DNS query to DNS2. DNS2 has forwarded the DNS query to DNS3. DNS3 was able to resolve www.yahoo.com to the address 204.71.200.72. It also returns that the TTL for this address is 45 minutes. When DNS2 adds the hostname/IP address combination to its cache, it also sets the TTL to 45 minutes, even though its default TTL for all records is 120 minutes. It does so because DNS3 can only guarantee this result for another 45 minutes. The same holds true when DNS1 adds the hostname/IP address combination to its cache. Configuring the TTL for a zone is covered tomorrow (Day 8, "Configuring Domain Name Servers").

7

NetBIOS Name Resolution

RFC 1001

RFC 1002

The NetBIOS names method also is used on networks to apply logical names to computers and their services. The NetBIOS interface is an Application Programming Interface that enables communications to take place between a client and a server computer using human names to represent each other. The following are services provided within NetBIOS:

- Name registration and release by clients
- Name resolution
- Session establishment and termination
- Support for reliable connection-oriented data transfer
- Support for connectionless datagram transfer

The NetBIOS names are restricted to 16 bytes in length. The first 15 bytes uniquely represent the NetBIOS resource on the network. The last byte represents the actual NetBIOS service that the NetBIOS resource is hosting. Each NetBIOS service has its own unique identifier that is used when registering the NetBIOS name.

COMPARING NETBIOS NAMES TO SOCKET NUMBERS

Both NetBIOS and WinSock have methods for identifying the applications and services running on a server or client. In NetBIOS, each service is assigned a NetBIOS name that includes a unique 16th character to represents that service. These service numbers are well known, and a client connects to the service using this NetBIOS name.

In WinSock, each service or application has a preconfigured port on which it listens for connections from clients. The clients know the port to which they should be connecting.

With both systems, the client also has a unique NetBIOS name or port that is used as its side of the communication system.

NetBIOS resources can include both unique names that can be registered only by a single computer and group names that can be registered by multiple computers. Table 7.2 lists some of the more common NetBIOS names.

TABLE 7.2. COMMON NETBIOS NAMES.

Name	NetBIOS Suffix	Type	Description
Computername	00	Unique	Workstation service.
msbrowse_	01	Unique	The master browser for the segment uses this NetBIOS name to broadcast and receive domain announcements on a segment.
Computername	03	Unique	Messenger service requests for a specific computer name.
Username	03	Unique	Messenger service requests for a specific user name.
Computername	06	Unique	RAS server service.
Domainname	1B	Unique	Domain master browser.
Domainname	1D	Unique	Master browser on a segment.
Computername	1F	Unique	NetDDE service.
Computername	20	Unique	Server service.
Computername	21	Unique	RAS client service.
Computername	BE	Unique	Network monitor agent.
Computername	BF	Unique	Network monitor application.
Domainname	00	Group	Domain or group membership.
Domainname	1C	Group	All domain controllers for a domain up to a maximum of 25 entries. The first entry always is the primary domain controller (PDC).
Domainname	1E	Group	Registered by all computers that participate in browser service elections.

A NetBIOS client must be configured to determine how it resolves NetBIOS names on the network. The *NetBIOS node type* is the property that determines this. The following different configurations can be set:

- A *B-node* client (broadcast) is configured to use only broadcasts for NetBIOS transactions. If the target NetBIOS computer is not on the same network segment, communication probably will not take place.
- A *P-node* client (peer) is configured to only perform NetBIOS transactions with a *NetBIOS name server (NBNS)*. The NBNS accepts the NetBIOS name registrations of all hosts configured to use the NBNS and stores them in an accessible database. If the NBNS does not have a record of the desired NetBIOS name, the client cannot connect to the desired host.

7

- An *M-node* client (mixed) first attempts to find the NetBIOS name on the network using a broadcast. If this fails, it then queries the configured NBNS to see whether it has a record of the NetBIOS name.

- An *H-node* client (hybrid) first attempts to resolve a NetBIOS name using a NBNS. If a record does not exist for the NetBIOS name on the NBNS, the client then resorts to a broadcast on the local network segment. This generally is the preferred configuration on a NetBIOS network because it reduces broadcast traffic yet still enables a broadcast to take place if a NetBIOS name has not been registered on the NBNS.

A MICROSOFT-SPECIFIC RESOLUTION METHOD

Microsoft clients can use another NetBIOS name-resolution method known as *enhanced B-node*. A NetBIOS name is first resolved using a broadcast message. If this does not work, the Microsoft client checks a locally configured file named LMHOSTS to see whether an IP address is stored in the file for the desired NetBIOS name. The LMHOSTS file is discussed in the section "TCP/IP Configuration Files."

NetBIOS Name-Resolution Process

NetBIOS name resolution is the process of resolving a NetBIOS name to an IP address. After the NetBIOS name has been resolved to an IP address, ARP enables the IP address to be translated to a MAC address.

The NetBIOS name-resolution process is shown in Figure 7.10. This process assumes the client is configured as an H-node client.

1. The first resolution attempt determines whether the NetBIOS name is a locally registered name. If it is, communication takes place using the localhost IP address (127.0.0.1) so that no network traffic is generated by the request.

2. The NetBIOS name cache is checked to see whether the NetBIOS name has been resolved recently. If found, the IP address related to the NetBIOS name is used.

3. A request is sent to the client's configured NetBIOS name server (NBNS). This server accepts automatic registration of NetBIOS name/IP address combinations from its configured clients. If the name is found in the NBNS database, the IP address is returned to the calling client.

4. A local broadcast is issued, asking the client that has registered the desired NetBIOS name to respond with its IP address.

FIGURE 7.10.

The NetBIOS name-resolution process for an H-node client.

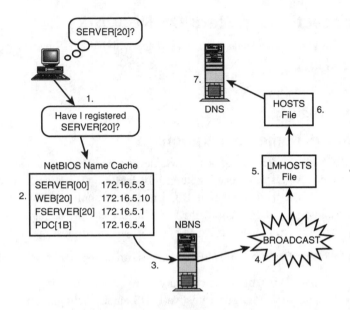

MICROSOFT-SPECIFIC NETBIOS RESOLUTION ISSUES

Microsoft clients have access to additional methods for resolving NetBIOS names. These additional resolution steps start at step 5. Non-Microsoft clients that use NetBIOS services cease their attempts to resolve a NetBIOS name at this point.

---

5. The NetBIOS name could exist in the computer's LMHOSTS file. If found, the configured IP address is used.

6. The NetBIOS name could exist in the computer's local HOSTS file. If found, the configured IP address is used.

7. The client's configured DNS server is queried to determine whether a host record exists for the desired NetBIOS name. If it does, the IP address is returned to the calling client.

If all these methods fail to resolve the NetBIOS name to an IP address, an error message informs the calling client that the NetBIOS name could not be found.

7

Transactions in NetBIOS Networks

The following basic transactions take place with NetBIOS names:

- Name registrations
- Name discoveries
- Name releases

NetBIOS Name Registrations

NetBIOS *name registration* occurs whenever a NetBIOS host is started. Each NetBIOS name a host wants to register is either broadcast on the network or sent directly to the NBNS. (This depends on the NetBIOS node-type configuration.) If the name registration is for a unique NetBIOS name, the name cannot already be registered on the network. If it is, the registering host receives a not-acknowledged message.

The following four types of NetBIOS names can be registered with a NetBIOS name server:

- *Unique.* This name type can only be registered to a single IP address. If another host attempts to register this NetBIOS name, the registration is rejected with a not-acknowledged message.
- *Normal group.* This name type is not registered to a specific host or hosts. It simply states that the normal group exists on the network and is assigned the limited broadcast address of 255.255.255.255.
- *MultiHomed.* This single, unique name type stores multiple addresses. It indicates a host with multiple network cards bound to NetBIOS over TCP/IP. Each multi-homed group name can contain a maximum of 25 IP addresses.
- *Domain name.* This NetBIOS name type includes up to 25 IP addresses for a single NetBIOS name. It is used for hosts that all can deliver an identical service, such as logon authentication in a Windows NT domain.

NetBIOS Name Discoveries

NetBIOS *name discoveries* occur any time a NetBIOS client needs to resolve another NetBIOS name to an IP address. Depending on the NetBIOS node-type configuration, this name discovery either is sent to an NBNS or is issued as a local network broadcast. Either the NBNS or the host that owns the NetBIOS name responds.

NetBIOS Name Releases

NetBIOS *name releases* occur whenever a NetBIOS application or service for which a NetBIOS name has been registered is stopped. This occurs, for example, when a user logs off the network. When a user performs the logoff sequence, the NetBIOS name USERNAME[03] is released because the user no longer is logged on to the network. When the user logs on again, the NetBIOS name is registered at the IP address of the host on which he is working. The messenger service can continue to reach him, even if he logs on to a different computer.

NetBIOS Name Servers

NetBIOS name servers provide a registration location for NetBIOS clients. A NetBIOS client sends its configured NetBIOS names and IP address to its configured NetBIOS name server. The NetBIOS name server either enters the NetBIOS name/IP address combination into its database or returns a Not Acknowledged message for the registration. When a Not Acknowledged message is received, the client must evaluate the severity of this error. If the error is for a computer-name registration, the host halts all TCP/IP services because a duplicate computer name has been found on the network. If it is simply a username registration, the Not Acknowledged message can be ignored. This is the case when a user is logged on to two or more hosts.

The advantage of a NetBIOS name server is that it can handle clients with dynamically assigned IP addresses. If a client receives a new IP address, the client sends a new NetBIOS name registration to register the new IP address.

Another advantage is the reduction in network traffic related to NetBIOS name services. Clients can send a directed packet to a NetBIOS name server when trying to resolve a NetBIOS name. This is much more efficient than using a local network broadcast that must be examined by all hosts on the network segment.

The most widely known implementation of a NetBIOS name server is Windows NT's Windows Internet Name Service (WINS). Configuration and troubleshooting of the WINS server is covered in Day 18, "IP over ATM and Configuring NetBIOS Name Servers."

Comparing NetBIOS Name Servers with DNS Servers

Although both NetBIOS name and hostname resolution ultimately provides logical name-to-IP address resolution, some key differences do exist, as follows:

- NetBIOS names must be registered on the network. If the name being registered is a unique NetBIOS name, then the name must not already be registered on the network. If the NetBIOS name is registered, the registration will fail.
- DNS servers can use aliases to assign multiple logical names to a single IP address for the same service.
- NetBIOS names can automatically be registered with a NetBIOS name server. A DNS server currently requires manual addition and modification of all resource records.

7

- NetBIOS names exist for each service a computer is hosting. A single computer can register numerous NetBIOS names. DNS only requires a single host record for a resource. Some additional records (such as Mail Exchanger records) indicate special services provided by a host.

- After NBNS replication is configured, NetBIOS name servers can exchange only changed records. The name servers perform an initial full replication to synchronize their databases. From that point on, they only send new and updated records. DNS servers require that all zone information be sent from the master name server to its slave name server when updates are requested.

- NetBIOS servers can handle a host changing its IP address in a speedier manner because of the automatic registration feature. DNS requires a manual configuration change.

Despite these differences, additional overhead is involved when both name resolution services are implemented in the same network. A new naming service that can handle automatic name registration and updates is now being defined. It is known as *dynamic DNS* and is discussed later today.

TCP/IP Configuration Files

As you have seen in the discussion of logical name resolution, several text files play a major part in the configuration of the TCP/IP protocol. These files are located in the UNIX /etc directory; on Windows NT clients, they are located in the %systemroot%\system32\drivers\etc directory.

The actual configuration files include the following:

- HOSTS
- NETWORKS
- SERVICES
- PROTOCOL
- LMHOSTS (Microsoft clients only)
- RESOLV.CONF

HOSTS

The HOSTS file is used by TCP/IP to resolve hostnames to IP addresses. The following is the syntax of the Hosts file:

```
127.0.0.1                    localhost
```

```
102.54.94.97          rhino.acme.com

38.25.63.10           x.acme.com

172.16.2.16           sideshowbri     brian     instructor
```

As you can see, the host named sideshowbri can be reached at IP address 172.16.2.16. The additional names on this configuration line are aliases. They also can be used instead of sideshowbri to refer to the host.

CONFIGURATION WARNING

As previously discussed, the HOSTS file is one of the first files referenced during the hostname resolution process. An IP address configured incorrectly in this file can result in a host never being reached, even if entered correctly at a DNS server.

Another issue with the HOSTS file is that, in some implementations of TCP/IP, hostnames are case sensitive. The most common way to represent a host-name is in lower case.

If you are considering implementing HOSTS files on your clients, a major issue to consider is that the files must be updated manually at each host on the network. For this reason, it is common to implement DNS instead.

NETWORKS

The NETWORKS file is used to create logical names for network IP addresses. The following is an example of a NETWORKS file:

```
loopback        127

winnipeg        172.16

calgary         172.17

minneapolis     192.168.5
```

By creating entries in the NETWORKS file, you can refer to these networks using their logical names in TCP/IP configuration commands, such as the creation of static route entries in a routing table.

7

SERVICES

The SERVICES file contains the text names for well-known port addresses used by both TCP and UDP. The following is a partial listing of a SERVICES file:

```
echo              7/tcp
echo              7/udp
discard           9/tcp       sink null
discard           9/udp       sink null
systat           11/tcp
systat           11/tcp       users
daytime          13/tcp
daytime          13/udp
netstat          15/tcp
qotd             17/tcp       quote
qotd             17/udp       quote
chargen          19/tcp       ttytst source
chargen          19/udp       ttytst source
ftp-data         20/tcp
ftp              21/tcp
telnet           23/tcp
smtp             25/tcp       mail
.
.
.
rscsa         10010/udp
rscsb         10011/udp
qmaster       10012/tcp
qmaster       10012/udp
```

The SERVICES file can be changed, but this should be done with great caution. If you change the ftp port from 21/tcp to 22/tcp, this only is changed in this system. All other systems in the network still assume that this transmission occurs on 21/tcp.

PROTOCOL

The PROTOCOL file contains the protocol ID numbers for the standard TCP/IP protocols. These protocol ID numbers are referred to in the IP header to designate which protocol is piggybacked on the IP protocol. The following is an example of the PROTOCOL file:

```
ip       0     IP      # Internet protocol
icmp     1     ICMP    # Internet control message protocol
ggp      3     GGP     # Gateway-gateway protocol
tcp      6     TCP     # Transmission control protocol
egp      8     EGP     # Exterior gateway protocol
pup     12     PUP     # PARC universal packet protocol
udp     17     UDP     # User datagram protocol
```

```
hmp       20    HMP       # Host monitoring protocol
xns-idp   22    XNS-IDP   # Xerox NS IDP
rdp       27    RDP       # "reliable datagram" protocol
rvd       66    RVD       # MIT remote virtual disk
```

This file is not changed very often. It can be edited, however, to add a new protocol that you want to refer to by a mnemonic.

LMHOSTS

The LMHOSTS (Lan Manager HOSTS) file is used only in Microsoft networks that require NetBIOS name resolution. This file provides the following capabilities:

- The capability to autoload NetBIOS names into the NetBIOS name cache
- The capability to refer to a centralized LMHOSTS file
- The capability to provide resolution to a login server located across a WAN boundary

---

LMHOSTS AND NetBIOS NAME SERVERS

If a NetBIOS name server is included in a network using NetBIOS name resolution, it is not necessary to implement LMHOSTS files. This is because the NetBIOS name-resolution method first attempts to resolve the NetBIOS name using a NetBIOS name lookup to the NetBIOS name server. You can, however, still include LMHOSTS files on key servers in case the NBNS fails. This ensures that remote NetBIOS hosts still can communicate if the NBNS fails.

The following is an example of an LMHOSTS file:

```
102.54.94.100      ntw
102.54.94.105      win95
102.54.94.97       rhino      #PRE    #DOM:networking
102.54.94.123      popular    #PRE
102.54.94.117      localsrv   #PRE

#BEGIN_ALTERNATE
#INCLUDE \\localsrv\public\lmhosts
#END_ALTERNATE
```

Placing the #PRE parameter in a line of the LMHOSTS file means that this name should be preloaded into the NetBIOS name cache. This results in faster NetBIOS name resolution.

The #DOM:Domain entry signifies that the entry can function as an authenticating server for the Domain domain.

7

The #INCLUDE line specifies the location of the centralized LMHOSTS file. The file always is noted using a *universal naming convention (UNC)* styled network reference. The UNC name is based on the following syntax:

```
\\SERVER\SHARED RESOURCE\FILE
```

In the preceding, SERVER is the NETBIOS name of the server on which the resource is located. SHARED RESOURCE refers to the logical name designated as an entry point to the server's files resources.

When you use the #INCLUDE line, it is important that the server name be referenced earlier in the LMHOSTS file. This is because the file is parsed sequentially. If the SERVER name is not previously referred to, the shared LMHOSTS file's location cannot be resolved. The server's entry must include a #PRE entry in its definition so that its IP address is loaded into the NetBIOS name cache.

The #Begin Alternate and #End Alternate tag lines indicate that a redirection is to occur. The redirection generally is to a centralized LMHOSTS file on a central file server. These lines provide multiple locations for storing a centralized LMHOSTS file.

ENTRIES TO INCLUDE IN AN LMHOSTS FILE

The **LMHOSTS** file should only contain name-resolution entries for NetBIOS computers not located on the same network segment. Local segment hosts are resolved using an NBNS lookup or broadcast before the **LMHOSTS** file even is consulted.

RESOLV.CONF

The RESOLV.CONF file is used on UNIX hosts to store their DNS configuration information. It generally is located in the /etc directory. The following is the format of the RESOLV.CONF file:

```
;
; Data file for a client
;
domain          online-can.com
nameserver      172.16.2.3
nameserver      172.16.3.3
```

- `domain` represents the domain portion of a fully qualified domain name.
- `nameserver` represents the IP addresses of your configured DNS servers. The order in which they occur in the file is the order in which connection is attempted.

If the RESOLV.CONF file does not exist on a UNIX host, it is assumed that the DNS service is running on the local host.

DNS CLIENT CONFIGURATION IN WINDOWS NT

The DNS configuration is performed entirely in the TCP/IP protocol's property pages. All information is entered on the DNS property page (see Figure 7.11).

FIGURE 7.11.

DNS configuration under Windows NT.

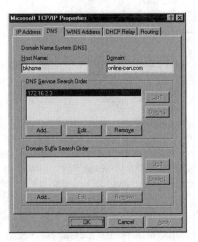

The Future of Name Resolution— Dynamic DNS

RFC 2136

RFC 2137

The domain name system currently in use does not provide dynamic updates. Any changes to the DNS database must be performed manually. With the advent of automatic configuration protocols such as DHCP (see Day 10), the need for dynamic registration with a DNS server has become more relevant.

The key to dynamic DNS (DDNS) is that, if a host receives a different IP address from the DHCP server, the DHCP server should send an UPDATE message to the DDNS server outlining the actual changes that should be applied to the related host record.

7

The DDNS server then sends this update to its secondary servers. This assumes that the cache time-to-live for these records is kept to a shorter duration so the updates propagate more efficiently through the domain name space.

DDNS Message Header Format

A DNS UPDATE message uses the message header format shown in Figure 7.12.

FIGURE 7.12.

The DNS UPDATE message header format.

ID			
QR	OPCODE	RESERVED	RCODE
ZOCOUNT			
PRCOUNT			
UPCOUNT			
ADCOUNT			

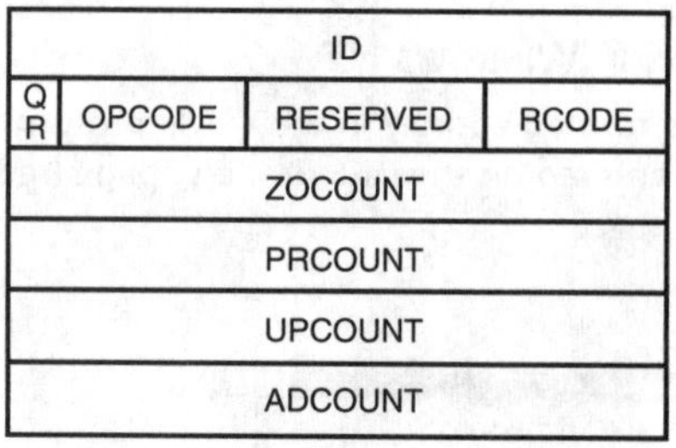

The ID field is a 16-bit identifier generated by the entity that generates the DNS UPDATE message. An example of this might be a DHCP server. This identifier is used by the requestor to match a reply from the DDNS server to an outstanding request.

The QR field is a 1-bit field that specifies whether the message is a query (0) or a response (1).

The OPCODE field is a 4-bit field that specifies the operation to be performed by the DNS message. For an UPDATE message, this value is set to 5.

The next 7-bit field is reserved for future use and should be set to a value of all zeros.

The RCODE field is used in DNS UPDATE response messages. Acceptable values are listed in Table 7.3.

TABLE 7.3. RESPONSE CODE OPTIONS.

Code	Value	Description
NOERROR	0	No error condition exists.
FORMERR	1	The name server was unable to parse the requested data because of a format error.
SERVFAIL	2	The name server encountered an internal error during the processing of the request.
NXDOMAIN	3	The name being updated does not exist.
NOTIMP	4	The name server does not support the UPDATE feature.

Code	Value	Description
REFUSED	5	The name server refused to perform the requested operation for a policy or security reason.
YXDOMAIN	6	A resource record already exists for the name being added.
YXRRSET	7	A resource record set that should not exist does exist.
NXRRSET	8	A resource record set that should exist does not exist.
NOTAUTH	9	The server is nonauthoritative for the zone named in the Zone section.
NOTZONE	10	A name used in the Prerequisite or Update section is not within the zone denoted in the Zone section.

The ZOCOUNT field contains the number of resource records in the Zone section.

The PRCOUNT field contains the number of resource records in the Prerequisites section.

The UPCOUNT field contains the number of resource records in the Update section.

The ADCOUNT field contains the number of resource records in the Additional Data section.

The Zone Section Format

Within each DNS message, a Zone section contains the DNS resource records to be updated. The format of the Zone section is shown in Figure 7.13.

FIGURE 7.13.

The DDNS Message Zone section.

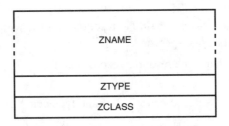

The ZNAME field contains the zone name to be updated. All records must be in the same zone; therefore, there is only one zone record per DDNS UPDATE message.

The ZTYPE record must contain the SOA record type.

The ZCLASS field contains the zone's class. This field most likely contains IN to indicate that it is an Internet class resource record.

7

New Functionality Provided by DDNS

The following are two new features DDNS adds to the existing DNS service:

- Propagation of updates to the primary DDNS server for a zone
- Notification of updates

Propagation of DDNS Updates

DDNS UPDATE messages provide a mechanism for the automatic addition, deletion, or modification of DNS resource records. With the implementation of IP addressing services such as DHCP, the possibility of new hosts requiring entries in DNS has grown dramatically. Previously, a manual update method could be used to maintain the DNS zone's master file. The possibility of rapidly changing IP address assignments, however, increases the need for this automated process. The DDNS update process is described in RFC 2136.

When a DNS UPDATE message is received by a DNS sever, a set of predefined prerequisites determines whether the UPDATE is processed. These prerequisites can include the following:

- *Resource record set exists (value independent).* At least one resource record with the specified NAME and TYPE must exist.

- *Resource record set exists (value dependent).* A set of resource records with the specified name and type must exist. In addition, this set of resource records must have the same members with the same resource data as the record set specified in the UPDATE message.

- *Resource record set does not exist.* No resource records with the specified NAME and TYPE can exist in the zone specified.

- *Name is in use.* At least one resource record with the specified NAME must exist in the specified zone.

- *Name is not in use.* No resource record of any type can exist in the zone.

Which prerequisite is used depends on the type of update performed on the resource records. An actual modification UPDATE, for example, cannot use the prerequisite "Name is not in use" because it depends on changing existing data. If the prerequisite is met, the processing of the UPDATE message can occur.

Updates are processed as follows:

1. If a system failure occurs during the processing of the Update section, the DDNS server sends an RCODE message of SERVFAIL to the requestor. All updates applied to the zone so far are rolled back to their previous state.

2. Any Update resource records whose CLASS matches the ZCLASS are added to the zone. If a duplicate record exists, it is replaced with the updated data.

3. If the Update resource record's CLASS and TYPE are both set to ANY, all zone resource records with the same name are deleted. The only exception is when NAME is the same as ZNAME. These deletion requests are ignored.

4. If the Update resource record's CLASS is NONE, all zone resource records that match the Update resource record for the fields NAME, TYPE, RDATA, and RDLENGTH are deleted. Again, the only exception is when NAME is equal to ZNAME. This represents an SOA or name server (NS) record.

After the updates are complete, the zone's serial number in the SOA record should be incremented. Remember, the secondary zones use this value to determine whether updates have been performed on the Zone database.

Notification of Updates

RFC 1996 RFC 1996 addresses the issue of slow propagation of new and changed data in a DNS zone. It introduces a new transaction known as a DDNS NOTIFY. This transaction enables master servers to inform their slave servers that a change has occurred in the zone.

This changes the typical zone update mechanism from a polling model to an interrupt model. This implementation only allows for changes to the zone's Start of Authority (SOA) record to be announced. This should meet the needs of DDNS because any changes to resource records should be accompanied by a change to the zone's serial number stored in the SOA record. The serial number tracks when changes occur to any resource records. By changing the zone's serial number, you can indicate that resource records have been added, deleted, or modified.

NOTIFY messages can use either UDP or TCP for transport. (UDP is the preferred method.) TCP must be implemented when a firewall prevents UDP datagrams from being transmitted or when a resource record's modified size is too large for a UDP datagram.

When the DNS NOTIFY datagram is received, the slave DNS server should behave as if it has reached its REFRESH interval. In other words, it immediately should query its Master DNS to determine whether the serial number stored in the SOA record is greater than the one currently stored in its zone files. If it is greater, a zone transfer should be initiated to update all the resource records for the zone.

If a DNS server functions as both a slave and a master DNS server, the NOTIFY protocol should be implemented so it only informs slave servers after the SOA record has been updated. In other words, the slave server should only function as a master server using the DNS NOTIFY protocol after it has successfully completed its own zone transfer from its master server.

7

Applying What You Have Learned

The following questions review some of the important concepts covered today and test your knowledge of the material.

Test Your Knowledge

1. What are some of the key differences between hostname resolution and NetBIOS name resolution?

2. What top-level domains exist on the Internet today? Why has there been a need to add additional generic top-level domains?

3. If a host's IP address is configured incorrectly in its HOSTS file but correctly in DNS, will communication occur successfully? Why or why not?

4. If a host's IP address is configured correctly in its HOSTS file but incorrectly in DNS, will communication occur successfully? Why or why not?

5. Compare and contrast a recursive DNS query with an iterative DNS query.

6. What can be done to increase performance on a DNS server?

7. What four NetBIOS node-type configurations can be set for a client? Which node types help reduce network traffic?

8. What three basic NetBIOS name transactions occur on a NetBIOS network?

9. What advantages does dynamic DNS provide over DNS?

10. If you want to use a centralized LMHOSTS file located on a server named PRIMARY in a share named NETLOGON, what lines need to be added to the LMHOSTS file? PRIMARY's IP address is 172.18.56.35.

Preview of the Next Day

Tomorrow you will examine domain name server configuration in more detail, starting with the DNS message formats.

After you have determined the format, you will look specifically at configuring a DNS server. You will approach this from the point of view of both a BIND-compliant DNS server and a Windows NT DNS server. This includes all configuration files and the various types of resource records that can be created.

DAY 8

Configuring Domain Name Servers

Today's material starts with an overview of the process that takes place when an organization registers a domain name on the Internet.

After this process is reviewed, you will inspect the DNS message format. The message format covers the message header, the Question section, and the format of a returned resource record. After you review the DNS message format, you will examine the actual configuration of a DNS server.

Two basic DNS servers are configured today: Berkeley Internet Name Daemon (BIND) compatible UNIX DNS servers and Windows NT Registry-based DNS servers. You will review the configuration of both DNS server types.

Finally, you will examine common configuration problems with these DNS implementations, and you will learn how the NSLOOKUP command can troubleshoot configuration problems.

Registering a DNS Name

To register a new domain name with InterNIC, use the following steps:

1. The person applying for the domain name first must determine whether the desired name already is in use. This can be done by searching the Whois database at `http://rs.internic.net/cgi/bin/whois`.

2. The applicant should contact an Internet service provider (ISP) to arrange for domain name space service. The ISP can provide a pool of IP addresses for use on the applicant's network and DNS name servers to host the domain name. In many cases, the ISP also assists the applicant with the domain name registration process.

3. The applicant next fills out a registration template at `http://rs.internic.net/help/templates.html`. The completed registration template becomes your contract with InterNIC for the requested domain name. On this registration form, the applicant names three contacts for the domain name: the administrative contact, the technical contact, and the billing contact.

4. The completed template is sent to InterNIC at the email address `hostmaster@internic.net`.

5. When InterNIC receives the registration request, it is assigned a tracking number. The requesting party receives an acknowledgment email with the assigned tracking number in the subject line. The tracking number uses the format `NIC-YYMMDD.#` in which # represents the unique number assigned to your request.

6. The registration request is parsed and checked for errors. If common errors are found, the template is returned to the registrant with an explanation of the problems and a suggested resolution. The corrected template must be re-sent to `hostmaster@internic.net` to undergo the parsing process again. The original tracking number is used each time the request is resubmitted. If the error is not a common error, the registration request is processed manually by InterNIC's staff.

7. When the registration template is accepted, the registrant is notified by email that the request has been approved. This generally takes place in less than 24 hours.

8. The information in the registration template is used to create a record for your new domain in InterNIC's Whois database. Your domain information also is placed in the zone files for your authoritative domain so that domain name requests can be processed against your domain.

9. As of April 1, 1998, registering your domain name costs $70 (US). You will be invoiced within seven days of your registration. This registration fee covers the first two years you use your domain name.

10. Following the initial two-year period, you are charged an annual fee on the anniversary of your initial registration. This registration fee is either:

- $50 (US) if the domain name was registered on or before March 31, 1998
- $35 (US) if the domain name was registered on or after April 1, 1998

This is due to the inclusion of a 30 percent Internet Infrastructure Fund for earlier registrations.

DNS Message Formats

RFC 1034

RFC 1035

Within a DNS message, the following major sections need to be detailed:

- The DNS message header
- The DNS Question section
- Resource record format

The DNS message header format is shown in Figure 8.1. It contains the following fields:

- *ID*. This 16-bit identifier is assigned by the program that generates a DNS query. This identifier also is used in the subsequent reply so the requestor can match the reply to the originating request.
- *QR*. This 1-bit field indicates whether the DNS message is a request (0) or a response (1).
- *OPCODE*. This 4-bit field specifies the type of query being formulated. A standard query has a value of 0, an inverse query has a value of 1, a server status request has a value of 2, and an update message has a value of 5. All other values up to 15 are reserved for future use.
- *AA*. This 1-bit field is only set in responses. When set, it indicates that the responding name server is an authority for the domain name in the DNS request message.

FIGURE 8.1.

The DNS message header format.

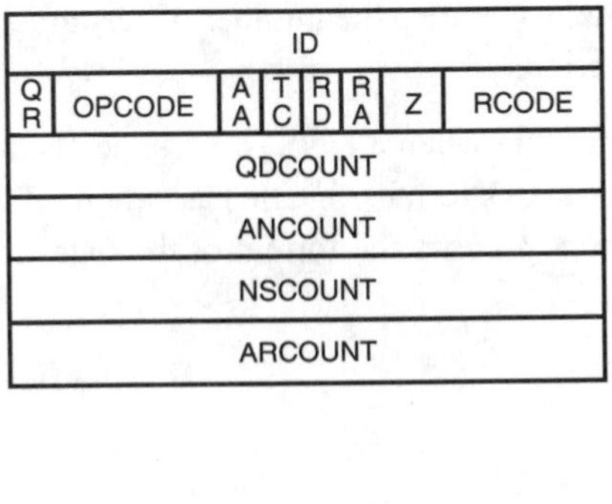

- *TC*. This 1-bit field stands for Truncation. It is set to 1 if the message was truncated because the length was longer than permitted on the transmission channel.
- *RD*. This 1-bit field stands for Recursion Desired. If set to 1, it indicates that the DNS resolver wants the DNS name server to use a recursive query.
- *RA*. This 1-bit field indicates that the responding name server can perform a recursive query. The RA stands for Recursion Available.
- *Z*. This 4-bit field is reserved for future use and should be set to all zeros.
- *RCODE*. The 4-bit Response Code field is only set in a DNS response message. It indicates whether an error has occurred. Allowed values include the following:
    - *(0) No Error Condition.* The DNS response was formulated with no errors.
    - *(1) Format Error.* The DNS name server could not interpret the DNS request.
    - *(2) Server failure.* The DNS name server was unable to process the query because of an error that occurred at the name server.
    - *(3) Name Error.* If the DNS response is from an authoritative name server, the name referenced in the DNS request does not exist.
    - *(4) Not Implemented.* The DNS name server does not support this DNS request message.
    - *(5) Refused.* The DNS name server has refused to process the DNS request because of a policy or security setting.
    - *(6) through (15).* Reserved for future use.
- *QDCOUNT*. This 16-bit field specifies the number of entries in the DNS Question section.
- *ANCOUNT*. This 16-bit field specifies the number of resource records returned in the Answer section.
- *NSCOUNT*. This 16-bit field specifies the number of name server resource records in the Authority Records section.
- *ARCOUNT*. This 16-bit field specifies the number of resource records in the Additional Records section.

The Question section contains data when a DNS resolver sends a DNS request message. The Question section follows the DNS message header when a DNS resolver sends a DNS request message. Figure 8.2 shows the format of the Question section.

FIGURE 8.2.

The Question section format for a DNS message.

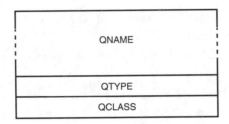

The Question section contains the following fields:

- *QNAME*. This variable-length field contains a requested domain name. It is represented as a sequence of labels, in which each label consists of a *length* octet followed by that number of octets.

- *QTYPE*. This 16-bit field specifies the type of the query. This field matches a type value for a specific resource record. Some general QTYPE values match more than one type of resource record.

- *QCLASS*. This 16-bit field specifies the class of the query. Valid classes include IN for Internet or CH for Chaos.

The Answer, Authority, and Additional sections all use the same format (see Figure 8.3). The Additional section contains resource records required in addition to the resource records returned in the Answer or Authority section. If a Start of Authority record is returned in the Authority section, for example, the related Answer (A) record for the authoritative name server also should be returned.

FIGURE 8.3.

The resource record format.

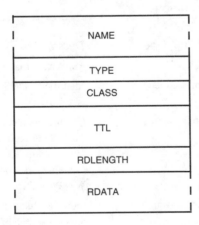

- *NAME*. This variable-length field contains the domain name to which the resource record information pertains.

- *TYPE*. This 16-bit field contains the type of resource record being returned in the information.

- *CLASS*. This 16-bit field contains the class of the data being returned in the RDATA field. The most common class returned is IN for Internet.

- *TTL*. This 32-bit field specifies the time (in seconds) that the resource record can be stored in cache before it must expire. If the value is set to zero, it may not be cached after being returned to the DNS resolver.

- *RDLENGTH*. This 16-bit field indicates the length in octets of the RDATA field.

- *RDATA*. This variable-length field describes the resource. The format of this field is based on the entries in the TYPE and CLASS fields.

Resource Records

A domain name server contains several resource records in its configuration files. These *resource records* help a DNS resolver find specific hosts on the network to which they need to connect. Although, most often, a host uses DNS to resolve a hostname to an IP address, DNS also is used to find a host that provides a specific service on the network (such as mail processing or name server service). Table 8.1 lists the resource records that can be included in the configuration files of a DNS server.

TABLE 8.1. DNS RESOURCE RECORD DEFINITIONS.

Record Alias	Numeric	Record Type	Description
A	1	Address	Maps a hostname to an IP address.
NS	2	Name server	Identifies a DNS authoritative name server for the DNS domain.
CNAME	5	Canonical name	Creates an alias for a specified hostname. The CNAME record cannot match any other existing DNS name. Common usage includes providing aliases such as WWW or FTP.
SOA	6	Start of Authority	Indicates that the named DNS server is the best source of information for the data within the named DNS domain.

8

Record Alias	Numeric	Record Type	Description
MB	7	Mailbox	An experimental record that indicates a DNS host with the specified mailbox.
MG	8	Mail group	An experimental record specifying that a mailbox is a member of a mailing group or list.
MR	9	Mailbox rename	An experimental record that specifies a mailbox is a proper rename of the other specified mailbox.
NULL	10		Null resource record.
WKS	11	Well-known service	Describes the services provided by a particular protocol on a particular interface.
PTR	12	Pointer	Maps an IP address to a hostname. It is used in reverse lookup zones to refer back to hostnames.
HINFO	13	Host information	Provides information about the specified hostname, including CPU Type and Operating System.
MINFO	14	Mailbox information	An experimental record that specifies a mailbox that is responsible for a mailing list or mailbox.
MX*	15	Mail exchanger	Indicates the mail server for a DNS domain name. This named host either processes or forwards mail for the DNS domain name.
TXT	16	Text	Associates general text information with an item in the DNS database. This is commonly used to indicate a host's location.
RP	17	Responsible person	Indicates the person responsible for the specified DNS domain or host.
AFSDB	18	AFS database	Provides the location of an Andrew File System (AFS) cell database server or a Distributed Computing Environment (DCE) cell's authenticated name server. AFS is a network file system similar to NFS, but it is meant to be deployed in a wide area network environment.

continues

TABLE 8.1. CONTINUED

Record Alias	Numeric	Record Type	Description
X.25	19	X.25	A variation of the address record that maps the hostname to an X.121 address used in an X.25 network. This resource record is used in conjunction with an RT record.
ISDN	20	Integrated Services Digital Network	A variation of the address record. Instead of mapping a hostname to an IP address, however, it is mapped to an ISDN address. This resource record is used in conjunction with the RT record.
RT	21	Route through (used with the X.25 and ISDN records)	Indicates an intermediate host that routes packets to a destination host. This is used in conjunction with ISDN or X.25 records.
AAAA	28	IPv6 address	Maps a hostname to an IPv6 address.

The mail destination (MD) and mail forwarder (MF) resource records are now extinct and have been replaced by the mail exchanger (MX) resource records.

Configuring a DNS Server

The following sections review the basics of configuring a DNS name server. This first section looks at the configuration of a DNS server from a UNIX perspective, focusing on the actual text configuration files for a BIND-compatible DNS server.

The second section reviews the configuration of a Windows NT 4.0 DNS server. The actual text files can be used from a UNIX BIND-compatible server and imported into Windows NT. If you are installing a new DNS server, however, the DNS interface in Windows NT provides a GUI format for inputting all relevant DNS zone information.

Configuring a BIND-Compatible DNS Server

The configuration of a Berkeley Internet Name Daemon (BIND) DNS server depends on the configuration of several text-based files and databases. They have to be either created from scratch or modified from a base template. The following files must be defined:

- The DNS boot file
- The DNS cache file

- The DNS forward lookup files
- The DNS reverse lookup files

The NAMED.BOOT File

A BIND-compatible DNS server uses the boot file NAMED.BOOT to indicate the following information:

- The directory in which the remaining DNS configuration files are located.
- The name of the named cache file that contains mappings to the Internet DNS root servers.
- The name of any primary domains for which the DNS server is authoritative and the database file that contains the resource records for that domain.
- The name of any secondary domains for which the DNS server is authoritative and the name of the local file that contains the resource records. There can be more than one secondary entry in the NAMED.BOOT file. These entries also indicate the IP address of the master DNS server for this zone file.
- The name of an alternative DNS name server that can be queried if this domain is not authoritative for the queried domain resource record.

This information is used by the named DNS daemon (or service) when it starts. The named daemon processes all DNS requests based on the configuration information in the configuration files.

The following is an example of the NAMED.BOOT file:

```
directory /etc/db

forwarders     172.16.2.1

cache          .                       named.cache

primary        0.0.127.in-addr.arpa    named.local
primary        2.16.172.in-addr.arpa   named.rev
primary        southpark.com           named.host

secondary      comedycentral.com              192.168.15.5
➥named.second.bak
```

The directory line indicates where the configuration files for the DNS server are located. In this example, the configuration files are located in the /etc/db subdirectory. This line should be the first line of the NAMED.BOOT file. If it is not, it is assumed that the configuration files are in the /etc directory.

The `forwarders` line indicates that, if the local name server cannot be used to resolve the request, the DNS request can be forwarded to the indicated DNS name server. In this example, that DNS name server is `172.16.2.1`. A common implementation of the forwarders entry is an internal DNS server. The `forwarders` entry is configured to point to the host functioning as a firewall with a DNS service.

The `cache` line indicates that the cache file is located in the default directory for the DNS configuration files. The name of the cache file is `named.cache`.

The `primary` lines itemize the domains for which this name server is authoritative. The `primary` line indicates the domain name and the configuration file that contains the resource records for the domain.

`in-addr.arpa` DOMAINS

The `in-addr.arpa` zones resolve reverse lookups. They contain pointer records that link a specific IP address to a hostname.

The `secondary` lines itemize the domains for which the DNS server will function as a secondary DNS server. The additional parameter in the `secondary` line is the IP address of the master DNS name server from which this server obtains its copies of the zone files.

BOOT CONFIGURATION FOR A WINDOWS NT DNS SERVER

Windows NT Server 4.0 also provides a DNS service. This DNS service, although RFC compatible, is not BIND compatible. The key missing component is a DNS boot file. Windows NT stores the configuration that commonly is located in the DNS boot file of the Windows NT Registry. If you want to implement DNS under Windows NT using a boot file, this can be accomplished by placing a copy of the NAMED.BOOT file in the `%system-root%\system32\dns` directory. More information specific to configuring DNS under Windows NT 4.0 can be found later in this chapter.

Cache File

The *DNS cache file* contains a list of the root domain name servers. This file can use any name as long as the name implemented matches the name referenced in the NAMED.BOOT file.

8

CONFIGURATION UPDATE

The DNS cache file's contents should be verified periodically. The root domain name servers change from time to time, and this file should be updated to include any new root servers that have been implemented. An updated version of the DNS cache file can be retrieved from the following location:

```
ftp://rs.internic.net/domain/named.cache
```

The contents of this file can be pasted into the existing DNS cache file, replacing its current contents.

The following is the latest version of the DNS cache file:

```
;
;         last update:    Aug 22, 1997
;         related version of root zone:    1997082200
;
;
; formerly NS.INTERNIC.NET
;
.                              3600000   IN   NS   A.ROOT-SERVERS.NET.
A.ROOT-SERVERS.NET.            3600000        A    198.41.0.4
;
; formerly NS1.ISI.EDU
;
.                              3600000        NS   B.ROOT-SERVERS.NET.
B.ROOT-SERVERS.NET.            3600000        A    128.9.0.107
;
; formerly C.PSI.NET
;
.                              3600000        NS   C.ROOT-SERVERS.NET.
C.ROOT-SERVERS.NET.            3600000        A    192.33.4.12
;
; formerly TERP.UMD.EDU
;
.                              3600000        NS   D.ROOT-SERVERS.NET.
D.ROOT-SERVERS.NET.            3600000        A    128.8.10.90
;
; formerly NS.NASA.GOV
;
.                              3600000        NS   E.ROOT-SERVERS.NET.
E.ROOT-SERVERS.NET.            3600000        A    192.203.230.10
;
; formerly NS.ISC.ORG
;
.                              3600000        NS   F.ROOT-SERVERS.NET.
```

```
      F.ROOT-SERVERS.NET.          3600000          A       192.5.5.241
      ;
      ; formerly NS.NIC.DDN.MIL
      ;
      .                            3600000          NS      G.ROOT-SERVERS.NET.
      G.ROOT-SERVERS.NET.          3600000          A       192.112.36.4
      ;
      ; formerly AOS.ARL.ARMY.MIL
      ;
      .                            3600000          NS      H.ROOT-SERVERS.NET.
      H.ROOT-SERVERS.NET.          3600000          A       128.63.2.53
      ;
      ; formerly NIC.NORDU.NET
      ;
      .                            3600000          NS      I.ROOT-SERVERS.NET.
      I.ROOT-SERVERS.NET.          3600000          A       192.36.148.17
      ;
      ; temporarily housed at NSI (InterNIC)
      ;
      .                            3600000          NS      J.ROOT-SERVERS.NET.
      J.ROOT-SERVERS.NET.          3600000          A       198.41.0.10
      ;
      ; housed in LINX, operated by RIPE NCC
      ;
      .                            3600000          NS      K.ROOT-SERVERS.NET.
      K.ROOT-SERVERS.NET.          3600000          A       193.0.14.129
      ;
      ; temporarily housed at ISI (IANA)
      ;
      .                            3600000          NS      L.ROOT-SERVERS.NET.
      L.ROOT-SERVERS.NET.          3600000          A       198.32.64.12
      ;
      ; housed in Japan, operated by WIDE
      ;
      .                            3600000          NS      M.ROOT-SERVERS.NET.
      M.ROOT-SERVERS.NET.          3600000          A       202.12.27.33
      ; End of File
```

DNS Forward-Lookup Files

Your DNS server hosts the zone configuration files for your domain. These configuration
files are called *forward-lookup zone files*. Each DNS server contains entries for these
forward-lookup configuration files in the NAMED.BOOT file. Remember, primary zones
have the actual configuration changes performed on the locally stored files. Secondary
zones receive a copy of the configured zone files from their master server, as indicated in
the secondary configuration lines of the NAMED.BOOT file.

The following is an example of a typical forward-lookup zone configuration file:

```
@                          IN    SOA   cartman.southpark.com.
➥hostmaster.southpark.com (
                                 1998030501    ; serial
                                 10800         ;refresh
                                 3600          ;retry
                                 604800        ;expire
                                 86400         ;TTL
                                 )

                          IN    NS    cartman.southpark.com.
                          IN    NS    stan.southpark.com.
cartman.southpark.com. IN    A     172.16.2.3
stan.southpark.com.    IN    A     172.16.2.4
kenny                     IN    A     172.16.2.5
kyle                      IN    A     172.16.2.6

www                       IN    CNAME cartman.southpark.com.
ftp                       IN    CNAME cartman.southpark.com.
proxy                     IN    CNAME kenny.southpark.com.
mail                      IN    CNAME stan.southpark.com.

southpark.com.         IN    MX    10    stan.southpark.com.
southpark.com.         IN    MX    20    kyle.southpark.com.
```

The following sections discuss the formatting of common resource records found in a forward-lookup configuration file.

Start of Authority (SOA) Resource Record   The key resource record in a forward-lookup configuration file is the Start of Authority (SOA) resource record. This resource record configures which host functions as the primary name server and how it treats the data configured for the domain.

The SOA resource record uses the following syntax:

```
@     IN    SOA   <Source host>  <contact email>      (
                  <Serial Number>
                  <Refresh Time>
                  <Retry Time>
                  <Expiration Time>
                  <Time to Live>

                  )
```

- @. This is used like a variable. It refers to the NAMED.BOOT file. In that file, it recorded that the named.host file contained the resource records for the southpark.com domain. If this file was saved as named.host, the @ character references the domain southpark.com.

- <Source Host>. This is the fully qualified domain name (FQDN) of the host that stores the master copy of the domain configuration file. Make sure you don't forget the period after the FQDN.

WARNING: DNS CONFIGURATION FILE SYNTAX

The period indicates that this is the absolute path to the host name. If you do not add a suffix period, DNS appends the domain name to the hostname. A missing period, for example, would cause cartman.southpark.com to be parsed to cartman.southpark.com.southpark.com. This is one of the most common DNS configuration file errors. Always double-check all your entries because it is easy to miss typing a period.

- <Contact Email>. This is the email address of the contact for this domain configuration file. Note that the @ character is replaced with a period in this resource record. This is because the @ symbol represents the domain name for the zone.

SOA RECORD CONFIGURATION

A problem can arise if the contact's email address contains a period. If the contact's email address is brian.komar@online-can.com, for example, the contact email name is formatted as brian\.komar.online-can.com. The backslash (\)indicates that the first period actually is part of the contact's mailbox name.

- <Serial Number>. The value in this field is used by a secondary name server to determine whether a zone transfer must take place to update the configuration files on the secondary name server. If the serial number on the master name server is higher than the serial number on the secondary name server, the secondary name server initiates a zone transfer.

8

SERIAL NUMBER CONFIGURATION TIP

You can use the date you make the configuration change as the serial number for the zone. The serial number in the sample file represents that this change was written March 5, 1998. The trailing 01 indicates that this was the first update performed on that date. This format ensures that the new serial number always is higher than any previous serial numbers.

- <Refresh Time>. This field configures how frequently a secondary name server checks to see whether its zone information is up to date. This value is stored in seconds. In the example, 10800 represents that the secondary server checks to see whether an update has taken place every three hours. If your DNS changes infrequently, a higher value can be configured.

- <Retry Time>. This field configures how the secondary server reacts if it fails to contact its master server at the refresh time interval. This usually is set to be a shorter value than the refresh time. In the example, the retry time is configured to 3600 seconds, or one hour.

- <Expire Time>. This field configures how long a secondary server can continue to provide DNS replies from out-of-date configuration files. In the example, the expire time is set to 604800 seconds, or 7 days. This means that, if a secondary server is unable to contact its master server for more than one week, it ceases to respond to DNS resolver requests for that domain.

- <Time to Live>. The Time to Live (TTL) field indicates how long another DNS name server can cache responses from this DNS server. This value can be set to a higher value if your resource record IP addresses do not change frequently. In the sample configuration file, the TTL was set to 86400 seconds, or 24 hours.

Name Server (NS) Resource Records *Name server (NS)* resource records indicate which DNS servers are authoritative for a domain. Make sure to include NS resource records for the primary name server and all secondary name servers.

The following is the syntax of an NS record:

```
<domain name>   IN    NS      <name server>
```

- <domain name>. The domain for which the indicated name server contains a zone configuration file and related resource records.

- <name server>. The FQDN for the name server that is authoritative for the indicated domain name.

In the sample forward-lookup configuration file, you might notice that the <domain name> field is missing. This is because of the NS resource records' location in the configuration file. If the first field is left blank in a resource record, it is assumed to have the same value as the previous resource record that *does* have a value in its first field. In the example, the SOA record has a value @ (the name of the domain) in its first field. Therefore, these NS resource records are both for the southpark.com domain.

NS RESOURCE RECORD CONFIGURATION

For an NS record, always refer to an address (A) record and not a canonical name (CNAME) record. An NS record must refer to a valid address record in the DNS resource records for a domain.

Address (A) Resource Record   The *address (A)*, or host, resource record resolves an IP address to a given host name. The following is the format of an address record:

```
<host name>    IN      A       <IP Address>
```

- <host name>. This field contains the logical name assigned to a host.
- <IP Address>. This field contains the IPv4 address assigned to the indicated host. If the address is an IPv6 address, an AAAA resource record is used.

In the sample configuration file, four address records have been configured. You might notice that cartman and stan are represented by FQDNs. Because kenny and kyle are represented by their hostnames, when they are resolved, the domain name southpark.com is appended to the hostnames.

ADDRESS RESOURCE RECORD

Make sure to include address resource records for all hosts that are commonly accessed on the network or that provide network services. Also make sure an address record exists for any hostnames referenced in Start of Authority (SOA), name server (NS), or mail exchanger (MX) resource records. These records *must* reference hosts with an existing address record.

Canonical Name (CNAME) Resource Records   *Canonical name (CNAME)* resource records provide the capability to create aliases for hosts. By using aliases, you can change which computer might host an Internet service (such as Web services) without having to modify an actual address (A) record. You are not restricted to naming your Web servers with the hostname WWW. The following is the syntax of a CNAME resource record:

```
<alias>      IN      CNAME      <hostname>
```

- `<alias>`. This field indicates the alias that also can be used to refer to the hostname.

- `<hostname>`. This field contains the actual hostname configured for the host using an address (A) record. Make sure to end the hostname with a period if you use an FQDN.

CNAME RESOURCE RECORD

It is not recommended to create a CNAME record that references another CNAME record. Although this actually works, it sometimes can become quite difficult to troubleshoot a DNS configuration error. You might have to refer to several CNAME records before you find the actual address record to which they all refer.

Mail Exchange (MX) Resource Records   A *mail exchange (MX)* resource record indicates where mail destined for the domain should be sent and processed. Multiple MX records can exist for a domain so load-balancing or fault tolerance can be provided for a domain's email services.

The following is the format of a mail exchanger resource record:

```
<domain name>   IN    MX       <cost>    <mail server>
```

- `<domain name>`. The domain name for which the mail exchanger processes mail.

- `<cost>`. This field enables a preference to be set for specific mail exchangers. The routing decision is based on a least-cost method. The lower the configured cost, the higher the preference for delivery. If you configure two MX records to have the same cost, load-balancing takes place between the two mail exchangers. Mail usually is routed to a higher-cost mail exchanger only if a lower-cost mail exchanger cannot be reached.

- `<mail server>`. This field represents the hostname of the mail exchanger that processes the mail. The hostname set in this field should be resolved by an address record rather than by a CNAME record. Some mailer software cannot resolve the MX record if it points to a CNAME record.

In the sample NAMED.HOST file, two MX records are configured: one for stan.southpark.com and one for kyle.southpark.com. Because the cost for stan is set to 10 and the cost for kyle is set to 20, mail most often is directed to stan.southpark.com for any mail addressed to name@southpark.com. If the stan host is down for any period of time, mail is directed to kyle.southpark.com.

Reverse Lookup Files

In some cases, a DNS resolver needs to resolve a given IP address to a hostname or an FQDN. A reverse-lookup file provides this functionality under DNS.

The zone files for the reverse-lookup zones are based on the network addresses for an IP network. The IP addresses are in reverse order in the reverse-lookup zone files. Table 8.2 shows the naming schemes required for Class A, Class B, and Class C networks.

TABLE 8.2. DNS RESOURCE RECORD DEFINITIONS.

IP Network Class	IP Address Format	Reverse Lookup Zone Name
Class A	w.x.y.z	w.in-addr.arpa
Class B	w.x.y.z	x.w.in-addr.arpa
Class C	w.x.y.z	y.x.w.in-addr.arpa

If the network address for your network is 10.0.0.0, for example, you name your reverse-lookup zone 10.in-addr.arpa. If your network address is 172.16.0.0, you name the reverse-lookup zone 16.172.in-addr.arpa. If your network address is 192.168.10.0, you name the reverse-lookup zone 10.168.192.in-addr.arpa.

REVERSE-LOOKUP CONFIGURATION ISSUE

It doesn't matter which subnet mask scheme you use for your network; the reverse-lookup zone should be based on the true class of the network address. You can use a less-specific reverse-lookup zone name, such as 168.192.in-addr.arpa for a 192.168.x.0 network addresses. You cannot, however, use a more-specific reverse-lookup zone for a Class B or Class A address.

The configuration file can have any name. One common naming routine is to name the file named.rev for the domain for which the DNS is authoritative. Another common naming scheme names the DNS configuration file db.y.x.w.in-addr.arpa for a Class C address. Windows NT uses the format y.w.x.in-addr.arpa.dns for its reverse-lookup files.

8

In the configuration of DNS reverse-lookup zone files, it is common to configure at least two reverse-lookup zones. This includes reverse-lookup zone files for the following:

- The local network address of 127.0.0.0
- The actual network address in use for the domain

Configuring the Local Network Reverse-Lookup Zone File The following is an example of a typical local network address reverse-lookup configuration file:

```
0.0.127.in-addr.arpa.        IN        SOA       cartman.southpark.com.
hostmaster.southpark.com (

                             1998030501          ; serial
                             10800               ;refresh
                             3600                ;retry
                             604800              ;expire
                             86400               ;TTL
                             )

                             IN        NS        cartman.southpark.com.

1                            IN        PTR       localhost.
```

An SOA record must exist within a reverse-lookup zone configuration file, just as in the forward-lookup zone file. The syntax of the SOA record is the same as in the forward-lookup zone file.

The NS server record also uses the same format as in the forward-lookup zone. The lack of hostname in the NS record indicates that the hostname should be the same as the previous resource record's hostname. In other words, this refers to 0.0.127.in-addr.arpa.

The *pointer (PTR)* resource record configures the IP address that is a pointer to a specific FQDN. Make sure you use periods correctly. If you want to append the address to the zone filename, enter the required address as previously shown with the entry for 1. This translates to the FQDN 1.0.0.127. in-addr.arpa.

Configuring the Reverse Lookup Zone File for Your Network Address The following is an example of the reverse-lookup zone for the southpark.com domain.

```
16.172.in-addr.arpa.         IN        SOA       cartman.southpark.com.
↪hostmaster.southpark.com (

                             1998030501          ; serial
                             10800               ;refresh
                             3600                ;retry
                             604800              ;expire
                             86400               ;TTL
                             )

                             IN        NS        cartman.southpark.com.
```

```
3.2          IN    PTR    cartman.southpark.com.
4.2          IN    PTR    stan.southpark.com.
5.2          IN    PTR    kenny.southpark.com.
6.2          IN    PTR    kyle.southpark.com.
```

As with the local network reverse-lookup zone, the reverse-lookup zone for your network address requires the following:

- A Start of Authority (SOA) record

- A name server (NS) record

- Pointer (PTR) records for any hosts named in address records in the forward-lookup zone configuration file

---

POINTER RECORD CONFIGURATION

Pointer records should only be configured to point to address (A) records, not to CNAME records. This results in a quicker reverse-resolution process.

Although reverse-lookup zones are not required for your DNS implementation, it is recommended that you implement this feature within DNS. This enables users to identify which machine they are logging in from using the logical name rather than just the IP address. If you plan to run the NSLOOKUP utility for troubleshooting a DNS server, the reverse-lookup zone for your domain must be configured correctly.

Configuring a Windows NT DNS Server

Windows NT Server includes a DNS service that can be optionally installed and implemented. The following section outlines the configuration of the southpark.com domain, including forward- and reverse-lookup zones.

Configuring the Server

Windows NT implements its version of a DNS server as a Windows NT service. The service is added to Windows NT from the Network Control Panel applet's Services tab (see Figure 8.4).

WINDOWS NT SERVICE PATCH WARNING

When adding the DNS service to a Windows NT server with service packs installed, you must reapply the service packs after the DNS service is installed. The DNS service has been heavily patched through the lifetime of Windows NT Server 4.0, and it needs to be repatched before you start configuring the DNS server.

FIGURE 8.4.

Adding the DNS service in Windows NT 4.0.

After the DNS service is installed, you can configure it using the DNS Manager utility (dnsadmin.exe) found under Administrative Tools (Common) in the Start menu.

Configuring DNS Forwarders

The DNS server service is not BIND compatible under Windows NT. Instead of using a boot file, the configuration of the DNS server as a whole is stored in the Windows NT Registry. If you prefer, you can configure the DNS service to use a boot file. This is not a requirement of the RFC, simply of a BIND implementation.

You can configure DNS forwarders in the property sheet of the DNS server. As previously mentioned, forwarders refer DNS requests when the DNS server is not authoritative for a requested DNS resource record. Forwarders can be configured by right-clicking your DNS server and selecting Properties. The dialog box in Figure 8.5 opens. Any DNS forwarders can be added to this dialog box.

FIGURE 8.5.

Configuring a DNS forwarder.

Configuring Reverse-Lookup Zones

The next step in configuring your Windows NT DNS server is to configure your reverse-lookup zone. As previously discussed, the reverse-lookup zone is named-based on the reverse order of the IP address for the network. The southpark.com domain assigns addresses in the 172.16.0.0 network.

To create a new reverse-lookup zone, first select the DNS server in the left window of the DNS Manager. Right-click the DNS server and select New Zone to add a new primary zone. In the first screen of the zone creation process, select Primary Zone and click Next. You will now see the screen in Figure 8.6.

FIGURE 8.6.

Creating the reverse-lookup zone file.

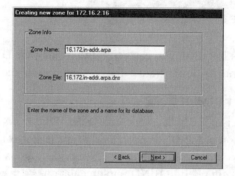

When you move the cursor into the Zone File field, Windows NT automatically suggests that the zone configuration file be named zone.dns. After the reverse-lookup zone has been configured, Windows NT automatically creates name server (NS) and start of authority (SOA) records (see Figure 8.7).

FIGURE 8.7.

SOA and NS records automatically are created by Windows NT.

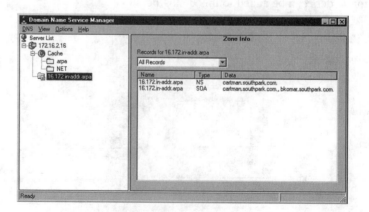

Not only are these records created automatically, the DNS Manager automatically increments the Serial Number field of the SOA record. This ensures that, when a secondary domain server exists, it always requests a zone transfer when it contacts the master name server. The SOA record also is configured with the following default values:

- The refresh interval is set to 60 minutes.
- The retry interval is set to 10 minutes.
- The expire time is set to 24 hours.
- The minimum default TTL is set to 60 minutes.

After the zone has been created, these values can be changed by changing the properties of the SOA record.

From now on, you should not have to manually configure any more records for the reverse-lookup zone. Windows NT allows automatic creation of PTR records in the zone when creating address (A) records. This reduces the chance that you will forget to create a pointer (PTR) record.

Creating a Forward-Lookup Zone File

Now you can create the actual domain zone file. Follow the same steps previously outlined for creating the reverse-lookup zone file. In this case, name the zone south-park.com. Windows NT automatically names the data file southpark.com.dns when you press Tab to move the cursor into the Zone File field.

The creation of the zone automatically creates name server (NS), start of authority (SOA), and address (A) records for the newly created zone. The address (A) record is created only if the Windows NT computer's DNS Properties tab is set to the same domain name as the one being created. In this case, it must be set to southpark.com.

Figure 8.8 shows the configuration screen for the SOA resource record. To modify this property sheet, double-click the SOA record in the DNS Manager.

FIGURE 8.8.

Configuring the SOA record for the domain.

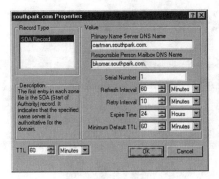

As you can see, this dialog box makes configuring the SOA record easier. The Refresh Interval, Retry Interval, Expire Time, and Minimum Default TTL can be changed by adjusting the values for each property.

New address records can be added by right-clicking the right pane of the DNS Manager and selecting New Host... (see Figure 8.9).

FIGURE 8.9.

Configuring an address (A) resource record.

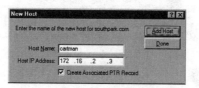

When configuring the address resource record, make sure to enter the correct IP address for the host. Also make sure you enable the Create Associated PTR Record option. This automatically creates a PTR resource record in the reverse-lookup zone created earlier.

WINDOWS NT IS TOO AUTOMATIC

When you first create a primary zone, DNS Manager automatically creates an address resource record for the DNS server. Unfortunately, it does not create an associated PTR record in the reverse-lookup zone. Always make sure this reverse-lookup record is created. If it isn't created, troubleshooting tools such as NSLOOKUP fail when they try to resolve the IP address of the DNS server to its hostname.

Figure 8.10 shows the configuration dialog box for configuring a canonical name (CNAME) resource record.

FIGURE 8.10.

Creating a CNAME resource record.

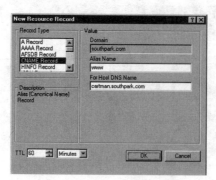

8

Right-click the domain name folder in the left pane and select New Record from the pop-up menu to create all other resource records. Make sure to reference the address record for the host to which the alias refers. It is inefficient to refer to another CNAME resource record.

Figure 8.11 shows the configuration dialog box for a mail exchanger (MX) resource record.

FIGURE 8.11.

Creating an MX resource record.

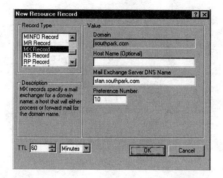

When configuring the MX resource record, make sure to indicate the address record for the computer that functions as the mail exchange for the domain. Remember that the preference value assigns a cost for using this mail exchanger. If multiple MX resource records exist, the MX server with the lowest preference value is accessed first.

After the zone's configuration has been completed, a text file is created to store the DNS zone information. The following configuration file is the DNS zone file created once all A, CNAME, NS, SOA, and MX records are created.

```
;
;  Database file southpark.com.dns for southpark.com zone.
;      Zone version:  21
;

@                       IN    SOA    cartman.southpark.com.
➥bkomar.southpark.com.    (
                        2           ; serial number
                        3600        ; refresh
                        600         ; retry
                        86400       ; expire
                        3600        ) ; minimum TTL


;
;  Zone NS records
;
```

```
@                               IN   NS    sideshowbri.online-can.com.

;
;  WINS lookup record
;

@                          0    IN    WINS    172.16.2.2

;
;  Zone records
;

@                          IN   MX    10     stan
@                          IN   MX    20     kyle
cartman                    IN   A     172.16.2.3
ftp                        IN   CNAME cartman
kenny                      IN   A     172.16.2.5
kyle                       IN   A     172.16.2.6
mail                       IN   CNAME stan
proxy                      IN   CNAME kenny
stan                       IN   A     172.16.2.4
www                        IN   CNAME cartman
```

Integrating WINS with DNS

In the zone file created, you might have noticed an additional resource record called WINS. The Windows Internet Name Service was described yesterday during the discussion about NetBIOS name resolution. The WINS server provides NetBIOS name resolution and registration on a Windows NT network.

Because all DHCP hosts can be configured to register their IP address dynamically with a WINS server, a WINS lookup (WINS) resource record can be configured. This resource record enables the Windows NT DNS server to query the configured WINS server for a hostname that does not exist in the zone file for the domain. The WINS server can provide the registered IP address, and the DNS server appends the zone's domain name when it returns the DNS response to the DNS resolver.

A WINS lookup record is configured in the property page for a DNS zone. To open this property page, right-click the DNS zone name in the left pane of the DNS Manager and select Properties (see Figure 8.12).

If an address record cannot be found for a queried hostname, the DNS server forwards requests to the configured WINS server.

A WINS reverse-lookup (WINS-R) resource record also can be configured in a reverse-lookup zone file. To configure this resource record, right-click the reverse-lookup zone and select Properties (see Figure 8.13).

FIGURE 8.12.

Configuring a WINS lookup resource record.

FIGURE 8.13.

Configuring a WINS-R resource record.

The WINS-R resource record enables the configuration of the actual WINS server used to resolve the queried IP address. It also configures which domain name is appended to the NetBIOS name that is returned to form the fully qualified domain name.

USING OF WINS IN DNS

Using a WINS server with a Windows NT 4.0 DNS server enables the functionality of dynamic DNS to be provided in the Windows NT operating system. Because the hosts might change IP addresses under DHCP and WINS, the TTL for WINS-resolved addresses is only 10 minutes by default rather than the default of 60 minutes for domain resource records.

Troubleshooting DNS with NSLOOKUP

The NSLOOKUP command can be used to troubleshoot hostname resolution problems. It also is quite useful when determining whether your DNS server has been configured correctly.

The NSLOOKUP command can be run in either interactive or batch mode. Batch mode enables quick name resolution to take place. The following is the syntax for interactive mode:

```
NSLOOKUP <hostname>    or NSLOOKUP <IP Address>
```

This returns the IP address for the queried hostname or the hostname for the queried IP address.

Interactive mode enables further inspection of the name space. Some common commands are shown in Table 8.3.

TABLE 8.3. NSLOOKUP INTERACTIVE COMMANDS.

Batch Command	Description
<hostname>	Print info about the host/domain NAME using default server.
<hostname> <DNS server>	Same as above, but use the indicated <DNS Server> as the name server.
<help> or <?>	Print info about common commands.
set all	Show all options currently in use.
set [no]recurse	Turn recursive queries on or off.
set querytype=X	Set query type, such as A, ANY, CNAME, MX, NS, PTR, or SOA.
set type=X	Synonym for querytype.
set class=X	Set query class to IN, CHAOS, HESIOD, or ANY.
set server <DNS Server>	Set default server to <DNS Server> using current default server.
ls [opt] DOMAIN	List addresses in DOMAIN: -a List canonical names and aliases -d List all records -t TYPE List records of the given type (such as A, CNAME, MX, NS, PTR, and so on)
Exit	Exit batch NSLOOKUP mode.

If you want to determine the SOA record for the southpark.com domain, for example, you can enter the following information in batch mode:

```
C:\>nslookup
Default Server:  sideshowbri.southpark.com
Address:  172.16.2.16

> set type=soa
> southpark.com
Server:  sideshowbri.southpark.com
Address:  172.16.2.16

southpark.com
        primary name server = cartman.southpark.com
        responsible mail addr = bkomar.southpark.com
        serial  = 3
        refresh = 3600 (1 hour)
        retry   = 600 (10 mins)
        expire  = 86400 (1 day)
        default TTL = 3600 (1 hour)
```

Applying What You Have Learned

Today's material reviewed the configuration of DNS servers in both BIND and non-BIND environments. Remember that the key is to configure DNS so hostname resolution is performed efficiently on your network. In the review questions, you will configure a DNS server using text files to make sure you understand the configuration of a DNS server.

Test Your Knowledge

The network diagram in Figure 8.14 is used to create a DNS server's configuration files. Use this network diagram for questions 1 through 3.

1. Create the NAMED.BOOT file for the Homer computer.

2. Create the zone file for simpsons.com that would be stored on HOMER.

3. Configure the reverse-lookup zone for this network that would be stored on HOMER.

4. How do you acquire an updated version of named.cache?

5. What NSLOOKUP command can be used to determine the mail exchange for the domain online-usa.com?

6. What NSLOOKUP command can be returned to determine all the name servers for the online-can domain?

FIGURE 8.14.

A sample network.

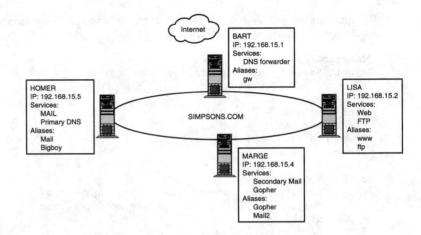

Preview of the Next Day

Tomorrow's material examines the specifics of routing in a TCP/IP internetwork. You will learn how to configure routing using both static routing tables and routing protocols to build your routing tables dynamically.

The material also covers the specific routing protocols in use today. It compares and contrasts the various routing protocols with one another.

Day 9

Gateway and Routing Protocols

Today's material examines various routing protocols that can be implemented in a network. The discussion starts with the basics of routing, including the following:

- Routing metrics
- Static routing
- Dynamic routing
- Common routing problems
- Methods for overcoming routing problems

After the basics are discussed, more detailed information is provided about the following:

- Static routing concepts
- Exterior gateway protocols (including EGP and BGP)
- Interior gateway protocols (including RIP and OSPF)

Finally, the last section reviews some troubleshooting techniques using the `traceroute` command.

Routing Basics

Routing is the process of moving a packet of information from one physical network segment to another. Ultimately, the packet is delivered to a destination host.

People often compare the term *bridging* with routing. Bridging occurs at the data link layer of the OSI model; routing takes place at network layer three of the OSI model (see Figure 9.1).

FIGURE 9.1.

Comparing bridging with routing.

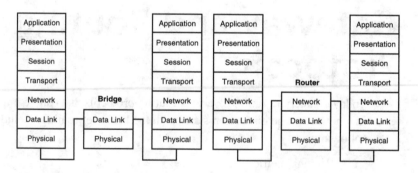

> **THE DIFFERENCES BETWEEN BRIDGES AND ROUTERS**
>
> A *bridge* examines the hardware destination address of a frame and, based on the tables it keeps of hardware addresses, either forwards or discards the frame. A new frame is generated to replace the original frame. Bridges only are used to connect locally managed networks.
>
> A *router* is more intelligent than a bridge. It can make additional decisions such as selecting the best route for a datagram to reach its destination. This enables routes to change and delivery still takes place to a destination host. Routers can connect both local and remotely managed networks.

Routers use various *metrics* to determine the best route for sending packets to a destination network. A metric is either a cost or a value assigned to a property of a network link. The following are some common metrics used by routing protocols:

- *Hop count.* This is the most common routing metric. The hop count measures how many routers are crossed by a packet as it moves from the source network to the destination network.

- *Delay.* This metric measures the amount of time it takes to move a packet from the source to the destination network. Factors that can affect the delay include: bandwidth of intermediate networks, size of queues waiting to be routed at each router, network congestion on intermediate networks, and total distance between two networks.

- *Throughput.* This metric measures the available traffic capacity of a network link. A 10Mbps ethernet link is preferred over a 56K frame-relay link.

- *Reliability.* This metric compares the reliability of network links. Some links are down more frequently than others, so the more reliable links are preferred. Other reliability ratings include determining how long it takes to get a failed link repaired and operational.

- *Communication costs.* Sometimes, delivering information to a destination network in the shortest amount of time is *not* the primary goal of the network designer. Reducing network transport costs often is the goal instead. It is less expensive to send data over privately owned lines than over public-switched networks.

Different routing protocols use different routing metrics. Some routing protocols enable you to use different combinations of the preceding routing metrics and enable the network administrator to apply different weights to each metric when calculating the optimal route to a remote network.

Types of Routing Configuration

There are two primary ways to configure routing in a network. The first, *static routing*, involves manually configuring all preferred routing paths through the internetwork.

Static routing works best in smaller networks that do not change much in topology. If a change occurs in the network, manual reconfiguration must take place. If the manual reconfiguration changes are not performed, routing does not take place correctly. If static routing is implemented and a router goes down, the network must be manually configured to bypass the failed network segment.

The other way to configure routing in a network, *dynamic routing*, makes use of routing protocols to build routing tables that describe the network automatically. If a change in topology occurs, the dynamic routing protocol advertises the network changes to all routers. The routers then re-evaluate the best path to each network segment.

The two most common types of routing protocols in use today are distance vector protocols and link state protocols.

Distance vector protocols are broadcast-based protocols that commonly use hop count as their primary routing metric. Distance vector protocols are widely implemented because they are easy to configure. When you add a new router running the distance vector protocol, it advertises and builds its own routing table.

Distance vector protocols do have some disadvantages. They do not scale well to larger networks because each routing packet contains paths to the entire network. This can lead to a large amount of network traffic dedicated to routing. The routing information is sent only to the router's neighbors. *Neighbors* are routers connected to the same physical segment as the sending router.

Distance vector protocols also are characteristically slow to converge. *Convergence time* is the amount of time it takes the network to adjust to a topology change and to recalculate all routing tables for the network.

Link state protocols flood routing information to all nodes in the network. This routing information only contains routes to directly attached networks. Even though these routing messages are sent to all routers on the network, their reduced size results in a more efficient exchange of routing information. Link state protocols also use multicasts or unicasts, which reduces the overall amount of network traffic.

Each router stores the best route to a network ID. This results in a shorter convergence time when a router or network segment goes down. The shorter convergence time is a key reason link state protocols are used in larger network implementations. The only disadvantage of link state protocols is that they require more planning, configuration, and CPU power for the routing configuration.

Common Routing Problems

Common routing problems that occur in routed networks include routing loops and counting-to-infinity problems.

Routing loops usually occur when static routing is implemented incorrectly. Figure 9.2 shows a common routing loop.

FIGURE 9.2.

A routing loop.

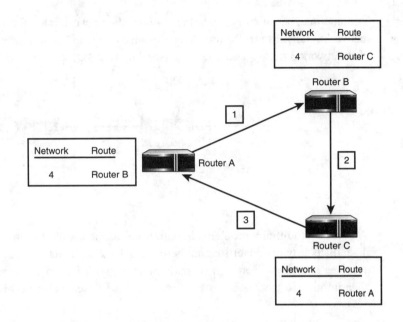

9

In the figure, Router A believes that any packets destined for network 4 must be routed to Router B. Router B is configured so that any packets destined for router 4 must be routed to Router C. Router C is configured so that packets destined for network 4 must be routed to Router A. You are now back to where you started from, and you will never get to network 4.

IP has some protection from routing loops in the Time-to-Live field. Every time the packet crosses a router, the TTL decreases by at least one. When the TTL reaches zero, the packet is discarded. This prevents a packet from continuing to circulate the network when there is no hope of it ever reaching its final destination.

A *counting-to-infinity* problem is more common in dynamic routing. Figure 9.3 shows a network about to suffer this type of problem.

FIGURE 9.3.

The network before a counting-to-infinity problem exists.

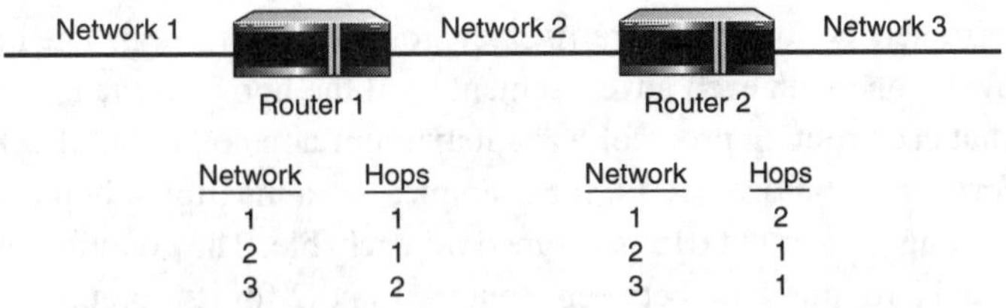

Network 1	Router 1	Network 2	Router 2	Network 3

Network	Hops		Network	Hops
1	1		1	2
2	1		2	1
3	2		3	1

Assume that, because of an interface failure, the network interface attaching Router 2 to network 3 fails. Router 2 immediately changes the hop count to infinity (∞) to indicate that network 3 no longer is available (see Figure 9.4).

FIGURE 9.4.

The router interface to network 3 fails.

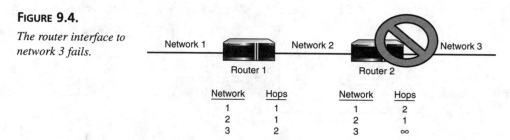

A counting to infinity problem also can occur as the result of a timing problem. If Router 1 sends its network advertisement before Router 2 sends its advertisement, Router 2 receives a routing advertisement stating that network 3 is only 2 hops away. This is better than infinity, so the 2 is incremented to 3 and is entered as the new hop count (see Figure 9.5).

FIGURE 9.5.

Router 2 receives incorrect routing information from Router 1.

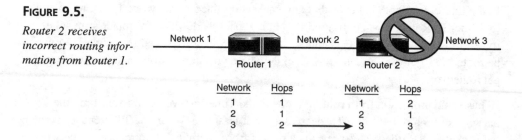

Router 2 now advertises its new routes. Router 1 receives a route update stating that network 3 is now 3 hops away. Router 1 must update its routing table because it originally learned about the route to network 3 from Router 2. The hop count is incremented by one and is recorded as 4 hops (see Figure 9.6).

The routers continue to advertise new routes to network 3. The hop count continues to grow by one with each advertisement until the hop count reaches infinity. The good news is that each routing protocol has a maximum hop count that it calls infinity. The Routing Information Protocol (RIP), for example, has a maximum hop count of 15 hops. Anything greater than 15 is deemed unreachable. The counting to infinity problem has created a routing loop between Routers 1 and 2 for its duration.

FIGURE 9.6.

Router 1 continues to update the incorrect information.

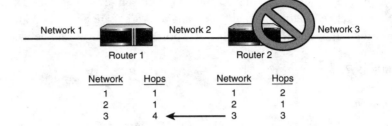

Common Techniques to Overcome Routing Problems

Some common techniques are used to prevent routing loops and counting to infinity problems. These techniques include the following:

- Implementing hold-downs
- Implementing split horizons
- Implementing poison reverse

Hold-downs prevent regular update messages from erroneously updating a route that should be removed. Routers that are directly attached to the network detect when a route goes down. They send routing update messages to inform their neighbors of the new hop counts. In the counting to infinity example, a neighboring router sent an update message indicating that network 3 was still reachable. A hold-down would have told Router 2 to maintain its configured change (that network 3 is unreachable) for a specified period of time (called the *hold-down time*). This would prevent Router 2 from updating its routing table with the incorrect information from Router 1. The hold-down time should be a longer period of time than the update interval used to announce the routing table.

Split horizons are based on the principle that it is not wise to send routing information back in the direction from which it came. If you go back to the network example in Figure 9.4, split horizons would have prevented the counting to infinity problem. The counting to infinity problem was caused by Router 1 advertising that it could reach network 3 in 2 hops. Router 1 should never pass this information to Router 2 because it learned about the route to network 3 *from* Router 2. This would prevent the two-node routing loops associated with counting to infinity problems.

Poison reverse helps to speed up convergence in a network. When a router learns about a network from a particular interface, it sends RIP advertisements to that same interface advertising that the network is unreachable. This prevents a counting to infinity problem because the hop count immediately is set to an unreachable state. If the network is reachable, that hop count is maintained by receiving routers.

Figure 9.7 shows the implementation of poison reverse. Router 2 sends a routing update packet (A) stating that network 2 and network 3 are both 1 hop away. Router 1 sends a routing update (B) stating that network 2 is 1 hop away and network 1 is 2 hops away.

FIGURE 9.7.

Poison reverse implementation.

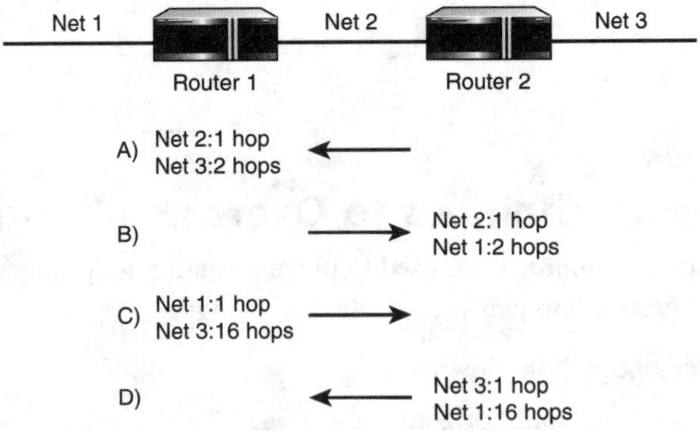

After Router 1 receives the network update from Router 2, it sends a poison reverse update back to Router 2. The update message sets the hop count to network 3 to 16 hops (or unreachable). Because this value is not lower than the current hop count of 2, the routing table is not updated. If Router 2 did not have a local interface to network 3, the counting-to-infinity problem would be prevented because the next update was set to an infinity value immediately.

Router 2 also sends an update message that sets the hop count to network 1 to 16 hops.

Static Routing

In *static routing*, all routes are set by a network administrator. This most often is used in smaller networks because any topological changes to the network result in the need to modify the static routing tables.

Static routing requires that routes be set to each network address for each router on the network. If a route is not created for a network segment, packets cannot be sent to that network segment.

A *default route* can be set as a catch-all route. Instead of explicitly naming each and every route to all segments of the network, several routes can be grouped together by a default route entry in the routing table.

Figure 9.8 shows a small network requiring that static routes be configured for each router. These routing tables determine how a packet is transferred from a source network to a destination network.

FIGURE 9.8.

Configuring static routing.

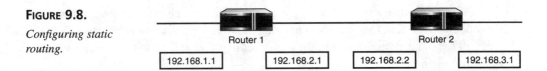

Router 1 has interfaces on both the 192.168.1.0 and 192.168.2.0 networks. The router automatically configures routes for these two networks through the local interfaces when the router is started (see Table 9.1).

TABLE 9.1. DEFAULT ROUTES AUTOCONFIGURED FOR ROUTER 1.

Net Address	Netmask	Gateway Address	Interface	Metric
192.168.1.0	255.255.255.0	192.168.1.1	192.168.1.1	1
192.168.2.0	255.255.255.0	192.168.2.1	192.168.2.1	1

These routes indicate that the 192.168.1.0/24 network is reachable through interface 192.168.1.1. The 192.168.2.0/24 network is reachable through the interface 192.168.2.1.

A static route entry must be added for information to travel from Router 1 to the 192.168.3.0 network. The entry is shown in Table 9.2.

TABLE 9.2. ADDITIONAL STATIC ROUTE REQUIRED FOR ROUTER 1.

Net Address	Netmask	Gateway Address	Interface	Metric
192.168.3.0	255.255.255.0	192.168.2.2	192.168.2.1	2

This indicates that the 192.168.3.0/24 network is reachable through the gateway at 192.168.2.2. Information destined for this network should be sent from the local interface with IP address 192.168.2.2.

Another method that could be used is to add a default gateway entry. Adding the entry in Table 9.3 accomplishes this.

TABLE 9.3. A DEFAULT GATEWAY STATIC ROUTE ENTRY.

Net Address	Netmask	Gateway Address	Interface	Metric
0.0.0.0	0.0.0.0	192.168.2.2	192.168.2.1	1

This route indicates that, if a network address is not explicitly entered in the routing table, all packets destined for the network must be sent to the router interface at 192.168.2.2 through the local interface 192.168.2.1.

The major disadvantage of static routes is that they must be changed manually every time the topology changes. This includes changing the routes when a router interface fails. As you will see in upcoming sections, the use of routing protocols enables dynamic updates to the routing table.

ROUTING TABLE CONFIGURATION

All static routing entries are made using the `route` command. The following is the syntax of the `route` command:

```
ROUTE [-f] [-p] [command [destination] [MASK netmask] [gateway]
➥[METRIC metric]]
```

- `-f`. Flushes the routing tables of all gateway entries. If this is used in conjunction with one of the commands, the tables are cleared prior to running the command.
- `-p`. When used with the ADD command, this option creates a persistent root that is re-created every time the router is restarted.
- `command`. Specifies one of four functions performed by the `route` command: Print, Add, Delete, or Change. Print shows the routing table on-screen, Add adds an additional route to the routing table, Delete removes a route from the routing table, and Change modifies an existing route in the routing table.
- `destination`. Specifies the destination IP address. This usually is a network address.
- `MASK netmask`. This indicates the subnet mask to be used with the destination address.
- `gateway`. This indicates the IP address to which packets destined for the indicated destination IP address/subnet mask should be sent.
- `metric`. This specifies the metric/cost for the destination network address.

Routing Protocols

Autonomous systems play a key part in defining whether a gateway protocol is an exterior gateway protocol (EGP) or an interior gateway protocol (IGP).

An autonomous system is a network managed by a single network management group. The phrase *autonomous system* usually represents your internal network. To identify the routers participating in your autonomous system, an *autonomous system number* can be acquired from InterNIC. Within an autonomous system, *interior gateway protocols* determine optimal routes between the locally managed networks.

Exterior gateway protocols transfer routing information between autonomous systems. If two companies want to establish an exchange of data between their networks, they use exterior gateway protocols to exchange routing information between the two autonomous systems.

The following sections discuss various implementations of exterior gateway protocols and interior gateway protocols.

Exterior Gateway Protocols

Exterior gateway protocols exchange of routing information between autonomous systems. When you need to exchange information with another organization's network, you can exchange entry-point information for each other's networks. This is much more efficient than exchanging entire routing tables.

The two most common exterior gateway protocols are Exterior Gateway Protocol and Border Gateway Protocol.

GATEWAY-TO-GATEWAY PROTOCOL

In the early days of ARPAnet, the Gateway-to-Gateway Protocol (GGP) exchanged routing information between the core routers of ARPAnet using a distance vector methodology. More information about GGP can be found in RFC 823.

Exterior Gateway Protocol (EGP)

`RFC 1884` The *Exterior Gateway Protocol (EGP)* was developed as an interdomain reachability protocol in April 1984. EGP served as the first exterior gateway protocol to enable autonomous systems to exchange routing reachability information on the Internet. Some problems with this protocol, however, have lead to its replacement by the *Border Gateway Protocol (BGP)* in most implementations.

Using EGP, information was passed from autonomous systems to the ARPAnet core routers by an EGP source router. This information was then exchanged throughout the core router network and was passed down to destination networks that belong to other autonomous systems (see Figure 9.9).

AS
AS
AS
EGP
EGP
EGP
Core Router
Core Router
Core Router
EGP
EGP
EGP
EGP
AS
AS
AS
AS

FIGURE 9.9.
EGP usage on the ARPAnet backbone.

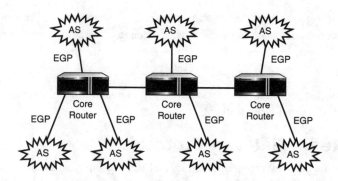

EGP is a dynamic routing protocol, but it does not calculate any routing metrics. As a result, it is unable to make intelligent routing decisions. The only time routing information from update messages can be used by EGP is when the routes being compared are from the same autonomous system. If the routes are from different autonomous systems, the results cannot be measured against each other. EGP only can inform another router of reachability to a remote network.

The following are the three primary functions of EGP:

- *Establishing neighbors.* Routers running EGP must define the routers with which it wants to share its reachability information.
- *Polling neighbors.* Neighboring routers are polled to make sure they are still up.
- *Sending update messages.* EGP routers send update messages that contain information about the reachability of networks within their autonomous system.

The packet format for an EGP message is shown in Figure 9.10.

EGP Version
Type
Code
Status
Checksum
Autonomous System Number
Sequence Number
Variable Length Data

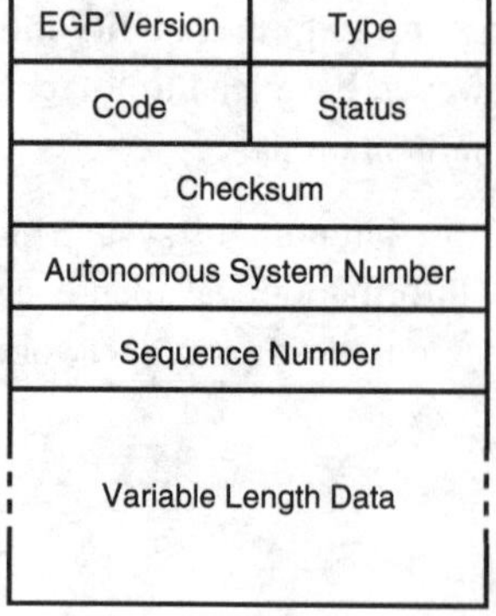

FIGURE 9.10.
EGP message format.

- *EGP Version.* This field identifies the EGP version that sent the EGP message. The EGP versions must be compatible between sending and receiving EGP routers.
- *Type.* This field indicates one of five EGP message types. The message types are shown in Table 9.4.

TABLE 9.4. EGP MESSAGE TYPES.

Message Type	Description
Neighbor acquisition	Establishes and de-establishes neighbors. This message includes the hello interval that establishes how frequently neighbor reachability messages should be sent and the poll interval that specifies how frequently routing update messages should be exchanged.
Neighbor reachability	Determines whether neighbors are alive. EGP uses an algorithm specifying that an EGP neighbor should be declared down only after a specified number of neighbor reachability messages have not been received.
Poll	Determines the reachability of the specified network. Using a poll message, an EGP router can determine the relative location of a host on a remote network. A poll message also provides reachability information about the remote network on which the host resides.
Routing update	Provides updated routing information. The routing update message contains additional fields in the Data section such as the number of interior gateways, the number of exterior gateways, and the IP source network address included in the message. A series of gateway blocks provides the IP address for a gateway and the networks reachable through that gateway. The gateway blocks also include a Distance field. This distance only can be used to compare paths within an autonomous system because the paths are only relative to that autonomous system.
Error	Indicates that an error condition exists, such as a bad EGP header format or an excessive polling rate.

- *Code.* This field distinguishes between message subtypes.
- *Status.* This field contains message-dependent status information. Possible entries include Insufficient Resources or Parameter Problem.
- *Checksum.* This field identifies corruption of the EGP message in transit.
- *Autonomous System Number.* This field identifies the autonomous system to which the sending router belongs.

- *Sequence Number.* This field enables a sending and receiving router to match a request to a reply. This sequence number is initialized with a zero value and is incremented by one for each request or response.

Border Gateway Protocol (BGP)

RFC 1884   The primary function of the BGP protocol also is to exchange network reachability information with other autonomous systems. BGP improves upon the functionality of EGP by including the full path of autonomous systems that traffic must transit to reach the destination network. Including the full path to each network provides enough information to construct a network layout graph that enables routing loops to be identified and removed from the routing tables.

BGP also includes some advertising rules that help prevent routing table corruption. An autonomous system can only advertise the routes it uses itself. If the autonomous system does not use a route, it cannot advertise that route because it is unsure whether that route is operational.

BGP uses the TCP protocol to transport routing messages between BGP routers. BGP uses port 179 to establish its connections. When two BGP systems communicate, they initially exchange the entire BGP routing table. After this occurs, only incremental updates are exchanged between the two BGP systems. BGP does not require a periodic refresh of the entire routing table.

To save time when a router goes down, each BGP router stores the most recent versions of its neighbors' routing tables. When the BGP router sends advertisements, it only sends the current optimal path in the routing messages. If a link goes down, it scans the neighbors' routing tables to determine a new optimal path.

In a BGP system, the routing metric assigns a degree of preference for a particular path to an autonomous system. These metrics are manually entered into router configuration files by network administrators. The degree of preference can be based on the number of autonomous systems that must be crossed, the type of link, the reliability of the link, or other preferences.

The BGP message header is shown in Figure 9.11.

FIGURE 9.11.

BGP message format.

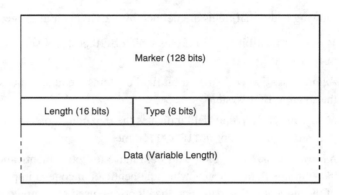

- *Marker.* This 128-bit field contains a value the recipient BGP system can predict. The computed value is based on the authentication mechanism. The Marker field also can identify when two BGP systems no longer are synchronized.

- *Length.* This 16-bit field indicates the total length of the BGP message in octets (including the header). This enables a stream of BGP messages to be sent one after the other. It also identifies where one message ends and the next one begins.

- *Type.* This 8-bit field indicates the type of BGP code transmitted by the BGP message and the format of the remaining fields in the BGP Data section. Possible types include OPEN, UPDATE, NOTIFICATION, and KEEPALIVE.

BGP Open Messages   After a TCP three-way handshake takes place between two BGP systems, the first message sent by each BGP system is an *open message*. If the open message is accepted by the receiving BGP system, a KEEPALIVE message is returned as confirmation.

The additional fields defined by a BGP open message are shown in Figure 9.12.

FIGURE 9.12.

BGP open message format.

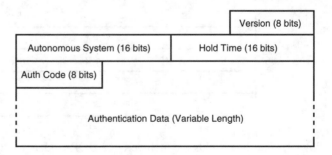

The following additional fields are defined by a BGP open message:

- *Version.* This 8-bit field indicates which BGP protocol version formed the BGP open message.

- *Autonomous System.* This 16-bit field contains the autonomous system number of the sending BGP system.

- *Hold Time.* This 16-bit field indicates the maximum interval between successive KEEPALIVE, UPDATE, or NOTIFICATION messages.

- *Authentication Code.* This 8-bit field indicates the authentication method used. The value in this field indicates which authentication code is implemented, the format of the authentication data, and the algorithm used to compute the values of the Marker field.

- *Authentication Data.* The contents of this variable-length field depend on the value set in the Authentication Code field. If the authentication code has a value of zero, the length of the Authentication Data field also must be zero.

BGP UPDATE Messages   BGP Update messages transfer routing information between BGP neighbors. The information from each BGP Update message is used to build a graph that describes the relationships between the autonomous systems. By inspecting all the relationships, the BGP system can detect potential routing loops and can remove them from the routing table.

The additional fields in a BGP Update message are shown in Figure 9.13.

FIGURE 9.13.

BGP Update message format.

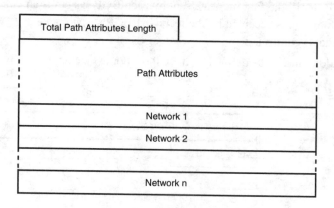

The following additional fields are included in a BGP Update message:

- *Total Path Attributes Length.* This 16-bit field indicates the total length of the Path Attributes field in octets.

- *Path Attributes.* This variable-length field contains three attributes: Type, Length, and Value.
- *Network #.* In this series of 32-bit fields, each field indicates a single network whose route is described by the Path Attributes field. This field does not report any information about subnet or host addresses.

Five different path attributes can be described in a BGP update message.

The *Origin* defines whether the path was learned from an IGP (part of the same autonomous system), an EGP (another autonomous system), or some other means (incomplete). Paths learned from IGP are preferred over paths learned from EGP.

The *AS path* attribute lists of autonomous systems that must be crossed to reach the destination network.

The *Next hop* attribute provides the IP address of the router to be used as the next hop en route to the network included in the update message.

The *Unreachable* attribute indicates that a formerly reachable network no longer is reachable.

The *Inter-AS metric* attribute provides a mechanism for a BGP router to advertise its cost to destinations within its own autonomous system. External BGP routers can choose the optimal route into the autonomous system to reach a destination network within the system.

BGP KEEPALIVE Messages   No explicit keep-alive mechanisms are defined within the BGP protocol. Instead, KEEPALIVE messages are exchanged between BGP neighbors at a more frequent rate than the configured hold time. This ensures that the hold timers do not expire. Keep-alive messages often are exchanged at a period equal to 1/3 the hold time.

A Keep-alive message does not contain any additional fields beyond the BGP header information.

BGP Notification Messages   BGP notification messages are sent whenever error conditions are detected. The notification message includes information about why the sending router is closing its connection to the destination router. Figure 9.14 shows the BGP notification message format.

- *Error Code.* This 8-bit field contains an integer value that indicates the type of error notification included in the notification message. Table 9.5 shows a list of configured error codes.

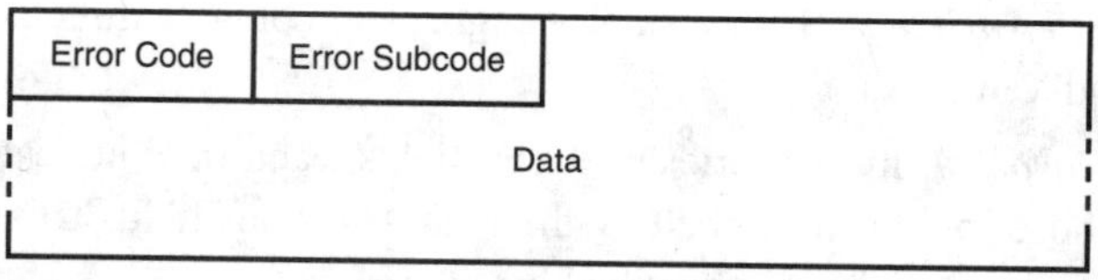

FIGURE 9.14.

BGP notification message format.

TABLE 9.5. EGP MESSAGE TYPES.

Error Code	Error Name	Description
1	Message Header Error	Indicates a problem with the format of the BGP message header.
2	OPEN Message Error	Indicates a problem with an open message format.
3	UPDATE Message Error	Indicates a problem with a BGP UPDATE message format.
4	Hold Timer Expired	Indicates that the hold-timer has expired. The BGP node is declared dead at this point.
5	Finite State Machine Error	Indicates that the sending BGP system has received an unexpected message.
6	Cease	Indicates that the sending BGP system wants to close its BGP connection with the recipient BGP system.

- *Error Subcode.* This 8-bit field provides more detailed information about the reported error code. If an error code does not have an associated subcode, a zero value is set in the Error Subcode field.

- *Data.* This variable-length field can be used to diagnose the cause of a notification error. The size of this field depends on the contents of the Error Code and Error Subcode fields.

Interior Gateway Protocols

Interior gateway protocols exchange routing information between routers belonging to the same autonomous system. Because all the information gathered is from within an autonomous system, interior gateway protocols can depend more on routing metrics to make accurate decisions when building routing tables.

As previously mentioned, the two most common types of interior routing protocols are distance vector protocols and link state protocols. The following sections discuss two common interior routing protocols: Routing Information Protocol (RIP), a distance vector routing protocol, and Open Shortest Path First (OSPF), a link state routing protocol.

THE HELLO PROTOCOL

The HELLO protocol sometimes is discussed in TCP/IP books as an example of an interior routing protocol. The HELLO protocol was used to synchronize clocks between hosts and to compute the path with the shortest delay between two hosts. RFC 891 contains more information about the HELLO protocol.

Routing Information Protocol Version 1 (RIPv1)

`RFC 1058`   The *Routing Information Protocol version 1 (RIPv1)* is a distance vector routing protocol originally developed for use in the Xerox Network Systems (XNS). RIP uses hop count as its routing metric. The hop count is the number of routers that must be navigated from the source network to the destination network.

RIP only maintains the best route to a destination network. RIP routers exchange routing information by sending RIP broadcast messages over UDP port 520. If a RIP router receives a broadcast suggesting a better route to a remote network, this better route replaces the existing route in the routing table.

Figure 9.15 shows a network structure and the resulting hop counts to each network segment.

Using a hop count metric might seem reasonable, but it does not show preference for routes that use fast network links over slower WAN links.

By default, RIP routers exchange routing information every 30 seconds. RIP broadcasts are sent out on all the routers' interfaces and contain a complete list of all network IDs to which they have been routed. The maximum number of networks that can be reported in a single RIP message is 25 networks. This can lead to scalability problems if a network grows to be quite large. It takes more than a single RIP packet to report the entire network layout. With broadcasts occurring every 30 seconds, a network easily can be overcome with RIP broadcast messages. The actual size at which this occurs is difficult to quantify. You need to consider the total number of RIP packets required to exchange the entire network routing table, the network utilization rates, and the total amount of network traffic.

To limit the number of paths reported by a single router, RIP assumes that a network located 16 or more hops away is considered unreachable.

Although RIPv1 is easy to implement, it has several key problems. The simplicity of the protocol does not lend itself to the routing problems faced by network administrators today. These problems include the following:

- *Subnet masks are not advertised.* RIP version 1 network advertisements do not include a Subnet Mask field. Without this field, it is assumed that networks use the default subnet mask based on the class of address. If a network interface on the router uses a variable-length subnet mask, it is assumed that any routes learned on that interface use the same subnet mask.

- *There is no authentication mechanism.* RIP version 1 does not implement any form of password. Nonauthorized RIP routers can be inserted into the network, potentially corrupting the routing tables.

- *The use of broadcast announcements.* The use of broadcast packets in RIP version 1 is an inefficient method of distributing routing information. Unicasts or multicasts are far more efficient.

FIGURE 9.15.

A sample network and the resulting hop counts.

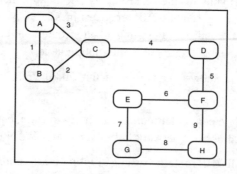

Network Router	1	2	3	4	5	6	7	8	9
A	1	2	1	2	3	4	5	5	4
B	1	1	2	2	3	4	5	5	4
C	2	1	1	1	2	3	4	4	3
D	3	2	2	1	1	2	3	3	2
E	5	4	4	3	2	1	1	2	2
F	4	3	3	2	1	1	2	2	1
G	6	5	5	4	3	2	1	1	2
H	5	4	4	3	2	2	2	1	1

RIP Version 2

RFC 1723 RIP version 2 was developed to overcome some of the shortcomings of RIP version 1. The following features have been added to RIP version 2:

- *Subnet Masks.* RIP version 2 router announcements include subnet masks with every network address. This enables network administrators to implement variable-length subnet masks and classless Internet domain routing in their networks.

- *Authentication.* RIP version 2 uses a password to make sure routes are accepted only from preferred routers on the network. If the password in a RIP packet does not match the necessary password, the RIP message is dropped.

- *Multicast announcements.* Instead of using inefficient broadcast announcements, RIP version 2 uses the multicast address 224.0.0.9 to send routing messages.

- *Route tags.* Route tags enable internal RIP routes to be distinguished from routes learned from other interior gateway protocols or from exterior gateway protocols. Route tags also can be configured to distinguish the source of external routes.

The RIP version 2 message format is shown in Figure 9.16.

- *Command.* The Command field indicates whether the RIP message is a request or a response. Response messages include all or part of the sending router's routing table.

- *Version.* This field indicates which RIP version was used to form the RIP message. In a mixed system that contains both RIP version 1 and RIP version 2, this field indicates whether a router can interpret a RIP message.

- *Address Family Identifier.* This field indicates the type of network addressing scheme in use. RIP can be implemented in non-TCP/IP environments such as IPX/SPX. For a TCP/IP environment, the address family identifier is set to a value of 2.

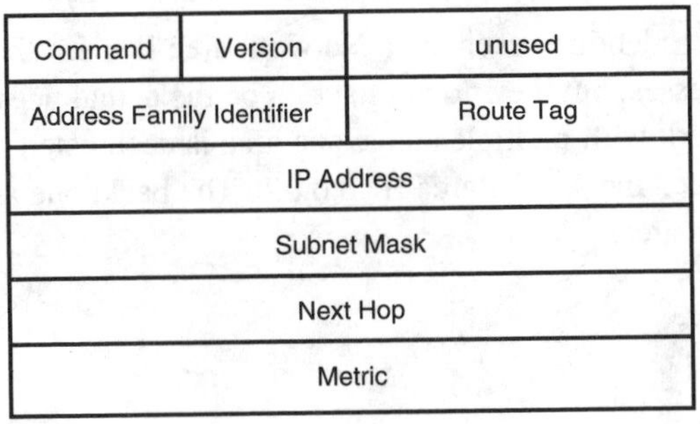

FIGURE 9.16.

The RIP version 2 message format.

Command	Version	unused	
Address Family Identifier		Route Tag	
IP Address			
Subnet Mask			
Next Hop			
Metric			

- *Route Tag.* This field enables a method of distinguishing the origin of a route. Route tags should be configured as arbitrary values to represent the source of a route. Another common implementation is to use the autonomous system number of the network from which the route was learned. In a RIP version 1 message, this field is set to all zeros.

- *IP Address.* This field contains the network IP address referred to in the RIP message.

- *Subnet Mask.* This field contains the subnet mask applied to the IP Address field to determine the network portion of the IP address. In a RIP version 1 message, this field is set to all zeros.

- *Next Hop.* This field indicates the next hop IP address to which packets destined for this network should be forwarded. This enables packets to be routed in a more efficient manner. This field is set to all zeros in a RIP version 1 message.

- *Metric.* This field specifies the hop count to the indicated network.

Open Shortest Path First (OSPF)

`RFC 1723` The *Open Shortest Path First (OSPF)* protocol is a link state routing protocol developed to overcome the shortcomings of the RIP protocol. OSPF is more scalable than RIP and enables dynamic routing to be configured in large, diverse networks.

The OSPF algorithm for finding the best route to a destination network is based on the Dijkstra algorithm. This algorithm finds the shortest path from a single source node to all other nodes in the network. It is applied at every router in the network.

OSPF Segmentation of the Network   The network can be divided into autonomous systems to make it easier to manage. OSPF is a routing protocol that can be implemented in an autonomous system. OSPF enables an additional hierarchy to be implemented that cannot be performed in a RIP environment. OSPF can subdivide an autonomous system into groups of networks called *areas* (see Figure 9.17).

A network number identifies each area. Network area IDs use the same dotted decimal format as IP addresses, but they do not have to be the actual network IP addresses in use. In an OSPF network with multiple areas, one area is designated as the *backbone area*. This area is assigned the special area ID 0.0.0.0. The backbone area acts as a routing hub for traffic between areas.

FIGURE 9.17.

OSPF areas within an autonomous system.

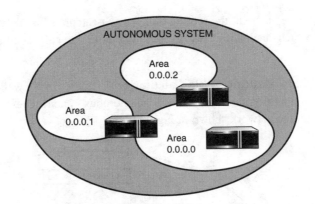

Dividing the autonomous system into areas reduces routing traffic for the entire autonomous system. If information needs to be routed entirely within an area, all routing information must be obtained from that area. No external area routing information is used.

Routing Table Construction under OSPF   Each OSPF router in an autonomous system maintains a network map called the *link state database (LSDB)*. The link state database is updated whenever an area of the network topology changes. If a router has interfaces on multiple areas, an LSDB is maintained for each separate area. The LSDB is evaluated every 10 seconds. If no changes have occurred to the area's topology, no changes are made to the LSDB.

The LSDB contains entries for all the networks to which each router in an area is attached. It also assigns an associated outgoing cost metric to each network interface of a router. This metric measures the cost of sending traffic through an interface to the connected network. By assigning costs, router preferences can be set based on line cost or line speed.

The entries in the LSDB are based on information sent in *link state advertisements (LSAs)*. An LSA contains the following information:

- Each OSPF interface on a router
- The attached networks for that router
- The cost to reach each of these networks

A network is in a *converged state* when the LSDB is the same for each router in the area. After the LSDB has reached this converged state, each OSPF router calculates the shortest path through the network for each network and each router. A *Shortest Path First (SPF) tree* stores this information. Every router maintains its own SPF tree.

After the SPF tree is built, the routing table can be calculated by determining the lowest-cost route to each destination network. Routing tables are calculated locally at each router.

A Sample OSPF Routing Table Calculation   This example walks you through the calculation of a routing table in an OSPF autonomous system. The routing table is calculated based on the network shown in Figure 9.18.

FIGURE 9.18.

A sample OSPF network.

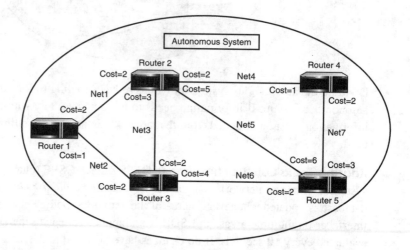

Based on the network in Figure 9.18, the following link state database would be built based on the link state advertisements sent by each router (see Table 9.5).

TABLE 9.5. DETERMINING THE LSDB.

Router	Attached Network	Network Usage Cost
Router 1	Net1	2
Router 1	Net2	1
Router 2	Net1	2
Router 2	Net3	3
Router 2	Net4	2
Router 2	Net5	5
Router 3	Net2	2
Router 3	Net3	2
Router 3	Net6	4

Router	Attached Network	Network Usage Cost
Router 4	Net4	1
Router 4	Net7	2
Router 5	Net5	6
Router 6	Net6	2
Router 7	Net7	3

Using this LSDB, a routing table now can be constructed by each router. To generate the routing table, determine the Shortest Path First tree for each router. The following shortest path first tree can be built for Router 1 (see Figure 9.19).

FIGURE 9.19.

The shortest path tree for Router 1.

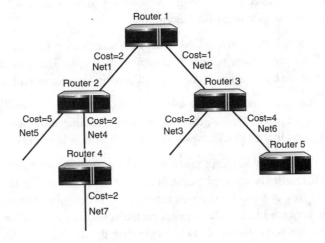

Based on the SPF tree for Router 1, Table 9.6 could be built for Router 1.

TABLE 9.6. ROUTER 1 ROUTING TABLE.

Network	Gateway	Interface	Metric
Net1	-	1	2
Net2	-	2	1
Net3	Router 3	2	3
Net4	Router 2	1	4
Net5	Router 2	1	7
Net6	Router 3	2	5
Net7	Router 2	1	6

Communication Within an OSPF Network   In an OSPF environment, the key is to make sure the link state databases at each router are synchronized for all routers within an area. To simplify this process, OSPF only requires that adjacent routers remain synchronized. Instead of worrying about all routers within an area, each router only synchronizes with routers on adjacent networks.

Before synchronization can take place between two OSPF adjacent routers, the routers must decide which will function as the Master for the synchronization process. The Master usually is chosen based on the router ID. The router with the highest ID acts as the Master.

After the Master and Slave roles are defined, the Master OSPF router sends *database description packets* to the Slave. These packets contain descriptions of the Master router's LSDB and contain a list of link state advertisements (LSAs). The Slave router responds with its own database description packets.

Based on the information received in the database description packets, each router builds a set of *link state request* packets to complete its LSDB. The routers respond to these packets with *link state update* packets that contain the requested LSAs.

After the link state requests are exchanged, the two routers are said to be *fully adjacent*. When they are fully adjacent, they can exchange routing information. The routing tables now can be built after the Shortest Path First algorithm is run at each router.

Because there can be several routers within an area, one router acts as the *designated router*. This router becomes the central contact point for routing information exchange within the area. All routing changes are sent to the designated router first. These changes then are distributed to all other routers on the network. For the sake of fault tolerance, a *backup designated router* also is elected in case the designated router fails.

The designated router is selected based on a *router priority*. Each router is manually assigned a priority value, and the router with the highest priority value is selected as the designated router. If more than one router has the same router priority, the router ID becomes the value used for the election.

Within the OSPF network, OSPF routers use one of the following multicast IP addresses for communication (if the router supports multicasting):

- *224.0.0.5.* This address sends information to *all* OSPF routers on a network.
- *224.0.0.6.* This address sends information to the designated router and the backup designated router. This address sends link state updates and link state acknowledgments to the designated router.

OSPF COMMUNICATION

In *Non-Broadcast Multiple Access (NBMA)* networks, such as an X.25 network, there is no capability for multicasts. In this form of networks, all neighbors' IP addresses must be configured manually on the routers.

Router Types Within an OSPF Network   Several types of routers can exist within an OSPF autonomous system. These routers are shown in Figure 9.20.

FIGURE 9.20.

Router roles in an OSPF autonomous system.

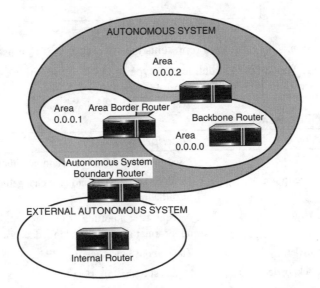

- An *internal router* is a router whose network interfaces are all connected to networks in the same area.
- An *area border router* is a router whose interfaces attach to networks belonging to multiple areas.
- A *backbone router* is any router with an interface to the backbone area. A backbone router can be either an area border router or an internal router that only connects to the backbone area.
- An *autonomous system boundary router* is a router that exchanges routing information with routers from an external autonomous system.

OSPF Message Header Format   Figure 9.21 shows the OSPF message header format.

FIGURE 9.21.

The OSPF message header.

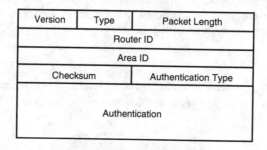

- *Version.* This 8-bit field represents the version of OSPF in use.
- *Type.* This 8-bit field defines the type of OSPF information contained in the data. The various type values are outlined in Table 9.7.

TABLE 9.7. OSPF MESSAGE TYPES.

Message Type	Description
Hello	Used to establish and maintain neighbor relationships.
Database description	Describes the LSDB and is exchanged during the establishment of full adjacency.
Link state request	A request for a portion of the destination router's LSDB, based on information exchanged in a database description message.
Link state update	The response message for a link state request.
Link state acknowledgment	Makes sure the link state update has been received successfully.
Router link advertisements	Describes the collected state of a router's links to a specific area. An RLA is sent for each area to which a router belongs. They do not go beyond the area.
Network link advertisements	Sent by the designated router, these messages describe all routers attached to a multiaccess network.
Summary link advertisements	These messages summarize routes to destinations outside the area but still within the autonomous network. Intra-area routes are advertised to the backbone area. Both intra-area and inter-area routes are advertised to all other areas.
AS external link advertisements	These messages describe routes to destination networks external to the autonomous system.

- *Packet Length.* This 16-bit field specifies the OSPF message length in bytes (including the OSPF header information).
- *Router ID.* This 32-bit field identifies the source router of the OSPF message.
- *Area ID.* This 32-bit field identifies the area to which the OSPF message belongs.
- *Checksum.* This 16-bit field makes sure the entire OSPF message has not been corrupted in transit. The checksum algorithm is performed against the entire OSPF message.
- *Authentication Type.* All OSPF messages are authenticated, and this 16-bit field designates the authentication method used. This can be configured uniquely for each area within an autonomous system.
- *Authentication.* This 64-bit field contains the authentication data based on the authentication type.

Troubleshooting Routing Problems

Most routing troubleshooting consists of inspecting the routing tables and tracing packets as they are routed through the network.

As previously mentioned in the "Static Routing" section, the ROUTE command can be used to inspect the routing table. You can type the following command to inspect the current routing table:

```
ROUTE PRINT
```

The default route (if defined) also should be inspected. Make sure the default route points to the correct gateway IP address.

Another command you can use to troubleshoot routing programs is the traceroute command. In Windows NT, the implementation of this command is TRACERT.EXE. The following is the syntax of the TRACERT command:

```
tracert [-d] [-h maximum_hops] [-j host-list] [-w timeout] target_name
```

- [-d]. This option suppresses the resolution of IP addresses to hostnames for each intermediate host crossed to the target name.
- [-h maximum hops]. This option specifies the maximum number of hops that can be crossed en route to the target name.
- [-j host-list]. This option indicates specific hosts that must be crossed en route to the target name. This is useful if you expect a route to be used and want to test that route.
- [-w timeout]. This option indicates the timeout in milliseconds implemented for each reply from each router crossed.

Applying What You Have Learned

Today's material covered key issues related to gateway and routing protocols. The following questions will help you determine how much of the information you retained.

Test Your Knowledge

1. Explain the use of multicast addresses in RIP version 2 and OSPF.

2. Explain the difference between exterior gateway protocols and interior gateway protocols.

3. Which command can be used to determine the route taken by a packet to a remote host?

4. What are some of the primary differences between distance vector and link state protocols?

5. What are some of the common problems faced in a dynamic routing environment?

6. What features can be implemented to overcome these routing problems?

Based on the following routing table information, answer the following questions:

Network Address	Netmask	Gateway Address	Interface	Metric
0.0.0.0	0.0.0.0	203.196.205.1	203.196.205.254	2
127.0.0.0	255.0.0.0	127.0.0.1	127.0.0.1	1
172.16.2.0	255.255.255.0	172.16.2.8	172.16.2.8	1
172.16.2.8	255.255.255.255	127.0.0.1	127.0.0.1	1
172.16.255.255	255.255.255.255	172.16.2.8	172.16.2.8	1
172.16.3.0	255.255.255.0	172.16.2.1	172.16.2.8	2
172.16.4.0	255.255.255.0	172.16.2.1	172.16.2.8	2
172.16.5.0	255.255.255.0	172.16.2.1	172.16.2.8	3
203.196.205.254	255.255.255.255	127.0.0.1	127.0.0.1	1
203.196.205.255	255.255.255.0	203.196.205.254	203.196.205.254	1
224.0.0.0	224.0.0.0	172.16.2.8	172.16.2.8	1
255.255.255.255	255.255.255.255	172.16.2.8	172.16.2.8	1

7. What is the address of the default gateway for this router?

8. List all local IP addresses of this router.

9. Are requests to the IP address 172.16.2.8 placed on the network?

10. What is the significance of the multicast address included in the routing table?

11. What metric is associated with reaching the network 172.16.4.0? Through which interface are packets destined for this network sent?

12. What metric is associated with reaching the network 172.16.5.0? Through which interface are packets destined for this network sent?

13. What Windows NT command would be used to add a static route to network 172.16.6.0/24 through the gateway at IP address 172.16.2.1?

Preview of the Next Day

Tomorrow's material examines different methods of assigning IP addresses automatically to hosts on the network. This greatly reduces the amount of time spent individually configuring each host and helps limit the possibility of duplicate IP addresses on the network.

The following three protocols currently enable the automatic configuration of TCP/IP on hosts:

- Reverse Address Resolution Protocol (RARP)
- Bootstrap Protocol (BOOTP)
- Dynamic Host Configuration Protocol (DHCP)

9

DAY 10

Auto Configuration of Hosts using RARP, BOOTP, and Dynamic Host Configuration Protocol (DHCP)

One of the most common challenges facing network administrators is the distribution of valid IP addresses to their clients. Addressing must be consistent across a subnetwork, and no duplicates are allowed. This lesson will review two techniques that can be used to auto-assign IP addresses to IP hosts. These methods reduce the initial configuration required for hosts and maintain an accurate pool of IP addresses without duplication.

The goals for today include the following:

- Determine when to use an auto-configuration solution
- Describe the RARP process
- Describe the BOOTP process
- Describe the DHCP process
- Configure a DHCP server

The Need for Auto Configuration

There are many scenarios in which the auto-configuration for IP addresses can be used successfully. These include

- *Diskless workstations*. Some clients do not have a hard disk on which to store their IP configuration. They cannot store this data on a network file server because they require an IP address to communicate with the file server.
- *Network hardware devices*. Some network hardware devices require an IP address to be assigned. These include devices such as HP Jet Direct cards. These clients require more information (such as a default gateway).
- *The allocation of IP addresses*. Rather than maintaining a table of IP addresses for each host, you can create a pool of IP addresses that can be dynamically assigned to each host on the network. This reduces the configuration time for each host.

By using an auto-assign method, network administrators ensure that clients have valid IP addresses with valid parameters.

Reverse Address Resolution Protocol (RARP)

RFC 903   The Reverse Address Resolution Protocol (RARP) builds on the Address Resolution Protocol (ARP). Rather than broadcasting an IP address for a target machine, the client broadcasts his MAC address on the network in a RARP message (see Figure 10.1).

A client host sends the RARP message to a RARP server. The RARP request specifies that the sending host is both the sender and target machine. The RARP request contains the sending host's MAC address in the target hardware address field. Only RARP servers respond to this message. These servers fill in the Target Protocol Address field and change the message type to a reply before sending the response packet. Due to the type of messaging being used, the RARP server must be on the same network segment as the calling host.

FIGURE 10.1.

The RARP process.

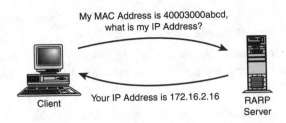

If the network is configured with only one RARP server, and it is unavailable, the client system could be locked up waiting for a response to the RARP request. You can remedy this by adding additional RARP servers. It is generally suggested to create a primary RARP server. The RARP servers that are designated as secondary RARP servers respond to a RARP request only when they receive a second RARP request from a calling system. This prevents the network from being flooded with RARP responses.

The final problem with RARP is that it cannot be used to dynamically assign IP addresses, because the RARP information is based on the client's MAC address. The following sections detail solutions that allow for the dynamic assignment of IP addresses.

Bootstrap Protocol (BOOTP)

RFC 1534 The BOOTP protocol uses the User Datagram Protocol (UDP) as an alternative to RARP. BOOTP addresses are the primary fallback of RARP in that it can send configuration beyond just the IP address of a client.

The BOOTP process uses UDP messages to obtain an IP address and its necessary configuration for a BOOTP client. How does a BOOTP client use IP datagrams before it has received its own IP address? By using the limited broadcast address of 255.255.255.255. This address can be used before the host has obtained its own unique IP address.

The BOOTP response is also sent in a UDP broadcast message. The client knows the broadcast is meant for its system by investigating the packet's Client Hardware Address field.

Ensuring Reliability in the BOOTP Process

Because UDP is used, the delivery of BOOTP messages is said to be *unreliable*. It is the responsibility of the BOOTP client to ensure that all messages are sent and received correctly. This is accomplished using two UDP options:

- *BOOTP requires UDP checksums.* The checksum is used to verify the information has not changed in transit.

- *BOOTP also requires that the Do Not Fragment bit is set.* Ensuring the information has not been fragmented prevents low memory clients from facing the scenario in which they do not have sufficient memory resources to reassemble the datagrams.

In addition, BOOTP uses the timeout and retransmission techniques to prevent data loss on the network. When the client transmits a BOOTP request, a timer starts. If the reply has not been received by when the timer expires, the request is retransmitted. The next time the data is retransmitted, the timer is set for double the previous duration.

The BOOTP Message Format

BOOTP messages use a simplified format. All fields are fixed length, and the same format is used for both BOOTP requests and BOOTP replies. Figure 10.2 shows the BOOTP message format.

FIGURE 10.2.

The BOOTP message format.

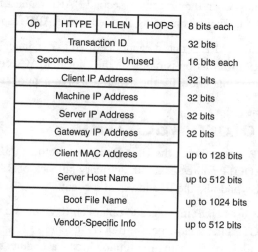

The fields used in a BOOTP message are as follows:

- Op—This 8-bit field indicates whether the message is a request (1) or a reply (2).

- HTYPE—This 8-bit field indicates what the client's network hardware type is. Ethernet uses a value of 1.

- HLEN—This 8-bit field indicates the client's hardware address length. Ethernet uses a hardware length of 6.

- HOPS—This 8-bit field indicates how many routers a BOOTP request has crossed on the way to a BOOTP server. The client initially sets this field to a value of 0. Each router that forwards this request increases this field by an increment of 1. This field generally indicates how many routers have been crossed by this BOOTP request.

- Transaction ID—This 32-bit field is used by diskless workstations to match the BOOTP reply to the proper BOOTP request. The client assigns this integer value.

- Seconds—This 16-bit field indicates the number of seconds since the client started its boot sequence.

- Unused—This 16-bit field is currently unused in the BOOTP message.

> The remaining fields contain the most important information in the BOOTP message. The client fills in as much information as it can in the BOOTP request. If a field is unknown, the IP address 0.0.0.0 is used. If a specific server IP address is indicated, only that BOOTP server can respond. If the IP address is left blank (or 0.0.0.0), any BOOTP server can respond.

10

- Client IP Address—This 32-bit field is filled in if the client knows its IP address (or prefers an IP address). This information can be a partial network address (such as 172.16.0.0).

- Machine IP Address—This 32-bit field is used by the BOOTP server when the client sends a client IP address of 0.0.0.0. The BOOTP server returns the assigned address for the client in the Machine IP Address field.

- Server IP Address—This 32-bit field contains either the IP address of a preferred BOOTP Server or 0.0.0.0 to allow any BOOTP server to respond to the BOOTP request.

- Gateway IP Address—This 32-bit field contains the IP address for the default gateway for the client.

- Client MAC Address—This field contains the MAC address of the BOOTP client. It can be up to 128 bits long as different hardware uses different length hardware addressing.

- Server Host Name—This field can be used in place of the Server IP Address field if the client is configured with the host name of its BOOTP server. This field can be up to 512 bits in length.

- `Boot File Name`—This field (up to 1,024 bits in length) specifies a filename from which a memory image can be retrieved to boot the diskless workstation. A different protocol (such as TFTP) is used to download this image from the boot image server. This boot image server can be a different machine than the BOOTP server.

- `Vendor-Specific Information`—This field contains optional information that is passed from the server to the client. The information is specific to each vendor. This variable length field has a maximum size of 512 bytes. Table 10.1 shows the BOOTP vendor-specific types. The first four octets of information are known as the *magic cookie*. The magic cookie defines the format used for the option fields. The standard format described in the table uses a magic cookie value of 99.130.83.99.

TABLE 10.1. BOOTP VENDOR-SPECIFIC TYPES.

Item Type	Item Code	Length	Contents
Padding	0	-	Used to pad messages
Subnet Mask	1	4	Subnet mask for local network
Time of Day	2	4	Time of day
Gateways (routers)	3	# of entries	IP addresses of all gateways
Time Servers	4	# of entries	IP addresses of all Time Servers
IEN116 Server	5	# of entries	IP addresses of all IEN116 Servers
Domain Name Server	6	# of entries	IP addresses of all DNS Servers
Log Server	7	# of entries	IP addresses of all Log Servers
Quote Server	8	# of entries	IP addresses of all Quote Servers
Lpr Server	9	# of entries	IP addresses of all Lpr Servers
Impress	10	# of entries	IP addresses of all Impress Servers
RLP Server	11	# of entries	IP addresses of all RLP Servers
Hostname	12	# of entries	Client hostname
Boot Size	13	2	Integer size of the boot file
Reserved	128-254	-	Reserved for site-specific use
End	255	-	End of item list

Dynamic Host Configuration Protocol (DHCP)

RFC 1534
RFC 1542

The Dynamic Host Configuration Protocol (DHCP) is the next logical extension of the BOOTP protocol. DHCP allows for additional configuration items and provides support for dynamic IP address assignments. The use of DHCP on a TCP/IP network enables easier configuration of hosts and helps to prevent duplicate IP address assignment.

The DHCP Process

The DHCP process is made up of four distinct phases (see Figure 10.3).

FIGURE 10.3.

The DHCP process.

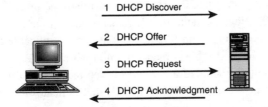

1.   DHCP Discover
2.   DHCP Offer
3.   DHCP Request
4.   DHCP Acknowledgment

10

1. The *DHCP Discover* is issued by the DHCP client computer when it attempts to acquire an IP address. Because the client does not have an IP address at this time, all information for the DHCP process is issued as broadcasts. The destination IP address used is 255.255.255.255. The client includes its MAC address in the DHCP Discover request to confirm the request was issued by that specific client.

2. The *DHCP Offer* is issued by any DHCP server that receives the DHCP Discover request. The DHCP server offers an IP address from a configured scope of IP addresses. The DHCP offer includes the requesting client's MAC address so that when the DHCP offer is sent, the appropriate client will know that the IP offer is meant for it. More than one DHCP offer can be received by the DHCP client.

3. The *DHCP Request* is issued by the DHCP client. This DHCP packet is also issued as a broadcast. The reason for this is that the client still does not have an IP address assigned; it is simply indicating which DHCP offer it has accepted. When multiple DHCP offers are received, the client uses the following decision process:

   a. The DHCP client always accepts the offer from the DHCP server from which it received its previous IP address.

b. If the previous DHCP server does not offer an IP address to the DHCP request, the DHCP client accepts the first DHCP offer that it received.

The DHCP request will also include a list of options that the DHCP client would like to receive from the DHCP server. The full list of available options is detailed later today in Table 10.2, "DHCP Options."

4. The *DHCP Acknowledgment* is issued by the DHCP server to acknowledge that the IP lease has been assigned to the requesting client. The DHCP Acknowledgment includes all the optional parameters that were requested by the client in the DHCP request. It also includes the total lease time and the renewal times for the IP address.

In some circumstances, the DHCP server can transmit an additional DHCP packet known as the *DHCP NACK* (Negative acknowledgment) packet. A DHCP NACK packet is sent when the DHCP client requests an IP address that is not applicable for the subnet in which it is presently located. This is most common with mobile users that obtain IP addresses on different segments of a network. When they request their previous IP address, the DHCP server sends a DHCP NACK that indicates the DHCP client should start the four-step process as if it has never been assigned a previous IP address.

DHCP Renewals

DHCP clients typically are assigned a limited lease on their IP addresses. The default lease duration is three days. Three automatic triggers cause a DHCP client to renew the IP lease from a DHCP server.

- *Every time a DHCP client restarts, it renews its IP lease by* using a two-packet stream starting with a DHCP request. All DHCP packets are sent as broadcasts.

- *At 50% of the lease duration, the DHCP client sends a directed packet to the DHCP server from which it received its IP lease.* The packet is a DHCP request to renew its present configuration. If the DHCP server receives the packet, it sends a DHCP acknowledgment resetting the DHCP lease interval.

- *At 87.5% of the lease duration, the DHCP client sends a broadcast DHCP request to renew its IP address.* If the original DHCP server receives the DHCP request, it renews the IP address lease. If a different DHCP server receives the request, it either allows the DHCP request if the requested IP address is available in its scope, or sends a DHCP NACK so that the client will restart the IP renewal process with a DHCP discover request.

Configuring a DHCP Server

Once you've decided to implement DHCP, you must configure the DHCP server to allow automatic IP address assignment for clients. Configuring a DHCP server is made up of three distinct phases, as follows:

- Installing the DHCP server software
- Configuring a scope of IP addresses
- Configuring options for the DHCP clients

The installation of the DHCP server software depends on your network operating system. The installation varies from vendor to vendor, but the actual configuration information remains the same, because the DHCP configuration options are defined in RFCs 1533, 1534, 1541, and 1542.

After the DHCP server has been installed, the first step is to create a scope (or pool) of IP addresses that can be leased to clients (see Figure 10.4).

10

FIGURE 10.4.

Configuring a DHCP scope.

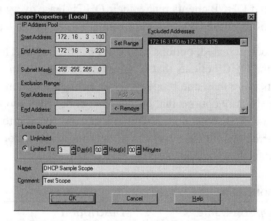

The DHCP scope definition can include the beginning and ending addresses for the pool of IP addresses and any exclusion ranges. Exclusions are commonly used for IP addresses that have already been allocated as static IP addresses to hosts. The scope also defines the duration for any IP leases. You can set the duration to either a finite time period or an unlimited duration. The following strategies are commonly applied when setting the lease duration for a pool of DHCP IP addresses:

- If the number of clients is very close to the number of IP addresses available to lease, the lease duration should be kept to a short duration (such as one day).

AN ALTERNATIVE SOLUTION

Another common solution that is implemented when the number of clients on a network is close to the total number of IP addresses available is to implement a proxy server solution. This is outlined in Day 16, "Firewalls and Security." On the internal network, a larger pool of IP addresses can be deployed. You can deploy a firewall with a proxy server component that hides the internal network addresses from the exterior network.

- If the number of clients is very low compared to the number of IP addresses available, a longer lease duration can be set (seven to fourteen days).
- You can set lease durations on a scope-by-scope basis.
- Remember that DHCP clients renew their DHCP lease every time the computer is restarted, at 50% of the lease duration, and at 87.5% of the lease duration.

Once a scope has been created, options can be set for the scope. These options are applied to any of the DHCP clients that acquire IP addresses from this scope. If the DHCP server hosts more than one scope, you can configure options on either a global or scope-by-scope basis. Any options that do not change between scopes can be applied a single time using a global scope option. Options that are specific to a scope of IP addresses (such as the default gateway) can be set in a scope option. Table 10.2 describes the full set of options that you can assign to DHCP clients.

TABLE 10.2. DHCP OPTIONS.

Option	Option Name	Description
Basic Options		
0	Pad	Causes subsequent fields to align on word boundaries.
1	Subnet mask	Specifies the subnet mask of the client subnet. This option is defined in the Create Scope or Scope Properties dialog box. It cannot be set directly in an Option dialog box.
2	Time offset	Specifies the Universal Coordinated Time (UCT) offset in seconds.

Option	Option Name	Description
3	Router	Specifies a list of IP addresses for routers on the client's subnet.
4	Time server	Specifies a list of IP addresses for time servers available to the client.
5	Name servers	Specifies a list of IP addresses for name servers available to the client.
6	DNS servers	Specifies a list of IP addresses for DNS name servers available to the client. Multihomed computers can have only one list per computer, not one per adapter card.
7	Log servers	Specifies a list of IP addresses for MIT_LCS UDP log servers available to the client.
8	Cookie servers	Specifies a list of IP addresses for RFC 865 cookie servers available to the client.
9	LPR servers	Specifies a list of IP addresses for RFC 1179 line-printer servers available to the client.
10	Impress servers	Specifies a list of IP addresses for Image Impress servers available to the client.
11	Resource location servers	Specifies a list of RFC 887 Resource Location servers available to the client.
12	Host name	Specifies the host name of up to 63 characters for the client. The name must start with a letter, end with a letter or digit, and have as interior characters only letters, numbers, and hyphens. The name can be qualified with the local DNS domain name.
13	Boot file size	Specifies the size of the default boot image file for the client, in 512-octet blocks.
14	Merit dump file	Specifies the ASCII path name of a file where the client's core image is dumped if a crash occurs.
15	Domain name	Specifies the DNS domain name the client should use for DNS host name resolution.
16	Swap server	Specifies the IP address of the client's swap server.
17	Root path	Specifies the ASCII path name for the client's root disk.

10

continues

TABLE 10.2. CONTINUED

Option	Option Name	Description
18	Extensions path	Specifies a file retrievable via TFTP containing information interpreted the same as the Vendor Extension field in the BOOTP response, except the file length is unconstrained and references to Tag 18 in the file are ignored.
255	End	Indicates the end of options in the DHCP packet.

IP Layer Parameters per Host

Option	Option Name	Description
19	IP layer forwarding	Enables or disables forwarding of IP packets for this client. 1 enables forwarding; 0 disables it.
20	Nonlocal source routing	Enables or disables forwarding of datagrams with nonlocal source routes. 1 enables forwarding; 0 disables it.
21	Policy filter masks	Specifies policy filters that consist of a list of pairs of IP addresses and masks specifying destination/mask pairs for filtering nonlocal source routes. The client discards any source routed datagram whose next-hop address does not match a filter.
22	Max datagram reassembly size	Specifies the maximum size datagram that the client can reassemble. The minimum value is 576.
23	Default time-to-live	Specifies the default time-to-live (TTL) that the client uses on outgoing datagrams. The value for the octet is a number between 1 and 255.
24	Path MTU aging timeout	Specifies the timeout, in seconds, for aging Path Maximum Transmission Unit (MTU) values (discovered by the mechanism defined in RFC 1191).
25	Path MTU plateau table	Specifies a table of Maximum Transmission Unit (MTU) sizes to use when performing Path MTU Discovered as defined in RFC 1191. The table is sorted by size from smallest to largest. The minimum MTU value is 68.

IP Parameters per Interface

Option	Option Name	Description
26	Interface MTU	Specifies the Maximum Transmission Unit (MTU) discovery size for this interface. The minimum MTU value is 68.

Option	Option Name	Description
27	All subnets are local	Specifies whether the client assumes that all subnets of the client's internetwork use the same MTU as the local subnet where the client is connected. 1 indicates that all subnets share the same MTU; 0 indicates that the client should assume some subnets may have smaller MTUs.
28	Broadcast address	Specifies the broadcast address used on the client's subnet.
29	Perform mask discovery	Specifies whether the client should use the Internet Control Message Protocol (ICMP) for subnet mask discovery. 1 indicates the client should perform mask discovery; 0 indicates the client should not.
30	Mask supplier	Specifies whether the client should respond to subnet mask requests using ICMP. 1 indicates the client should respond; 0 indicates the client should not respond.
31	Perform router discovery	Specifies whether the client should solicit routers using the router discovery method in RFC 1256. 1 indicates the client should perform router discovery; 0 indicates that the client should not use it.
32	Router solicitation address	Specifies the IP address to which the client submits router solicitation requests.
33	Static route	Specifies a list of IP address pairs that indicate the static routes the client should install in its routing cache. Any multiple routes to the same destination are listed in descending order or priority. The routes are destination/router address pairs. The default route of 0.0.0.0 is an illegal destination for a static route.

Link Layer Parameters per Interface

34	Trailer encapsulation	Specifies whether the client should negotiate use of trailers (RFC 983) when using the ARP protocol. 1 indicates the client should attempt to use trailers; 0 indicates the client should not use trailers.

10

continues

TABLE 10.2. CONTINUED

Option	Option Name	Description
35	ARP cache timeout	Specifies the timeout in seconds for ARP cache entries.
36	Ethernet encapsulation	Specifies whether the client should use Ethernet v. 2 (RFC 894) or IEEE 802.3 (RFC 1042) encapsulation if the interface is Ethernet. 1 indicates the client should use RFC 1042 encapsulation; 0 indicates the client should use RFC 894 encapsulation.

TCP Parameters on a per Interface Basis

Option	Option Name	Description
37	Default time-to-live	Specifies the default TTL the client should use when sending TCP segments. The minimum value of the octet is 1.
38	Keepalive interval	Specifies the interval, in seconds, the client TCP should wait before sending a keepalive message on a TCP connection. A value of 0 indicates that the client should not send keepalive messages on connections unless specifically requested by an application.
39	Keepalive garbage	Specifies whether the client should send TCP keepalive messages with an octet of garbage data for compatibility with older implementations. 1 indicates a garbage octet should be sent; 0 indicates that it should not be sent.

Application Layer Parameters per Interface

Option	Option Name	Description
40	NIS domain name	Specifies the Network Information Service (NIS) domain name as an ASCII string.
41	NIS servers	Specifies a list of IP addresses for NIS servers available to the client.
42	NTP servers	Specifies a list of IP addresses for Network Time Protocol (NTP) servers available to the client.
43	Vendor specific info	Specifies binary information used by clients and servers to exchange vendor-specific information. Servers not equipped to interpret the information ignore it. Clients that expect but don't receive the information attempt to operate without it.

Option	Option Name	Description
NetBIOS over TCP/IP		
44	WINS/NBNS servers	Specifies a list of IP addresses for NetBIOS Name Servers (NBNS).
45	NetBIOS over TCP/IP NBDD	Specifies a list of IP addresses for NetBIOS Datagram Distribution servers (NBDD).
46	WINS/NBT node type	Allows configurable NetBIOS over TCP/IP clients to be configured as described in RFC 1001/1002, where 1=b-node, 2=p-node, 4=m-node, and 8=h-node. On multihomed computers, the node type is assigned to the entire computer, not to individual adapter cards.
47	NetBIOS scope ID	Specifies a string that is the NetBIOS over TCP/IP scope ID for the client, as specified in RFC 1001/1002. On multihomed computers, the scope ID is assigned to the entire computer, not to individual adapter cards.
X Window Options		
48	X Window system font	Specifies a list of IP addresses for X Window font servers available to the client.
49	X Window system display	Specifies a list of IP addresses for X Window System Display Manager servers available to the client.
DHCP Extensions		
51	Lease time	Specifies the time, in seconds, from address assignment until the client's lease on the address expires. Lease time is specified in the Create Scope or Scope Properties dialog box. It cannot be set directly in a DHCP Options dialog box.
58	Renewal (T1) time value	Specifies the time, in seconds, from address assignment until the client enters the renewing state. Renewal time is a function of the Lease time option, which is specified in the Create Scope or Scope Properties dialog box. It cannot be set directly in a DHCP Options dialog box.

10

continues

TABLE 10.2. CONTINUED

Option	Option Name	Description
59	Rebinding (T2) time value	Specifies the time, in seconds, from address assignment until the client enters the rebinding state. Rebinding time is a function of the Lease time option, which is specified in the Create Scope or Scope Properties dialog box. It cannot be set directly in a DHCP Options dialog box.

MICROSOFT CLIENT DHCP OPTIONS

Whereas there are several options that can be configured for a DHCP scope, a Microsoft client is very specific in the list of options it can receive from a DCHP server (see Figure 10.5).

FIGURE 10.5.

DHCP scope options that apply to Microsoft clients.

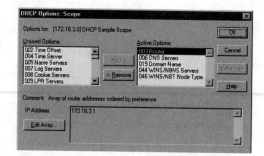

When a Microsoft DHCP client places a DHCP request on the network, it requests only the following options:

- 001 Subnet Mask
- 003 Router
- 006 DNS Servers
- 015 Domain Name
- 044 WINS/NBNS Servers
- 046 WINS/NBT Node Type
- 047 NetBIOS Scope ID

If you are configuring your DHCP server to support only Microsoft clients, configure these options only; the Microsoft client will ignore all other options that are configured.

Advanced DHCP Deployment

Before wrapping up our discussion of DHCP, we need to address a few of the advanced configuration options that can be implemented with DHCP. These include the use of DHCP reservations and implementing DHCP in a multisegment network.

Using DHCP Client Reservations

Figure 10.6 shows the configuration screen for setting a client IP address reservation. The reservation ensures the desired client will lease a specific IP address. The most common use of this is to ensure that a server-class computer always leases the same IP address. The client lease is based on the MAC address of the client.

FIGURE 10.6.

Configuring a client IP address reservation.

10

Leases are also a good tactic when multiple DHCP servers exist on an intranet. You can set up DHCP servers with overlapping scopes as long as the overlapping addresses have been configured as IP lease reservations. This ensures the host is assigned the predetermined IP address no matter which DHCP server offers the successful lease.

Deploying DHCP Servers in a Multisegmented Network

One of the most difficult questions when deploying DHCP servers is: How many DHCP servers do I need for my network? A common misconception is that you need a separate DHCP server for each segment of the network. This is not true.

In place of a DHCP server, you can install a DHCP Relay Agent on a network segment. A DHCP Relay Agent listens for DHCP broadcasts on its segment of the network. When it identifies a DHCP Discovery or DHCP Request broadcast packet on its segment of the network, the DHCP Relay Agent forwards the request as a directed packet to preconfigured DHCP servers. When the packet is forwarded, the IP address of the DHCP Relay Agent is added to the DHCP packet. This Relay Agent IP address is used to determine which scope of IP address should be used for the client's IP address assignment (see Figure 10.7).

Clients on Net1 are assigned addresses from Scope 1. The DHCP server knows this scope should be used because the DHCP Relay Agent includes its address in all DHCP Discover and DHCP Request packets. Likewise, clients on Net2 are assigned addresses from Scope 2. The DHCP server knows to assign addresses from Scope 2 based on the fact that the DHCP Discover and DHCP Offer packets are broadcast on the local network.

FIGURE 10.7.

Using a DHCP Relay Agent.

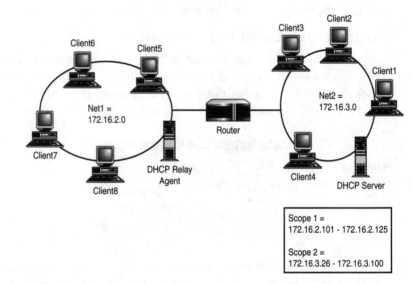

By using DHCP Relay Agents, you can reduce the number of DHCP servers for an intranet. DHCP Relay Agents can also be located on segments that have a DHCP server. These provide backup capabilities in case the DHCP server on that segment fails. You can use the DHCP Relay Agent to forward the DHCP client requests to a remote DHCP server.

The last issue that needs to be dealt with is configuring multiple scopes on a single DHCP server. The most common implementation is to place the majority of the IP addresses for a network segment on a DHCP server located on that segment. It is also suggested to configure a smaller portion of the scope on a remote DHCP server. You should configure a DHCP Relay Agent that forwards DHCP requests to that remote DHCP server.

RFC 1542-COMPLIANT ROUTERS

Another alternative to DHCP Relay Agents is to implement RFC 1542-compliant routers. These routers forward BOOTP requests across subnets. It is often preferred that you not forward any broadcasts across segments of the network.

Applying What You Have Learned

The use of automated IP address distribution is becoming more widespread in corporate networks. This chapter reviewed the three most common ways to assign IP addresses automatically to hosts.

The process of assigning IP addresses has evolved from RARP (which can assign an IP address only to a host), to BOOTP (which allows additional parameters such as a default gateway), to DHCP (which allows for automatic configuration and random IP address assignments). The exercise in the following section details how to configure a DHCP server under Windows NT Server.

Test Your Knowledge

The following exercise details the steps of installing a DHCP server under Windows NT Server:

10

1. Log in as Administrator to your Windows NT Server computer.

2. Right-click the Network Neighborhood and select Properties. The Network Properties dialog box appears.

3. Select the Services tab.

4. Click the Add button and select Microsoft DHCP Server from the list of installable network services. Click OK to validate your selection.

5. Insert the CD-ROM. Assuming you are running Windows NT Server on the Intel platform, the CD:\i386 directory is required for installation.

WINDOWS NT SERVICE PACK WARNING

After you install the DHCP server files, you must know whether any Windows NT Service Packs have been applied to your server. If they have, they should be reapplied before restarting the server. DHCP has been drastically updated from the original release of Windows NT 4.0 to allow a DHCP server to also function as a BOOTP server.

If you do not reapply the Service Pack, the mix of drivers could result in a blue screen condition during the startup of Windows NT 4.0 Server.

---

6. When prompted to restart the computer, select Yes only if there have been no Service Packs applied to the server. If a Service Pack has been applied, reapply the latest Service Pack before restarting the server.

After the Windows NT Server has restarted and you have once again logged in as the Administrator of the Windows NT Server, you can create an initial scope of IP addresses.

1. From the Start menu, select Programs, Administrative Tools (Common), DHCP Manager.

2. Select the Local Machine icon in the left pane.

3. From the Scope menu, select Create.

4. Enter the following information into the Create Scope dialog box:
   - Start Address = 192.168.1.10
   - End Address = 192.168.1.100
   - Subnet Mask = 255.255.255.0
   - Lease Duration = 5 days
   - Name = Your Name

5. After you have entered all the parameters in the Create Scope dialog box, click OK to confirm the settings.

6. When prompted, click Yes to activate the scope.

7. From the DHCP Options menu, select the Scope option.

8. Add the following options:
   - 003 Router = 192.168.1.1
   - 006 DNS Servers = 192.168.1.2
   - 015 Domain Name = experiment.org

   Each option is configured by clicking the Add button to install the option. The actual value is assigned by clicking the Value button and entering the desired value.

9. Click the OK button to confirm the options.

Preview of the Next Day

The next four days dig into specific applications that use a TCP/IP network as their transport protocol. Each day is broken into a specific category of network application. The categories covered include

- Remote command applications
- File transfer applications
- Electronic mail applications
- Network management applications

Each Day investigates specific TCP/IP application-level protocols that provide such functionality.

DAY 11

Remote Command Applications

Remote command applications enable users to perform tasks and run processes on a server while they are physically located at a remote host. The processes will run as if the users are operating at the server console.

Telnet is a protocol commonly used for this type of functionality. It enables remote users to use a standardized interface to communicate with a remote server. This chapter will detail

- Telnet communication flow
- Negotiation of additional Telnet options
- Telnet control functions
- The Telnet USASCII character set
- Telnet escape sequence commands

In addition, this chapter will look at some of the Berkeley UNIX "R-Utilities." These remote commands enable a user to execute processes on a remote system. The security involved with these remote commands will also be reviewed.

Finally, some of the optional TCP/IP services will be reviewed. This section will include definitions of the optional TCP/IP utilities, installation of the utilities in a Windows NT environment, and using Telnet to inspect these optional services.

Telnet

RFC 854 The Telnet protocol provides a bi-directional communication session between two hosts. It allows the calling system to connect to a Telnet server service running on a TCP/IP host. Once connected, the calling host can run commands and processes as if it were sitting at the console of the Telnet server.

Three key features are provided to the two hosts participating in a Telnet session:

- *Network Virtual Terminal (NVT)*. An NVT provides a common endpoint at each end of a Telnet communication session that defines what functionality is provided (see Figure 11.1).

FIGURE 11.1.

A Telnet communication session.

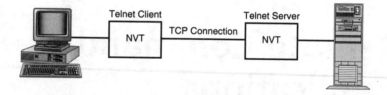

This eliminates the need for specific client and server software to be required. If you are running Telnet server software from one software vendor, you are not required to use that same vendor's client software to communicate with the Telnet server. The NVT creates an environment that can be extended if the client and server portion can agree to what options can be implemented beyond the scope of the NVT. It is also a minimum set of standards that must be provided. Therefore, a client that does not support all the options of a server will be able to operate using this minimum set of functions.

- *Negotiated options*. If a Telnet server or client is able to provide options above the base NVT, they can negotiate what options each will support to create a more option-inclusive Telnet session. Both the client and the server side of a Telnet session can request that options either be implemented or not implemented. In addition, the requesting system can ask for the option to be set on its NVT or on the server's NVT.

- *Symmetric view.* Because the negotiation syntax of options takes place in a symmetrical fashion, it can result in option loops. An option loop occurs when one NVT's acknowledgment of an option is mistakenly interpreted as a request to set an option on the other NVT. The Telnet protocol implements the following features to prevent option loops from occurring:

  - Option requests can be sent to another NVT only if they are requesting a change in option status. Option requests should not be sent simply to announce what an option is currently set to.

  - If an NVT receives a request to set an option and it already has that option set, it should not send an acknowledgment for this option. This helps to prevent option loops from starting.

  - Most options are set at the beginning of a Telnet session. If you need to change an option during a Telnet session, it can be implemented midstream. In other words, you can place the option in a data stream where it needs to take effect. All transmission of data beyond the point where the option is set follows the rules of that option being set.

WHAT IF THE OPTION IS REJECTED?

The NVT that requests the option change must keep a send buffer of all the data sent after the option change request has been sent. This way, if the option change is rejected, the NVT can resend the data with the option set to the original setting. If the option is accepted, the send buffer can be flushed.

The Telnet protocol uses the TCP protocol to ensure that reliable delivery of information takes place between the two hosts. The calling Telnet system uses a random TCP port above port 1024 and connects to the Telnet server's TCP port 23.

The Option Negotiation Process

The negotiation of options between two NVTs generally occurs during the initial creation of a Telnet session. The actual setting of options makes use of four negotiation options (see Table 11.1).

TABLE 11.1. NVT NEGOTIATION REQUEST TYPES.

Negotiation Option	Meaning as Offer/Request	Meaning as Acknowledgment
DO	Requests that the receiving NVT implements the requested option.	Indicates that the receiving NVT agrees to the requesting NVT implementing the indicated option.
DON'T	Requests that the receiving NVT ceases to implement the requested option.	Indicates that the receiving NVT does not agree to the requesting NVT implementing the indicated option.
WILL	Offers to implement the indicated option.	Indicates that the receiving NVT has implemented the requested option.
WON'T	Offers to cease supporting the indicated option.	Indicates that the receiving NVT did not implement the requested option.

The option negotiation asks either that the remote NVT implements an option or that the remote NVT accepts the local NVT setting an option. Figure 11.2 shows the sending of a WILL and DO option request and the expected acknowledgments that follow.

FIGURE 11.2.

The option negotiation process.

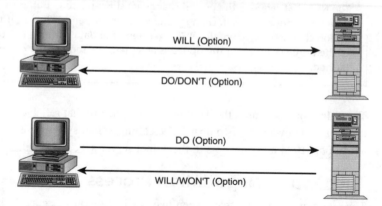

As you can see, the acknowledgment of an option uses the same negotiation options as a request. This is what can lead to option loops.

The options that can be set through negotiation include

- Echo options—If enabled, the configured side of the Telnet session will echo the data it receives.

- `Transmit Binary`—This option changes the transmission from 7-bit US ASCII to 8-bit binary.

- `Terminal Type options`—This option allows information to be exchanged about the type and model of a terminal being used. This allows output to be optimized for that terminal type.

- `End of Record options`—This option indicates whether data will be terminated with an End of Record Code.

- `Suppress Go Ahead (GA)`—This option suppresses the sending of a Go Ahead signal after data has been transmitted.

- `Status`—This option requests the status of other Telnet options from a remote host.

- `Timing-Mark`—This option inserts a timing mark in a return data stream to allow the two ends of the connection to synchronize their clocks.

- `Linemode`—This option allows a Telnet client to perform local editing on input lines. This will send complete lines rather than individual characters to the Telnet server.

- `Com Port Control`—This option provides the client with the ability to send COM port configuration information to the access server that is connected to the outbound modem if connecting to the Telnet server via a serial line.

- `Character Set`—This option allows a negotiation to take place to determine what character set to use for transmission between the client and server.

- `Environment`—This option allows the exchange of environment variable information between two hosts. This includes both global and user environment variables.

- `Authentication`—This option provides a framework to be created for the passing of authentication information through a Telnet session. This removes the security risk of sending clear text authentication—the default with Telnet.

- `Remote Flow Control`—This option provides a method of remotely toggling flow control between a user Telnet process and the attached terminal. This flow control pertains only to data being transmitted over the Telnet session.

Standard Control Functions

Because you can implement Telnet servers and clients on heterogeneous systems, some standard control functions had to be implemented in the Telnet protocol. The standardization of these functions recognizes that different systems might implement these functions differently, but the functions must be defined the same. One Telnet client, for example, might use Control-C to represent an `Interrupt Process (IP)` function whereas another client might use the Esc key. The caveat is that if the local system does not implement one of the seven control functions locally, it does not have to provide support for that function to remote users.

The seven common control functions are

- `Interrupt Process (IP)`
- `Abort Output (AO)`
- `Are You There (AYT)`
- `Erase Character (EC)`
- `Erase Line (EL)`
- `Synchronize (SYNCH)`
- `Break (BRK)`

The `Interrupt Process (IP)` control function enables you to suspend or interrupt a process running on the Telnet server. A common use for this function is to terminate a looping process that the user feels has not completed in a timely fashion. The `Interrupt Process (IP)` control function is also used by protocols other than Telnet; if other protocols are used, the `Interrupt Process (IP)` control function must be implemented.

The `Abort Output (AO)` function allows the running process to continue running until it's completed, but it stops the sending of output to the remote user's terminal screen. This function often will also clear output that has been produced but not yet sent to the remote terminal. Typically, the remote terminal will be placed back at a prompt screen and ask for its next command to be issued.

The `Are You There (AYT)` function enables remote users to determine whether their connection to the Telnet server is still functioning. The Telnet server may appear to be "down" due to heavy usage or a large computation.

The `Break (BRK)` function is used by many systems to indicate that the Break or Attention key has been invoked. This function emulates these keys in a Telnet session.

The `Erase Character (EC)` function deletes the last character inputted by the remote user. This is most commonly used when a remote user wants to edit his input before submitting it to the Telnet server.

The `Erase Line (EL)` function is used to delete the contents of the current "line" of input. This is the case in which the entire line needs to be erased and replaced with an alternate command.

The Synchronize (SYNCH) function provides a method for remote users to ensure that they are able to regain control of the Telnet session in the case of a runaway process. The IP and AO functions provide this function commonly, but in the case of a remote host, these commands might not reach the Telnet server and will have no effect. The SYNCH function consists of a TCP segment with the URGENT flag set and the Telnet Data Mark (DM) command. The TCP URGENT flag ensures the receiving host reads the accompanying data stream immediately. The DM command discards all the characters between the remote host that sent the SYNCH function and the Telnet server.

Definitions of ASCII Control Characters

Within the NVT, the US ASCII character set is used to represent all input and output characters on the screen. This includes all printable characters, such as lower case letters, upper case letters, and punctuation. Table 11.2 shows the standard definitions of the recognized US ASCII control codes between characters 0 and 31.

TABLE 11.2. US ASCII CURSOR CONTROL CODES.

US ASCII Decimal Value	US ASCII Control Code	Meaning
0	Null [NUL]	No operation.
7	Bell [BEL]	Produces a sound at the terminal. This character does not move the cursor one character position towards the right margin.
8	Back Space [BS]	Moves the cursor one character position towards the left margin.
9	Horizontal Tab [HT]	Moves the cursor to the next horizontal tab stop. The location of the tab stop is configured in the Telnet client software.
10	Line Feed [LF]	Moves the cursor to the next print line, keeping the cursor in the horizontal location on screen.
11	Vertical Tab [VT]	Moves the cursor to the next vertical tab stop. The location of the tab stop is configured in the Telnet client software.

continues

11

TABLE 11.2. CONTINUED

US ASCII Decimal Value	US ASCII Control Code	Meaning
12	Form Feed [FF]	Moves the cursor to the top of the next page, keeping the cursor in the same horizontal location on screen.
13	Carriage Return [CR]	Moves the cursor to the left margin of the current line.

The most common combination of these control codes is the combination of [CR][LF]. You should treat this combination as a single "new line" character. It moves the cursor to the left-most column of the next line when sent to the Telnet server.

Telnet Escape Sequence Commands

Commands issued in a Telnet session are actually made up of a two-command sequence. The first command is always the Interpret as Command (IAC)–Escape character sequence. The second command is the actual code for the command being issued. When the command codes are not preceded by the Interpret as Command code, they do not have the same meaning.

Requiring the IAC character to precede each command sequence leaves no doubt whether a data stream is intended to be a command or simply some data sent to the other host. Table 11.3 shows the defined Telnet commands.

TABLE 11.3. TELNET COMMAND CODES.

US ASCII Decimal Value	Control Code	Meaning
240	SE	End of sub-negotiation parameters.
241	NOP	No operation.
242	Data Mark	The data stream portion of a SYNCH operation. This should always be accompanied by a TCP Urgent notification.
243	Break	The Break (BRK) function.
244	Interrupt Process	The Interrupt Process (IP) function.
245	Abort Output	The Abort Output (AO) function.
246	AYT	The Are You There (AYT) function.
247	EC	The Erase Character (EC) function.

US ASCII Decimal Value	Control Code	Meaning
248	EL	The Erase Line (EL) function.
249	GA	The Go Ahead signal.
250	SB	Indicates the following data stream is a sub-negotiation of the indicated option.
251	WILL [Option code]	If sent initially, indicates the desire to begin performing the indicated option. If sent as an acknowledgment, indicates a confirmation that the receiving host is currently performing the indicated option.
252	WON'T [Option code]	If sent initially, indicates the desire to not perform the indicated option. If sent as an acknowledgment, indicates a confirmation that the receiving host has ceased to perform the indicated option.
253	DO [Option code]	If sent initially, indicates the desire for the receiving host to perform the indicated option. Can also represent an acknowledgment that the receiving host will perform the indicated option.
254	DON'T [Option code]	If sent initially, indicates the desire for the receiving host to cease performing the indicated option. Can also represent a response that the receiving host should not implement the indicated option.
255	IAC	The Interpret as Command (IAC) function that precedes all the command functions.

11

Connecting to a Telnet Server

To connect to a Telnet server, you need to use Telnet client software. Most operating systems now come with Telnet software, including Windows for Workgroups (with the WFW-TCP32 protocol installed), Windows 95, and Windows NT. On most systems, the executable for the Telnet client is TELNET.EXE.

After running `TELNET.EXE`, you need to indicate the host you want to connect to for a Telnet session. Select Remote System from the Connect menu. The connection dialog box shown in Figure 11.3 appears.

FIGURE 11.3.

Connecting to a Telnet server.

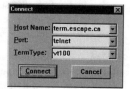

After you connect to the Telnet server, you need to authenticate with the Telnet server. This includes providing your user account and password combination when prompted (see Figure 11.4). The account and password are commonly transported using clear text.

FIGURE 11.4.

Authenticating with a Telnet server.

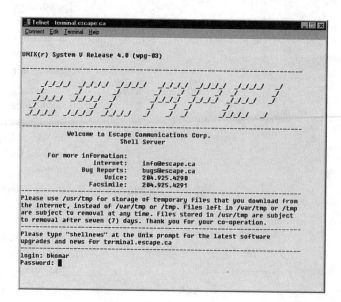

VARIANTS OF TELNET

Depending on the version of your OS, you can have either a graphical version of Telnet (as shown in Figure 11.4) or a text-based version. The actual syntax does not differ much. For a text-based Telnet client, launch the client with the following sequence:

```
/home/orgs/online/users/b/bkomar 5% telnet
telnet> open ds.internic.net
Trying 198.49.45.10...
Connected to ds.internic.net.
Escape character is '^]'.
```

This sequence shows a connection to the Telnet server at
ds.internic.net. Note that rather than using menu options, the open
command is used to connect to the Telnet server.

After you connect to the Telnet server, the level of commands you can execute depends
on your privilege level on the system hosting the Telnet server. Table 11.4 shows some of
the common Telnet commands.

TABLE 11.4. TELNET COMMANDS.

Telnet Command	Description
? [specific command]	Shows a list of available commands. If [specific command] is included, this command will provide help information about [specific command].
Close	Closes the connection to the Telnet server and returns you to the Telnet command prompt.
Display [argument]	Displays all the set and toggle values if no arguments are specified. The arguments limit the listing to only those values that match the argument.
Open [host] [port]	Opens a connection to the indicated host. The host can be represented as either an IP address or a hostname. The use of a hostname requires a functioning hostname resolution process. If no port is indicated, Telnet will default to TCP port 23.
Quit	Closes a connection and terminates the Telnet program.
Control-D	Has the same effect as the Quit command when in command mode.
Status	Shows the status of the Telnet session, including the current mode and connected remote host.
Z	Opens a shell on the local host as specified in the SHELL environment variable.

11

ANONYMOUS ACCESS IN TELNET

When you attempt to connect to a Telnet server with an anonymous account, the most common account you use is the GUEST account with no password. If the server does not support anonymous clients, your authentication request will be rejected.

Remote UNIX Commands

A set of remote commands, known as the *Berkeley R-Utilities*, was developed at the University of California at Berkeley. The "R" stands for "remote." These utilities enable remote users to run processes and applications as if they were local users on the systems running the remote daemons. They are found most often in UNIX systems, but several of the R-utilities have been ported to other operating systems.

OTHER REMOTE COMMANDS

This section covers only the rlogin, rsh, and rexec commands. Day 12, "File Transfer Protocols," discusses the rcp (remote copy) command. Other R-Utilities include rwho (remote who) and ruptime (remote uptime). The rwho command displays a list of users on the network. The ruptime command displays a list of all machines on the network. It includes statistics on their status, the time they have been up, the number of active users, and their current load.

Configuring Security

Determining who can run these remote commands is a key issue when configuring the security level of your network. Two files can be configured to grant remote users access to a system to run the R-Utilities: HOSTS.EQUIV and .RHOSTS. The combination of entries in these two files and entries in the /etc/passwd file control which users can access the local system using the R-Utilities and without having to provide a password.

THE /ETC/PASSWD FILE

For a remote user to connect to the local system, not only must there be an entry in either HOSTS.EQUIV or .RHOSTS for his hostname or login name, the /etc/passwd file must have an entry for the user's login name on both the machines. The remote user's login name must exist in both the remote host's /etc/passwd file and in the local host's /etc/passwd file.

The HOSTS.EQUIV File

The HOSTS.EQUIV file is located in the /etc directory on a UNIX system. The file can contain entries for trusted hosts or for specific users on a host. The danger in trusting all users on a remote system is that if a single account were compromised on the remote system, the system with the remote system in its HOSTS.EQUIV file is also compromised.

The following is an example of a HOSTS.EQUIV file:

```
#Sample HOSTS.EQUIV file
ironman tlangmade
obscgy ephillips
online_mb_ca gseburn
development
```

Any user that has a valid account on development can connect to the system with this HOSTS.EQUIV file. The other three systems name specific users that can connect from the remote system to the local system.

ADDITIONAL SECURITY CONCERNS FOR HOSTS.EQUIV

The HOSTS.EQUIV file should never contain an entry of "+," which allows all hosts to be trusted. Another issue to watch is the misuse of the HOSTS.EQUIV file. The HOSTS.EQUIV file grants access for the R-utilities and for the lpd print services. If you want to grant access to use print services, the host entries should be placed only in the HOSTS.LPD file.

11

The .RHOSTS File

The .RHOSTS file allows specific accounts to be named for a remote host for granting access to the local host. The .RHOSTS file contains entries for hosts and users that can gain access to the local system. Each entry consists of a hostname and a login name. The following is a sample .RHOSTS file:

```
#Sample .RHOSTS file
ironman tlangmade
ironman mbrown
ironman bkomar
obscgy ephillips
obscgy bkomar
online_mb_ca gseburn
online_mb_ca dplummer
online_mb_ca bkomar
```

The .RHOSTS file commonly resides in the user's home directory. This means that the network administrator can lose control of the security environment. It is very possible that a user could place an undesirable user in the .RHOSTS file.

ADDITIONAL SECURITY CONCERNS FOR .RHOSTS

The .RHOSTS file should never contain an entry of "+ +," which enables all users from all hosts to access the local system with the R-utilities.

---

rlogin (Remote Login)

RFC 1282 The rlogin command enables a user to remotely log in to another system on the network. The host that accepts the remote login runs the rlogind daemon to allow this connection.

The rlogin command connects using TCP port 513. Once connected, the client sends the following four null-terminated strings:

- <NULL>—An empty string to begin the session.
- CLIENT-USER-NAME<NULL>—The username the client uses at the client host.
- SERVER-USER-NAME<NULL>—The username the client uses on the remote server. Generally, this is the same as CLIENT-USER-NAME, but it can be different.
- TERMINAL-TYPE/SPEED<NULL>—The final string contains the name and transmission speed of the remote user's terminal.

An example of this initialization sequence could occur as follows:

```
<NULL>
bkomar<NULL>
briank<NULL>
VT100/14400<NULL>
```

The server returns a zero byte to indicate that it received these three strings and is ready for data transfer.

The syntax of the rlogin command is as follows:

```
rlogin rhost [-ec] [-8] [-L] [-l username]
```

- rhost—The name of the remote host you are connecting to.
- [-ec]—Enables you to define an alternate escape character. The default is the tilde (~) character.

- [-8]—Sets the data input path to be 8 bits all the time.
- [-L]—Runs the session in litout mode. This provides backward compatibility with version 4 of Berkeley Software Development (BSD) UNIX. Litout mode enables 7 bit with parity data transmission. All lowercase characters are translated to uppercase.
- [-l *username*]—Indicates the username you want to use on the remote system. If not indicated, uses your current login name.

The following is a sample `rlogin` command for logging into the `ironman` remote server using the `pscott` login name:

```
rlogin ironman –l pscott
```

After your `rlogin` session has completed, you must type the following on a separate line to exit the session:

```
~.
```

WHEN DOES *RLOGIN* PROMPT YOU FOR A PASSWORD?

If the login name you specify in the `rlogin` command or the host you are working at is not found in either the HOSTS.EQUIV or .RHOSTS file, you will be prompted for a password when you connect with the `rlogin` command. This password will be transmitted in clear text across the network.

11

rsh (Remote Shell)

The `rsh` (remote shell) utility enables you to execute a single command on a remote host without logging in to the remote host. If you need to run multiple commands, you should use either `rlogin` or Telnet.

The `rsh` command is not suited for processes that return data to the screen, because the connection is completed before the data would be returned. Likewise, no return codes are ever returned to the calling system when using the `rsh` command.

The `rsh` command also uses the HOSTS.EQUIV and .RHOSTS files to determine whether the calling user is authorized to execute remote commands on the local host.

A host must run the `rshd` daemon to allow remote users to run the `rsh` command against it.

The syntax of the `rsh` command is as follows:

```
rsh [-l username] rhost command
```

- [-l *username*]—Indicates the username you want to use on the remote system. If not indicated, `rsh` uses your current login name.
- `rhost`—The name of the remote host you are connecting to.
- `command`—The command you want to execute on the remote host.

For example, if you want to concatenate the file `remote_file_1` on the remote host `Earl` to the local file `myfile`, use the following command:

```
rsh Earl cat remote_file_1 >>myfile
```

rexec (Remote Execute)

The `rexec` (remote execute) command allows remote execution of programs to take place. Unlike `rlogin` and `rsh`, `rexec` does not use the `HOSTS.EQUIV` or `.RHOSTS` files to determine trusted hosts. Instead, the client must specify the username, password, and command that it wants to execute. Depending on the version of the `rexec` and `rexecd` being run, the password may be sent in encrypted format across the network.

The syntax of the `rexec` command is as follows:

```
rexec [-l username] [-p password] rhost command
```

- [-l *username*]—Indicates the login name that should be used on the remote host.
- [-p *password*]—Provides the password for the login name on the remote host.
- `rhost`—The name of the remote host being communicated with.
- `command`—The command to be executed on the remote host.

The Optional TCP/IP Services

A TCP/IP network has several optional services that users and applications can use. These optional services are

- Active Users
- Character Generator
- Daytime
- Discard
- Echo

- Quote of the Day
- Time

The *Active Users* service returns a message to the calling system informing it of all the users currently active on the system running the Active Users service. The Active Users service monitors both TCP and UDP port 11 to establish a session.

The *Character Generator* service returns a list of all 95 printable ASCII characters. Both TCP and UDP port 19 are monitored for connections, but they behave differently. A connection on TCP port 19 returns the list of printable characters until the connection is broken. A connection on UDP port 19 responds with a datagram that contains a random set of the printable ASCII characters (with a maximum of 512 characters being returned). This service is useful for testing whether a printer is capable of printing all ASCII characters correctly.

The *Daytime* service returns a message that contains the current date and time to the connection system. The format of the response is Day of Week, Month, Day, Year, HH:MM:SS, with each field separated by a single space. The Daytime service monitors both TCP and UDP port 13 for connections.

The *Discard* service discards all information sent to it on either TCP or UDP port 9. Although this might seem rather pointless, it can be quite useful for testing routing.

The *Echo* service returns any information passed to it. In the case of a TCP connection on port 7, the Echo service returns whatever data is sent until the connection is broken. For a UDP connection on port 7, the exact datagram that is received is retransmitted back to the originating host. This can be used to measure response times on the network. The ping utility uses this service to test whether another host is reachable.

The *Quote of the Day* service returns a quotation from a central file of quotations. This central file must exist for the service to function. The Quote of the Day service listens for requests on both TCP and UDP port 17.

The *Time* service returns the number of seconds that have elapsed since midnight, January 1, 1900. This number is sent as a 32-bit binary number that must be translated by the requesting host. All requests to the Time service are sent to TCP or UDP port 37. This service is useful for synchronizing clocks on the network.

Installing the Optional TCP/IP Services in Windows NT

In a Windows NT environment, these optional TCP/IP services are referred to as the *Simple TCP/IP services*. They are installed through the Network applet in the Control Panel.

To install the Simple TCP/IP services, follow these steps:

1. Start the Control Panel.

2. Start the Network applet.

3. Select the Services tab of the Network applet.

4. Select Simple TCP/IP Services from the Select Network Service dialog box (see Figure 11.5).

FIGURE 11.5.

Installing the Simple TCP/IP Services in Windows NT.

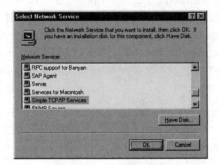

5. You will be required to reboot the Windows NT Server before using the Simple TCP/IP services.

OPTIONAL TCP/IP SERVICES INCLUDED WITH WINDOWS NT

Windows NT includes the following optional TCP/IP services: Character Generator, Daytime, Discard, Echo, and Quote of the Day. The Simple TCP/IP Services do not include Active Users and Time. These services are provided in native Windows NT utilities.

Testing the Optional TCP/IP Services

If you want to connect to the optional TCP/IP services, you can use a Telnet client. The catch is that you must change to the port of the optional TCP/IP service that you are connecting to.

To connect to the Quote of the Day service on the host named simple, for example, execute the following commands:

```
/home/orgs/online/users/b/bkomar 13% telnet simple 17
Trying 207.161.165.73...
Connected to 207.161.165.73.
Escape character is '^]'.
```

```
"Oh the nerves, the nerves; the mysteries of this machine called man!
 Oh the little that unhinges it, poor creatures that we are!"
 Charles Dickens (1812-70)
Connection closed by foreign host.
```

Likewise, to check out the current date and time using the Daytime service on simple, use the following sequence of commands:

```
/home/orgs/online/users/b/bkomar 14% telnet 207.161.165.73 13
Trying 207.161.165.73...
Connected to 207.161.165.73.
Escape character is '^]'.
Saturday, March 14, 1998 21:01:00
Connection closed by foreign host.
```

You can also generate these commands from within the Telnet client software that ships with Microsoft operating systems. Figure 11.6 shows the dialog box that is configured to connect to the Echo service on simple from the Windows NT Telnet client software.

FIGURE 11.6.

Connecting to the Echo service.

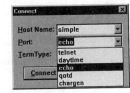

11

As you can see, you can choose from Telnet, Daytime, Echo, Qotd (Quote of the Day), and Chargen (Character Generator). If you are connecting to another system that is running Time or Active Users, simply type the port number in the Port drop-down list. For example, you would fill the Connect dialog box as shown in Figure 11.7 to connect to the Active User service on the host name Earl.

FIGURE 11.7.

Connecting to the Active User service.

Applying What You Have Learned

Today's material investigated the Telnet process, the R-utilities, and the optional TCP/IP services. The following section tests your knowledge of these topics and indicates areas you might want to review further.

Test Your Knowledge

1. Complete Table 11.5 to associate the correct TCP port numbers to the appropriate TCP/IP Service.

TABLE 11.5. ASSOCIATING PORT NUMBERS WITH THE CORRECT TCP/IP SERVICE.

Service	Port
1. Telnet	A. 19
2. rlogin	B. 9
3. Quote of the Day	C. 7
4. Daytime	D. 23
5. Echo	E. 17
6. Discard	F. 13
7. Character Generator	G. 37
8. Time	H. 513

2. Compare the security implications of a Telnet session with an rlogin session.

3. What is the syntax of an rlogin command to connect to a host named BART using the username LISA?

4. Describe the interaction between the DO/DON'T and WILL/WON'T functions during a Telnet option negotiation.

5. What is the significance of the Interpret as Command sequence?

6. Describe the concept of the Network Virtual Terminal?

7. What are some uses of the Telnet client software besides connecting to a Telnet server?

8. What optional TCP/IP services are supported under Windows NT Server?

Preview of the Next Day

Tomorrow's material will investigate the next class of application software that runs on a TCP/IP network: file transfer applications. Specifically, we will investigate

- FTP (File Transfer Protocol)
- TFTP (Trivial File Transfer Protocol)
- rcp (remote copy)
- HTTP (HyperText Transfer Protocol)

We will also review several of the popular Web servers available today.

DAY 12

File Transfer Protocols

Today's material presents an overview on the major protocols used for transferring files on a TCP/IP network. These include the following:

- File Transfer Protocol (FTP)
- Trivial File Transfer Protocol (TFTP)
- Remote Copy (RCP)
- Gopher
- Hypertext Transmission Protocol (HTTP)

In addition to discussing common connection sequences, security, and characteristics of these protocols, I also discuss some of the search mechanisms that can be used to search for resources that can be accessed via these protocols.

Search mechanisms discussed include the following:

- Archie
- Veronica
- Jughead
- Web search engines

File Transfer Protocol (FTP)

RFC 959   *File Transfer Protocol* (FTP) is the most commonly used protocol for transferring data files from one host to another in a TCP/IP network. The advantage of FTP is that it uses the TCP protocol to provide a session-oriented, reliable method to transfer data between two hosts.

The FTP protocol uses two separate processes during the transfer of data:

- The *Data Transfer Process* (DTP) is used for the actual transmission of data between an FTP client and an FTP server. The DTP on the client listens for a connection from the server's DTP process.

- The *Protocol Interpreter* (PI) is used to transmit the commands between the FTP client and the FTP server. The PI initiates the FTP process and is used to govern the FTP client-side DTP service.

The actual FTP session is really two separate sessions between the client and the FTP server (see Figure 12.1).

FIGURE 12.1.

An FTP session.

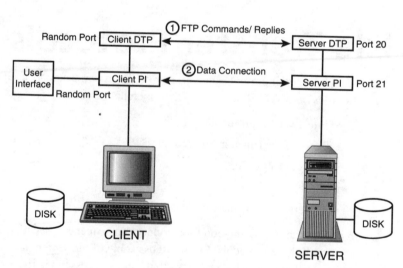

The following transactions take place when an FTP session is established between an FTP client and an FTP server:

1. The first session takes place between the server and client PI services. The user-side protocol interpreter initiates the control connection between the client and server sides. For each command sent to the FTP server, a response is returned over

the control connection to the FTP client. The user side of this connection uses a randomly assigned port number and connects to TCP port 21 on the FTP server.

2. When a data transfer is requested, the server's DTP initiates a connection with the client's DTP service. Only data is transmitted over the data connection.

During the actual transmission of data, the control connection must remain established so that commands and responses can be exchanged between the server and client processes. Both the control connection and the data connection will allow data to flow in both directions between the client and server.

Common Commands Used in FTP

The following sections outline many of the common commands used during an FTP session. They are broken out into the following categories:

- Access control commands
- Transfer parameter commands
- File transfer commands
- Directory and file management commands
- Help and status commands
- FTP server responses

Access Control Commands

FTP access control commands are used during the establishment and termination of an FTP session between client and server. These commands are often issued in a specific sequence. The PASS command, for example, is always expected to follow the USER command to provide the accompanying password for a user account. Table 12.1 shows the FTP access control commands.

12

TABLE 12.1. FTP ACCESS CONTROL COMMANDS.

Command	Description
OPEN [hostname]	The OPEN command is used to establish an FTP session with the FTP service running on [hostname].
USER [username]	The USER command is used to identify the user who is performing the FTP commands. This command is the first command sent after the control connection is established.

continues

TABLE 12.1. CONTINUED

Command	Description
PASS [password]	The PASS command immediately follows the USER command. It is used to pass the user's password via the Telnet protocol to the FTP server. An FTP client will generally not display the user's password onscreen. Unfortunately, the default FTP specification does transmit the password over the network using clear text.
ACCT [account]	This optional parameter is required by some FTP servers to identify the user's account on the FTP server. The account does not have to be related to the USER command.
SMNT	The SMNT (Structure Mount) command allows a different file system data structure to be mounted without having to re-log on to the FTP server.
REIN	The REIN (Reinitialize) command terminates the session for the current user account. All input/output information is terminated (except for a current transfer). This places the user in the same state as when he initially connected to the FTP server.
QUIT	The QUIT (Logoff) command terminates the session between the FTP client and server. Some implementations also use the command BYE with the same meaning.

ANONYMOUS FTP SESSIONS

The FTP protocol allows anonymous connections to take place between an FTP client and server. The account used for the session is commonly ANONYMOUS or FTP. Commonly, the FTP server asks the client to provide his or her email address as the password when logging on anonymously. Although it may seem insecure to run an anonymous FTP server, in many ways it is more secure. By allowing only read access to FTP clients, you prevent the uploading of unexpected data. Likewise, you prevent the clear-text transmission of user passwords over the network when they authenticate with the FTP server.

Transfer Parameter Commands

The FTP transfer parameter commands allow the default parameters for an FTP session to be changed. The FTP server will generally have defaults preserved. They need to be modified only if your implementation requires new methods to be used. Table 12.2 shows the FTP transfer parameter commands.

TABLE 12.2. FTP TRANSFER PARAMETER COMMANDS.

Command	Description
PORT ##	This command allows for the FTP client-side socket to be defined. The ## parameter includes the 32-bit IP address of the host that the DTP connection should be established with and the 16-bit port address on that host.
PASV	The PASV (Passive) command changes the behavior of the server during a data session establishment. Rather than initiating the establishment of the data connection, the server listens on a data port and waits for the client to initiate the data connection.
TYPE	The TYPE (Representation Type) command indicates whether the data representation on the server is ASCII, EBCDIC, or Image.
STRU	The STRU (File Structure) command is a single code that indicates whether the default file structure is files, records, or pages.
MODE	The MODE (Transfer Mode) command specifies the transfer mode that will be used during the transmission of data. Options include Stream, Block, and Compressed.

FTP File Transfer Commands

After you have established your session with the FTP server and have set any defaults that you want for the data transfer session, you are ready to start the transfer of data files. Table 12.3 illustrates some of the more common file transfer commands used within FTP client software.

TABLE 12.3. FTP FILE TRANSFER COMMANDS.

Command	Description
ASCII	This file transfer type is used to transfer text files. This is the default transfer type.
BINARY	The BINARY file transfer type should be used to transfer all non-text files. This includes graphics, archives, and executables.
TYPE	The TYPE command indicates whether the data transfer method has been set for BINARY or ASCII.
RECV [remfile] [locfile]	This command copies the file [remfile] from the remote FTP server to the local file [locfile]. If [locfile] is not specified, the file will be copied using the same filename as on the remote FTP server.

continues

12

TABLE 12.3. CONTINUED

Command	Description
SEND [*locfile*] [*remfile*]	This command copies the local file [*locfile*] to the FTP server using the filename [*remfile*]. If [*remfile*] is not indicated, the remote file will use the filename [*locfile*].
GET [*remfile*] [*locfile*]	The GET command works the same as the RECV command.
PUT [*locfile*] [*remfile*]	The PUT command works the same as the SEND command.
MGET [*remfile*]	The MGET (Multiple Get) command allows multiple files to be transferred from the FTP server to the local host. This command allows the use of wildcards when designating the remote file to copy.
MPUT [*locfile*]	The MPUT (Multiple Put) command allows multiple files to be transferred to the FTP server. This command also allows the use of wildcard characters.
PROMPT	This command enables/disables the use of prompts when using an MPUT or MGET command. If enabled, you are prompted whether to transfer the files on a one-by-one basis. If disabled, no prompts display.

Directory and File Management Commands

After you have connected to the FTP server, you may have to do some file or directory management in addition to transferring files to and from the FTP server. Table 12.4 shows many of the directory and file management commands used by an FTP client.

TABLE 12.4. FTP DIRECTORY AND FILE MANAGEMENT COMMANDS.

Command	Description
DELETE [*remfile*]	The DELETE command deletes the indicated [*remfile*] on the FTP server.
MDELETE [*remfile*]	The MDELETE command deletes all files that match the wildcard indicated in [*remfile*].
LCD	The LCD (Local Change Directory) command changes the default directory on the local host. This is commonly used to choose a new location to transfer files to the local host.
CD	The CD (Change Directory) command is used to change the current directory on the FTP Server.
CDUP	The CDUP (Change Directory Up) command changes the directory to the parent directory of the current working directory. This command was created to handle the various representations of the parent directory that are implemented by different systems.

Command	Description
MKDIR	The MKDIR (Make Directory) command is used to create a new directory on the FTP server.
RMDIR	The RMDIR (Remove Directory) command is used to remove a directory on the FTP server.
DIR	The DIR command shows a detailed listing of the contents of the FTP server's current directory.
LS	The LS (List) command can be used to view the contents of the FTP server's current directory. Common flags used with the LS command include -F and -all. The -F flag shows subdirectory names with a following slash (/) character. The -all flag produces the same screen output as the DIR command.
PWD	The PWD command displays the name of the current directory on the FTP server.
RENAME [*fromfile*] [*tofile*]	The RENAME command renames the [*fromfile*] filename to the new name [*tofile*] on the FTP server.

FTP Help and Status Commands

The FTP help and status commands help you to investigate the syntax of an FTP command if you are unsure of its parameters. You can also use them to determine what options have been currently set for your FTP sessions. Table 12.5 shows some of the more common help and status commands for FTP.

TABLE 12.5. FTP HELP AND STATUS COMMANDS.

Command	Description
!	The ! command shells out of FTP to a local shell or command interpreter. Most often you will return to your FTP session by typing in the command EXIT.
?	The ? command displays all the available commands in the FTP client software.
HELP	The HELP command works the same as the ? command.
STATUS	The STATUS command displays the current status information for your FTP session. This includes the transfer mode, connection status, prompt status, and timeout value.
VERBOSE	The VERBOSE command toggles between VERBOSE and non-VERBOSE screen output. VERBOSE output includes all FTP server responses and transmission rates on file transfers.

12

FTP Server Reply Codes

When an FTP client issues a command to the FTP server, the FTP server returns a reply code to indicate whether the command was carried out successfully. If not, an error code is returned so that the FTP client is informed on how to proceed from this point.

All FTP server reply codes are three-digit alphanumeric codes. The first digit of the three-digit code indicates the general status of the preceding command. In general, the first digit indicates the next appropriate action the FTP client should take. Table 12.6 shows the five values that can be returned in the first digit of the FTP reply code.

TABLE 12.6. THE FIRST DIGIT VALUES OF AN FTP SERVER-REPLY CODE.

Value	Definition	Description
1yz	Positive Preliminary Reply	A value of 1 in the first digit of the FTP reply code is a *Positive Preliminary Reply*. It indicates that the request action has been started and another reply will be sent before the next command should be issued. Only a single 1yz reply can be sent in a row.
2yz	Positive Completion Reply	A value of 2 in the first digit of an FTP server response indicates that the requested action has been performed successfully and the FTP server is ready for the next client command.
3yz	Positive Intermediate Reply	A value of 3 in the first digit of an FTP server reply code indicates that the command has been accepted from the FTP client, but more information is required. This is the common response when a sequence of commands is expected, such as a USER command followed by a PASS command.
4yz	Transient Negative Completion Reply	A value of 4 in the first digit of an FTP server reply code indicates that the submitted command did not execute correctly. But, the failure was due to a temporary error connection and the command should be tried again.
5yz	Permanent Negative Completion Reply	A value of 5 in the first digit of an FTP server reply code indicates that the requested action could not be performed. This could result from a mistyped command or a security privilege not being assigned to the current user.

The second digit of the reply code provides further detailed information about an FTP server reply. Table 12.7 details the possible values set to the second digit of the FTP server reply codes.

TABLE 12.7. THE SECOND DIGIT VALUES OF AN FTP SERVER REPLY CODE.

Value	Definition	Description
x0z	Syntax	This indicates that an error is returned because of a syntax error. It is also used for a syntactically correct command issued at the incorrect time.
x1z	Information	This reply code is used in responses to FTP status commands such as STATUS or HELP.
x2z	Connections	This reply code is used for replies that refer to maintenance of data connections.
x3z	Authentication and Accounting	This reply code is used during the user authentication process.
x4z	Unspecified	This reply code is not implemented as of yet.
x5z	File System	This reply code indicates the status of the FTP server file system or the local client file system.

The final digit gives even more granular information about the reply code that is dependent on the specific first and second digits of the reply code. It is recommended to always include a text field with the error code to better explain the meaning of the reply code. RFC 959 provides details on specific third-level reply codes.

FTP Security Issues

RFC 2228   The recently released RFC 2228 outlines the need for a standardized security mechanism for the FTP protocol. Currently, passwords are passed in FTP using clear text. This can lead to passwords being captured by *network sniffers*.

These security mechanisms will also ensure that servers are authenticated to prevent masquerading, and the encryption of information transferred on the data channel.

RFC 2228 introduces new commands that can be optionally implemented in an FTP system. Table 12.8 outlines these new commands.

12

TABLE 12.8. FTP SECURITY EXTENSION COMMANDS.

Command	Description
AUTH	The AUTH (Authentication/Security Mechanism) command is used by the client to state what mechanism it wants to use for a secure transfer of information. This command may be sent several times as the authentication method is negotiated between client and server.
ADAT	The ADAT (Authentication/Security Data) command sends additional information to implement any optional features for the chosen security mechanism.
PROT	The PROT (Data Channel Protection Level) command indicates what level of protection the client and server will implement on the data channel. If set to Clear, this indicates that only raw data will be transmitted. If set to Safe, data integrity will be verified. If set to Confidential, the data will be transmitted in an encrypted state. Finally, if set to Private, the data will be both encrypted and verified for data integrity.
PBSZ	The PBSZ (Protection Buffer Size) command indicates the maximum in size of the encoded data blocks that will be transmitted during a file exchange. This size is indicated in bytes.
CCC	The CCC (Clear Command Channel) command is used to quit using the security implementation. This is commonly used when TCP security is implemented on a network. After the authentication has taken place, the CCC command can be used to terminate all authentication and data integrity checks.
MIC	The MIC (Integrity Protected Command) is used for the transmission of data when the data protection level is set to Safe.
CONF	The CONF (Confidentiality Protected Command) is used for the transmission of data when the data protection level is set to Confidential.
ENC	The ENC (Privacy Protected Command) is used for the transmission of data when the data protection level is set to Private.

An actual security exchange begins with an FTP client telling the security mechanism that it wants to enable a secure FTP session by using the AUTH command. The FTP server accepts the mechanism requested in the AUTH command, rejects the mechanism, or rejects the command entirely (when the server does not implement FTP security).

If any additional security information is required by the FTP server, it requests that the client using an ADAT command send this information. This exchange continues until a security association has been established.

After the secure connection has been established, the data protection can be set using the PROT command. Depending on the level set, MIC, CONF, or ENC commands will be used to transport the data in a secure manner over the data connection. The size of these packets of data is determined using the PBZ command.

A Typical FTP Session

The following set of commands shows a typical FTP session. All commands are preceded by either CLIENT> or SERVER> to indicate the source of the information.

```
CLIENT> D:\>ftp
CLIENT> ftp> open sideshowbri
SERVER>  Connected to sideshowbri.
SERVER>  220 sideshowbri Microsoft FTP Service (Version 3.0).
CLIENT> User (sideshowbri:(none)): ftp
SERVER>  331 Anonymous access allowed, send identity (e-mail name) as
➥password.
CLIENT> Password:
SERVER>  230-Welcome to the Sideshowbri FTP Server
SERVER>  ====================================
SERVER>   Anonymous access allowed!

SERVER>  230 Anonymous user logged in.
CLIENT> ftp> ls -F
SERVER>  200 PORT command successful.
S 150 Opening ASCII mode data connection for /bin/ls.
SERVER>  lanma256.bmp
SERVER>  Telnet Utilities/
SERVER>  226 Transfer complete.
SERVER>  33 bytes received in 0.01 seconds (3.30 Kbytes/sec)
CLIENT> ftp> cd "Telnet utilities"
SERVER>  250 CWD command successful.
CLIENT> ftp> ls
SERVER>  200 PORT command successful.
SERVER>  150 Opening ASCII mode data connection for file list.
SERVER>  teld4_x86_beta.exe
SERVER>  telftp32.exe
SERVER>  226 Transfer complete.
SERVER>  34 bytes received in 0.01 seconds (3.40 Kbytes/sec)
CLIENT> ftp> binary
SERVER>  200 Type set to I.
CLIENT> ftp> get telftp32.exe
SERVER>  200 PORT command successful.
SERVER>  150 Opening BINARY mode data connection for telftp32.exe(743758
➥bytes).
SERVER>  226 Transfer complete.
SERVER>  743758 bytes received in 3.11 seconds (238.84 Kbytes/sec)
CLIENT> ftp> bye
SERVER>  221 Thanks for visiting!
```

12

As you can see, the actual commands used are generally limited to the commands you require for acquiring a file. In this example, the FTP server SIDESHOWBRI was connected to. The FTP session used anonymous authentication by supplying the username FTP. After the session was established, the command ls -F was used to determine the contents of the FTP server's current directory. The -F option enabled us to distinguish between directories and files on the FTP server. After we changed directory to the directory Telnet Utilities, the file telftp32.exe was transferred using a binary transmission.

Using Archie to Search for FTP Resources

The toughest part about using FTP is knowing where to find the files on the Internet that you need to download.

Archie servers maintain an index of the anonymous FTP archives maintained on the Internet. Archie can respond to filename searches and file description searches.

You can use actual Archie utilities to find FTP file locations, but you can also use the Telnet utility to connect to an Archie server. Table 12.9 shows some of the Archie servers available around the world.

TABLE 12.9. A LISTING OF ARCHIE SERVERS BY COUNTRY.

Country	Archie Site
Canada	archie.mcgill.ca
Finland	archie.funet.fi
Japan	archie.wide.ap.jp
Taiwan	archie.ncu.edu.tw
United Kingdom	archie.doc.ic.ac.uk
USA	archie.internic.net
	archie.rutgers.edu

After you have decided on which Archie server to connect to, follow these steps to find a file on a remote FTP server.

1. Telnet to the appropriate Telnet server and log on as Archie.

```
/home/orgs/online/users/b/bkomar 1% telnet archie.mcgill.ca
Trying 192.77.55.2...
Connected to services.bunyip.com.
Escape character is '^]'.

SunOS UNIX (services.bunyip.com)
```

```
login: archie

# Bunyip Information Systems, Inc., 1993, 1994, 1995

# Terminal type set to 'vt100 24 80'.
# 'erase' character is '^?'.
# 'search' (type string) has the value 'sub'.
archie>
```

2. Set the Sortby option to indicate the display order for the returned information.

```
archie> set sortby time
```

3. Set the maximum hits that you want to have returned to you. Many times, you will receive more locations than you will know what to do with.

```
archie> set maxhits 10
```

4. You are now ready to type in your search. If you want to find the file winzip95.exe, type the following command:

```
archie> find winzip95.exe
# Search type: sub.
working...

    ftp://ftp.cam.org/downloads/w95/winzip95.exe
            Date: 20:41  4 Jun 1997      Size: 500684 bytes

    ftp://ftp.cam.org/systems/win95/extra/winzip95.exe
            Date: 05:00 13 Dec 1996      Size: 77512 bytes

    ftp://ftp.colorado.edu/cns/pc/Win95/HelperApps/winzip95.exe
            Date: 10:32 11 Dec 1996      Size: 628991 bytes

    ftp://ftp.cs.umass.edu/pc/win95/apps/WinZip95/winzip95.exe
            Date: 07:26 29 Oct 1996      Size: 628991 bytes

    ftp://infoserv.cc.uniaugsburg.de/pub/pc/windows/util/archive
    ➥/winzip/old_61/winzip95.exe.v61.gz
            Date: 17:00 26 May 1996      Size: 278 bytes

    ftp://ftp.cs.mun.ca/pub/win95/winzip95.exe
            Date: 19:00 17 Apr 1996      Size: 345015 bytes

    ftp://knot.queensu.ca/pub/win95/zip/winzip95.exe
            Date: 19:00  4 Mar 1996      Size: 367969 bytes
```

12

```
ftp://hubcap.clemson.edu/pub/pc_shareware/Windows95/Archive/winzip95.
exe
            Date: 19:00 30 Aug 1995      Size: 345015 bytes

     ftp://ftp.PHYSICS.OHIO-STATE.EDU/win3/winzip95.exe
            Date: 19:00 17 Aug 1995      Size: 345015 bytes

      ftp://igc.org/pub/INTERNET/windows/Misc/winzip95.exe
            Date: 05:00 15 Jun 1995      Size: 246352 bytes
```

5. After you have noted which FTP server you are going to connect to, you should
   end the Telnet session by typing the QUIT command

```
archie> quit
# Bye.
```

Trivial File Transfer Protocol (TFTP)

RFC 1350   *Trivial File Transfer Protocol* (TFTP) allows the transfer of files between two
           hosts using the UDP protocol. It does not provide as many features as FTP, but
does allow for the reading and writing of data files between two TCP/IP hosts. TFTP is
commonly implemented to download initializing code to printers, hubs, and routers.
DHCP or BOOTP clients that are diskless workstations use another implementation of
TFTP. A reference is supplied to a TFTP server from which the client can download an
image of its initialization code.

All data transferred using TFTP uses fixed-length packets of 512 bytes. If a packet is less
than 512 bytes, this indicates that this is the last packet of the data transfer. After a data
packet is sent to the destination host, the data is held in a buffer space until an acknowledgment is received to indicate that the data has been received successfully. If the sending host does not receive the acknowledgment before the retransmit timer expires, the
data packet will be re-sent. This does add a level of protection to the data stream above
and beyond the UDP checksum. Only the last packet must be maintained to ensure reliable delivery, as there is only a single outstanding data packet at any one time.

TFTP Message Formats

The following five types of messages can be sent during a TFTP session:

- Read Request (RRQ)
- Write Request (WRQ)
- Data (DATA)

- Acknowledgment (ACK)

- Error (ERR)

Both the *Read Request* (RRQ) and *Write Request* (WRQ) use the same message format (see Figure 12.2).

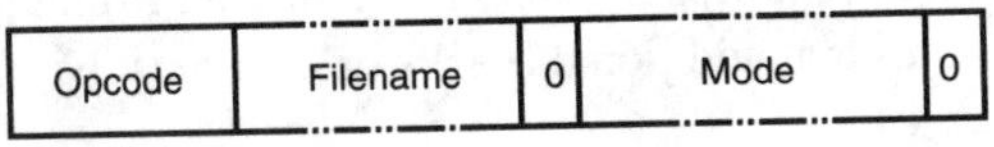

FIGURE 12.2.

A Read Request/Write Request TFTP packet format.

| Opcode | Filename | 0 | Mode | 0 |

- The Opcode *field* contains 1 for a Read Request and a 2 for a Write Request.

- The Filename indicates the name of the file that is either being uploaded or downloaded from the TFTP server. The filename is transmitted as NETASCII characters using a variable-length field.

- The 0 is used to indicate the end of the filename field.

- The Mode field indicates the type of transfer that is to take place. Allowable values include NETASCII and OCTET. The NETASCII mode is used to transfer text documents. *NETASCII* is 8-bit ASCII as used in the Telnet protocol. *OCTET* is used for the transfer of binary data using raw 8-bit bytes.

- The 0 is used to indicate the end of the Mode field.

ANOTHER TFTP TRANSFER MODE

There is also an obsolete mode that was originally implemented in TFTP known as Mail mode. This allowed NETASCII characters to be transmitted to a user's email address rather than to a file destination.

12

Actual data is transferred in TFTP using the DATA message format (see Figure 12.3). The DATA message will contain the actual file contents as the file is transferred from one host to another.

- The Opcode field will be set to a value of 3 to indicate that data is being transmitted the TFTP message.

- The Block # field will be set to a value of one for the initial DATA packet. Each additional packet will be incremented by 1 until the entire file has been transmitted.

FIGURE 12.3.

A TFTP DATA message.

The Data field will be up to 512 bytes in length. If the Data field is less than 512 bytes, this indicates that it is the final block of data from the file. If it is 512 bytes long, this indicates that additional blocks of data must be transmitted to complete the file transfer.

Figure 12.4 shows a TFTP *Acknowledgment* (ACK) packet. Each DATA packet and WRQ packet are responded to with either an ACK packet (if received successfully) or an ERROR packet if the data was corrupted or incorrect.

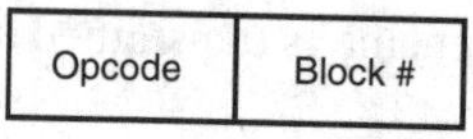

FIGURE 12.4.

A TFTP Acknowledgment (ACK) packet.

The Opcode field in an ACK packet will have a value of 4. The Block # field will contain the Block # of the DATA packet that is being acknowledged. If the acknowledgment is in response to a Write Request (WRQ) packet, the Block # will be set to 0 to indicate that data transfer can commence.

Table 12.10 shows the TFTP error codes that can be returned when an error takes place during a TFTP transmission.

TABLE 12.10. TFTP ERROR CODES.

Error Code	Description
0	Undefined error, the error message will provide any additional information as to the cause of the error.
1	File not found. An incorrect filename has been provided.
2	Access violation. Insufficient security rights have caused an error during the transmission of the data.
3	Disk full or allocation exceeded.
4	Illegal TFTP operation.
5	Unknown transfer ID.
6	File already exists.
7	No such user.

Figure 12.5 shows the *TFTP Error* (ERR) message format.

FIGURE 12.5.
The TFTP Error packet.

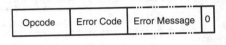

The Error packet will have an Opcode field set to a value of 5. The Error Code field will be set to one of the values shown in Table 12.1. The Error Message field is stored in NETASCII format and adds a text description to assist in debugging TFTP error messages. Because the Error Message field is of variable length, the error message is always terminated with a 0.

Connecting to a TFTP Server

Two common transactions take place when a client connects to a TFTP server. The client either uploads data to the TFTP server using a Write Request or downloads data from the TFTP server using a Read Request.

Figure 12.6 shows the communication sequence that takes place when a Write Request is sent to the TFTP server.

FIGURE 12.6.
A Write Request to a TFTP server.

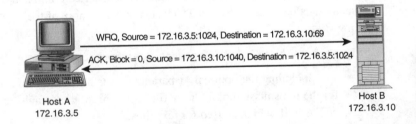

12

The sending host (Host A) will send a TFTP message with the Opcode set to 2 for a Write Request. Within the TFTP message, the source port will be set to a random port number over port 1024. The destination port for the Write Request will always be UDP port 69 by default. The TFTP server (Host B) responds with a TFTP acknowledge message. This message will set the block # to be a value of 0. This indicates that the TFTP server is ready to begin receiving data from the sending host. Within the TFTP message, the TFTP server will now set the UDP port that it will listen on for future data transmissions for this data transfer. Data will now be transferred in 512-byte packets until the data has been sent. The final packet will be less than 512 bytes.

Figure 12.7 shows the communication sequence that takes place when the TFTP client wants to download a file from the TFTP server.

FIGURE 12.7.

*A Read Request to a
TFTP server.*

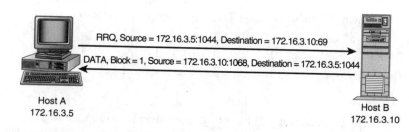

RRQ, Source = 172.16.3.5:1044, Destination = 172.16.3.10:69

DATA, Block = 1, Source = 172.16.3.10:1068, Destination = 172.16.3.5:1044

Host A
172.16.3.5

Host B
172.16.3.10

Host A sends a TFTP Read request message to Host B. The Opcode will be set to a value
of 1 to indicate that the request is a Read Request. Within the Read Request message,
Host A sets its Transport ID to be the random UDP port that it has selected for the data
transmission. In this case, port 1044 was selected. The Read Request will always be sent
to UDP port 69 on the TFTP server by default. The TFTP server responds with a TFTP
DATA packet. The initial DATA packet will have a block # of 1 and will include the first
512 bytes of data. Within the first DATA packet, the TFTP server will set its Transport
ID. Each successive DATA packet will contain 512 bytes of data and increment the block
by 1 for each DATA packet. The final packet will have a size less than 512 bytes.

TFTP Client Software

The TFTP command in most UNIX shells is a text-based command that enables you to
transmit data either to or from a TFTP server. The syntax of the TFTP command is as
follows:

TFTP [-i] *host* [GET ¦ PUT] source [*destination*]

- -i   Including the optional –i parameter sets the data transfer to use OCTET mode
  for the transmission of a binary file. If not used, the default transfer mode is
  NETASCII, which is used for text files.
- host   Indicates the hostname of the TFTP server.
- GET   This transaction copies a file from the TFTP server to the host running the
  client software.
- PUT   This transaction copies a file from the host running the TFTP client software
  to the TFTP server.
- Source   The name of the file to be downloaded from or uploaded to the TFTP
  server.
- destination   The name that is to be used for the file after it has been transferred.
  This is often referred to as the *Target filename.*

Common Uses of TFTP

The TFTP protocol is not used that often for actual transmission of data. It is most commonly used for downloading configuration information to hosts. The two most common implementations include the configuration of routers and the configuration of BOOTP hosts.

Routers can store the configuration parameters on a TFTP server. This provides a method of fault tolerance for routers. If a router crashes, the correct configuration can be downloaded from the TFTP server to either the repaired router or to a replacement router.

ROUTER CONFIGURATION ISSUES

Make sure the router being used as a replacement router has the same router operating system and if possible is the same version of the router. In the case of CISCO routers, the router operating system allows different configuration parameters to be used.

The BOOTP protocol contains a reference to a TFTP server that can contain the configuration files for the BOOTP client. After an initial IP configuration has been retrieved from the BOOTP server, the TFTP server is contacted for downloading the operating system. This is an extremely efficient method for transferring the data to the BOOTP client. This can also be performed in some implementations of the DHCP protocol.

Remote Copy Protocol (RCP)

12

The *Remote Copy Protocol* (RCP) is part of the Berkeley R-Utilities suite. It enables you to copy directories and their contents to and from a remote host.

As with the RSH and RLOGIN utilities discussed in yesterday's material, the RCP command makes use of the hosts.equiv and .rhosts files to determine which hosts and users can run the RCP command.

The syntax of the RCP command is as follows:

```
RCP [-r] host1:file1 host2:file2
```

- [-r]   This option allows a recursive copy to take place. This will include the contents of the indicated directory and all of its subdirectory contents.
- host1:file1   This is the file to be copied from. If host1 is the local computer, the directory and filename are all that must be provided.
- host2:file2   This is the destination file and directory for the copy process.

If you wanted to copy the file budget.txt from the local directory
/usr/bkomar/reports to the remote host PSCOTT in the directory /usr/pscott, for
example, you would use the following syntax:

```
RCP /usr/bkomar/reports/budget.txt pscott:/usr/pscott
```

Likewise, if you wanted to copy the entire contents of the /data/accounting directory
to the /data/budget directory on the remote host named IRONMAN, you would use the
following command:

```
RCP -r /data/accounting ironman:/data/budget
```

Finally, if you wanted to copy the directory structure /data/marketing on the host
named PSCOTT to the directory structure /data/marketing/1998 on the host named
IRONMAN, you would use the following command:

```
rcp -r pscott:/data/marketing ironman:/data/marketing/1998
```

Gopher

 Gopher was the first attempt at making the Internet easier to access. Gopher provided a menu-based system that enabled a user to navigate through
gopherspace—the collection of all Gopher servers on the Internet.

Gopher was developed at the University of Minnesota and literally means that it will
"Go For" you and satisfy your requests. A gopher also happens to be the mascot for the
University of Minnesota. Although most people are presently using Web browsers for
navigating the Internet, Gopher is still a good resource for text-based documents.

Gopher provides a client/server model document delivery system. Clients connect to a
Gopher server on TCP port 70. Once connected, they can connect to any information via
a hierarchical menu system. This structure was chosen because it is very familiar to DOS
and UNIX users. They can navigate though a series of menus to acquire the files that
they are looking for.

When the Gopher client communicates with the Gopher server, it opens a connection to
the Gopher server on TCP port 70 and sends the request to the Gopher server using a

---

GRAPHICAL GOPHER CLIENTS

If the client supports a graphical environment, users can use a mouse to
point and click on the resources they want to view.

selector. The Gopher server sends the response and then closes the connection. When the server sends the response, the first character returned in a line of information describes the type of information being returned. A [CR][LF] combination is used to indicate the end of a line of information. The values sent in the first character include the following:

- 0   Document.
- 1   Directory.
- 2   Item is a CSO phonebook server.
- 3   Error.
- 4   Item is a BinHexed Macintosh file.
- 5   Item is a DOS binary archive of some sort.
- 6   Item is a UNIX uuencoded file.
- 7   Item is a reference to a Gopher search service.
- 8   Item points to a text-based Telnet session.
- 9   Item is a binary file.
- +   Item is a redundant server.
- T   Item points to a text-based TN3270 session.
- G   Item is a GIF format graphics file.
- I   Item is an image file—client will decide how to display.

In a graphical Gopher client, the first character of each line is used to determine an icon to display to the left of each line of information. The final line returned by the server just includes a period (.). This indicates that all server data has been sent and the connection should be terminated.

Common Uses of Gopher

Some of the more common uses of Gopher include the following:

- Checking local area weather reports
- Searching for text archives of the Internet
- Browsing text-based information on the Internet

Searching Gopherspace

When connected to a Gopher server, you can use the following three common search engines to find information in gopherspace:

12

- *Veronica*. Very Easy Rodent-Oriented Netwide Index to Computerized Archives
- *Jughead*. Jonzy's Universal Gopher Hierarchy Excavation and Display
- *WAIS*. Wide Area Information Server

A DESPERATE NEED FOR ACRONYMS

You may have noticed a definite Archie connection in the search engines for FTP and Gopher. Although it is denied in all journals that there is any relation to the Archie comic books, you can't help noticing the desperate measures used to create meanings for these acronyms in the Gopher search engines.

Veronica maintains an index of all the menus in gopherspace. Queries can be performed against the index to find a menu with your search keywords included. Search strings can include logical operators such as AND, OR, and NOT to create a more succinct query. The advantage of a Veronica server over an Archie server is that the responses are returned in a Gopher model that enables you to link to the Gopher servers that contain the data that you were searching for.

Jughead takes a Veronica search to the next level. Rather than just maintaining an index of top-level menus, a Jughead index also includes nested menus. This can lead to more accurate search results.

A *WAIS* search enables you to search the actual text of documents stored on a Gopher server. In addition, queries do not have to be performed using Boolean strings, but rather simple English.

Hypertext Transfer Protocol (HTTP)

RFC 2068 The *Hypertext Transfer Protocol* (HTTP) is the protocol used when exploring the *World Wide Web* (WWW). The HTTP protocol is implemented as a request/response protocol. A client requests that a page be transferred to him from the Web server. The Web server responds with the contents of that page.

The HTTP protocol is currently on its third revision. This protocol works at the application level. A client sends a request to the HTTP server (normally on TCP port 80); the HTTP server interprets the request and sends an appropriate response to the client. The actual communication is connectionless and stateless. After the HTTP server has responded to the client's request, the connection is dropped until the next request is posted. The exception to this scenario is when the client implements HTTP keep-alives that are supported under HTTP 1.1. In this case, the client would maintain the connection rather than establish a new session.

Several methods are used in HTTP requests, including the following:

- The GET method
- The HEAD method
- The POST method
- The PUT method
- The DELETE method
- The TRACE method
- The CONNECT method

The GET method is used to retrieve the indicated information in an HTTP request. GET allows additional flexibility through the use of IF statements. This can lead to what is known as a *conditional GET*. When the condition in the IF statement is met, the data is transferred. This enables HTTP clients to utilize cached copies of Web pages if they have not been recently updated. This leads to a better utilization of network bandwidth.

The HEAD method works much the same as the GET method except that the message body is not returned to the client. This method is often used to determine whether a link is still valid or has been recently modified. The modification is tested by comparing the information sent in the REQUEST header with the response received in the RESPONSE header.

The POST method is used to request that the HTTP server accept the attached data as a new posting to the HTTP server. This can be used to post messages to a newsgroup, the submission of an HTML form to the HTTP server, or the addition of a record of data to a database hosted on an HTTP server.

The PUT method is used to request that the data sent in the request be stored on the resource indicated in the REQUEST message. This differs from the POST method in that the target can be specified for the data. If the data already exists, the data should be considered to be a modification of the existing data.

The DELETE method is used to request that the HTTP server delete the resource indicated in the REQUEST message. This method may be overridden by human intervention or by security set on the HTTP server. A success response should be sent only if the HTTP server intends to delete the resource.

The TRACE method is used to ensure that the data received at the HTTP server is correct. The TRACE response is the actual HTTP request that was received by the HTTP server. This allows for testing and debugging of the HTTP request to take place.

12

The CONNECT method is reserved for use by *SSL* (Secure Socket Layer) *tunneling*.

HTTP 1.1 is currently being defined as the new standard for the HTTP protocol. Some of the new features that have been added to the newest version of the HTTP protocol include the following:

- *Persistent connections*. HTTP 1.1 now allows for multiple requests to be service in the same connection. Previous implementations of the protocol required that a separate connection be established for each graphic embedded on a Web page.

- *Pipelining*. This feature allows additional requests to be sent to a Web server before the response to their initial request has been received. This results in a greater performance boost.

- *Caching directives*. The implementation of caching directives allows default caching algorithms on both the client and server to be overridden and optimized.

- *Host headers*. This HTTP 1.1 option allows multiple hostnames to be associated with a single IP address. This eliminates the need for multiple IP addresses to be assigned to a Web server that is hosting many virtual servers. The host header is used to determine which virtual server the request should be directed to.

- *PUT and DELETE options*. These commands enable a remote administrator to post and remove content from a Web server by using a standard Web browser.

- *HTTP redirects*. This feature enables an administrator to redirect a user to an alternative page or Web site if the original page is unavailable or has been removed.

COMMON HTTP SERVERS

Three common HTTP servers are being implemented today. The most popular being the shareware APACHE Web server that runs on most UNIX systems. Other popular Web servers include Netscape's Enterprise Server and Microsoft's Internet Information Server. The Netscape Enterprise Server runs on the most platforms including Windows NT, LINUX, and SCO UNIX. Internet Information Server (IIS) runs only on the Windows NT Server platform.

Security in HTTP

Several methods can be implemented for securing information transmitted via an HTTP connection. The two most common methods involve *encryption* of the actual data transmission and *authentication* of both the client and server components.

One of the most common methods used for security in an HTTP environment is the use of a *Secure Sockets Layer* (SSL). SSL functions as a layer between the TCP/IP transport layer and the application layer. All transmissions between the client and server are encrypted and decrypted by the SSL. The implementation of SSL is accomplished through the use of SSL *digital certificates*.

Figure 12.8 shows a typical SSL communication sequence.

FIGURE 12.8.

The SSL handshake process.

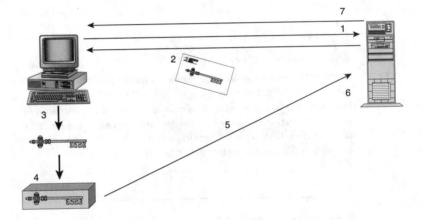

1. The client makes a security request to the server.
2. The server sends to the client its certificate. This certificate contains the client's public key and the client's cipher preferences.

PUBLIC AND PRIVATE KEYS

Many encryption mechanisms use what are known as public/private key pairs. If a private key is used to encrypt a package, only its matching public key can be used to decrypt the package. Likewise, if the public key is used to encrypt a package, only its matching private key can be used to decrypt the package. Day 16, "Firewalls and Security," discusses public/private key technology in detail.

---

3. The client generates a master key.
4. The client encrypts the master key using the server's public key that it received in step 2. The master key of the client can now only be decrypted by the server's private key that is only located on the server.

12

5. The client transmits the encrypted master key to the server.

6. The server decrypts the client's master key using the server's private key.

7. The server authenticates with the client by returning a message to the client that is encrypted using the client's master key. This authenticates both sides of the session.

All following data will be encrypted and decrypted using the master key that was sent to the server.

BASIC AUTHENTICATION OPTION

Many Web servers can also implement a basic security option. This will prompt the visitors of a Web page for a valid user account and password before access to the Web page is granted. The major problem with this form of authentication is that the username and password are passed on the network as clear text. Anyone running a network sniffer can capture this account and password and break in using this account.

HOW TO KNOW WHEN SSL IS BEING USED

All Web pages that institute SSL will have HTTPS:// in the *Universal Resource Locator* (URL) for the Web page. If you do not see HTTPS:// for what is supposed to be a secure Web site, do not input any valuable information such as a credit-card number. You will also see additional indicators that a secure connection has been established in both Netscape and Internet Explorer. In Netscape, a key appears at the bottom of the window. Likewise, in Internet Explorer, a lock appears at the bottom of the window.

Finding Resources on the Web

You can use several search engines to find resources on the Web. The following sites can currently be used to search for information. I do not prefer any one site, and have found that I will repeat the same search on multiple sites when researching information.

- www.infoseek.com
- www.excite.com
- www.altavista.digital.com
- www.yahoo.com

- www.lycos.com
- www.hotbot.com
- www.dejanews.com
- www.webcrawler.com
- www.metacrawler.com
- www.mamma.com

ADVANCED SEARCH ENGINES

The search engines located at www.metacrawler.com and www.mamma.com (the mother-of-all search engines) are meta search engines. Rather than perform their own searches, they act as brokers for your search request. They use multiple instances of other search engines and return the results from multiple search engines.

SO WHAT DO I USE TO SEARCH?

This chapter has reviewed several methods for searching for information on the Internet. More and more people are moving toward using Web search engines exclusively, because more and more information is only being stored in Web archives. The search engines also perform searches of FTP servers.

12

Applying What You Have Learned

Today's material reviewed many of the file transfer protocols available in a TCP/IP network. Most of the file transfers that you will be performing on a TCP/IP network will probably involve the FTP protocol. Remember that several freeware and shareware utilities can be used for file transfers, and that these are much more intuitive than the text-based methods discussed in the book. An excellent GUI-based FTP client is the WS_FTP32 client.

Test Your Knowledge

1. What are some of the key differences between the FTP and TFTP protocols?
2. What is meant by the term *anonymous FTP*?
3. Compare the security of Remote Copy Protocol (RCP) and the File Transfer Protocol (FTP).

4. What are some of the methods that can be used to search for a file in gopherspace?

5. What are some of the methods that can be used to search for a topic on the World Wide Web?

6. What are the two communication channels used during an FTP session? What ports are used on the server side during this session?

7. Describe the steps involved in the establishment of a Secure Socket Layer session?

Preview of the Next Day

Tomorrow's material focuses on the use of electronic mail in a TCP/IP network. Topics include the protocols used for mail transport. These include Simple Mail Transfer Protocol (SMTP), Post Office Protocol 3 (POP3), and Internet Mail Access Protocol (IMAP).

The material also looks into the issues involved with mail attachments. Various methods for implementing attachments are also overviewed.

Finally, we look at the directory services provided by the Lightweight Directory Access Protocol (LDAP).

DAY **13**

Electronic Mail over TCP/IP

Today's material investigates the various protocols required to implement an email system in a TCP/IP network. The protocols—used to send and retrieve email—discussed include the following:

- Simple Mail Transfer Protocol (SMTP)
- Post Office Protocol 3 (POP3)
- Internet Mail Access Protocol (IMAP)

Other email-related topics discussed in today's material include the need for directory services to find email addresses. The Lightweight Directory Access Protocol (LDAP) provides this functionality.

I also discuss the topic of email attachments. Many people receive attachments and find it difficult to open them. I review the common methods of attaching documents to email and discuss some of the tools that exist for extracting these attachments.

Internet Email at a Glance

Internet email is probably the most used of all applications running on a TCP/IP network. With the explosive growth of the Internet, the use of email in the business place is becoming more and more a required tool.

FOR THOSE OF YOU WHO ARE FAMILIAR WITH EMAIL

If you are familiar with the concepts involved with Internet email, you might want to skip ahead to the next section in today's material titled "Simple Mail Transfer Protocol" where we start looking at the specifics of SMTP.

Some of the reasons that offices are moving toward using email as a standard of communication include the following:

- It is a cheaper alternative than faxing or sending a floppy disk through the post office or courier.

- Email offers quick delivery of a message to the recipient. Time is generally measured in terms of seconds and minutes rather than days and weeks.

- Email can reach a recipient even if he is not at his normal location (such as being on a business trip). The recipient can connect to his mail server from anywhere in the world and access new mail.

- Through the use of tools such as *PGP* (Pretty Good Privacy), data can be transported in a secure manner using email.

Although there are many positives, email has some negative points also, including the following:

- You require a computer or access to a computer to view your email. This is slowly becoming less of a requirement as technologies such as digital phones (with email access) and Web TV start to become available.

- Email does not offer the same response time as just talking to the other party via a phone call or in person.

- Sometimes email is abused. Receiving items such as chain letters and "junk" email is one of my biggest frustrations.

Internet email uses a unique method of addressing for recipients. The address contains both the mailbox of the recipient whom you wish to contact and the domain that is hosting the recipient's mailbox.

The format of an Internet email address is `mailbox@domain`, in which the `mailbox` is generally the recipient's account name and the `domain` is the name of the company or Internet service provider's domain name on the Internet.

My email address is `bkomar@online-can.com`, for example. This indicates that my mailbox name is `bkomar` and it is hosted by the Internet domain `online-can.com`. In addition to addresses for mailboxes, there are also addresses known as *aliases*. Aliases are commonly used for email addresses that serve some functionality in the organization. At Online Business Systems where I work, for example, applicants can send email to `personnel@online-can.com`. This is an alias for Online's Human Resources director. Rather than give out their personal address, we use the alias "personnel" for their account. All the actual email arrives at the same mailbox.

Another common type of email address is known as a *distribution list*. The addresses do not have to be members of the same Internet domain. They are just referred to by a single name. I could create a distribution list named `instructors@online-can.com`, for example, and include the addresses `bkomar@online-can.com`, `psmith@online-can.com`, `djones@online-can.com`, `jkeel@online-can.com`, and `swant@online-can.com` as members of the distribution list. Rather than addressing the email individually to each instructor, you could send email to `instructors@online-can.com`.

Simple Mail Transfer Protocol (SMTP)

RFC 821 *Simple Mail Transfer Protocol* (SMTP) provides message transfer between two hosts. SMTP uses the TCP protocol for transport. An SMTP server listens on TCP port 25 for connections.

SMTP defines both the message format and the methods that will be used for transferring email between two SMTP hosts. The sending host uses SMTP commands to transfer the email to the receiving host. After the transport has completed, the connection is closed between the two hosts.

The SMTP Process

A typical SMTP connection involves six steps (see Figure 13.1).

1. The SMTP client initiates a connection to the SMTP server. The client uses a random port above 1024 and connects to the server's TCP port 25. On accepting the connection, the SMTP server will respond with a `220 <Ready>` message.

13

FIGURE 13.1.

The SMTP process.

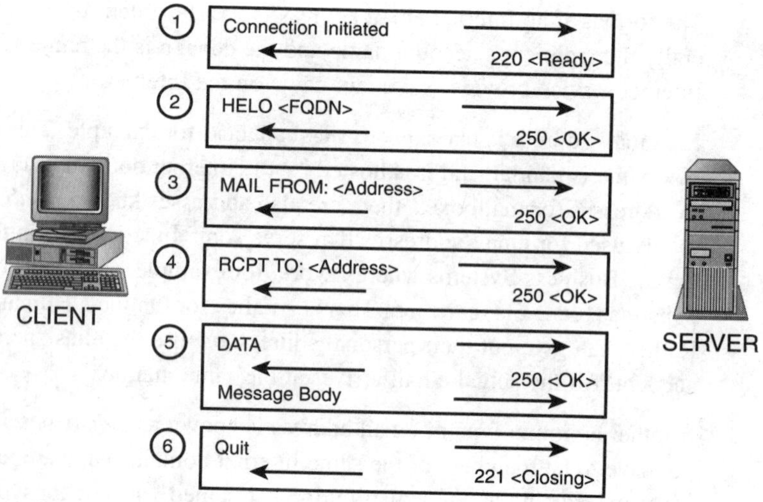

2. The SMTP client requests that the SMTP session be established by sending a HELO (Hello) command. This command should include the Fully Qualified Domain Name (FQDN) of the SMTP client. The SMTP server should respond with a 250 <OK> message.

3. The SMTP client informs the SMTP server who is sending the message with the MAIL FROM: <Address> command, in which the <Address> parameter is the Internet email address of the sending user. This is generally configured as the reply address in the email client software. The SMTP server should respond with a 250 <OK> message.

4. The SMTP client now identifies all the recipients for whom the message is intended using the RCPT TO: <Address> command. If multiple recipients are hosted on the SMTP server, a RCPT TO: command is issued for each of the recipients. The SMTP server responds to each of the recipients with a 250 <OK> message.

5. The SMTP client indicates that it is prepared to transmit the actual email message by issuing the DATA command. The server responds with a 250 <OK> message. It also indicates the string that it will expect to end the body text of the message. Most often this is the string [CR][LF].[CR][LF]. The actual message is now transmitted to the SMTP server. The message is transmitted using 7-bit ASCII characters. If any attachments exist in the message, the attachments must be encoded into a 7-bit stream using BinHex, uuencode, or MIME.

6. After the message has been successfully transmitted, the SMTP client sends a QUIT command to terminate the SMTP session. The SMTP server responds with a 221

<Closing> message to indicate that the session termination has taken place. If the SMTP client had another message to transmit, it could issue the MAIL FROM: command again.

The following code sample shows a typical SMTP connection. Client commands are shown in bold in the transcript.

```
/users/bkomar% telnet mail.escape.ca 25
220 wpg-01.escape.ca ESMTP Sendmail 8.8.7/8.7.5 ready at Sun, 22 Mar 1998
➥19:35:25 -0600 (CST)
helo
250 wpg-01.escape.ca Hello bkomar@wpg-03.escape.ca [198.163.232.252],
➥pleased to meet you
mail from:bkomar@escape.ca
250 bkomar@escape.ca... Sender ok
rcpt to:bkomar@online-can.com
250 bkomar@online-can.com... Recipient ok
data
354 Enter mail, end with "." on a line by itself
subject:This is a test

This was sent by connecting to an SMTP server
.
250 TAA16829 Message accepted for delivery
QUIT
```

This session connected to the SMTP server mail.escape.ca. Once connected, issuing the command HELO started an SMTP session. After the SMTP session was established, a message was sent from bkomar@escape.ca to bkomar@online-can.com. This message sent had the subject This is a test. To complete the message, a single period was entered on a line as the SMTP server indicated.

Other SMTP Requirements

For mail to be successfully delivered to an SMTP server, the SMTP client must be able to resolve the domain portion of the Internet email address to an IP address. This is normally done through DNS. For more information on the DNS, review Day 8, "Configuring Domain Name Servers."

DNS has special records that indicate the *mail exchanger* for a domain. This is represented using an *MX* (mail exchanger) record. When a client is sending email to bkomar@online-can.com, for example, the SMTP client performs a resolution for the MX record for the domain online-can.com. The MX record indicates the hostname of the mail exchanger for online-can.com. An additional DNS lookup may have to take place to determine the IP address of the mail exchanger so that the SMTP process can be established to the SMTP server.

13

> **MX RECORD CONFIGURATION**
>
> MX records in DNS should refer *only* to A (address) records in DNS. They
> should not refer to CNAME records. This causes additional resolution to have
> to take place. This could lead to inefficient mail delivery and potential mail
> failure.

Within the DNS configuration files, MX records appear as follows:

```
online-can.com          IN    MX    10    mail.online-can.com.
online-can.com          IN    MX    20    mail2.online-can.com.
```

There can be more than one MX record for a domain to provide alternative delivery
points for Internet email. The preference number in the MX record is used to rank the
preference of mail servers for a domain. The SMTP servers are contacted in an order
based on the preference numbers. A lower preference number indicates a higher priority
for the mail exchanger. In the example shown, email is sent to `mail.online-can.com` for
the `online-can.com` domain. If `mail.online-can.com` is not available, it is sent to
`mail2.online-can.com`.

Post Office Protocol 3 (POP3)

RFC 1939   The *Post Office Protocol 3* (POP3) protocol is the most common client protocol
that is used for the retrieval of email messages. Initially, SMTP was used for
both sending and receiving email. This worked well in an environment when all hosts
were on the same network and were available at all hours of the day. As time has pro-
gressed, most people are now connecting to the email servers from varying computers or
from different locations. This intermittent checking for messages has resulted in the
development of protocols such as POP3.

A POP3 server is best compared to a mail-drop system. The POP3 server holds the mail
until the user connects and removes the mail from the server. Some POP3 clients do
allow you to leave the mail on the POP3 server, but this is a client configuration. It is not
part of the POP3 protocol itself. POP3 servers do sometimes *not* support this feature or
limits are imposed on the amount of mail that can be left on a POP3 server.

Figure 13.2 shows the steps involved in a POP3 session.

FIGURE 13.2.

A POP3 client session.

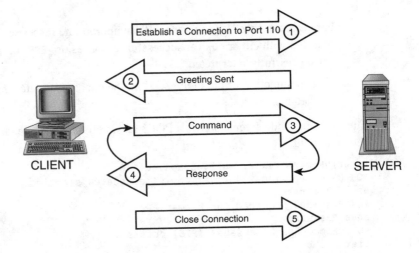

1. The POP3 client connects to the POP3 server. The POP3 server will be listening on port 110 for client connections.

2. The POP3 server sends the client a greeting. The greeting generally contains the name and version of the POP3 server that is running.

3. All of the following steps consist of commands and responses from the POP3 server. The initial command involves authentication with the POP3 server. The client must identify himself with a USER *<username>* and PASS *<password>* command. After the user has been authenticated, several commands can be executed. Table 13.1 itemizes the specific POP3 commands that can be sent from the client to the server.

TABLE 13.1. POP3-SUPPORTED COMMANDS.

Command	Description
AUTH	This command is used to specify the type of authentication that is to be used for the session.
USER *<username>*	This command is used to identify the mailbox that the user is connecting to.
PASS *<password>*	This command sends the password for the mailbox to the POP3 server. This password is sent by clear text by default. Secure Socket Layers can be implemented in some cases to better protect the user's password.
QUIT	This command terminates the POP3 session.
STAT	This command indicates the number of messages that are stored on the server and the total amount of disk space that they occupy.
LIST *<msg #>*	This command indicates the approximate size of the indicated message.
RETR *<msg #>*	This command retrieves the indicated message number.
NOOP	This command indicates that no operation should take place.
TOP *<msg #> n*	This command displays the first *n* lines of the indicated message number.

4. For each command, the server sends an appropriate response. The responses are prefaced with either +OK for successful responses or -ERR for commands that were not successfully interpreted.

5. Upon completion of the POP3 session, the client terminates the session using the QUIT command.

The following code sample shows a POP3 session transcript. The client commands are shown in bold.

```
/user/bkomar% telnet mail.escape.ca 110
+OK QPOP (version 2.4b2) at wpg-01.escape.ca starting.
user bkomar
+OK Password required for bkomar.
pass Password
+OK bkomar has 2 messages (2767 octets).
stat
+OK 2 2767
retr 2
+OK 1057 octets
Return-Path: bkomar@online-can.com
Received: by wpg-01.escape.ca (8.8.7/8.7.5) with SMTP id TAA16267 for
➥<bkomar@escape.ca>;
 Sun, 22 Mar 1998 19:33:08 -0600 (CST)
Message-ID: <000301bd55fc$20eb8f30$080810ac@bkhome.online-can.com>
From: "Brian Komar" <bkomar@online-can.com>
To: <bkomar@escape.ca>
Subject: Another Test Message
Date: Sun, 22 Mar 1998 19:36:38 -0600
MIME-Version: 1.0
        charset="iso-8859-1"
Content-Transfer-Encoding: 7bit
Content-Type: text/plain;

Did you receive this okay!!!

Brian
QUIT
+OK Pop server at wpg-01.escape.ca signing off.
Connection closed by foreign host.
```

As you can see, the client bkomar connected to the POP3 server using the password of Password. The STAT command showed that there were two messages on the POP3 server using a total disk space of 2767 bytes. The second message was retrieved. This was a message from bkomar@online-can.com with the subject Another Test Message.

Internet Message Access Protocol (IMAP)

RFC 2060 *Internet Mail Access Protocol* (IMAP) is a newer form of email transport protocol. It has been built with more features than the older POP3 protocol, but has not been implemented in as great of numbers.

IMAP offers the following advantages over the POP3 protocol:

- IMAP clients are not sent the contents of every mail file. The IMAP server sends only a short menu of waiting messages; this results in quicker transmission times.
- IMAP allows messages to be stored in a hierarchical structure on the IMAP server. Rather than storing the messages locally (as the default is for POP3), the messages are stored on the server.
- Because the messages are stored on the IMAP server, the messages can be accessed from multiple IMAP clients and users can still see the same status information for all messages. This includes Read and Reply status.
- IMAP servers understand MIME file extensions. This enables an IMAP client to select which portions of a message he wants to retrieve. If an important message also includes a 5MB AVI attachment, for example, the client could choose to retrieve only the text message.
- IMAP supports online, offline, and disconnected access modes. POP3 supports only the online mode.

IMAP Message Attributes

One of the key features of IMAP mail is that messages are stored on a central IMAP server. This allows multiple clients to connect to the same mailbox. This requires the implementation of flags to indicate the current status of a message. Each message can be assigned one or more separate flags to indicate the status of a message.

Currently defined system flags include the following:

- \Seen—This flag indicates that the message has been previously read.
- \Answered—This flag indicates that a Reply has been sent in response to this message.
- \Flagged—This flag indicates that an Urgent or Special Attention flag has been set for this message.
- \Deleted—This flag indicates that this message has been marked for deletion by an EXPUNGE command.

13

- \Draft—This flag is set on a message that has been saved for later delivery on the IMAP client. This is commonly referred to as a draft message.

- \Recent—This flag is assigned to messages that have just arrived in the mailbox. This flag exists only during the first session in which the message arrives. Thereafter, this flag is not set.

IMAP States and Their Associated Commands

The following four different states can exist for an IMAP session between an IMAP client and an IMAP server:

- Non-authenticated state
- Authenticated state
- Selected state
- Logout state

Within each of these states, the client can execute associated IMAP commands. Each command is issued with an alphanumeric prefix used to tie a response back to the original command. If you were to request the language capabilities of the IMAP server, for example, you would proceed through the following command sequence:

```
Client: 0001 Capability
Server: * CAPABILITY IMAP4 IMAP4rev1 AUTH=Kerberos_v4 AUTH=NTLM
Server: 0001 OK Capability Completed
```

where 0001 is the alphanumeric prefix that indicates that the response was in regard to the CAPABILITY command issued in the first line.

Some IMAP client commands can be issued in any of the four states. Table 13.2 shows these commands.

TABLE 13.2. IMAP COMMANDS VALID IN ANY STATE.

Command	Description
CAPABILITY	This command requests a listing of all the capabilities that the server will support. If a capability is prefixed by "Auth=", this represents an authentication method that can be used to authenticate with the server.
NOOP	This command will always succeed. It is used commonly as a polling mechanism for new messages and to prevent the session from disconnecting because of the auto-logout timer expiring.
LOGOUT	This command is used to inform the server that the client is ready to terminate the connection. The server will send a BYE response before responding OK to the LOGOUT request.
QUIT	This command terminates the POP3 session.

Non-Authenticated State Commands

The *non-authenticated state* is very limited in the commands that can be issued. The goal of this state is to authenticate users so that they can start to manage their server-based email store. This state is entered after the connection has been started between the IMAP client and the IMAP server.

Table 13.3 shows the two commands that are available in the non-authenticated state.

TABLE 13.3. IMAP COMMANDS VALID IN THE NON-AUTHENTICATED STATE.

Command	Description
AUTHENTICATE *method*	This command indicates the authentication *method* that will be used for this session. If the server supports the authentication mechanism, it performs the selected authentication routine. The actual exchange depends on the authentication mechanism indicated. After the mechanism is negotiated, it is applied to all subsequent data transmitted in the session.
LOGIN *user password*	This command identifies the *user* to the server and sends the associated *password*. This *password* may or may not be sent as clear text across the network, depending on the authentication method selected.

Authenticated State Commands

The *authenticated state* is entered after the IMAP client has successfully authenticated with the IMAP server. In this state, the client's primary task is to indicate the mailbox to which he will be connecting. This is the mailbox to which the client will be issuing mail management commands. Other tasks that can be performed in this state include creating and deleting mailboxes, adjusting subscriptions, and checking the status of mailboxes. Table 13.4 shows the commands available in the authenticated state.

TABLE 13.4. IMAP COMMANDS VALID IN THE AUTHENTICATED STATE.

Command	Description
Select *mailbox*	This command is used to select the *mailbox* to be inspected in the selected state. If another mailbox is currently selected, the select command automatically de-selects the preceding mailbox.

continues

13

TABLE 13.4. CONTINUED

Command	Description
Examine *mailbox*	This command is much like the Select command. The difference is that the Examine command gives read access only to a mailbox; the Select command can provide read/write access.
Create *mailbox*	This command allows a new mailbox to be created with the mailbox name. If the mailbox that is named includes parent folders in its name, these parent folders will also be created if they do not exist beforehand.
Delete *mailbox*	This command is used to permanently remove the indicated mailbox. The indicated mailbox cannot be removed if subfolders exist below it.
Rename *mailbox newmailbox*	This command renames the existing mailbox to newmailbox. There is one special case for this command. If the mailbox being renamed is the Inbox, all the messages in the original Inbox are moved to the new mailbox. However, the original Inbox will remain with no messages in it.
Subscribe *mailbox*	This command adds the specified mailbox to the list of "Active" mailboxes displayed in the IMAP client software.
Unsubscribe *mailbox*	This command is used to remove the specified mailbox from the list of "Active" mailboxes displayed in the IMAP client software.
List *reference mailbox*	This command returns a subset of names from the complete set of all names available to the client. The *reference* parameter allows the hierarchy in which the *mailbox* exists to be indicated.

Command	Description
LSUB *reference mailbox*	This command returns only a subset of names from the mailboxes that the user has subscribed to by marking "Active." This is very common when a user subscribes to various IMAP folders.
Status *mailbox status item*	This command indicates the status of the *mailbox*. This allows a different mailbox to be inspected without terminating the connection to the current mailbox. Status items that can be inspected include messages, \Recent flagged files, the next UID value that will be assigned to the next new message, the number of unread messages, and the unique identifier validity value for the mailbox.
Append *mailbox message*	This command appends a new mail *message* to the specified *mailbox*.

Selected State Commands

The *selected state* is entered after the IMAP client has selected a mailbox to work with. At this point, commands can be entered to investigate the contents and manage the contents of the selected mailbox. In addition to the selected state commands listed in Table 13.5, all authenticated state commands can also be issued in this state.

TABLE 13.4. IMAP COMMANDS VALID IN THE SELECTED STATE.

Command	Description
Check	This command is used to launch any native housekeeping functionality implemented by the IMAP server. If the IMAP server does not have any housekeeping functionality, this command is the equivalent of the NOOP command.

continues

13

TABLE 13.4. CONTINUED

Command	Description
Close	This command is used to return to the authenticated state from the selected state. It also will permanently remove all messages that have the \Delete flag set.
Expunge	This command will permanently remove all messages with the \Delete flag set, but it will continue in the Selected state.
Search [Charset] parameters	This command is used to search the mailbox for all messages that meet the indicated search parameters. Optionally, the character set can be specified by using the Charset option.
Fetch message_set Message data_items	This command is used to retrieve data associated with a message in the mailbox. When used, the specific contents of a message can be retrieved. Message _data items include ALL, BODY, ENVELOPE, FLAGS, FULL, and UID.
Store message_set message_data_item value	This command can be used to alter the data associated with a message in the mailbox. This is generally used to change the flags associated with a message.
Copy message_set mailbox	This command copies the specified message(s) to the mailbox indicated. The copy operation will maintain the flags and date stamps.
Uid command arguments	This command allows commands to be executed against Unique ID numbers rather than message sequence numbers. The UID command can be used with the COPY, FETCH, STORE, and SEARCH commands.

Logout State Commands

In the *logout state*, the connection is being prepared for termination. After the server is prepared, it closes the connection between client and server. This state is entered after a client performs a CLOSE request or the auto-logout timer expires.

Lightweight Directory Access Protocol (LDAP)

RFC 2251   *Lightweight Directory Access Protocol* (LDAP) has been developed by the IETF to standardize access to X.500 and non-X.500 directory systems. Several email systems have been deployed on the Internet. Each of these systems has its own proprietary directory service. What LDAP provides is a methodology that uses a common framework for finding names in the diverse directory services.

LDAP's Evolution from X.500

LDAP has evolved from the *X.500 directory service*. The X.500 standard defines different object classes that can be used to identify objects within the directory services tree. These objects include the following:

- Aliases
- Country codes
- Localities
- Organizations
- Organizational units
- People

Within these object classes, several common objects have a defined set of attributes. Some of the more common objects that are used within X.500 include the following:

- Common Name (CN)
- Organization Name (O)
- Organizational Unit Name (OU)
- Country (C)
- State or Province (S)

Figure 13.3 shows a typical X.500 tree structure.

13

FIGURE 13.3.

An X.500 tree structure.

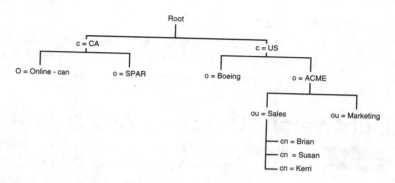

Within this tree, the *distinguished name* (dn) for Kerri would be this:

```
cn=Kerri, ou=sales, o=Acme, c=US
```

This name is generated by starting at the lowest part of the X.500 tree and working your way back to the root of the X.500 tree.

The LDAP protocol provides a method of access to the directory. Within the protocol, the operations of searching, addition, deletion, and modification are all defined. When you perform a search of the directory using LDAP, the following parameters are provided:

- A base distinguished name, where the search is to be started. You could limit the search to start in "c=US, o=Acme", for example.

- A filter can be applied that sets the criteria for the search. The criteria can include attribute types and wildcard characters.

- A scope is set that indicates which part of the directory to search. The scope can just include the base distinguished name, the level just below the distinguished name, or the entire subtree starting at the distinguished name.

LDAP Operations

All LDAP queries are directed to the LDAP server on TCP port 389 by default. When the client initially contacts the LDAP server, this is known as the *bind operation*.

The LDAP client will initiate the LDAP protocol session between the client and the server and perform client authentication. The Bind Request uses the following format:

```
BindRequest ::=
    [APPLICATION 0] SEQUENCE{
            version            INTEGER (1..127)
            name               LDAPDN,
            authentication CHOICE {
                simple      [0] OCTET STRING,
                krbv42LDAP    [1] OCTET STRING,
```

```
                        krbv42DSA              [2] OCTET STRING
                    }
            }
```

- `Version`—This indicates the LDAP protocol version being used.
- `Name`—The name that the client is using to bind to the directory object. This is used for authenticating the client.
- `Authentication`—This parameter is used to authenticate the name indicated in the Bind Request. The simple authentication method passes the password as clear text. This should be used only in anonymous situations because of the possibility of passwords being compromised. Other authentication methods supported include Kerberos authentication to the LDAP server and to the Directory Service Agent. The `OCTET` string passed with these would be the Kerberos authentication ticket. Kerberos authentication is discussed in greater detail in Day 16, "Firewalls and Security."

After the bind operation has been processed, the LDAP server must send a *Bind Response* in the following format:

```
BindResponse ::= [Application 1] LDAPResult
```

The `LDAPResult` will be the notification of a successful or unsuccessful authentication with the LDAP server.

The most common operation that is performed next by the LDAP client is a search operation. This is performed by using a *Search Request*. The Search Request uses the following format:

```
SearchRequest ::=
    [Application 3] SEQUENCE {
            baseObject      LDAPDN,
            scope           ENUMERATED {
                                    baseObject       (0),
                                    singleLevel      (1),
                                    wholeSubtree     (2)
                            },
            drefAliases     ENUMERATED {
                                    neverDerefAliases      (0),
                                    derefInSearching       (1),
                                    derefFindingBaseObj    (2),
                                    derefAlways            (3)
                            },
            sizeLimit       INTEGER (0 .. maxInt),
            timeLimit       INTEGER (0 .. maxInt),
        attrsOnly       BOOLEAN,
        filter          Filter,
        attributes      SEQUENCE of AttributeType
```

13

```
        }
    Filter ::=
        CHOICE {
                and                     [0] SET OF Filter,
                or                      [1] SET OF Filter,
                not                     [2] Filter,
                equalityMatch           [3] AttributeValueAssertion,
                substrings              [4] SubstringFilter,
                greaterOrEqual          [5] AttributeValueAssertion,
                lessOrEqual             [6] AttributeValueAssertion,
                present                 [7] AttributeType,
                approxMatch             [8] AttributeValueAssertion,
            }
    SubstringFIlter
        SEQUENCE {
                Type                    AttributeType,
                SEQUENCE OF CHOICE      {
                Initial                 [0] LDAPString,
                        Any             [1] LDAPString,
                        Final           [2] LDAPString
                }
            }
        }
```

Within the search request, the following parameters are used:

- BaseObject—This is the directory entry used as the starting point for the search.

- Scope—This indicator represents the scope of the search. This can be set to be only the base object, the layer below the base object, or the entire subtree starting at the base object.

- derefAliases—This is an indicator as to how alias objects should be handled when performing the search. You can set to never use aliases in searching, only use aliases when searching for a directory entry (not the base object), only use aliases for locating the base object of the search, or to freely use aliases at any time during a search.

- sizeLimit—This parameter restricts the number of entries that are returned by a search request. Setting this parameter to 0 indicates that all entries should be returned that match the criteria of the search.

- timeLimit—This parameter sets a maximum amount of time (in seconds) for the search. If set to 0, there are no time limit constraints on the search.

- attrsOnly—This indicator is used to set that the search results should contain attribute types and values, or just attribute types.

- Filter—This parameter defines the criteria for the search to be performed.

- `Attributes`—This is a listing of the attributes the search wants returned for each matching directory object. If this parameter is `null`, all attributes are returned.

The server responds with a *Search Response*, using the following format:

```
Search Response ::=
        CHOICE {
                Entry           [APPLICATION 4] SEQUENCE {
                                        ObjectName      LDAPDN,
                                        Attributes      SEQUENCE OF SEQUENCE
                                                        {
                                                                AttributeType,
                                                                SET OF
                                                                AttributeValue
                                                        }
                                },
                ResultCode      [APPLICATION 5] LDAPResult
        }
```

The Search Response contains zero or more matching objects based on the filter set in the Search Request. Each entry contains all the attributes specified in the Search Request and their associated values. In addition, a `resultCode` is returned that indicates whether the search was a success or failure.

After the LDAP process is complete, the LDAP client sends an *unbind operation* to terminate the protocol session. The unbind operation uses the following syntax:

```
UnbindRequest ::= [Application 2] NULL
```

There will be no associated response to the unbind operation. Upon receipt of the unbind request, the protocol server assumes the client has disconnected. If there are any outstanding requests, they are discarded at this point.

Email Attachment Issues

With the continued use of email, the need for translating attachments is becoming a common support issue for email administrators. The following three common methods are used for attaching non-text attachments to email messages:

- BinHex
- uuencode/uudecode
- Multipurpose Internet Mail Extensions (MIME)

The basic purpose of each of these *file-encoding* schemes is to convert binary data into text data for transmission by SMTP clients. The biggest problem encountered is having the correct decoding software installed on the client. The following sections detail specifics about each of the file-encoding schemes.

13

BinHex

BinHex is a storage protocol that was developed initially for use by Macintosh systems. BinHex translates a binary data file into an encrypted text version using hexadecimal. This enables email clients to send the "BinHexed" version of a binary file.

A BinHex attachment is generally stored with the extension .hqx. If you do receive an attachment with the .hqx extension, you need a BinHex utility such as Stuffit or WinZip 6.3+.

BinHex is the preferred method of file encoding on Macintosh systems because BinHex can handle data fork and resource fork information. BinHex preserves this information when file encoding so that this information is correctly transferred between systems.

BinHex is also available as an attachment method in Eudora and Pegasys email clients.

uuencode/uudecode

uuencode (UNIX to UNIX encoding) is an alternative method for converting raw binary data into a text representation. This is mainly performed for the purpose of sending binary attachments via a text-based Internet email system.

uuencode converts the binary file into a series of 7-bit ASCII characters. The encoded files do not have a standard naming convention, but you will often see .uu on UNIX systems and .UUE on DOS- and Windows-based systems.

A uuencoded file can also be identified by the very first line of the file. It always appears in this format:

```
Begin ### afile.avi
```

The ### represents a permissions flag for the file. This is used in UNIX systems. The afile.avi represents the name of the file that the uudecode will use for the re-expanded file. Each additional line will begin with the letter *M*. If this is not the case, either the file is not a uuencode file or the file is damaged. Each line is terminated with a [CR][LF] character combination.

The utility uudecode is used for translating the uuencoded file back into its native format. Most versions of uuencoding software available today has both the uuencode and uudecode programs built in to one software interface.

cc:Mail is an example of an email system that uses uuencoding for binary attachments.

MIME

RFC 2045 The *Multipurpose Internet Mail Extensions* (MIME) standard was developed by the IETF to provide a mechanism for formatting non-ASCII messages so that they can be transmitted over the Internet. Most current email clients now support the MIME standard. The added benefit of MIME is that it supports character sets other than ASCII.

The existence of MIME data in an email message is determined by examining an email's message header. A text-only email message header might look something like this:

```
From: bkomar@online-can.com
To: rick_boivin@faneuil.com
Subject: How have you been doing
... Message Text ...
```

If an email message has MIME data included, five additional fields can be included within the message header. These additional fields are as follows:

- MIME-Version
- Content-Type
- Content-Transfer Encoding
- Content-ID
- Content-Description

The MIME-Version Field

The *MIME-Version* field is used to indicate the MIME version that was used to create the email message. Currently, this would be version 1.0. This field must be located at the top level of a message. If the message is a multipart message, the MIME-Version needs to be declared only once at the top of the message.

The Content-Type Field

RFC 2046 The *Content-Type* is used to indicate the type of data contained in the message body. The recipient's email client software can select the correct application to present the data based on the Content-Type field. The Content-Type is based on a top-level media type and a subtype value. The top-level media type declares the general type of data. There are five discrete top-level media types.

- *Text*. This media type is used for encoding text-based information. Two subtypes are predefined for the Text media-type: plain and enriched. This encoding is used when the text can be displayed as is. Recently, more and more email products are using the HTML subtype so that *Hypertext Markup Language* can be used to generate graphic email solutions.

13

- *Image*. This media type is used for graphic attachments, and requires that a display device be present. Two subtypes were initially defined for the media type: JPEG and GIF.

- *Audio*. This media type is used for sound producing attachments and requires headphones or speakers for output. Several subtypes are defined, such as BASIC and WAV.

- *Video*. This media type is used for video attachments. Defined subtypes includes MPEG, QT (QuickTime), and AVI.

- *Application*. This media type is used for data that must be processed by a native application. PostScript is one of the most common subtypes.

There are also two composite top-level media types.

- *Multipart*. This media type is used when data from multiple entities is included within a single email message. Four basic subtypes exist, as follows:
    - The *Mixed* subtype is used to specify that there are multiple attachments using different media types in the message.
    - The *Alternative* subtype is used to indicate that the data is attached in multiple formats to facilitate different clients reading the information.
    - The *Parallel* subtype is used to indicate that the MIME attachments should be viewed simultaneously at the receiving host.
    - The *Digest* subtype is used to represent that the message has many entities and all the entities have a default type of message/rfc822.

- **Message**—This media type indicates that an encapsulated message is included in the message body. The message can be an entire message or part of a message.
    - The *rfc822* subtypes indicates that the message is plain text and shorter than 1,000 characters as per RFC 822.
    - The *Partial* subtype is used when an RFC822 message has been broken apart because of size restrictions.
    - The *External-body* subtype is used to reference an external data source for the message instead of including the actual message.

If the Content-type is not indicated, it is assumed that the content type is text/plain, using the US-ASCII character set.

The Content-Transfer-Encoding Header Field

Because the natural format of many attachments is not compatible for transport across the SMTP protocol, the attachments must be encoded into a 7-bit ASCII format. MIME uses several methods for encoding the data into a 7-bit short-line format. The *Content-Transfer-Encoding* field is used to indicate the method of encoding that was used and provides the decoding method for the receiving client to use when reading the attachment.

Accepted encoding mechanisms include the following:

- *7-bit*. This is used when the data is exclusively using ASCII characters that are no greater than value 127 and do not contain `null` characters. Each line is less than 998 octets and ends with the `[CR][LF]` sequence. No actual encoding is performed for this mechanism.

- *8-bit*. This is used when data includes octets with values greater than 127 from the ASCII character set. As with 7-bit encoding, each line is less than 998 octets and each line is terminated with a `[CR][LF]` combination. No actual encoding is performed for this mechanism.

- *Binary data*. This mechanism is not currently valid in today's Internet email. It has been provided for the time when a binary attachment can be transmitted over the Internet without being encoded. This mechanism would transmit the data without any encoding.

- *Quoted-printable*. This mechanism transforms the original attachment into material that is 7-bit in nature. This mechanism is used when the data is largely made up of data from the 7-bit US-ASCII character set. The following rules are used for encoding under Quoted-printable:

  - Any 8-bit characters will be represented with `"="` followed by the two-digit hexadecimal representation of the characters ASCII number. The hexadecimal digit must be represented in uppercase letters.

  - Lines will be truncated to no more than 76 characters per line. A "soft line break" will be implemented. Simply put, an `"="` symbol is used as the last character on an encoded line.

- *Base64*. This mechanism converts binary data into a format that is humanly unreadable. Unfortunately, an encoded document will be roughly 33% larger after this encoding has been performed.

  The Base64 encoding process breaks the binary data into 24-bit streams of data by concatenating three 8-bit input groups. These 24 bits will be treated as four 6-bit groups. These 6-bit groupings are translated into a single digit of the Base64 alphabet (see Table 13.5).

13

TABLE 13.5. THE BASE64 ALPHABET.

Value	Encoding	Value	Encoding	Value	Encoding	Value	Encoding
0	A	16	Q	32	g	48	w
1	B	17	R	33	h	49	x
2	C	18	S	34	i	50	y
3	D	19	T	35	j	51	z
4	E	20	U	36	k	52	0
5	F	21	V	37	l	53	1
6	G	22	W	38	m	54	2
7	H	23	X	39	n	55	3
8	I	24	Y	40	o	56	4
9	J	25	Z	41	p	57	5
10	K	26	a	42	q	58	6
11	L	27	b	43	r	59	7
12	M	28	c	44	s	60	8
13	N	29	d	45	t	61	9
14	O	30	e	46	u	62	+
15	P	31	f	47	v	63	/

If less than 24 bits are available at the very end of the data being encoded, the data will be padded with the "=" character to provide 24 bits for conversion. These bits will be considered to be zero bits when calculations are performed.

The Content-ID Header Field

This field is an optional field used when referencing one body to another body. These Content-ID fields must be globally unique so that duplicate IDs are not created. This field is required in the case where the MIME media type is set to `message/external-body`.

The Content-Description Header Field

This field is provided to associate a descriptive text phrase to an attachment. This is generally displayed as the attached document's icon title when working in a graphical interface. This field is an optional MIME header field.

A Sample MIME Header

The following message was transmitted using Outlook Express. This product allows messages to be sent using HTML formatting.

```
From: scrim@scrimtech.ca
To:bkomar@online-can.com
Subject: How is it going.
Date: Sun, 22 Mar 1998 12:32:58 -0600
MIME-Version: 1.0
Content-Type: text/html;
        charset="iso-8859-1"
Content-Transfer-Encoding: quoted-printable

<!DOCTYPE HTML PUBLIC "-//W3C//DTD W3 HTML//EN">
<HTML>
<HEAD>

<META content=3Dtext/html;charset=3Diso-8859-1 =
http-equiv=3DContent-Type>
<META content=3D'"MSHTML 4.72.2106.6"' name=3DGENERATOR>
</HEAD>
<BODY bgColor=3D#ffffff>
<DIV><FONT color=3D#000000 size=3D2>Talk to you =
next week!</FONT></DIV></BODY></HTML>
```

Note that the MIME-Version is set to version 1.0. Also note that the Content-type is set to text/html. The Content-type also used the optional parameter to indicate the character set that was used for the message.

This message was encoded using Quoted-printable. You will notice that the longer HTML lines were split into multiple lines by using "=" as the last character of the line.

Applying What You Have Learned

Today's material reviewed the common methods of implementing email applications in a TCP/IP environment. Although SMTP is still the most common method for sending mail, there seems to be more and more of a movement toward using IMAP for retrieving messages because of the performance gains over POP3 clients.

We also reviewed the issue of attachments. The key thing to remember when dealing with attachments is that you may require additional software to read attachments that have been encoded using a method that your email software does not support.

13

Test Your Knowledge

1. What are the steps involved in an SMTP session between an SMTP client and an SMTP server?

2. With an Internet email client, what function does the SMTP protocol provide? What function does POP3 or IMAP provide?

3. What type of record is queried in DNS by an SMTP client?

4. What advantages do IMAP mail clients offer over POP3 mail clients?

5. Why is the LDAP protocol being developed?

6. Describe the meaning of the following X.500 style name.

```
cn=Crooks, Malcolm; ou=Winnipeg; o=Online Business Systems, c=CA
```

7. If you were working primarily with Macintosh systems, which method of file encoding would you use for email attachments?

8. What are the field headers used when a MIME attachment exists in an email message?

Preview of the Next Day

Tomorrow's material looks at managing a TCP/IP network using the Simple Network Management Protocol (SNMP). It looks at how SNMP tackles the task of managing a network and overviews some of the common products used for managing an SNMP network.

DAY 14

Managing a Network with SNMP

Today's material looks at the use of the *Simple Network Management Protocol* (SNMP) to manage the infrastructure of a network. The material includes an overview of the following:

- Roles in a network management system
- SNMP communities
- The structure of the Management Information Base (MIB)
- SNMP transactions
- Security considerations

An Overview of Network Management

Two different thoughts come to mind when the term *network management* is brought up. The first thought deals with the management of resources of the network. These include user accounts, file resources, and print resources. This management is specific to the network operating system implemented.

Network management can also encompass the management of the physical devices that make up the network, such as routers, bridges, and hubs. The management of these devices is many times a reactive style of management. When failures occur, users notify the network administrator that they cannot perform normal day-to-day activities. Although this eventually leads to the solution of the problem, early notification would assist greatly in solving the problem.

Simple Network Management Protocol (SNMP) enables the network administrator to detect problems before the user base even notices the problem. SNMP management systems can determine immediately when a network interface on a router has failed and starts to build a solution to the problem. SNMP provides a standard for the monitoring and controlling of a network. SNMP most commonly runs on TCP/IP networks, but it can also run on AppleTalk, IPX, and OSI networks.

SNMP Management Systems and SNMP Agents

There are two key components in an SNMP system: the *SNMP management system* and the *SNMP agents*. SNMP management systems are used to issue queries to the systems running SNMP agents. The SNMP agents respond with values filled in for the queried information. SNMP management systems are able to query and manage network devices remotely. A key feature of some network devices is the fact that they are *SNMP-enabled*. This means they have been configured to respond to SNMP requests from an SNMP management system. SNMP agents are implemented via either software loaded on the host or firmware loaded on the actual device.

You can also configure SNMP agents to initiate conversations with an SNMP management system, by using *SNMP traps*. Traps are messages issued by the SNMP agent because a specified threshold has been exceeded for an SNMP-monitored resource. A router, for example, might send an SNMP trap when one of its configured interfaces fails.

In some cases, the SNMP agent cannot be implemented on the device that needs to be managed. Instead, the agent is loaded onto a different system that functions on behalf of the network device. This system is known as a *SNMP proxy agent*. When the proxied network device needs to be managed, the SNMP management system sends the management request to the proxy agent. The proxy agent then contacts the proxied device. The device either uses a different protocol to query the device or monitors the device using other methods to determine the results to any queries.

SNMP AGENT IMPLEMENTATIONS

You are likely to see SNMP agents implemented as firmware on actual networking hardware devices, such as routers, switches, bridges, and hubs. Generally, host computers implement SNMP agents as actual software packages or services.

SNMP Communities

Each SNMP transaction contains a tag known as the *community name*. The community name is used as a low-level method of security. When the request is made, the SNMP agent determines whether the request has come from a management system within the same community. If the community name does not match, the request is not processed.

Community names are *case-sensitive* and can be a maximum of 32 characters. It is imperative that all systems within the same management domain share the same community name.

Three types of communities exist in an SNMP implementation. They include

- *Monitor community*. The management system in the Monitor community is able to perform read-only queries of all SNMP agents that belong to the same community name. For each query that is posed, the SNMP management system includes the Monitor community name in the request. This is compared to the monitor agent's community name as a low-level security check. If they match, the request is responded to.

- *Control community*. The management system in the Control community is able to perform read/write functions to the SNMP agents. Write operations are allowed only for properties that can be modified by a management system. This community is normally disabled to protect against accidental modification of properties of the SNMP agents.

- *Trap community*. The Trap community name is set on the SNMP agent system. When a trap event occurs, the SNMP agent sends a message to its configured SNMP management system. The Trap community name configured in the SNMP trap message must match the community name of the SNMP network management system.

14

> **A Warning About Community Names**
>
> Most implementations of SNMP use the default community name of PUBLIC. Although this is convenient, it is often considered a security issue. When configuring your SNMP system, use any name other than PUBLIC.

The Components of an SNMP System

The following are two requirements for implementing SNMP:

- The traffic involved with network management should not adversely affect the network traffic within the system as a whole.

- The network monitor agent should not cause additional processor usage.

Several components make up the SNMP system, including

- The Structure of Management Information (SMI)
- The SNMP protocol
- Management Information Bases (MIB)

Structure of Management Information (SMI)

`RFC 1155` The *Structure of Management Information (SMI)* provides a standardized framework for defining the information that an SNMP manager can manage. It does not describe the actual objects that can be managed. Instead, it provides the basic format for all managed objects.

In addition, the SMI defines the hierarchy used to store MIB database information. By defining the hierarchy, it is guaranteed that there will be no ambiguity when an SNMP request is made.

Each object within the SNMP hierarchy is assigned a unique *object identifier*. Object identifiers are allocated in a hierarchical tree method (see Figure 14.1).

When an object is referred to within the object identifier tree, either the object identifiers or the object descriptions are used. When discussing the management object in the object identifier hierarchy, for example, you can refer to it by its object identifiers, or as follows:

```
iso.org.dod.internet.management
```

FIGURE 14.1.

*The object identifier
hierarchy.*

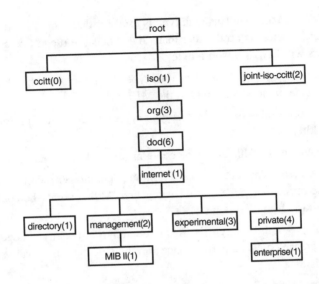

This can also be identified using the following object identifier values:

```
1.3.6.1.2
```

Each object is defined using *Abstract Syntax Notation One (ASN.1)*, which provides a
common mechanism for defining objects so that there is no ambiguity with the function
and properties of the object. Each object contains the following properties:

- name
- syntax
- encoding

The name property is used to identify each managed object. The name is based on the
actual object identifier for the managed object. Each managed object must have a unique
object identifier based on the SMI. The object identifier is created by traversing the
object hierarchical tree starting at the root and ending at the managed object.

The syntax property is used to define the structure of the object type. This is defined
using the ASN.1 notation. The use of ASN.1 removes any ambiguity as to the contents
and properties of each managed object. Within the syntax, the following defined *types*
are used for the properties of an object:

- Integer—This data type is a whole number between 1 and the largest integer
  value allowed on the host system.

14

- `Octet_String`—This data type is used for data stored in strings of 8-bit *bytes* (the term "octet" is used rather than "byte" because it can't be assumed that all computers will have 8 bits in a byte).

- `Object_Identifier`—This data type is used to store the object identifiers used to name unique objects within the MIB.

- `NetworkAddress`—This data type is used to define the protocol family for an address.

- `IpAddress`—This data type contains an IPv4 32-bit address.

- `Counter`—This data type is a non-negative integer incremented by values of 1 until the maximum value of $2^{32}-1$ is reached. At this point, the count reverts to 0 and restarts from that point.

- `Gauge`—This data type is used to contain non-negative integers that can increase or decrease based on performance variables. A maximum value of $2^{32}-1$ is allowed for this data type.

- `TimeTicks`—This data type is used to indicate the time in hundredths of a second since a specific event occurred.

- `Opaque`—This data type is used to pass arbitrary ASN.1 syntax. A value is first encoded using ASN.1 rules into a string of octets. This is then encoded again as an Octet_string. This second encoding is performed so that a recognized ASN.1 format is used for the transport of the data. The receiving system needs only to know how to interpret the octet_string data, not the encoded internal data.

The encoding property is used to transmit the value of an object to a management station based on the syntax describing the object type.

INTERNET OBJECTS WITHIN THE OBJECT IDENTIFIER HIERARCHY

All Internet-based object identifiers are located within the `iso.org.dod.internet` hierarchy. The Internet Architecture Board (IAB) manages the allocation of new values to this hierarchy.

The SNMP Protocol

RFC 1441   SNMP is a simple protocol that uses the following UDP destination ports during transmission:

- *Port 161.* This is the destination port for all SNMP request and response messages. Remember that the SNMP management station initiates SNMP requests.

- *Port 162.* This is the destination port for all SNMP trap messages. Remember that the SNMP agent initiates SNMP trap messages when a preconfigured event takes place.

WHY NOT USE TCP?

The UDP protocol is used as the transport protocol, rather than TCP, because of the requirement for timely delivery of SNMP messages. The need to get the information to the SNMP management system as quickly as possible outweighs the need for reliable transmission. Using UDP bypasses the additional transmission packets involved in establishing a TCP session.

Within the SNMP protocol, six basic operations have been defined. Each operation is encoded using ASN.1 and is defined in separate *Protocol Data Units (PDUs)*. These PDUs define the format of the SNMP message.

`RFC 1448`   The defined operations include

- `GetRequest`—The SNMP management station uses the `GetRequest` PDU to query an MIB on an SNMP agent (see Figure 14.2).

FIGURE 14.2.

The traffic flow for an SNMP GetRequest PDU.

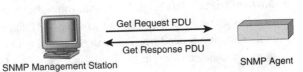

SNMP Management Station

Get Request PDU →

← Get Response PDU

SNMP Agent

- `GetNextRequest`—The `GetNextRequest` PDU is used by an SNMP management station to read sequentially through an MIB. The `GetNextRequest` allows a value in a table to be retrieved without knowing its exact object ID. This is extremely valuable when the SNMP management station is unaware of the number of instances of an object that exist.
- `GetBulk`—The `GetBulk` PDU has been added in SNMP v2. It was created to provide a more efficient retrieval mechanism for values in a table. Rather than having to send a `GetNextRequest` for each entry in a table, `GetBulk` allows the table to be retrieved in a single request.
- `SetRequest`—The SNMP management station uses the `SetRequest` PDU to change the value of an MIB object. This object must allow Read/Write access.
- `GetResponse`—The `GetResponse` PDU is sent by the SNMP agent to the SNMP management station. Its format is identical to `GetRequest` except that the `Type` and `Value` portions of the variables are completed with the current values.

14

- Trap—The Trap PDU (see Figure 14.3) is the only PDU initiated by the SNMP agent. It provides a mechanism for the agent to signal out the occurrence of an event that may require special attention.

FIGURE 14.3.

The SNMP Trap message flow.

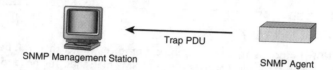

SNMP Management Station   Trap PDU   SNMP Agent

The following seven traps have been predefined for use:

- coldStart—This trap is sent when the SNMP agent is in the state of reinitializing itself and has significant changes to its configuration. Rebooting the system causes this trap to be sent.

- warmStart—This trap is sent when the SNMP agent reinitializes itself with no changes in its configuration.

- linkDown—This trap is sent to indicate that one of the communication links of the sending SNMP agent has failed.

- linkUp—This trap is sent by the SNMP agent to indicate that a downed communication link has been restored to normal operation.

- authenticationFailure—This trap implies that an SNMP management station has made an SNMP request to the SNMP agent and has failed the authentication procedure. This can be due to a non-matching community name or non-inclusion in the list of accepted SNMP management stations.

- egpNeighborLoss—This trap is sent by an SNMP agent when an EGP peer relationship has been lost.

- enterpriseSpecific—This trap is an enterprise-specific defined trap event.

Management Information Base (MIB)

RFC 1213   The *Management Information Base* (MIB) is used to specify the details that a managed device will report to an SNMP management system. There are actually several MIB files that can be implemented. Each vendor can produce a unique MIB for its hardware device that will have specific management objects exposed for queries. Objects within the MIB are defined based on the structures and object types defined in the SMI. These objects are stored together within a subtree of the object identifier hierarchy. Several different MIBs exist for each distinct part of the object hierarchy.

The current version of the MIB is MIB-II. The MIB is divided into logically related groups of objects. These groups are defined using the following criteria:

- The object must be essential for either fault or configuration management to be included in the MIB.
- Objects included in the MIB should allow only limited damaged when an SNMP manager tampers with them.
- The object must be in current use.
- Each object must be independent. If an object can be derived from others in the MIB, it should not be included in the MIB.
- Implementation-specific objects are not included in the MIB.

Internet MIB-II is divided into the following categories:

- System
- Interfaces
- Address Translation
- IP
- ICMP
- TCP
- UDP
- EGP
- Transmission
- SNMP

All SNMP-capable devices must implement these groups. The only caveat is that an SNMP-capable device must implement only groups that are relevant to that device. If the device does not use EGP, it is not required to implement the EGP group.

THE MIB TABLES

Tables 14.1–14.9 define all the default objects included in the Internet MIB-II. You do not have to know every object within this MIB. This information is provided so that you can utilize these tables to troubleshoot specific SNMP events or to perform specific SNMP requests.

14

The System Group

The System group is used to contain general information about the network device. Table 14.1 shows some of the more commonly used objects within the System group.

TABLE 14.1. THE MIB-II SYSTEM GROUP OBJECTS.

Object	Object ID	Description
SysDescr	.1.3.6.1.2.1.1.1	A textual description of the device. It should include the full name of the device.
SysObjectID	.1.3.6.1.2.1.1.2	The vendor's authoritative identification of the network management subsystem. This is the hierarchy object ID for the vendor's enterprise MIB.
SysUpTime	.1.3.6.1.2.1.1.3	The time, in seconds, since the device was last initialized.
SysContact	.1.3.6.1.2.1.1.4	The contact person for the network device. This should include information on how to contact this person.
SysName	.1.3.6.1.2.1.1.5	The fully qualified domain name of the device.
SysLocation	.1.3.6.1.2.1.1.6	The physical location of the device.
SysServices	.1.3.6.1.2.1.1.7	A value that indicates the set of services the device offers as its primary function.

The Interfaces Group

The Interfaces group defines information about a network interface. This includes both physical network interfaces such as ethernet or token ring and point-to-point links. Table 14.2 shows the objects in the Interfaces group.

TABLE 14.2. THE MIB-II INTERFACES GROUP OBJECTS.

Object	Object ID	Description
IfNumber	.1.3.6.1.2.1.2.1	The number of network interfaces present on a device.
IfTable	.1.3.6.1.2.1.2.2	A list of interface entries. The total number of entries in the table is the value of IfNumber.
IfEntry	.1.3.6.1.2.1.2.2.1	An interface entry that contains objects at the subnetwork layer and below for a particular interface.
IfIndex	.1.3.6.1.2.1.2.2.1.1	A unique value for each interface. The value ranges between 1 and the value of IfNumber.

Object	Object ID	Description
IfDescr	.1.3.6.1.2.1.2.2.1.2	A textual description of the interface, which commonly contains the manufacturer, the product name, and the version of the interface.
IfType	.1.3.6.1.2.1.2.2.1.3	The type of interface. This defines whether the device is an ethernet card, a token ring card, an ISDN interface, or others.
IfMTU	.1.3.6.1.2.1.2.2.1.4	The size of the largest datagram that can be sent/received on the interface.
IfSpeed	.1.3.6.1.2.1.2.2.1.5	An estimate of the interface's current bandwidth in bits per second.
IfPhysAddress	.1.3.6.1.2.1.2.2.1.6	The physical address of the network interface. If the device (such as a serial line) does not have a physical address, the object should contain an octet string of length zero.
IfAdminStatus	.1.3.6.1.2.1.2.2.1.7	This describes the desired state of the interface. It can be listed as up, down, or in testing mode.
IfOperStatus	.1.3.6.1.2.1.2.2.1.8	This describes the current state of the interface in terms of up, down, or testing.
ifLastChange	.1.3.6.1.2.1.2.2.1.9	The value of sysUptime at the time the interface entered its current operational state.
ifInOctets	.1.3.6.1.2.1.2.2.1.10	The total number of octets received on the interface.
ifinUcastPkts	.1.3.6.1.2.1.2.2.1.11	The number of subnetwork unicast packets delivered to a higher-level protocol.
ifInNUcastPkts	.1.3.6.1.2.1.2.2.1.12	The number of non-unicast packets delivered to a higher-layer protocol. This is the total number of broadcasts and multicasts received.
ifInDiscards	.1.3.6.1.2.1.2.2.1.13	The number of inbound packets that were discarded without an error condition existing.

14

continues

TABLE 14.2. CONTINUED

Object	Object ID	Description
InInErrors	.1.3.6.1.2.1.2.2.1.14	The number of inbound packets that contained errors and were not delivered to a higher-level protocol.
ifInUnknownProtos	.1.3.6.1.2.1.2.2.1.15	The number of inbound packets that contained unknown or unsupported protocols and were discarded.
IfOutOctets	.1.3.6.1.2.1.2.2.1.16	The total number of octets transmitted out the interface.
IfOutUcastPkts	.1.3.6.1.2.1.2.2.1.17	The total number of unicast packets transmitted out the interface.
IfOutNUcastPkts	.1.3.6.1.2.1.2.2.1.18	The total number of non-unicast packets transmitted out the interface. This includes both broadcasts and multicasts.
IfOutDiscards	.1.3.6.1.2.1.2.2.1.19	The total number of outbound packets discarded even though no error condition existed.
IfOutErrors	.1.3.6.1.2.1.2.2.1.20	The number of outbound packets that were not transmitted due to errors.
IfOutQlen	.1.3.6.1.2.1.2.2.1.21	The length, in packets, of the output packet queue.
IfSpecific	.1.3.6.1.2.1.2.2.1.22	A reference to MIB definitions specific to the media being used by the interface.

The Address Translation Group

The Address Translation group exists solely for compatibility with MIB-I nodes. It is used to contain address translation information. The information is contained in a single table used to convert a network address (such as an IP address) into subnet-specific addresses (such as a physical address). Table 14.3 shows the objects contained in the Address Translation group.

TABLE 14.3. THE MIB-II ADDRESS TRANSLATION GROUP OBJECTS.

Object	Object ID	Description
AtTable	.1.3.6.1.2.1.3.1	This table contains the network address to physical address entries.
AtEntry	.1.3.6.1.2.1.3.1.1	Each entry contains a single network address to physical address mapping.
AtIfIndex	.1.3.6.1.2.1.3.1.1.1	The interface for which the network address to physical address mapping is based.
AtPhysAddress	.1.3.6.1.2.1.3.1.1.2	The media-dependent physical address of the interface.
AtNetAddress	.1.3.6.1.2.1.3.1.1.3	The network address that corresponds to the physical address (such as an IP address).

The IP Group

The IP group contains information specific to the IP protocol. Table 14.4 shows the primary objects contained in the IP group.

TABLE 14.4. THE MIB-II IP GROUP OBJECTS.

Object	Object ID	Description
IpForwarding	.1.3.6.1.2.1.4.1	This indicates whether the device is functioning as an IP router or as a nonrouting IP host.
IpDefaultTTL	.1.3.6.1.2.1.4.2	The default value inserted into the TTL field of an IP header for datagrams that originate at this device. This is used only if an upper layer protocol does not supply a TTL value.
IpInReceives	.1.3.6.1.2.1.4.3	The total number of IP datagrams received from interfaces (including errors).
IpInHdrErrors	.1.3.6.1.2.1.4.4	The number of input errors discarded due to errors in the IP header.

continues

14

TABLE 14.4. CONTINUED

Object	Object ID	Description
IpInAddrErrors	.1.3.6.1.2.1.4.5	The number of input datagrams discarded at the device because the IP address in their IP header's destination field was not a valid address to be received at this device. This can be due to a destination address of 0.0.0.0 or a non-supported class of IP address (such as a Class E address).
IpForwDatagrams	.1.3.6.1.2.1.4.6	The number of input datagrams that were received that this device was not the final destination and they were forwarded. This includes source route packets that were routed via this device successfully.
IpInUnknownProtos	.1.3.6.1.2.1.4.7	The number of locally addressed datagrams received successfully but that were dropped due to an unknown or unsupported protocol.
IpInDiscards	.1.3.6.1.2.1.4.8	The number of IP datagrams that were discarded even though an error condition was not detected. This includes IP fragment packets that were discarded while awaiting reassembly.
IpInDelivers	.1.3.6.1.2.1.4.9	The total number of input datagrams successfully delivered to IP user protocols (including ICMP).
IpOutRequests	.1.3.6.1.2.1.4.10	The total number of IP datagrams that local IP user protocols (including ICMP) supplied to IP in requests for transmission.

Object	Object ID	Description
IPOutDiscards	.1.3.6.1.2.1.4.11	The number of output datagrams that were discarded even though no error conditions were detected.
IpOutNoRoutes	.1.3.6.1.2.1.4.12	The number of IP datagrams discarded because no route could be determined for the next hop.
IPReasmTimeout	.1.3.6.1.2.1.4.13	The maximum number of seconds an incoming fragment is held for the reassembly process.
IPReasmReqds	.1.3.6.1.2.1.4.14	The number of IP fragments received that need to be reassembled at this device.
IpReasmOKs	.1.3.6.1.2.1.4.15	The number of IP datagrams successfully reassembled at this device.
IpReasmFails	.1.3.6.1.2.1.4.16	The number of failures detected by the IP reassembly process.
IpFragOKs	.1.3.6.1.2.1.4.17	The number of IP datagrams that have been successfully fragmented by this device.
IpFragFails	.1.3.6.1.2.1.4.18	The number of IP datagrams that have been discarded because they needed to be fragmented but could not be. This can be caused by a datagram having the Don't Fragment flag set.
IPFragCreates	.1.3.6.1.2.1.4.19	The number of IP fragments that have been generated by the fragmentation process by this device.
IpAddrTable	.1.3.6.1.2.1.4.20	The table of addressing information for this device's IP addresses.

14

continues

TABLE 14.4. CONTINUED

Object	Object ID	Description
IpAddrEntry	.1.3.6.1.2.1.4.20.1	The addressing information for one of this device's IP addresses.
IpAddEntAddr	.1.3.6.1.2.1.4.20.1.1	The IP address to which this entry's addressing information pertains.
IpAdEntIfIndex	.1.3.6.1.2.1.4.20.1.2	The index value that uniquely identifies the interface to which this entry is applicable.
IpAdEntNetMask	.1.3.6.1.2.1.4.20.1.3	The subnet mask associated with the IP address of this entry.
IpAdEntBcastAddr	.1.3.6.1.2.1.4.20.1.4	The value of the least significant bit in the IP broadcast address used for sending datagrams on the (logical) interface associated with the IP address of this entry.
IpAdEntReasmMaxSize	.1.3.6.1.2.1.4.20.1.5	The size of the largest IP datagram this entry can reassemble from incoming IP fragmented datagrams received on this interface.
IpRouteTable	.1.3.6.1.2.1.4.21	The IP routing table for a device.
IpRouteEntry	.1.3.6.1.2.1.4.21.1	A route to a specific destination.
IpRouteDest	.1.3.6.1.2.1.4.21.1.1	The destination IP address of this route. An entry with the value 0.0.0.0 is considered to be the default route.
IpRouteIfIndex	.1.3.6.1.2.1.4.21.1.2	The index value that uniquely identifies the local interface through which the next hop of this route should be reached.

Object	Object ID	Description
IpRouteMetric1	.1.3.6.1.2.1.4.21.1.3	The primary routing metric for this route. The specifics of the metric are based on the IPRouteProto.
IpRouteMetric2	.1.3.6.1.2.1.4.21.1.4	An alternate routing metric for this route. If this route is not used, the value is set to -1.
IpRouteMetric3	.1.3.6.1.2.1.4.21.1.5	An alternate routing metric for this route. If this route is not used, the value is set to −1.
IpRouteMetric4	.1.3.6.1.2.1.4.21.1.6	An alternate routing metric for this route. If this route is not used, the value is set to −1.
IpRouteNextHop	.1.3.6.1.2.1.4.21.1.7	The IP address for the next hop in this route.
IpRouteType	.1.3.6.1.2.1.4.21.1.8	The type of route. Generally, this value is set to either direct or indirect.
IpRouteProto	.1.3.6.1.2.1.4.21.1.9	The routing mechanism by which the route was learned. This can include protocols such as RIP, OSPF, and BGP.
IpRouteAge	.1.3.6.1.2.1.4.21.1.10	The number of seconds since this route was last updated or otherwise determined to be correct.
IpRouteMask	.1.3.6.1.2.1.4.21.1.11	The subnet mask to be used for the ANDing process with the destination IP address value in the ipRouteDest field.
IpRouteMetric5	.1.3.6.1.2.1.4.21.1.12	An alternate routing metric for this route. If this route is not used, the value is set to −1.

continues

14

TABLE 14.4. CONTINUED

Object	Object ID	Description
IpRouteInfo	.1.3.6.1.2.1.4.21.1.13	A reference to MIB definitions specific to the particular routing protocol responsible for this route, as determined by the value specified in the route's ipRouteProto value.
IpNetToMediaTable	.1.3.6.1.2.1.4.22	The IP Address Translation table used for mapping from IP addresses to physical addresses.
IpNetToMediaEntry	.1.3.6.1.2.1.4.22.1	Each entry contains one IP address to physical address mapping.
IpNetToMediaIfIndex	.1.3.6.1.2.1.4.22.1.1	The interface on which this IP address to physical address mapping is based.
IpNetToMediaPhysAddress	.1.3.6.1.2.1.4.22.1.2	The media-dependent physical address.
IpNetToMediaNetAddress	.1.3.6.1.2.1.4.22.1.3	The IP address corresponding to the physical address.
IpNetToMediaType	.1.3.6.1.2.1.4.22.1.4	The type of mapping. Valid entries include Invalid, Static, Dynamic, or Other.
IpRoutingDiscards	.1.3.6.1.2.1.4.23	The number of IP routing entries that were chosen to be discarded even though they were valid.

The ICMP Group

The ICMP group contains information specific to the ICMP protocol. Table 14.5 shows the primary objects contained in the ICMP group.

TABLE 14.5. THE MIB-II ICMP GROUP OBJECTS.

Object	Object ID	Description
icmpInMsgs	.1.3.6.1.2.1.5.1	The total number of ICMP messages the device has received.
icmpInErrors	.1.3.6.1.2.1.5.2	The number of ICMP messages the device received but that were determined to have ICMP-specific errors.
icmpInDestUnreachs	.1.3.6.1.2.1.5.3	The number of ICMP destination unreachable messages received.
icmpInTimeExcds	.1.3.6.1.2.1.5.4	The number of ICMP time exceeded messages received.
icmpInParmProbs	.1.3.6.1.2.1.5.5	The number of ICMP parameter problem messages received.
icmpInSrcQuenchs	.1.3.6.1.2.1.5.6	The number of ICMP source quench messages received.
icmpInRedirects	.1.3.6.1.2.1.5.7	The number of ICMP redirect messages received.
icmpInEchos	.1.3.6.1.2.1.5.8	The number of ICMP echo request messages received.
icmpInEchoReps	.1.3.6.1.2.1.5.9	The number of ICMP echo reply messages received.
icmpInTimestamps	.1.3.6.1.2.1.5.10	The number of ICMP timestamp request messages received.
icmpInTimestampReps	.1.3.6.1.2.1.5.11	The number of ICMP timestamp reply messages received.
icmpInAddrMasks	.1.3.6.1.2.1.5.12	The number of ICMP address mask request messages received.
icmpInAddrMaskReps	.1.3.6.1.2.1.5.13	The number of ICMP address mask reply messages received.
IcmpOutMsgs	.1.3.6.1.2.1.5.14	The total number of ICMP messages this entity attempted to send, including all IcmpOutErrors.
IcmpOutErrors	.1.3.6.1.2.1.5.15	The number of ICMP messages the device did not send due to problems discovered within ICMP. This does not include errors discovered outside the ICMP layer.

continues

14

TABLE 14.5. CONTINUED

Object	Object ID	Description
IcmpOutDestUnreachs	.1.3.6.1.2.1.5.16	The number of ICMP destination unreachable messages sent.
IcmpOutTimeExcds	.1.3.6.1.2.1.5.17	The number of ICMP time exceeded messages sent.
IcmpOutParmProbs	.1.3.6.1.2.1.5.18	The number of ICMP parameter problem messages sent.
IcmpOutSrcQuenchs	.1.3.6.1.2.1.5.19	The number of ICMP source quench messages sent.
IcmpOutRedirects	.1.3.6.1.2.1.5.20	The number of ICMP redirect messages sent.
IcmpOutEchos	.1.3.6.1.2.1.5.21	The number of ICMP echo request messages sent.
IcmpOutEchoReps	.1.3.6.1.2.1.5.22	The number of ICMP echo reply messages sent.
IcmpOutTimestamps	.1.3.6.1.2.1.5.23	The number of ICMP timestamp request messages sent.
IcmpOutTimestampReps	.1.3.6.1.2.1.5.24	The number of ICMP timestamp reply messages.
IcmpOutAddrMasks	.1.3.6.1.2.1.5.25	The number of ICMP address mask request messages sent.
IcmpOutAddrMaskReps	.1.3.6.1.2.1.5.26	The number of ICMP address mask reply messages sent.

The TCP Group

The TCP group contains information specific to the TCP protocol. In the TCP group, objects that represent specific TCP connections exist only for the duration of the TCP session. Table 14.6 shows the primary objects contained in the TCP group.

TABLE 14.6. THE MIB-II TCP GROUP OBJECTS.

Object	Object ID	Description
TcpRtoAlgorithm	.1.3.6.1.2.1.6.1	The algorithm used to determine the timeout value for the retransmission timer.
TcpRtoMin	.1.3.6.1.2.1.6.2	The minimum value, in milliseconds, permitted by a TCP implementation for the retransmission timeout.

Object	Object ID	Description
TcpRtoMax	.1.3.6.1.2.1.6.3	The maximum value, in milliseconds, permitted by a TCP implementation for the retransmission timeout.
TcpMaxConn	.1.3.6.1.2.1.6.4	The limit on the total number of TCP connections a device can support.
TcpActiveOpens	.1.3.6.1.2.1.6.5	The number of times TCP connections have made a direct transition to the SYN-SENT state from the CLOSED state.
TcpPassiveOpens	.1.3.6.1.2.1.6.6	The number of times TCP connections have made a direct transition to the SYN-RCVD state from the LISTEN state.
TcpAttemptFails	.1.3.6.1.2.1.6.7	The number of times TCP connections have made a direct transition to the CLOSED state from either the SYN-SENT state or the SYN-RCVD state. This also includes the number of times a connection made a direct transition to the LISTEN state from the SYN-RCVD state.
TcpEstabResets	.1.3.6.1.2.1.6.8	The number of times TCP connections made a direct transition to the CLOSED state from either the ESTABLISHED state or the CLOSE-WAIT state.
TcpCurrEstab	.1.3.6.1.2.1.6.9	The number of TCP connections for which the current state is ESTABLISHED or CLOSE-WAIT.
TcpInSegs	.1.3.6.1.2.1.6.10	The total number of TCP segments received, including TCP

continues

14

TABLE 14.6. CONTINUED

Object	Object ID	Description
		segments that were received with errors.
TcpOutSegs	.1.3.6.1.2.1.6.11	The total number of TCP segments sent. This does not include segments that contained only retransmitted octets.
TcpRetransSegs	.1.3.6.1.2.1.6.12	The total number of segments that were contained in one or more of the previously transmitted octets.
TcpConnTable	.1.3.6.1.2.1.6.13	A table that contains TCP connection-specific information.
TcpConnEntry	.1.3.6.1.2.1.6.13.1	Information about a specific, currently existing TCP connection. The connection is removed when the connection state enters the CLOSED state.
TcpConnState	.1.3.6.1.2.1.6.13.1.1	The state of this TCP connection. Allowable values include CLOSED, LISTEN, and ESTABLISHED.
TcpConnLocalAddress	.1.3.6.1.2.1.6.13.1.2	The local IP address for this TCP connection. If the connection is in a LISTEN state that is willing to accept connection on any available IP interface on the device, the IP address 0.0.0.0 is used.
TcpConnLocalPort	.1.3.6.1.2.1.6.13.1.3	The local port number for this TCP connection.
TcpConnRemAddress	.1.3.6.1.2.1.6.13.1.4	The remote IP address for this TCP connection.

Object	Object ID	Description
TcpConnRemPort	.1.3.6.1.2.1.6.13.1.5	The remote port number for this TCP connection.
TcpInErrs	.1.3.6.1.2.1.6.14	The total number of segments received with errors (such as bad TCP checksums).
TcpOutRsts	.1.3.6.1.2.1.6.15	The number of TCP segments sent with the RST flag set.

The UDP Group

The UDP group contains information specific to the UDP protocol. Table 14.7 shows the primary objects contained in the UDP group.

TABLE 14.7. THE MIB-II UDP GROUP OBJECTS.

Object	Object ID	Description
UdpInDatagrams	.1.3.6.1.2.1.7.1	The total number of UDP datagrams delivered to UDP users.
UdpNoPorts	.1.3.6.1.2.1.7.2	The total number of received UDP datagrams for which there was no application at the destination port.
UdpInErrors	.1.3.6.1.2.1.7.3	The number of received UDP datagrams that could not be delivered for reasons other than the absence of an application at the indicated UDP destination port.
UdpOutDatagrams	.1.3.6.1.2.1.7.4	The total number of UDP datagrams sent from this device.
UdpTable	.1.3.6.1.2.1.7.5	A table containing information about all UDP listeners.
UdpEntry	.1.3.6.1.2.1.7.5.1	Information about a specific, currently operating UDP listener.
UdpLocalAddress	.1.3.6.1.2.1.7.5.1.1	The local IP address for this UDP listener. If the device is able to accept datagrams on any of its IP interfaces, the value 0.0.0.0 is used.
UdpLocalPort	.1.3.6.1.2.1.7.5.1.2	The local port number for this UDP listener.

14

The EGP Group

The EGP group contains information specific to the EGP protocol. The EGP protocol is used by exterior routers to allow autonomous systems to exchange routing reachability information on the Internet. Table 14.8 shows the primary objects contained in the EGP group.

TABLE 14.8. THE MIB-II EGP GROUP OBJECTS.

Object	Object ID	Description
EgpInMsgs	.1.3.6.1.2.1.8.1	The number of EGP messages received that have no errors.
EgpInErrors	.1.3.6.1.2.1.8.2	The number of EGP messages received that have errors.
EgpOutMsgs	.1.3.6.1.2.1.8.3	The total number of locally generated EGP messages.
EgpOutErrors	.1.3.6.1.2.1.8.4	The number of locally generated EGP messages not sent due to resource limitations within an EGP device.
EgpNeighTable	.1.3.6.1.2.1.8.5	The EGP neighbor table.
EgpNeighEntry	.1.3.6.1.2.1.8.5.1	Information about this device's relationship with a specific EGP neighbor.
EgpNeighState	.1.3.6.1.2.1.8.5.1.1	The EGP state of the local system with respect to this entry's EGP neighbor.
EgpNeighAddr	.1.3.6.1.2.1.8.5.1.2	The IP address of this entry's EGP neighbor.
EgpNeighAs	.1.3.6.1.2.1.8.5.1.3	The autonomous system of this EGP peer. This is set to zero if the AS number is not known at this time.
EgpNeighInMsgs	.1.3.6.1.2.1.8.5.1.4	The number of EGP messages received from this EGP peer that did not have errors.
EgpNeighInErrs	.1.3.6.1.2.1.8.5.1.5	The number of EGP messages received from this EGP peer that were found to have errors.

Object	Object ID	Description
EgpNeighOutMsgs	.1.3.6.1.2.1.8.5.1.6	The number of locally generated EGP messages to this EGP peer.
EgpNeighOutErrs	.1.3.6.1.2.1.8.5.1.7	The number of locally generated EGP messages not sent to this EGP peer due to a resource limitation on this EGP device.
EgpNeighInErrMsgs	.1.3.6.1.2.1.8.5.1.8	The number of EGP-defined error messages received from this EGP peer.
EgpNeighOutErrMsgs	.1.3.6.1.2.1.8.5.1.9	The number of EGP-defined error messages sent to this EGP peer.
EgpNeighStateUps	.1.3.6.1.2.1.8.5.1.10	The number of EGP state transitions to the UP state with this EGP peer.
EgpNeighStateDowns	.1.3.6.1.2.1.8.5.1.11	The number of EGP state transitions from the UP state to any other state with this EGP peer.
EgpNeighIntervalHello	.1.3.6.1.2.1.8.5.1.12	The interval, in hundredths of a second, between EGP Hello command retransmissions.
EgpNeighIntervalPoll	.1.3.6.1.2.1.8.5.1.13	The interval, in hundreths of a second, between EGP poll command transmissions.
EgpNeighMode	.1.3.6.1.2.1.8.5.1.14	The polling mode of the EGP device. This is set to either passive or active.
EgpNeighEventTrigger	.1.3.6.1.2.1.8.5.1.15	A control variable used to trigger an operator-initiated Start or Stop event. This returns the most recent value set for this object.
EgpAs	.1.3.6.1.2.1.8.6	The autonomous system number of this EGP device.

The Transmission Group

The objects in the Transmission group are based on the actual transmission media used by each interface. Currently, as the definitions for transmission media progress through the standardization process, they reside in the experimental portion of the MIB.

14

The SNMP Group

The SNMP group contains information specific to the SNMP protocol. Table 14.9 shows the primary objects contained in the SNMP group.

TABLE 14.9. THE MIB-II SNMP GROUP OBJECTS.

Object	Object ID	Description
SnmpInPkts	.1.3.6.1.2.1.11.1	The total number of messages delivered to the SNMP device from the transport service.
SnmpOutPkts	.1.3.6.1.2.1.11.2	The total number of SNMP messages passed from the SNMP protocol device to the transport services.
SnmpInBadVersions	.1.3.6.1.2.1.11.3	The total number of SNMP messages delivered to the SNMP protocol device from an unsupported SNMP version.
SnmpInBadCommunityNames	.1.3.6.1.2.1.11.4	The total number of SNMP messages that contained an unrecognized community name.
SnmpInBadCommunityUses	.1.3.6.1.2.1.11.5	The total number of SNMP messages delivered to the SNMP protocol device that requested an SNMP operation not allowed by the referenced SNMP community name.
SnmpInASNParseErrs	.1.3.6.1.2.1.11.6	The total number of ASN.1 errors encountered by the SNMP protocol device when decoding an SNMP message.
SnmpInTooBigs	.1.3.6.1.2.1.11.8	The total number of SNMP PDUs delivered to the SNMP protocol device that had the error status value set to tooBig.
SnmpInNoSuchNames	.1.3.6.1.2.1.11.9	The total number of SNMP PDUs delivered to the SNMP protocol device that had the error status value set to noSuchName.
SnmpInBadValues	.1.3.6.1.2.1.11.10	The total number of SNMP PDUs delivered to the SNMP protocol device that had the error status value set to badValue.

Object	Object ID	Description
SnmpInReadOnlys	.1.3.6.1.2.1.11.11	The total number of SNMP PDUs delivered to the SNMP protocol device that had the error status value set to readOnly.
SnmpInGenErrs	.1.3.6.1.2.1.11.12	The total number of SNMP PDUs delivered to the SNMP protocol device that had the error status value set to genErr.
SnmpInTotalReqVars	.1.3.6.1.2.1.11.13	The total number of MIB objects retrieved successfully by the SNMP protocol device as the result of receiving valid SNMP Get-Request and Get-Next PDUs.
SnmpInTotalSetVars	.1.3.6.1.2.1.11.14	The total number of MIB objects retrieved successfully by the SNMP protocol entity as the result of receiving valid SNMP Set-Request PDUs.
SnmpInGetRequests	.1.3.6.1.2.1.11.15	The total number of SNMP Get-Request PDUs accepted and processed by the SNMP protocol device.
SnmpInGetNexts	.1.3.6.1.2.1.11.16	The total number of SNMP Get-Next Request PDUs accepted and processed by the SNMP protocol device.
SnmpInSetRequests	.1.3.6.1.2.1.11.17	The total number of SNMP Set-Request PDUs accepted and processed by the SNMP protocol device.
SnmpInGetResponses	.1.3.6.1.2.1.11.18	The total number of SNMP Get-Response PDUs accepted and processed by the SNMP protocol device.
SnmpInTraps	.1.3.6.1.2.1.11.19	The total number of SNMP Trap PDUs accepted and processed by the SNMP protocol device.

14

continues

TABLE 14.9. CONTINUED

Object	Object ID	Description
SnmpOutTooBigs	.1.3.6.1.2.1.11.20	The total number of SNMP PDUs generated by the SNMP protocol device that had an error status value set to tooBig.
SnmpOutNoSuchNames	.1.3.6.1.2.1.11.21	The total number of SNMP PDUs generated by the SNMP protocol device that had an error status value set to noSuchName.
SnmpOutBadValues	.1.3.6.1.2.1.11.22	The total number of SNMP PDUs generated by the SNMP protocol device that had an error status value set to badValue.
SnmpOutGenErrs	.1.3.6.1.2.1.11.24	The total number of SNMP PDUs generated by the SNMP protocol device that had an error status value set to genErr.
SnmpOutGetRequests	.1.3.6.1.2.1.11.25	The total number of SNMP Get-Request PDUs generated by the SNMP protocol device.
SnmpOutGetNexts	.1.3.6.1.2.1.11.26	The total number of SNMP Get-Next Request PDUs generated by the SNMP protocol device.
SnmpOutSetRequests	.1.3.6.1.2.1.11.27	The total number of SNMP Set-Request PDUs generated by the SNMP protocol device.
SnmpOutGetResponses	.1.3.6.1.2.1.11.28	The total number of SNMP Get-Response PDUs generated by the SNMP protocol device.
SnmpOutTraps	.1.3.6.1.2.1.11.29	The total number of SNMP Trap PDUs generated by the SNMP protocol device.
SnmpEnableAuthenTraps	.1.3.6.1.2.1.11.30	Indicates whether the SNMP agent process is permitted to generate authentication-failure traps.

The SNMP object IDs .1.3.6.1.2.1.11.7 *and* .1.3.6.1.2.1.11.23 *are not implemented.*

Deploying an SNMP Management System

The deployment of SNMP management software requires two separate configuration tasks. First, SNMP agent software must be acquired for all devices you want to manage on the network. You must configure each device to load the SNMP agent software. Second, an SNMP management software package must be acquired, from which all SNMP management operations are performed.

Configuring the SNMP Agent

In a Windows NT environment, the SNMP agent software is distributed freely with the Windows NT software. Complete the following steps to configure the SNMP agent on a Windows NT workstation:

1. From the desktop, right-click on the Network Neighborhood and select Properties.

2. In the Network dialog box, select the Services tab.

3. Select SNMP Service from the Select Network Service dialog box, and then select OK to install the service (see Figure 14.4).

FIGURE 14.4.

Installing the SNMP Service.

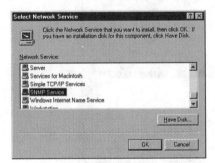

4. After the necessary files for SNMP have been installed, you need to configure the property pages of the SNMP service. The Agent tab of the Microsoft SNMP Properties page (see Figure 14.5) enables you to configure information such as contact name and location. It also determines which levels of the network will be monitored by SNMP.

5. On the Traps tab of the Microsoft SNMP Properties page (see Figure 14.6), you can configure the destination IP address for SNMP trap messages. You also can configure the SNMP Trap Community name. You should change the default community name from Public, because this is generally considered a security weakness.

14

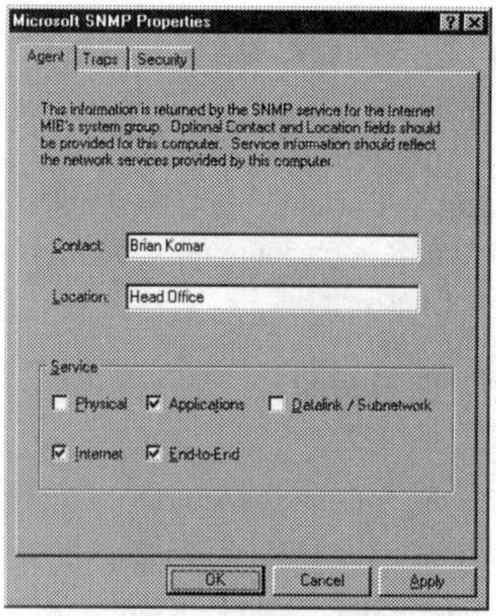

FIGURE 14.5.

Configuring the SNMP agent properties.

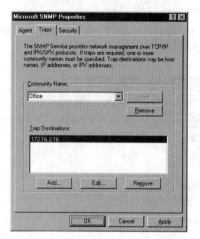

FIGURE 14.6.

Configuring the SNMP trap properties.

6. On the Security tab of the Microsoft SNMP Properties page (see Figure 14.7), you can configure the accepted community names for SNMP Get requests. The Security tab is also used to configure which IP addresses will be allowed to perform SNMP requests to this SNMP agent. For added security, you can configure to send authentication traps when an SNMP request is issued from an SNMP management station that does not match the community name or list of approved management stations.

7. After you have installed the service, reapply your most recent service pack before restarting the Windows NT system. This ensures the current versions of all files are installed on the system.

FIGURE 14.7.

Configuring the SNMP security properties.

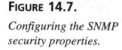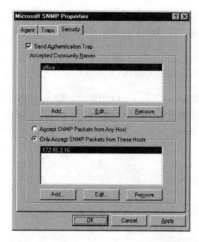

Using an SNMP Management Station

Windows NT does not ship with a prepackaged SNMP management station. Several SNMP management packages are available to provide SNMP management capability to Windows NT including

- HP OpenView
- Intel LanDesk
- CA-Unicenter

ADVANTAGES OF USING SNMP MANAGEMENT TOOLS

The main benefit in using third-party SNMP management tools is that you do not have to remember actual MIB object IDs. The graphical interface enables you to navigate the MIB object tree using the English names for the objects, rather than the numeric object IDs.

The Windows NT Resource Kit provides a command-line utility called SNMPUTIL, which uses the following syntax:

```
snmputil [get|getnext|walk] agent community oid
```

This command enables you to configure whether you want to perform a Get, Getnext, or Walk operation. The Walk operation shows the text equivalents of the object IDs. You must also provide the agent name you want to send the GetRequest PDU to and the community name you want to use.

14

If you want to determine how long the SNMP device named Router1 has been operating, for example, and the SNMP community that Router1 belongs to is Marketing, issue the following command:

```
SNMPUTIL get router1 marketing .1.3.6.1.2.1.1.3
```

Although SNMPUTIL provides the ability to perform SNMP queries, it does not provide a mechanism to perform SNMP SetRequest operations. GUI versions of SNMP management software provide many benefits, including

- More intuitive features
- Network mapping capabilities
- Increased functionality

Figure 14.8 shows an example of how CA-Unicenter is able to show a network mapping of the 131.107.3.0 network segment.

FIGURE 14.8.

The 131.107.3.0 network segment.

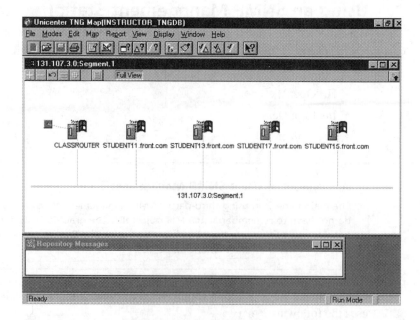

Note how each device on the network segment is identified. The identification includes the hostname for each device and an icon to indicate that these are all Windows NT Server hosts.

The same request for determining the system uptime is much easier when using a graphical SNMP manager. Figure 14.9 shows the same SNMP request being performed to the device named classrouter in the 131.107.3.0 network.

FIGURE 14.9.

A query on sysUpTime using CA-Unicenter.

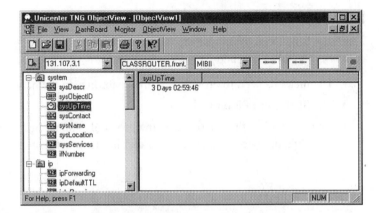

Applying What You Have Learned

The material discussed today walked you through the various aspects of network management using the SNMP protocol. SNMP is used widely in enterprise networks because of its capability to attack problems at an early stage.

Test Your Knowledge

1. What are the two major categories of network management?

2. What protocols (in addition to IP) can an SNMP system be implemented on?

3. What role does the SNMP management system play in the SNMP process?

4. What role does the SNMP agent play in the SNMP process?

5. What additional network management functionality does the SNMP Trap PDU provide?

6. What measures can you apply in an SNMP environment to provide additional security?

7. What are the three types of community names used in an SNMP implementation?

8. How are object identifiers assigned to objects in the MIB?

9. What are the major categories in the MIB-II database?

10. What advantage does the GetBulk PDU provide in SNMP v2?

14

Preview of the Next Day

Tomorrow's material looks into the issues involved with providing remote access to your network. The topics include

- The methods used to provide dial-in capabilities to the network
- The SLIP and PPP protocols
- An overview on the use of tunneling protocols, including two of the more common tunneling protocols available today and in the near future: PPTP and L2TP

DAY 15

Dial-Up Networking Using TCP/IP

Today's material examines the technology used to remotely access networks. A comparison is provided of the two methods used to access networks through public phone networks: Serial Line Internet Protocol (SLIP) and Point-to-Point Protocol (PPP).

After the technology of dialing into networks is discussed, you will learn how to implement Dial-Up Networking in a Windows NT environment. Configuration is examined from both the server and client sides.

You also will learn about a new technology being implemented in more and more networks. Tunneling enables public networks to be used as secure connections between two remote networks. Implementing tunnels between clients over a public network also is covered.

Connecting to Networks Remotely over Phone Lines

This book so far has discussed connecting systems over traditional network media including ethernet, token ring, and wide-area networking technologies. This section discusses implementation over analog phone lines. The following are the two most commonly implemented protocols:

- Serial Line Internet Protocol (SLIP)
- Point-to-Point Protocol (PPP)

These protocols are similar to frame types implemented on local area networks. They define how data is formatted as it transmits over the analog phone lines.

Serial Line Internet Protocol (SLIP)

RFC 1055 The *Serial Line Internet Protocol (SLIP)* is the original method developed for TCP/IP communication over serial phone lines. SLIP forms a point-to-point connection that runs the TCP/IP protocol.

The SLIP protocol is implemented as a packet-framing protocol. SLIP defines a specific sequence of characters that frame each IP packet as it is transported over the serial line. SLIP does not have a standardized maximum packet size. The two most common sizes are 1,006 bytes or 1,500 bytes.

Two special characters are defined—the END character (decimal 192) and the ESC character (decimal 219). This ESC character should not be confused with the ASCII Escape character.

The END character indicates the end of the packet being transmitted. If the data packet contains the decimal 192 character, the END character is represented with a two-byte sequence comprising the ESC character and the decimal 220 character.

The ESC character is used when the END character has to be represented as a two-byte sequence because the decimal 192 character exists in the data stream.

Although the SLIP protocol is a simple protocol to implement, the following deficiencies exist:

- Both computers need to know each other's IP address for routing purposes. A script often is required to allow the server to assign an IP address to the client at dial-in. No mechanism is provided to automatically assign the IP address to the client.

- SLIP is designed for use with the IP protocol. Without a Type field, it is impossible to use an alternative protocol, such as IPX, over the connection.
- No error detection or error correction is provided. SLIP leaves these tasks to the transport protocols instead of implementing its own checksums. This leads to inefficiencies because it is up to a higher-level protocol to determine whether a packet has been corrupted in transit.
- The user's account and password are transmitted as clear text across the phone network.
- No compression is provided. Many of the packets transmitted over a SLIP connection are fragmented. A compression algorithm can be implemented on the common fields of the fragmented packets, including the IP header and the TCP header. If these fields are included in compression algorithms, only the changed fields between fragmented fields can be transmitted.

COMPRESSED SLIP

A modified version of the SLIP protocol, *Compressed Serial Line Internet Protocol (CSLIP)*, can perform a compression algorithm on the common fields in fragmented packets.

Point-to-Point Protocol (PPP)

`RFC 1661` The *Point-to-Point Protocol (PPP)* is a standardized protocol developed to solve the problem of encapsulating the IP protocol over point-to-point links. PPP has the following features:

- Automatic assignment and management of IP addresses for remote clients
- The capability to transmit multiple protocols over a single point-to-point link
- Negotiation of options between the client and server, including network addresses and data-compression options
- Automatic error detection

The following are the main components of the PPP protocol:

- A method to encapsulate multiple-protocol datagrams.
- A *Link Control Protocol (LCP)* used to establish, configure, and test the data link connection. This actually is an extension to the PPP protocol.
- A family of *Network Control Protocols (NCPs)* used to establish and configure different network-layer protocols.

The PPP Packet

The PPP protocol can transmit multiple protocols during a single communication session. To accomplish this, the PPP packet uses framing to indicate the beginning and end of the encapsulated data. The PPP packet is shown in Figure 15.1.

FIGURE 15.1.

The PPP packet format.

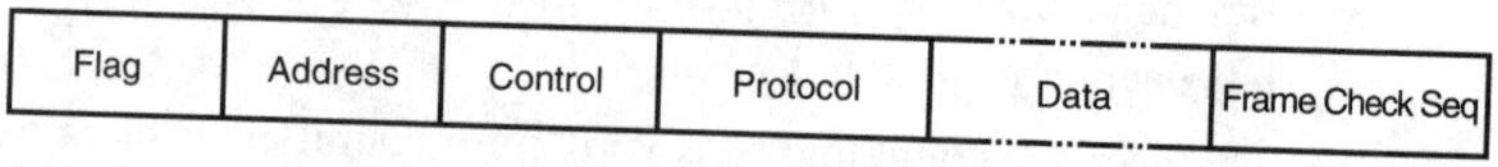

Flag	Address	Control	Protocol	Data	Frame Check Seq

- *Flag.* This 8-bit field indicates the beginning or end of a frame of data. It is a static value set to the binary sequence 01111110.
- *Address.* This 8-bit field is set to the standard broadcast address 11111111. PPP does not assign addresses to each station in the point-to-point link.
- *Control.* This 8-bit field contains the binary sequence 00000011, which calls for the transmission of user data in unsequenced frames.
- *Protocol.* This 16-bit field identifies the protocol encapsulated in the data payload. This protocol ID is based on the values stored within the current STD002, the Assigned Numbers standard document. The following protocol IDs have been reserved by the PPP specification:
  - *c021.* Link Control Protocol (LCP)
  - *c023.* Password Authentication Protocol (PAP)
  - *c025.* Link Quality Report
  - *c223.* Challenge Handshake Authentication Protocol (CHAP)
- *Data.* This variable-length field contains the actual protocol data encapsulated within the PPP packet. The maximum length of this field, called the *Maximum Receive Unit (MRU)*, is set to the default of 1,500 bytes. Two hosts can negotiate for this to be set to a different value. The end of the data field is indicated by the 01111110 flag sequence.
- *Frame Check Sequence (FCS).* This 16-bit checksum makes sure the PPP packet has not been corrupted in transit. Some implementations can use a 32-bit checksum for improved error detection.

Link Control Protocol Phases

The Link Control Protocol provides the PPP protocol with a methodology for establishing, configuring, maintaining, and terminating a point-to-point connection. The following four phases are involved in the Link Control Protocol:

15

- The link establishment phase
- The authentication phase
- The network-layer protocol phase
- The link termination phase

The Link Establishment Phase The link establishment phase uses the Link Control Protocol to establish a point-to-point connection by exchanging configuration packets.

At the beginning of the negotiation, it is assumed that all configurations are set to their default value. Negotiation only needs to occur for values being changed from their default.

Options configured during this phase are network-layer protocol independent. Network protocol-specific configuration is handled by the separate network-control protocol during the network-layer configuration phase.

The following options can be configured during this phase:

- *Maximum Receive Unit (MRU)*. This option informs their peer that they can receive larger packets than the default size of 1,500 bytes. It also can request smaller packets for transmission.
- *Authentication Protocol*. This option selects a protocol for authentication. Valid options include the Password Authentication Protocol and the Challenge Authentication Protocol.
- *Quality of Link Protocol*. This option determines whether link monitoring is enabled. Link monitoring can determine how often the link drops data.
- *Magic Number*. This option detects a looped-back link. When a magic-number request is sent, the receiving host compares the magic number received to the magic number in the last configuration request sent to the peer. If the magic numbers do not match, the link is not looped back. If they match, the link might be looped back. To determine whether it gets looped back, a new magic number is selected by the protocol, and a new configure request is sent using this new magic number. If the magic numbers match again when the next configure request is received, the link is in a looped-back state.
- *Protocol field compression*. This option enables the compression of the PPP protocol field. Protocol field values are chosen so they can be compressed into a single octet (rather than the default 16 bits). If both peers agree to this option, the smaller, 8-bit version of the protocol field can be transmitted.

- *Address and Control field compression.* This option provides a method to negotiate the compression of the address and control fields. In a PPP link, the address and control fields have static addresses that easily can be compressed during transmission.

The Authentication Phase

This optional phase enables a peer to authenticate before network-layer protocols are exchanged. If authentication takes place, it should occur as soon as possible after the link is established. Two common protocols used to authenticate a peer in this phase: Password Authentication Protocol (PAP) and Challenged Handshake Authentication Protocol (CHAP).

The PAP protocol follows a basic login procedure using a two-step process. The client authenticates by sending the user's name and password to the server. For additional security, this password can be passed in an encrypted format. The server compares the user/password combination with its secrets database and either acknowledges or rejects the credentials supplied.

RFC 1994 The CHAP protocol uses a three-step authentication procedure. The server sends a string to the client. This string contains a randomly generated challenge string and the hostname of the server. The client uses the hostname to look up the implemented secret between the client and server. This secret is used to encrypt the challenge string. The result of this encryption process is sent to the server with the client's name. The server uses the same procedure and considers the client authenticated if it arrives at the same result. CHAP not only performs this procedure during the initialization of a session, it challenges at regular intervals to make sure the line has not been hijacked during the session.

Network-Layer Protocol Phase

After the link establishment and authentication phases are complete, each network-layer protocol to be implemented during the session must be configured using the appropriate Network Control Protocol (NCP). Remember that PPP can be used to transport multiple protocols during the same session. After the network-layer protocol negotiation is complete, the link can transmit those protocols.

An example of network-layer protocol negotiation is the negotiation of an IP address for a remote client.

Link Termination Phase

PPP can terminate a link at any time. All of the following can cause the termination of a link:

- Loss of carrier
- Authentication failure

15

- Link-quality failure
- Expiration of the idle-time timer
- Administrative closing of the link

The termination of the link is processed through an exchange of terminate packets.

Configuring Dial-Up Networking in a Microsoft Environment

Now that the theory behind Dial-Up Networking has been discussed, you will examine the configuration of dial-in server and dial-in client software using Windows NT Server and Windows NT Workstation.

Configuring the Remote Access Service

Windows NT can function as a PPP dial-up server by installing the Remote Access Service (RAS). Windows NT does not support SLIP dial-in clients because the clear-text passwords are considered too insecure.

SIMULTANEOUS DIAL-UP CONNECTIONS

Windows NT Server can support up to 256 simultaneous dial-up connections. Windows NT Workstation can support only a single dial-up connection.

To install the Remote Access Service, you first need to install the modems attached to your system. Modems can be installed using the following steps:

1. Log in to the server as a member of the Administrators local group.
2. Open Control Panel.
3. Double-click to start the Modems applet in Control Panel.
4. Click the Add button to install the drivers for your new modem.
5. The Install New Modem Wizard starts. If you know the model of your modem and the port to which it is attached, you can configure the modem manually. Otherwise, you can have the wizard detect your modem.

6. If the wizard does not detect the modem correctly (this is common with newer modems), you can either select the modem from the list of installable drivers or click the Have Disk button to install a third-party driver (see Figure 15.2).

FIGURE 15.2.

Selecting a modem driver.

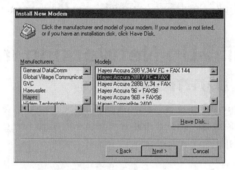

7. After you select the model of your modem, you must select the port to which the modem is attached (see Figure 15.3).

FIGURE 15.3.

Selecting the port for a newly installed modem.

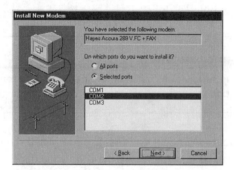

8. Click the Finish button to complete the Install New Modem Wizard.

9. Click the Close button to complete the installation of your new modem.

MODEM DRIVERS IN WINDOWS NT

Many modem manufacturers do not include Windows NT drivers with their modems. This is not a major issue because the same modem drivers are used by both Windows 95 and Windows NT.

15

Now that your modem is installed, Windows NT Server automatically installs the Remote Access Service. The Remote Access Service configures both the client and server services involved with Dial-Up Networking. A dialog box states that you must configure Dial-Up Networking to use the newly installed modem (see Figure 15.4).

FIGURE 15.4.

The Modem Setup warning dialog box.

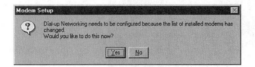

The Remote Access configuration dialog box is now displayed. The following steps can be used to add a new modem:

1. Click the Add button and select the newly installed modem from the Add RAS Device dialog box.

2. After the modem has been added to the list of available ports, you can select each modem and click the Configure button to determine how the modem functions (see Figure 15.5).

FIGURE 15.5.

Configuring the port usage for a modem.

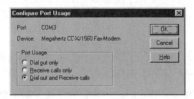

Valid options include: Dial Out Only, Receive Calls Only, or Dial Out and Receive Calls. This enables you to configure whether the modem is used for server or client functionality (or both).

3a. If you select Dial Out Only, the Network configuration dialog box opens (see Figure 15.6).

This dialog box enables you to select which protocols should be used by the modem for dialing out.

FIGURE 15.6.

Configuring the dial-out protocols.

3b. If you select Receive Calls Only, the Network configuration dialog box has additional parameters to configure (see Figure 15.7).

FIGURE 15.7.

Configuring dial-out and dial-up protocols.

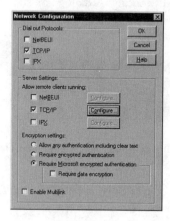

This dialog box enables you to configure the following properties:

- *Dial out protocols.* Select the protocols to be used by a dial-up client.
- *Server settings.* Select which protocols remote clients can use to connect to the remote access server. The Configure button for TCP/IP properties is discussed in step 3c.
- *Encryption settings.* Set the minimum level of encryption a client must support for a connection to be established.
- *Enable multilink.* Set whether this modem can connect or accept connections using the multilink PPP protocol.

3c. The TCP/IP Configure button enables you to determine how TCP/IP should be configured for dial-up clients (see Figure 15.8).

This dialog box enables you to configure the following properties:

- *Access to network.* This property determines whether dial-up clients can use only network resources on the RAS server or can access the entire network.
- *IP address assignment.* This property enables you either to use a DHCP server for assigning IP addresses to dial-up clients or to configure a static pool for use by dial-up clients.

- *Request static IP address.* This option enables clients to request a specific IP address upon connection.

4. After you configure all installed modems, click the Continue button to proceed with the installation.

5. The installation program reconfigures the network bindings based on the protocols and modem configuration in the previous steps.

6. You are prompted to restart your computer for the setting changes to take effect.

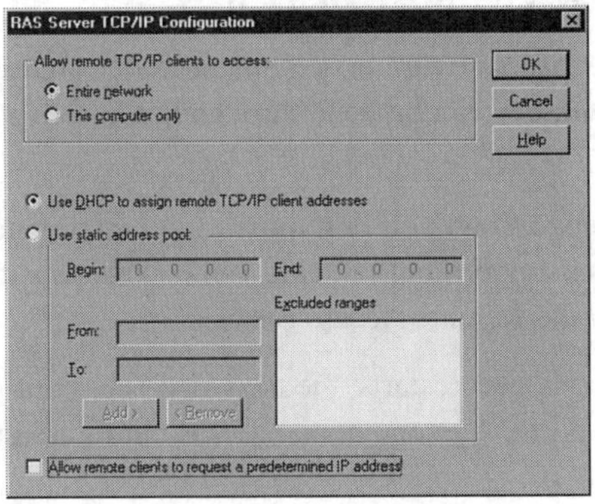

FIGURE 15.8.

Configuring TCP/IP properties for the Remote Access Server.

SERVICE PACK WARNING

If you have applied any service packs, the most recent version of the service pack must be reinstalled after the Remote Access Service (or anything else from the original CD) has been configured.

After the server restarts, you can perform the last step in configuring the Remote Access Server—deciding which users can connect to the Remote Access Server. This is best accomplished using the User Manager for Domains utility.

Each user has a Dial-In Properties tab (see Figure 15.9).

This tab enables you to configure whether the user account can remotely access the network using Dial-Up Networking. It also enables you to configure the level of callback security. Valid security levels include No Call Back, Set by Caller, and a preset phone number.

FIGURE 15.9.

Configuring dial-up rights for a user.

Configuring Dial-Up Networking

The client also is required to configure his computer to dial-in to the network. In a Windows NT environment, this can be done through the Dial-Up Networking option in My Computer.

To configure Dial-Up Networking, you first must install a modem and configure the Remote Access Service to support dial-out calls only. (This was discussed in the preceding section "Configuring the Remote Access Service.")

After the Windows NT computer restarts, the next step is to configure a phone book entry for Dial-Up Networking. A phone book entry is configured using the following tabs:

- The Basic tab (see Figure 15.10) enables you to configure a name for the new entry, its phone number, and the modem used to connect to the remote network (if multiple modems exist).

FIGURE 15.10.

Adding a new phone book entry.

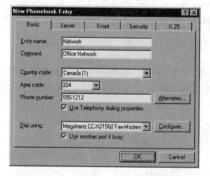

You also can configure alternate phone numbers. These are used if a connection cannot be established using the primary phone number.

- The Server tab enables you to configure the type of dial-up server to which you are connecting (see Figure 15.11).

FIGURE 15.11.

The Server tab of Dial-Up Networking.

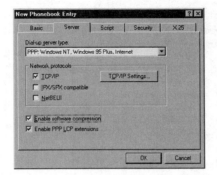

15

For TCP/IP connectivity, you can configure the client to use SLIP or PPP. The general dialog box also enables you to support software compression and Link Control Protocol (LCP) negotiation.

In the Server tab, you also can configure the TCP/IP protocol (see Figure 15.12).

FIGURE 15.12.

Configuring the TCP/IP protocol for Dial-Up Networking.

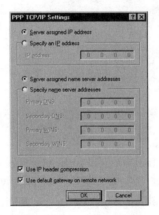

This tab enables you to configure the IP address, the name server addresses, the IP header compression, and whether packets can be routed to the remote network.

- The Script tab enables the phone book to be associated with scripts that can be executed before or after a session is established (see Figure 15.13).

PPP servers using Link Control Protocol negotiations generally do not require scripting.

- The Security tab enables the authentication mechanism to be configured (see Figure 15.14).

FIGURE 15.13.

Configuring scripting options for Dial-Up Networking.

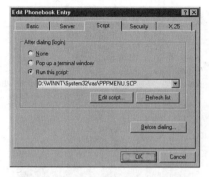

FIGURE 15.14.

Configuring the Security tab.

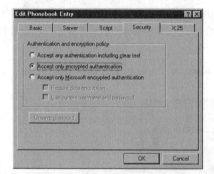

If you select Accept Any Authentication Including Clear Text, any authentication protocol can be negotiated during a connection. Accept Only Encrypted Authentication prevents PAP from being used for authentication. Accept Only Microsoft-Encrypted Authentication configures the client to use MS-Chap for the authentication protocol. It also can be used to encrypt the transmitted data.

- The X.25 tab configures X.25 options if the modem device is an X.25 device.

Tunneling Extensions

Many organizations are examining other methods of enabling remote users to access the internal network. One method being implemented more frequently is tunneling. *Tunneling* enables a routable protocol (such as IP) to transfer the frames of another protocol to a destination network.

At the sending end of the connection, software encapsulates the network packets so it can be transferred to the remote network. At the destination network, the receiving router decapsulates the original frame and sends it to the destination host.

Windows NT includes the Point-to-Point Tunneling Protocol (PPTP), which enables Internet Protocol (IP), NetBEUI, or IPX to be encapsulated within an IP header for transmission across an intermediary network. All encapsulated data is encrypted before it is encapsulated for transmission over the network. This technology also can be implemented over public networks such as the Internet. The completed link between the remote client and the tunneling server is called a *Virtual Private Network (VPN)*.

FUTURE OF TUNNELING PROTOCOLS

The IETF is preparing an RFC about a protocol known as *Layer 2 Tunneling Protocol (L2TP)*. This protocol combines the technology of Microsoft's PPTP and Cisco's Layer 2 forwarding.

Components of a Virtual Private Network

Figure 15.15 shows the components in a Virtual Private Network.

FIGURE 15.15.

Components of a Virtual Private Network.

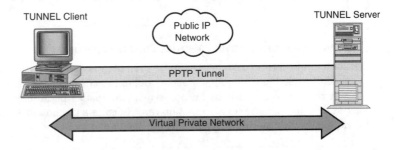

- *Tunnel server.* The tunnel server is configured with a protocol (such as PPTP) that can support a Virtual Private Network. The tunnel server can be configured to host multiple virtual network interfaces to enable connections from remote clients.

- *Tunnel client.* The tunnel client is configured with the same tunneling protocol as the tunnel server. The virtual network interface on the tunnel client must be configured to provide dial-out access.

- *Tunnel.* The tunnel is a logical connection established between the tunnel client and the tunnel server. Although the tunnel might cross several routers between the client and the server, it logically appears to be a single network hop. All data transmitted over the tunnel can be encrypted for secure communications.

The Tunneling Process

The network in Figure 15.15 shows a scenario in which the tunneling client is directly attached to the network. It is more common, however, for the remote-tunneling client to connect to a public network (such as the Internet) using a serial line protocol such as PPP (see Figure 15.16).

FIGURE 15.16.

Connecting to a tunnel server using a dial-up client.

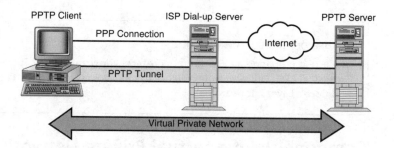

In this figure, the PPTP client first establishes a PPP connection to the Internet service provider's dial-up networking server. This establishes an IP address for the PPTP client.

ADVANTAGES OF DEPLOYING VIRTUAL PRIVATE NETWORKS

Configuring clients to connect to an ISP's remote networking services eliminates the need to configure a modem pool to provide access to the internal network. This provides huge savings to many companies because they do not have to purchase serial expansion cards (such as a Digiboard). They also do not have to provide 7×24 support for the modem pool.

After the connection to the PPP server is established, the client launches a second Dial-Up Networking connection. This connection does not use a modem as the dialing device. Instead, it uses a Virtual Private Network adapter (see Figure 15.17).

The only difference between a VPN phone book entry and a modem phone book entry is that the VPN dials an IP address (or hostname) rather than a phone number. All other settings can be configured as described in the section "Configuring Dial-Up Networking in a Microsoft Environment," earlier in this chapter.

FIGURE 15.17.

Configuring Dial-Up Networking to use a VPN.

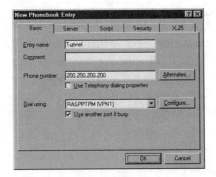

SUPPORT FOR THE PPTP PROTOCOL

Windows NT Server, Windows NT Workstation, and Windows 95 all can be configured to use the PPTP protocol. Windows 95 requires that the upgrade for Dial-Up Networking be applied to the operating system. This file is available from the Microsoft Web site at http://www.microsoft.com. Virtual Private Network adapters can be configured by adding the Point-to-Point Tunneling Protocol to an NT class system through the Network applet in Control Panel.

The following characteristics are true for every PPTP tunnel:

- The PPTP client uses a random TCP port number over 1024.

- The PPTP client connects to the PPTP server's TCP port 1723.

`RFC 1702`   • The Virtual Private Network transports all data in *Generic Routing Encapsulation (GRE)* packets. GRE packets encapsulated within the IP protocol use IP protocol identifier 47.

Applying What You Have Learned

Today's material provided information about technologies that enable remote users to connect to an organization's internal network. As more users take part in mobile computing, the need to provide remote access to the internal network increases. Expect to see more implementations of tunneling solutions. They provide access to internal networks over public networks without the hardware requirements of setting up modem pools.

Test Your Knowledge

1. What are some of the deficiencies of the SLIP protocol?

2. What forms of authentication can the PPP protocol use?

3. How does SLIP frame the data it transmits over a serial line?

4. Can PPP be used to transmit multiple protocols over a single dial-up session?

5. Which service in Windows NT enables you to configure a dial-up server?

6. What role does the Link Control Protocol (LCP) play in a PPP connection?

7. What are the three main components of a Virtual Private Network (VPN)?

8. What ports are used by a PPTP tunnel?

9. How are dial-in rights configured in Windows NT Server?

Preview of the Next Day

Tomorrow's material provides an in-depth look at security on a TCP/IP network. Specifically, it investigates the role that firewalls play in network security.

Other topics covered in tomorrow's material include the following:

- Common threats to network security
- Planning a network security methodology
- Types of firewalls
- Advanced authentication methods

DAY **16**

Firewalls and Security

Today's material overviews one of the most contentious topics discussed when referring to networks—network security. The discussion starts with some of the issues you face when configuring the security of a network.

After learning about common network threats, you will look at various implementations of firewalls that can protect your network from external sources. The following firewalls are discussed:

- Packet-filter firewalls
- Circuit-level firewalls
- Proxy application firewalls
- Dynamic packet-filter firewalls
- Kernel proxy firewalls

The chapter closes with information about protecting local network resources. An implementation becoming more popular is the use of Kerberos authentication. You'll learn how Kerberos authentication is implemented and the advantages associated with this authentication.

Threats to Network Security

As networks become more common, several security issues are becoming more apparent. Some standard technologies currently used on the Internet are not secure. Awareness is key if you want to further secure your network from infiltration. The following are common security holes in networks today:

- The use of clear-text passwords for authentication
- The ease of performing network monitoring
- The capability to spoof network addresses
- The poor quality of security implementations

Clear-Text Authentication

Many common, networked business applications in use today utilize clear-text passwords. These applications include the following:

- FTP
- Telnet
- POP3 mail clients

Anyone running a network monitor can capture network packets and reassemble them to determine account and password information.

Despite countless warnings, many passwords in use today are not secure. Passwords should not be names of family members or pets, birth dates, favorite colors, or phone numbers. Many users are guilty of sharing passwords with other users or even leaving passwords in readily accessible areas of the office. Some even stick Post-it notes on monitors or under keyboards with passwords written on them.

Even if more obscure passwords are used, it still is common practice to use words found in the dictionary. These passwords still are very insecure. Almost every operating system has password-cracking programs that use dictionary files to crack passwords. These password-cracking programs encrypt the contents of the dictionary file using the same encryption algorithm used by the network operating system to encrypt the password file. The contents are compared until a match is found.

How do you protect yourself from this network hacking routine? The key is to select alphanumeric, non-dictionary words. Do not just tag a number to the end of a word. Many password-cracking programs tag the numbers 1 through 99 to the end of each word in its dictionary.

Proliferation of Network-Monitoring Software

Network-monitoring software packages (also called *network sniffers*) are readily available and can view packets as they traverse the network wire. If applications utilizing clear-text passwords are implemented, this security flaw enables anyone running network-monitoring software to capture passwords and account information for reuse later. The threat is not limited to the local network; it encompasses all network segments that the packets must cross from the user to the server. Any network-monitoring equipment between the two endpoints can capture the account and password information.

Network-monitoring software can be an expensive proposition, but several shareware and bundled versions of network-monitoring software are readily available.

Windows NT includes the Network Monitor Tools and Agent as a service for use in Windows NT Workstation and Windows NT Server. This utility sniffs out any traffic destined for the station running the network-monitoring software. This includes any traffic directed to the monitoring station and broadcast traffic destined for the host. System Management Server includes a full-service version of the network-monitoring software. This version has the capability to monitor all network traffic on the network, not just traffic destined for the station running the network-monitoring software. Figure 16.1 shows a network capture of a user's FTP account and password.

FIGURE 16.1.

A network capture of the password go4It for the account bkomar.

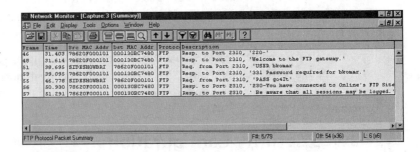

Network monitoring not only is related to external attempts to access the secure network; it also can be performed from within the interior network. Network administrators need to be aware of this. Verifying that no unauthorized network monitors are operating should be part of your regular monitoring activities.

In a Windows NT environment, the following NetBIOS name is registered whenever a client is running a network-monitoring software application:

```
SIDESHOWBRI™ ™ ™ ™ <BF>   UNIQUE        Registered
```

The <BF> entry also can be observed within the WINS database (if implemented) to determine which users have executed a network-monitoring software application.

Spoofing

Several methods are available for a host to masquerade as another host. This technique is commonly known as *IP spoofing*. The following steps show a common method of spoofing an IP address:

1. The attacking station changes its IP address to that of client it wants to spoof.

2. The attacking station next creates a source route packet. This packet indicates the path an IP packet takes from the server on a return path. The trusted client being spoofed is the last hop in the indicated source route before reaching the server. This makes it appear that the packet originated at the masqueraded workstation.

3. The attacking station next sends a packet destined for the server using the source route packet.

4. Because the packet has been routed through the trusted client, the server accepts the packet.

5. The server returns its response to the trusted client.

6. Because of the source route implemented, the trusted client forwards the response to the attacking station.

This is one common method of spoofing an IP address. Another method consists of masquerading as the trusted host when the trusted host is turned off. As long as the correct account/password combination is used, the attacking station can masquerade as the trusted host.

Spoofing also can be performed with email services. It is easy to use a Telnet application to connect to a SMTP server. Using SMTP commands, an email message can be sent using any return address you want. This is accomplished using the SMTP MAIL FROM: command.

Flawed Security Configuration

The most common form of network security breach relates back to improper configuration of security. This usually is the result of one of the following:

- Lack of experience on the part of the network administrator
- Security patches not being applied to the operating system
- Lack of security on a single host that compromises the entire network

Lack of experience is a major cause of insecure networks. Many network administrators inherit their networks without knowing all the inherent risks involved in managing them. They learn their trade on the job, and the results can be disastrous. Sometimes default accounts and default passwords are not changed. Many networks are broken into using the default administrative account names and passwords.

As security holes are discovered in operating systems, patches or fixes are created to close these holes. A network administrator must keep up with the latest patches to make sure the system remains secure. If patches are not applied to the server, the network is left open to hackers who can exploit the unpatched security hole.

16

WINDOWS NT SECURITY HOLES

Many patches have been created for security holes in the Windows NT operating system. The site `http://www.ntsecurity.net` is an excellent source for information about the most recent security holes found in the Windows NT operating system. In addition to listing security holes, this site also suggests solutions to them.

Another URL that should be bookmarked in your Web browser is the service-pack directory on Microsoft's FTP site. The following is the location of this site:

`ftp://ftp.microsoft.com/bussys/winnt/winnt-public/fixes/usa/nt40/`

This site contains recent service packs and hot fixes. Within each subdirectory, Microsoft knowledge-base articles document which security hole each hot fix addresses.

On most networks, if a single system is compromised, it can lead to the entire network being compromised. The Berkeley R-utilities, discussed on Day 11, "Remote Command Applications," can lead to this situation.

On one hand, the R-utilities improve security because no text-based passwords are transmitted on the network. This reduces the possibility of a network monitor capturing a text-based password. These utilities, however, can open up other security holes.

If a single host is compromised as a result of bad or captured passwords, it can lead to other hosts being compromised. If the compromised system is included in an .rhosts file on another system, the hacker then can compromise that system as well. After that system has been compromised, the hacker can attack other systems that include a compromised system in the .rhosts file.

Planning a Network Security Policy

Before security can be implemented on a network, the organization must draft a security policy. This document should detail the following information:

- What information should be accessible to all internal users of the network?
- What information should be accessible to remote users of the network?
- What external resources should be accessible to internal users of the network?
- What rules are in place for the removal of data from the office? These rules should include both physical and electronic forms of data.
- What rules of conduct should be implemented for electronic mail?
- What rules of conduct should be implemented for Web browsing?
- A password policy should be established. This policy should include how frequently passwords are changed, the minimum length of a password, and the password requirements. Password requirements can force a password to be alphanumeric or to be a minimum length of characters.

If you predocument the network policy before implementing network security, you can determine the optimal network security rather than making the policy match the existing network. This leads to a more secure network.

Firewalls

A *firewall* provides a boundary service to the local area network. A firewall usually is located between the external world and the internal network (see Figure 16.2).

FIGURE 16.2.

Locating a firewall between the interior and exterior networks.

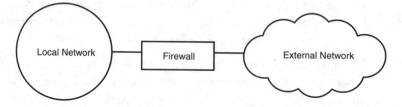

Making sure that all connections to and from the internal network pass through the firewall inspection enforces security. A firewall can be configured to allow specific protocols to pass through the firewall if predefined criteria are met. Criteria also can be set to reject a packet if it does not pass inspection.

The two most common implementations of firewalls are based on the following:

- Permitting all services to pass unless they are explicitly denied
- Denying all services unless they are explicitly allowed

The second implementation is the most common because it prevents newly developed protocols and applications from easily passing through the firewall. All unknown protocols are rejected by default.

Placing the firewall between the interior and exterior networks masks the internal network characteristics from the exterior network. Common protocols that are blocked from revealing the interior network's characteristics include NIS, DNS, and FINGER. These protocols have the potential to reveal network configuration information that is invaluable to a hacker attempting to circumnavigate the firewall mechanism.

In addition to enforcing security on the network, a good firewall also includes reporting and alert facilities. Usage reports can be generated to show commonly visited sites. They also can reveal security holes missed during the configuration of the network security policy. Alert services enable the firewall to notify a network or a security administrator when an intruder attempts to gain access using a prohibited service.

Additional Security Issues

After its initial configuration, a firewall must be maintained to provide continued protection against newer attack methods. As new services are released, a determination must be made whether each service will be allowed to navigate through the firewall. The following questions must be answered:

1. Is the service located on the internal network or the external network?
2. If the service is located on the external network, will all users on the internal network be allowed to connect to the service? Or will only a specific group of hosts be allowed to connect?
3. When connecting to the external service, will the clients connect directly or will they use a proxy service on the firewall?
4. If the service is located on the internal network, will external users be allowed to connect to the service?
5. If external users are allowed to connect, will a security mechanism be implemented to authenticate the users and to limit access?

6. What are the characteristics of the traffic related to the new service? Does it use UDP or TCP? What ports are used by the server service? What ports are used by the client service? Are any high-level protocols used that can be identified by a protocol ID number?

By answering these questions for a new service, you can make sure the service is implemented in a secure method that follows the security policy of the network.

The firewall should not be the last line of defense on your network. Make sure the actual network security for your network operating system is implemented correctly. If someone can crack your firewall, they should still have to break through your network security before data is compromised. Do not depend entirely on a firewall to provide all the security for your network.

You also need to be aware of backdoors to your network. It does not matter how well your firewall is configured if the network can be entered through a modem pool on the interior network that is not inspected by the firewall. Modem implementations must include authentication to make sure only known users are accessing the network.

Certain data on the internal network should have a restrictive access policy. Data encryption and secure transmissions can help make sure data is transported in a secure manner on the internal network. Implementing a Kerberos authentication scheme is discussed at the end of today's material. This provides secure authentication of users and services. It also provides secure, encrypted data transmission over the network.

Common Implementations

Firewall technology has five basic implementations. These implementations have evolved over the years to increasingly protect the internal network from external attacks.

The following are the five implementations:

- Packet-filter firewalls
- Circuit-level firewalls
- Application-level firewalls with proxies
- Dynamic packet-filter firewalls
- Kernel proxy firewalls

Packet-Filter Firewalls

Packet-filter firewalls are the earliest form of firewall. They analyze network traffic at the transport layer of the OSI model. Each packet is compared to a set of rules configured for the interface. Rules can be set for both incoming and outgoing packets.

The rules are based on information in the transport protocol header and the IP header. Table 16.1 shows some of the packet-filter rules that can be established on a firewall.

TABLE 16.1. PACKET-FILTER RULES.

Rule #	Interface	Protocol	IP Source	Source Port	IP Destination	Destination Port
1	Internal	TCP	172.16.2.*	*	*	80
2	Internal	TCP	172.16.2.*	*	*	23
3	Internal	TCP	172.16.2.*	*	192.168.3.5	25
4	Internal	TCP	172.16.2.*	*	192.168.3.5	110
5	Internal	UDP	172.16.2.*	*	*	69
6	External	TCP	*	*	172.16.2.100	80

An asterisk (*) is a wildcard character that allows any valid entry for an IP address or port address to replace it.

16

This set of rules denies all packets except specified protocols and ports that are explicitly allowed through the firewall. The rules in Table 16.1 accomplish the following tasks:

1. Rule 1 allows any hosts in the 172.16.2.* network to browse Internet resources with a Web browser on port 80.

2. Rule 2 allows any hosts in the 172.16.2.* network to connect to Telnet servers on the external network.

3. Rule 3 allows any host in the 172.16.2.* network to send mail through SMTP to the SMTP server at IP address 192.168.3.5.

4. Rule 4 allows any host in the 172.16.2.* network to receive POP3 mail from the POP3 server at IP address 192.168.3.5.

5. Rule 5 allows any host in the 172.16.2.* network to use TFTP to connect to any TFTP servers on the external network.

6. Rule 6 allows all external hosts to connect to the internal Web server at IP address 172.16.2.100.

Packet filters often are implemented because they offer the following advantages:

- Client computers require no special configuration. The rules are based on traffic patterns that occur when a host attempts communication that traverses the firewall.

- Packet filters can be implemented with a strategy called *network address translation (NAT)*. The internal network can use a pool of IP addresses hidden from the external network. These addresses are overwritten with a common external address when a packet is sent through the firewall to the external network.

- Packet filters provide the best performance because of the small number of packet evaluations that have to be performed.

Despite these advantages, several disadvantages are related to packet-filtering firewalls. The following are some common disadvantages:

- Packet-filtering firewalls do not provide any additional capabilities such as Web page caching.

- Packet filters function based only on transport-layer information. They cannot determine application-level commands. This prevents more refined rules from being implemented, such as allowing FTP GET commands but disallowing FTP PUT commands. The only rules that can be implemented are to allow or disallow access to TCP ports 20 and 21.

- Packet filters cannot prevent access to the actual firewall host. The rules only affect traffic that navigates through the firewall. This leaves the firewall itself open to attacks from the external network.

- Packet filters often have little or no audit functionality. This can prevent you from determining whether an attack occurred if it was not initially noticed on the internal network.

Circuit-Level Firewalls

Circuit-level firewalls use this assumption about network traffic: Each packet that passes through the firewall either is a connection request or is data being transported across a current connection that exists between a client and a server host.

A circuit-level firewall functions as a referee. When a TCP session is established, it makes sure a valid TCP three-way handshake occurs. If it does not occur, the connection is terminated.

For each connection established through the firewall, a table of valid connections is maintained. This includes the current session state and the sequence information for both the client and host systems. By interpreting the sequence information, it can be determined whether another host is attempting to hijack a session and place its own packets into the TCP stream.

After a connection is terminated, its entry from the session state is removed.

The following advantages are associated with circuit-level firewalls:

- Circuit-level firewalls are quite efficient at moving traffic through the firewall.
- Connections can be prohibited from an entire network or from specific hosts in the rules table.
- Network address translation can be implemented to protect the internal network address scheme.

The following disadvantages are associated with circuit-level firewalls:

- Circuit-level firewalls cannot restrict access to protocols other than TCP. UDP protocol transactions are connectionless and no session is established.
- It is difficult to test the firewall rules unless they are implemented from the actual host to which restrictions are being applied.
- Packet-filtering firewalls do not provide any additional capabilities such as Web page caching.
- Circuit-level firewalls cannot perform higher-level protocol rule evaluations.

Application-Level Firewalls with Proxy Services

Application-level firewalls evaluate data at the application layer before allowing a connection to take place between two hosts. Information that can be evaluated includes connection state and sequencing information, user passwords, and service requests.

Application-level firewalls also generally include proxy services. A *proxy server* functions as a go-between for a client connecting to an external server. An internal client sends external network requests to a specific proxy server, which is configured in the client software. Figure 16.3 shows the configuration of proxy services in the Netscape Navigator browser.

FIGURE 16.3.

Configuring proxy services in Netscape Navigator.

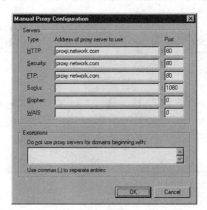

After a client has been configured to use a proxy server, all requests are issued by the client as if it is directly communicating with the external server. The proxy service is transparent to the client after the proxy is configured.

When a client uses a proxy server, all requests for external network services are sent directly to the proxy server. The proxy server evaluates the request and compares it to rules configured for the proxy service. If the request is allowed, the proxy server issues the request on behalf of the calling client system. When the response is returned to the proxy server, it is forwarded on the internal network to the calling client. From the external service's point of view, the request originated at the proxy server and was returned to the source of the request.

Because proxy services understand the protocol used by the client, more precise rules can be developed based on the application data. This also provides the capability to log detailed session information by proxy clients.

Proxy servers cache the Web resources they acquire for proxy clients. When subsequent requests are sent to the proxy server, it checks its cache to determine whether a cached copy of the page is stored locally. If it exists in cache, the client is served the resource from the cache. This results in faster delivery to the proxy client. It also reduces the amount of traffic sent over the network link from the internal network to the external network.

When a proxy service is implemented, packet-filtering services can be modified to only allow the proxy server to initiate communications from the internal network to the external network. Table 16.2 shows the modified packet-filtering rules based on the usage of a proxy server.

TABLE 16.2. MODIFIED PACKET-FILTERING RULES BASED ON A PROXY SERVER AT 172.16.2.7.

Rule #	Interface	Protocol	IP Source	Source Port	IP Destination	Destination Port
1	Internal	TCP	172.16.2.7	*	*	80
2	Internal	TCP	172.16.2.7	*	*	23
3	Internal	TCP	172.16.2.7	*	192.168.3.5	25
4	Internal	TCP	172.16.2.7	*	192.168.3.5	110
5	Internal	UDP	172.16.2.7	*	*	69
6	External	TCP	*	*	172.16.2.100	80

The following are some common proxy services provided on firewalls:

- Telnet
- FTP
- HTTP
- NNTP
- Gopher
- Socks
- WAIS
- POP3
- SMTP
- IMAP
- Real Audio

The following advantages are associated with application firewalls:

- The implementation of proxy services allows enforcement on application-level protocols such as HTTP and FTP.
- The proxy service hides the internal network addressing scheme from the external network.
- All allowed communications from the internal network must be performed by proxy services on the firewall. All other attempts to communicate with the external network can be denied.
- Client software can be configured so the use of proxy services is transparent to the clients using them.
- Proxy services can be configured to route external requests to specific internal servers without revealing their actual hostname or internal IP address. The service appears to be running on the proxy server, not the internal server where it truly resides.
- Proxy services keep detailed records of all the requests they handle.

The following disadvantages are associated with application servers:

- Proxy services run on the same ports as the applications they support. This prevents the implementation of the actual services on the firewall host.
- Performance delays can occur when using a proxy because all incoming data is processed twice—once by the proxy service and once by the actual client application.

16

- New protocols require that a specific proxy be created for them. In many cases, however, you can configure the protocol to work using a generic proxy.

- In most cases, client software has to be configured manually to allow usage of the proxy server.

- Some proxy services require clients to first authenticate with the proxy server before they can use the proxy services. This can cause frustration with the user base.

Dynamic Packet-Filter Firewalls

Dynamic packet-filter firewalls combine the services of application-level firewalls and packet-filter firewalls. As an added benefit, this firewall technology allows firewall security rules to be created on-the-fly.

This technology also can support protocols that use UDP as their transport protocol. As previously mentioned, it is more difficult to monitor UDP communications because a session is not established between the client and the server. A dynamic packet-filter firewall remembers all UDP packets that cross it. When the other host sends a response message, the firewall makes sure it is destined for the original requestor. If this is the case, the UDP packet is allowed to cross the firewall boundary. If not, the packet is dropped. If the UDP response is not returned within a specific time frame, the association is deemed invalid and the response is dropped.

Kernel Proxy Firewalls

Kernel proxy firewalls are implemented at the kernel level of the underlying operating system. When information is discarded, it is done before the data is passed up the network stack.

When a new session request is received by the kernel proxy firewall, a new TCP/IP stack is generated on-the-fly. These stacks only contain the protocol proxies required for the requested session. This allows for additional customization to be implemented that will investigate the data transmission.

As data is transferred up through the levels of the network stack, the network packet can be examined and re-examined at each level. If any rules are broken at any level, the packet can be discarded immediately. There is no need to transfer data all the way up to the application level before the packet is discarded.

Network Address Translation

RFC 1918   Network address translation hides internal network addressing. External networks only see the external IP address of the proxy server. All transactions between the internal network and the external network are handled by the proxy services on the firewall. As a result, a different addressing scheme can be maintained for the internal network. This addressing scheme does not have to be revealed to the external network.

RFC 1918 outlines three network address ranges reserved for internal networks:

- 10.0.0.0–10.255.255.255
- 172.16.0.0–172.31.255.255
- 192.168.0.0–192.168.255.255

These addresses are labeled as internal network addresses on firewall implementations that use network address translation. Other address pools can be used, but if you try to connect to any outside resource in the same network range, the connection fails because the range has been designated as part of the internal network.

If someone attempts to access the internal network from the external network using an address located in the internal network, the transaction is rejected because the internal network address is located on the wrong side of the firewall.

Creating a Demilitarized Zone

One of the more common firewall implementations is known as a *demilitarized zone* (see Figure 16.4).

In a demilitarized zone network implementation, all services made available to external network clients are located on a separate network segment. Access to this segment only is allowed through the firewall. This way, firewall rules can be applied to any traffic that traverses the firewall. This ensures that only desired traffic streams reach the servers in the demilitarized zone.

The internal network also is located behind the firewall. This protects the internal network from external clients. By removing all servers that grant access to external clients, no access needs to be granted to the internal network for external clients.

If hosts in the demilitarized zone require access to resources on the internal network, rules can be configured to allow these hosts to communicate through the firewall. Because you control all hosts in the demilitarized zone, you can be sure proper traffic streams take place.

FIGURE 16.4.

A demilitarized zone firewall implementation.

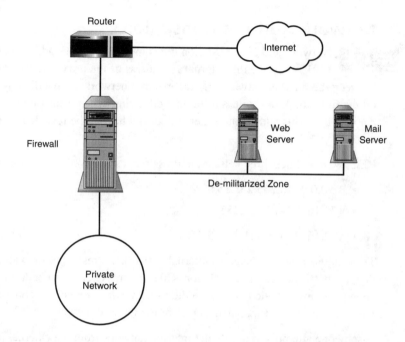

By implementing a proxy service on the firewall, all internal clients can be forced to use proxy services if they want to access resources on the Internet. This prevents internal clients from using unapproved resources on the external network.

Kerberos Data Encryption

The threat of data interception through network monitoring has increased the emphasis on encryption of data as it is transported on the network. This prevents clear-text transportation of authentication information and data from taking place on the network.

One of the best methods of authentication and data encryption is *Kerberos authentication.* Kerberos enables users and services to authenticate each other. This prevents impersonation of both the client and the server. Kerberos provides a methodology for users and services to authenticate each other. This is accomplished using private/public key technology.

Private/public key technology is based on the paradigm that a secure message can be encrypted using half of the key pair. The recipient only can open the message using the other key of the set.

Each user and network service registers key pairs with an *authentication server (AS)*. The user's key is derived from his chosen password. (This is based on the assumption that the user will select a good password.) The service's key is based on a randomly generated password. The service does not actually enter a password when it is invoked.

The Kerberos Authentication Process

The following steps are involved in a Kerberos authentication:

1. The user sends a message to the authentication server (AS) indicating that he wants to start communications with the data server.

2. The AS creates two copies of a *session key*, which is used for any transactions between the user and the data server.

3. The first copy of the session key is placed in a message. Also included in this message is an indication that the session key has been created for a session with the data server. This message is locked using the copy of the user's key stored on the AS.

4. The second copy of the session key is stored in another message called a *ticket*. This message contains an identifier that indicates the name of the user who wants to communicate with the data server. This message is locked using the service's key stored on the AS.

5. Both messages are sent to the user.

6. The user opens the message addressed to him using his private key. By opening this message, he has securely extracted the session key for communicating with the data server.

7. The user must now create a third message called the *authenticator*. This message contains the current time in its contents. Other information might be included to further authenticate the user with the server to prevent impersonation. This message is locked using the newly created session key.

8. The ticket and the authenticator are sent to the data server for verification of the user.

9. The data server opens both the ticket and the authenticator. The ticket is opened using the server's private key, which extracts its copy of the session key. After the session key has been extracted, it is used to open the authenticator. The authenticator is opened to make sure the messages have been received in a timely manner. If a long delay takes place between the issuing of the ticket and the creation of the authenticator, it is possible that the ticket has been captured in transit and is being sent from a system impersonating the client.

16

10. Depending on the security required for the transaction, the user also might want to verify the identity of the data server. To accomplish this, the data server places the time stamps from the authenticator message in a new message with an identifier containing the data server's name. This information is locked using the session key and is returned to the user.

11. The user opens the return authentication message using the session key. If the name of the server is correct, transactions now can begin between the user and the data server. All further communications can be encrypted using the session key established for this session.

Advantages and Disadvantages of Kerberos

The advantage of using Kerberos for authentication is that new session keys are created each time communication is established between the user and the server. This prevents a network-monitoring agent from capturing the session key and using it later. The session key will have expired by that point.

The only disadvantage with this exchange is that, every time a user wants to contact the data server, he must enter his password to open the message containing the session key from the authentication server. Some clients might start to cache this password, which can lead to someone reading the password from cache. The system is then compromised until the user changes his password.

The Ticket-Granting Server

Another agent, called a *ticket-granting server (TGS)*, can be implemented in a Kerberos environment to provide additional security and to protect against password caching. The TGS is distinct from the authentication server, but both services can run on the same physical system.

The user first requests a ticket to contact the TGS. It treats the TGS as another available service on the network. The ticket issued for this session is called a *ticket-granting ticket (TGT)*. After the user receives the ticket-granting ticket, he requests tickets from the ticket-granting server rather than the authentication server. All replies from the ticket-granting server are encrypted using the session key granted for the session with the ticket-granting server. The reply contains the session key for communication with the indicated data server. This password is more secure, does not require the user to enter it every time he wants to establish a connection to a server, and expires after eight hours.

Applying What You Have Learned

The following questions review the concepts discussed in today's material.

Test Your Knowledge

1. What are some of the common security threats faced on a network?
2. How does network address translation protect an interior network?
3. What rules can be applied to a password policy to protect a network?
4. Complete the following table of packet-forwarding rules based on the network configured in Figure 16.5.

16

FIGURE 16.5.

A sample network.

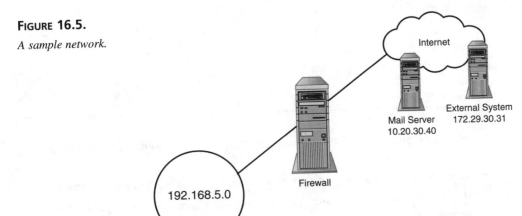

The following proxy rules should be established:

- All clients in the internal network (192.168.5.0) should be allowed to connect to the mail server using POP3, SMTP, or IMAP as protocols.
- All clients in the internal network should be allowed to connect to any Web server on the Internet.
- All clients in the internal network should be allowed to connect to any gopher server on the Internet.
- All clients in the internal network should be allowed to connect to any Telnet server on the Internet.
- Only the external client at IP address 172.29.30.31 should be allowed to telnet to the internal server at 192.168.5.10.

Rule #	Interface	Protocol	IP Source	Source Port	IP Destination	Destination Port
POP3						
IMAP						
SMTP						
HTTP						
Gopher						
Telnet out						
Telnet in						

All source and destination port information can be found in the services file in your \etc directory.

5. How does a ticket-granting ticket increase security in a Kerberos environment?

6. What advantage does Kerberos provide over other forms of private/public key encryption?

7. Describe a process by which an intruder can spoof another host's address.

Preview of the Next Day

Tomorrow's material examines one of the most common network file-sharing methodologies used in TCP/IP networks—network file system (NFS). The material delves into the methods used to connect to remote NFS servers and to utilize their file resources.

The material also looks at how the network information service (NIS) can provide a common directory in a UNIX environment when working with products such as NFS.

DAY **17**

NIS and NFS

Today's material examines two services that provide centralized account management and shared file services in a TCP/IP environment.

The network information system (NIS), or Yellow Pages, provides a uniform directory across a UNIX environment. Instead of each UNIX host maintaining its own account and password information, the hosts can share a common NIS directory.

The Network File System (NFS) is a common method used to share files from a central UNIX server. Clients can use these files as if they are local files. Later sections detail how Remote Procedure Calls (RPCs) and external data representation (XDR) play a part in the communications involved in NFS transactions.

Network Information System (NIS)

The *network information system (NIS)* provides a global and centralized database of information about a UNIX network. NIS provides a service to keep user account information synchronized between hosts. This is of great importance in the NFS environment, where the same account information must be used on both client and server hosts.

NIS comprises both NIS clients and NIS servers. An NIS client requests data from the NIS database on an NIS server. A system can function as both an NIS client and an NIS server. NIS (like NFS) uses Remote Procedure Calls and external data representation. This makes NIS portable between operating systems.

> **THE YELLOW PAGES**
>
> When NIS was first released, it was known as the Yellow Pages. Unfortunately, this broke several copyright laws. Many people, however, still refer to NIS as the Yellow Pages. In fact, many implementations still run the daemon ypserv for the NIS service.

NIS comprises the following key features:

- Master and slave servers
- NIS maps
- NIS domains

Server Roles in NIS

NIS servers take on one of two roles. They are either master servers or slave servers. *Master servers* maintain the original copy of the NIS databases. Any new information or updates are added to this copy of the database. A *slave server* maintains a duplicate copy of the master database. The information in the slave server database is kept up-to-date by the *propagation* process. If the NIS databases are kept in synch, it does not matter which NIS database an NIS client contacts when it is providing authentication information. This is known as a *steady state* situation.

The NIS Database

The NIS database comprises several files known as *NIS maps*. These files initially are stored in ASCII text files. To provide better performance when querying the NIS database, NIS tools convert the text files to DBM format. The maps contain keys and values. A *key* is a specific field in the map that the client specifies when it submits a query to the NIS server. A *value* is an attribute of the key returned in the response from the NIS server. In the map hosts.byname, for example, the keys are the individual names of the hosts, and the values returned are their assigned IP addresses.

NIS Domains

NIS domains comprise all hosts sharing the same NIS database. The actual name of the NIS domain often is not relevant to the users participating in the domain. The only part of NIS they see is that their user/password combination is accepted on all participating hosts. They do not have to set up separate accounts on each host on the network.

An application is configured to query a specific NIS domain. The application uses the `ypbind` daemon to detect a suitable NIS server in the NIS domain. The `ypbind` daemon broadcasts on the local network for an NIS server. The first server to respond is assumed to be the fastest NIS server and is used for all subsequent NIS queries.

Network File System (NFS)

17

RFC 1094

RFC 1813

The *network file system (NFS)* was created by Sun Microsystems to enable transparent access to remote file services for network clients. Transparent means the client does not realize it is accessing files from a remote server. The files appear to be stored locally. The network client performs an action called *mounting* to create a file handle that connects them to the remote file source. This file handle makes the network file source appear to be a local file resource. Assigning a drive letter to the remote file source accomplishes this. This functionality is provided by using Remote Procedure Calls (RPCs) at the session level and external data representation at the presentation level of the OSI model (see Figure 17.1).

FIGURE 17.1.

NFS software implementation.

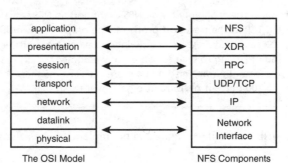

The OSI Model   NFS Components

NFS usually runs on the UDP protocol, but it now can run on TCP with its latest revision (NFS 3.0). The client connects to TCP or UDP port 2049 on the NFS server when accessing remote file sources.

NFS is implemented as a stateless protocol. The server does not keep track of any ongoing disk transactions. It is the responsibility of the client to manage and track all operations. This model of operation is known as *idempotent*. The client must fully describe the operation it is going to perform. It cannot depend on the server to remember anything about previous transactions.

If a write transaction is taking place, for example, the client has to specify the following information:

- The file to be written to (using the file handle)
- The number of bytes to be written
- The starting point for the write operation

Because NFS operations usually run on UDP, the NFS client must wait for an acknowledgment before proceeding with its next transaction. If an acknowledgment is not received, the client retries the transaction when its retransmit timer reaches zero. This is repeated until the client's retry threshold fails. At this time, the transaction fails.

Although this seems to be an inefficient method of operation, it removes complexity from the NFS server. The NFS server can fail, restart, and still maintain client connections. The clients retry their operations until the server once again is available.

USING NFS WITH TCP

NFS 3.0 introduces the capability for an NFS client and an NFS server to communicate using TCP as the transport protocol. The primary advantage of using TCP is the capability to use sliding windows when transmitting transactions. Instead of having to wait for an acknowledgment of every request, multiple requests can be transmitted in a more efficient manner. This provides roughly a 200-percent performance gain over using UDP.

The following distributed file systems can be implemented as alternatives to NFS:

- *AFS*. Andrew file system
- *DFS*. Distributed file system
- *RFS*. Remote file system
- *NetWare*. Novell-based systems
- *NetBIOS*. NetBIOS over UNIX or Windows NT systems

Remote Procedure Calls (RPCs)

Remote Procedure Calls (RPCs) play a major role in the implementation of NFS. Using RPCs, a client can utilize the file resources of a remote server. RPCs make the remote file-sharing process on the NFS server appear to be a local file resource.

The manner in which RPCs are implemented is similar to a function call in programming. When the RPC is executed on the remote host, the RPC is run at the security level of the calling user. This ensures that security is maintained, even though the procedure actually is running on a remote host.

Figure 17.2 shows the communications involved when a Remote Procedure Call is executed on a remote host.

FIGURE 17.2.

RPC communications.

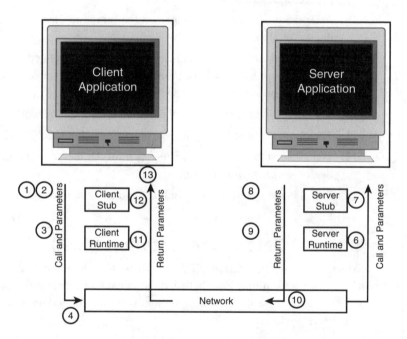

1. The client application issues a normal function call to the client stub.
2. The client stub converts the input arguments from the local data representation to a common data representation that can be used between hosts that utilize different internal data representations. In this example, data representation refers to the scheme the local host uses to store all characters and data internally. An example of data representations differing is when an ASCII-based machine requires communication with an EBCDIC-based machine.

3. The client stub calls the client runtime. The client runtime usually is a library of routines that provides functionality to the client stub.

4. The client runtime transmits a message containing the encapsulated XDR representation of the function call across the network to the server runtime. The server runtime also is a library of routines that provides the necessary functionality to the server stub.

5. The server runtime issues a call to the server stub.

6. The server stub converts the encapsulated arguments from the common data representation to its native data representation.

7. The server stub calls the server application and passes the original client inputs for processing.

8. After the processing has completed, the server application returns the result set to the server stub.

9. The server stub converts the result set and any associated arguments to the common data representation for transmission. This is encapsulated within a message passed to the server runtime.

10. The server runtime transmits this message over the network to the client runtime.

11. The client runtime passes the message to the client stub.

12. The client stub extracts the result set from the message and converts the message to the local data representation.

13. The client stub returns the result set and any accompanying arguments to the calling function.

External Data Representation (XDR)

External data representation (XDR) provides the common data representation used by RPCs when transmitting data between the client and server systems. The XDR format was created to solve the following problems when binary data is exchanged between heterogeneous systems:

- Different byte orders
- Different data type representation (EBCDIC versus ASCII)
- Structure alignment

Whenever data is transmitted between client and server systems, XDR is used as the data's format during transmission. This ensures that the data is presented in a format with which the receiving system can work.

Portmapper

NFS is not the only application that makes use of Remote Procedure Calls. Because different applications can use Remote Procedure Calls simultaneously, a *portmapper* program operates on all servers that provide client/server connectivity using RPCs. When a client connects to the server to communicate with a server application using RPCs, the portmapper first determines whether the application is running on the server. If it is, the correct port number is returned to the client system. The client continues to use this port number until the application terminates.

The portmapper uses UDP and TCP port 111. When an RPC-based service is launched on the server, it reports its port usage to the portmapper.

NFS RPC Procedure Calls

The following Remote Procedure Calls have been defined for use with NFS. These Remote Procedure Calls provide functionality to NFS clients.

- *NULL*. The do-nothing procedure tests whether the NFS server is responding. It does not perform an actual task.
- *GETATTR*. The Get File Attributes procedure gets the attributes of a file found on the server. These attributes include protection, owner, size, and access times.
- *SETATTR*. The Set File Attributes procedure changes the attributes of a file.
- *ROOT*. This procedure now is obsolete. It originally was used to mount file systems. (The mount protocol, discussed later today, now accomplishes this.)
- *LOOKUP*. The Lookup Filename procedure performs a directory lookup for the client. This procedure returns both a file handle for the client to use to access the file and the attributes of the file.
- *ACCESS*. The Access procedure checks the access permissions for the user.
- *READLINK*. The Read From Symbolic Link procedure reads the value stored within a symbolic link.
- *READ*. The Read From File procedure is used by the client to read data from a file.
- *WRITE*. The Write to File procedure is used by the client to write data to a file.
- *CREATE*. The Create File procedure creates a file in a directory.
- *MKDIR*. The Create Directory procedure creates a directory.
- *SYMLINK*. The Create Symbolic Link procedure creates a symbolic link to an existing file.
- *MKNOD*. The Create Special Device procedure creates device files or named pipes.
- *REMOVE*. The Remove File procedure deletes a file.

17

- *RMDIR*. The Remove Directory procedure removes an empty directory.

- *RENAME*. The Rename procedure renames a file or a directory.

- *LINK*. The Link Procedure creates a hard link to an existing file.

- *READDIR*. The Read From Directory procedure views the contents of a directory. This procedure requires the client and server to maintain the state of the connection so a long directory listing can be returned fully to the client. This is accomplished with a magic cookie. The *magic cookie* contains the state information to be maintained between client and server. The READDIR function returns the filename and the file ID.

- *READDIRPLUS*. The Extended Read From Directory procedure also returns the contents of a directory using the same methodology as the READDIR function. In addition to the filename and file ID, attributes and file handles also are returned. This function greatly increases the performance of directory browsing.

- *FSSTAT*. The Dynamic File System Information procedure returns volatile file system state information. If the NFS server does not support all attributes, it makes a best effort and returns all the attributes it can. This command previously was implemented as STATFS in earlier versions of NFS.

- *FSINFO*. The Get Static File System Information procedure retrieves nonvolatile file system state information and general information about the NFS version 3 protocol server implementation.

- *PATHCONF*. The Retrieve POSIX Information procedure returns POSIX-specific information including the maximum number of hard links, the maximum object name length, how to handle name truncation, and case-sensitivity issues.

- *COMMIT*. The Commit procedure forces or flushes cached data to permanent disk storage that was previously written with a WRITE procedure call. This prevents data from being lost because it was not committed from cache.

Authentication Methods

Remote Procedure Calls enable authentication of the calling client. This ensures that the client performing the Remote Procedure Call has sufficient permissions to perform the desired task. The following authentication mechanisms are supported under NFS 3.0:

- AUTH_NONE

- AUTH_UNIX

- AUTH_SHORT

- AUTH_DES

- AUTH_KERB

AUTH_NONE

The AUTH_NONE authentication method is a misnomer. It means no authentication is required. This often is used for read-only data stores that are not confidential. User authentication is not required to access this type of data store.

AUTH_UNIX

The AUTH_UNIX authentication method is based on traditional UNIX authentication. When using this mechanism, the NFS client provides a user ID (UID), a group ID (GID), and group information to the NFS server.

When implementing AUTH_UNIX as the authentication mechanism, it generally is best to use the network information service (NIS). This provides a common and consistent account database for all participating hosts.

The major issue with the AUTH_UNIX mechanism is that all authentication information is transmitted in clear text. It is possible a network sniffer might intercept the data transmission and then spoof the calling client to connect to the server.

AUTH_SHORT

In the AUTH_SHORT authentication method, the client generates an authentication sequence. The server returns the authentication mechanism. This generally is used when an RPC connection previously has been established. This previous RPC connection is referenced to shorten the authentication process.

AUTH_DES

The AUTH_DES method uses *data encryption standard (DES)* authentication when transferring RPC packets. Session keys are exchanged using a public/private key model.

The following are advantages of using DES rather than UNIX authentication:

- The authentication method is not tied to a specific operating system.
- The authentication mechanism utilizes encrypted transfer of authentication information.
- For outsiders to perform impersonation, they must acquire the private key or the client's network password.

AUTH_KERB

The AUTH_KERB authentication mechanism utilizes the Kerberos authentication mechanism. Kerberos differs from other encryption methods because the need to demonstrate the existence of a private key is not divulged by exposing the information itself.

17

In a Kerberos authentication scheme, the client presents a ticket issued by a Kerberos authentication server (AS). The advantage of Kerberos security is that the client also can authenticate the service. In other words, the client can make sure that the service to which it is connecting is the correct service, not an imposter.

Mounting a File System

The *mount protocol* is a separate protocol used in an NFS implementation. The mount protocol provides NFS with the necessary tools to launch base on the underlying operating system. The following tasks are assigned to the mount protocol:

- Determining server pathnames
- Validating of users
- Verifying access permissions
- Providing clients with access to the root of a remote file system (by providing a file handle to the access point)

This information is kept separate from the NFS protocol so that methods of access and validation can be changed without having to change the NFS protocol. The mount protocol currently uses AUTH_NONE, AUTH_UNIX, AUTH_SHORT, AUTH DES, and AUTH_KERB for authentication mechanisms.

After the mount of a file system is complete, all further communication between the client and server uses the NFS protocol.

The following procedures have been defined for the mount protocol:

- *NULL.* The NULL procedure does not have any actual functionality. It simply tests server response times and availability.
- *MNT.* The mount procedure adds a mount entry. This procedure maps a pathname on the server to a file handle. A successful server response returns the NFS file handle and a vector containing the supported authentication mechanisms the client can use to connect to the file resource.
- *DUMP.* The DUMP procedure returns a list of currently mounted file systems. The list includes the mounted directory and the associated hostname. The entries remain in the list until an UMNT or UMNTALL procedure is executed by the client.
- *UMNT.* The UMNT procedure is used by the client to remove a mount list entry and disconnect from the remote file resource.

- *UMNTALL*. The UMNTALL procedure removes all mount entries established by a client. (This can include multiple servers.) Clients generally use this procedure when they have suffered an ungraceful shutdown. This prevents the UMNT procedure from executing correctly. The UMNTALL procedure ensures that servers are not preserving mounted file systems from previous sessions. This procedure uses a broadcast RPC so all possible servers are reached on the network segment.

- *EXPORT*. The EXPORT procedure returns a list of all exported file systems the client is allowed to mount. This list specifies which clients are configured to mount each file system. The client list includes hosts and groups of hosts.

File Locking Under NFS

Because NFS is implemented as a stateless protocol, an additional protocol is required to implement file locking. File locking ensures that multiple clients cannot access a data file simultaneously (unless this is required by the application). The *network lock manager (NLM)* provides this functionality for NFS. NFS 3.0 uses NLM 4.0 for file-locking functionality.

The NLM protocol indicates which client holds a lock on a file. A lock can be either an *exclusive lock* (access to the file is not allowed until the lock is removed) or a *shared lock* (multiple clients can connect to the file in question).

Timers also are implemented in NLM. Timers prevent a file from being permanently locked if a client crashes while the lock is still in place.

Implementing NFS in a Windows NT Environment with FTP Software

Windows NT does not provide an NFS server service with its default software options. Several third-party versions are available. InterServe from FTP Software, one of the more common third-party solutions, is used here to discuss implementing NFS in a Windows NT environment. FTP Software has been distributing its own proprietary TCP/IP protocol suite for several years.

Installing the NFS Server Software

The NFS server software from FTP Software can be installed from the Services tab of the Network applet in the Control Panel. To add the service, use the Have Disk option and indicate the distribution files directory. This opens the dialog box in Figure 17.3.

17

FIGURE 17.3.

Adding the NFS server service to a Windows NT 4.0 server.

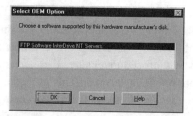

After the service is installed, the exported file systems can be configured using the Server Control utility installed with the NFS server software.

Exported file systems can be configured from the Configure Server dialog box (see Figure 17.4).

FIGURE 17.4.

Configuring the NFS server.

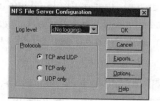

You can click the Exports button to add new exported directories using the Currently Exported Directories dialog box. You also can use the Add button to configure the directory to be exported and the access rights to be assigned to the exported directory (see Figure 17.5).

FIGURE 17.5.

Configuring the download's export directory.

The e:\downloads directory has been exported, and all users have read-only access to the directory. In addition to configuring the initial access to the exported directory, permissions for new files and directories created by remote users can be configured using the Options button in the Currently Exported Directories dialog box (see Figure 17.6).

FIGURE 17.6.

Configuring options for the NFS export directories.

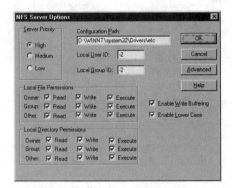

The following options can be configured for the InterDrive NFS server:

- Setting the server priority. This determines how the NFS server performs in relation to other applications running on the host NT Server.

- Setting the configuration path where the NFS configuration files will be stored. This commonly is left as the Windows NT default directory for TCP/IP configuration files %Systemroot%\system32\drivers\etc.

- Setting local user and group IDs. These IDs differentiate files created locally from files created by remote NFS clients.

- Setting the permissions for a file or directory after it has been created and stored within the export directory. The permissions can differ between the creator of the file, the members of the same group as the creator, and everyone else.

- Enabling a write cache to provide better performance for NFS clients when writing to the NFS server.

- Setting whether the NFS server will send all file and directory listings as lowercase. This can be helpful if any of your clients do not support mixed-case filenames.

From the NFS Users and Printers window, users and groups can be configured for accessing the NFS server. When adding a new user (see Figure 17.7), you can specify the following: the full name, the password user ID, and the groups to which the user belongs for NFS security purposes.

17

FIGURE 17.7.

Adding a new user for accessing the NFS server.

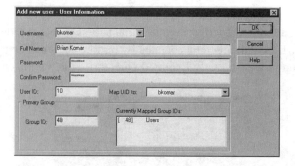

After all the information has been configured for the users and export directories, the NFS server services can be started.

ALTERNATIVE NFS SERVERS

Several other third-party NFS servers can be implemented. Alternatives include Omni-NFS from Xlink Technology, Inc. and Chameleon32NFS from NetManage.

Using the Windows NT NFS Client Software

Windows NT, by default, does not ship with an NFS client. Again, FTP software offers a good NFS client. The client can be installed by running the Setup program on the distribution media.

After the client is installed, the network access order can be configured from the Network applet in Control Panel (see Figure 17.8).

FIGURE 17.8.

Configuring the network access order.

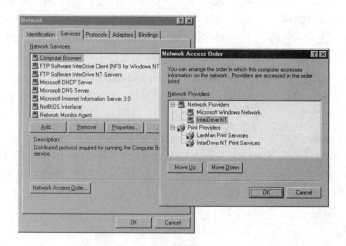

Configuring the network access order is important if NFS is your primary file-sharing methodology. Windows NT, by default, prefers to use its own native file-sharing scheme before using NFS. This can be configured in this dialog box by moving the InterDrive NT client to a higher position for both the network providers and print providers (if you also are using the LPD service provided with InterDrive NFS Server).

An NFS export directory can be mounted in Windows NT using the Map Network Drive option. To use this option, right-click the Network Neighborhood icon and select Map Network Drive... from the pop-up menu (see Figure 17.9).

FIGURE 17.9.

Selecting to map a Network Drive.

In the Map Network Drive dialog box, two network systems are available: InterDrive NT and Microsoft Windows Network. The NFS servers are available under the InterDrive NT network. Figure 17.10 shows the configuration information for connecting to the DOWNLOADS export directory on the BKHOME NFS Server (see Figure 17.10).

FIGURE 17.10.

Connecting to an NFS export directory.

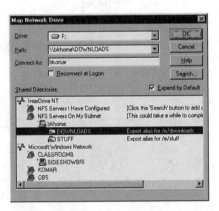

Applying What You Have Learned

Today's material discussed how the network information service provides a common user directory for security purposes. It also detailed how the network file system protocol can be used to provide remote file access to clients.

Test Your Knowledge

1. What functionality does NFS provide in a networked environment?

2. What service does NIS provide to an NFS deployment?

3. How does a portmapper function?

4. Describe the process involved with an RPC function call.

5. What functionality is provided to an NFS server by the mount protocol?

6. Explain the concept of file locking. Why is it important in a network environment?

7. Name the three key configuration issues involved with NIS.

8. Of the various authentication mechanisms supported by NFS, which offer the strongest protection for data and password transmissions?

Preview of the Next Day

Tomorrow's material examines the concept of implementing NetBIOS on a TCP/IP network. Specifically, the material covers the following key concepts:

- Tuning the NetBIOS resolution method for the underlying network
- Configuring a NetBIOS name server
- Optimizing NetBIOS traffic on a network
- Common NetBIOS network implementations

DAY 18

IP over ATM and Configuring NetBIOS Name Servers

Today's material covers two unrelated TCP/IP topic areas. These technologies are not implemented in every network, but it is important to be familiar with them. In the first half of the day, you will examine the issues involved with implementing TCP/IP on an ATM network. These issues exist because ATM devices do not have a physical hardware address. The following details of implementing TCP/IP over ATM are discussed:

- Using TCP/IP in an ATM environment
- The ATMARP packet structure
- Implementing an ATMARP server
- ATMARP transactions

In the second half of the day, you will examine the configuration of NetBIOS name servers (NBNS) in an enterprise network. Specifically, you will look at configuring Windows NT Server's Windows Internet Naming Service (WINS). NetBIOS name servers are required only in networks that have implemented NetBIOS names (such as Windows NT 4.0). The following issues are discussed:

- Installing a NetBIOS name server
- Configuring clients to reduce NetBIOS-related traffic
- Integrating WINS and non-WINS clients on the same network
- Configuring NetBIOS name replication between NetBIOS name servers

Using TCP/IP in an ATM Network

RFC 1577 Asynchronous Transfer Mode (ATM) is used to transmit data, voice, and video over a network at speeds exceeding 145Mbps. This enhanced speed enables simultaneous transmission of all three data types. With the increasing demand for multimedia presentations over TCP/IP networks, the use of technologies such as ATM will continue to grow.

A major issue with running IP over an ATM network is that ATM devices do not have a hardware address. Instead, they have an ATM address that can be extended to represent the hardware address for ATM device. For TCP/IP to function correctly in an ATM network, a modified version of the address-resolution protocol *ATMARP* must be used to resolve an IP address to an ATM address. A modified version of reverse ARP, *InATMARP*, resolves an ATM address to an IP address.

Another issue when TCP/IP is implemented in an ATM network is that ATM does not support the use of broadcasts. As a result, there is no way to map an IP broadcast address to an ATM broadcast address. If an ATM host receives an IP broadcast or an IP subnet broadcast for its IP network, the ATM host must process the packet as if it were addressed directly to that host.

The ATMARP Packet

An IP address is assigned directly to each ATM device, independent of its ATM address. For IP addressing to function in an ATM environment, each host must have the following configuration information:

- The ATM host must know its ATM address.
- The ATM host must know its IP address and subnet mask configuration.
- The ATM host must respond to any address-resolution requests to resolve an IP address to its ATM address or vice versa.
- The ATM host must use ATMARP and InATMARP to resolve IP addresses to ATM addresses when necessary.
- Each ATM host must have an ATMARP request address configured. This is the ATM address of an ATMARP server located on their network. In a switched virtual-connection environment, all ATMARP requests are sent to this address for resolution of IP addresses to ATM addresses.

An ATMARP and InATMARP packet is similar in format to an ARP packet. Figure 18.1 shows the detailed ATMARP packet format.

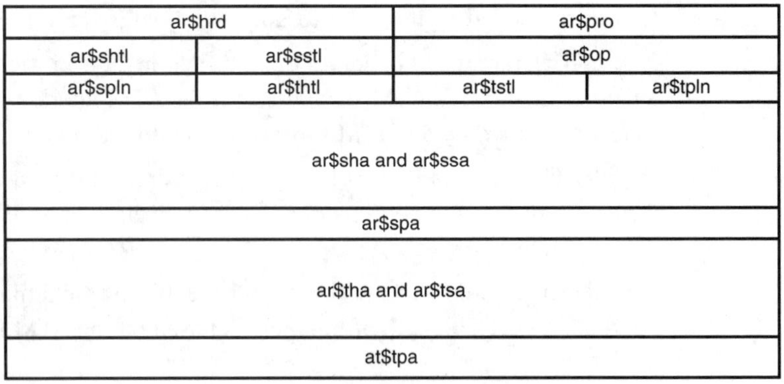

FIGURE 18.1.

The ATMARP packet.

ar$hrd		ar$pro	
ar$shtl	ar$sstl	ar$op	
ar$spln	ar$thtl	ar$tstl	ar$tpln
ar$sha and ar$ssa			
ar$spa			
ar$tha and ar$tsa			
at$tpa			

18

- *ar$hrd.* The Hardware Type field is a 16-bit field that contains the hexadecimal value 0x0013 to indicate that the hardware in use is an ATM device.
- *ar$pro.* The Protocol Type field is a 16-bit field that contains the hexadecimal value 0x0800 to indicate that the protocol in use is IP.
- *ar$shtl.* The Sender's Hardware Length field is an 8-bit field that contains the length of the sender's ATM address. If the ATM address implemented is a 20-octet address (as recommended by the ATM forum), this field is set to a value of 20.
- *ar$sstl.* The Sender's Subaddress Length field in an 8-bit field that contains the length of the sender's ATM subaddress. If the ATM address scheme is implemented as recommended by the ATM forum, this field is set to a value of zero.
- *ar$op.* The Operation Type field is an 8-bit field that contains the operation in the ATMARP packet. Table 18.1 shows the allowed values for the operation type.

TABLE 18.1. THE ATM OPERATION TYPES.

Operation Code	Description
1	An ATMARP request
2	An ATMARP reply
8	An Inverse ATMARP request
9	An Inverse ATMARP reply
10	An ATMARP negative acknowledgment

- *ar$spln.* The Sender's Protocol Address Length field is an 8-bit field that contains the length of the source protocol address in octets. For an IP address, this field is set to a value of 4.

- *ar$thtl.* The Target's Hardware Length field is an 8-bit field that contains the length of the target's ATM address. If the ATM address implemented is a 20-octet address (as recommended by the ATM forum), this field is set to a value of 20.

- *ar$tstl.* The Target's Subaddress Length field in an 8-bit field that contains the length of the target's ATM subaddress. If the ATM address scheme is implemented as recommended by the ATM forum, this field is set to a value of zero.

- *ar$tpln.* The Target's Protocol Address Length field is an 8-bit field that contains the length of the source protocol address in octets. For an IP address, this field is set to a value of 4.

- *ar$sha.* The Source ATM Address field is a 160-bit field that contains the source's ATM address. The length of this field is based on the ATM forum recommended addressing scheme.

- *ar$ssa.* The Source ATM Subaddress field is not shown in Figure 18.1 because the figure shows the ATMARP packet structure when the ATM forum recommended addressing scheme is utilized.

- *ar$spa.* The Source Protocol Address field's length is based on the information stored in the ar$spln field. For an IP address, the length of this field is 32 bits, and it contains the source host's IP address.

- *ar$tha.* The Target ATM Address field is a 160-bit field that contains the target's ATM address. The length of this field is based on the ATM forum recommended addressing scheme.

- *ar$tsa.* The Target ATM Subaddress field is not shown in Figure 18.1 because the figure shows the ATMARP packet structure when the ATM forum recommended addressing scheme is utilized.

- *ar$tpa.* The Target Protocol Address field's length is based on the information stored in the ar$tpln field. For an IP address, the length of this field is 32 bits, and it contains the target host's IP address.

Dividing the Network into Logical IP Subnets

Logical IP subnets (LISs) are used in an ATM environment to group ATM hosts into a closed IP subnetwork. Every ATM host in an LIS has the same network and subnetwork IP addressing scheme. If two hosts in the same LIS want to communicate with each other, they do so using a direct connection. To communicate with an ATM host that is not a member of the same LIS, IP transmission must take place through an IP router. In this case, the IP router is an ATM device configured as a member of one or more LISs. They also can have an alternate interface that is not an ATM device.

The following conditions must be met for all ATM hosts participating in an LIS:

- All members must be part of the same IP network and subnetwork.
- All members in an LIS must be directly connected to the same ATM network.
- All members outside the LIS must be accessed using an IP router.
- All members of the LIS must implement a mechanism to resolve IP addresses to ATM addresses (ATMARP).
- All members of the LIS must implement a mechanism to resolve ATM addresses to IP addresses (InATMARP).
- The ATM network must be fully meshed. All members of an LIS must be able to communicate with all other members of their LIS.

18

MULTIPLE LISs ON THE SAME PHYSICAL NETWORK

Multiple LISs can exist on the same ATM network. A different IP network address must be implemented for each LIS. Even though multiple LISs can exist on the same physical network, communication between hosts in different LISs must occur using an IP router that is a member of both LISs (see Figure 18.2).

In this figure, the ATM hosts are broken into two LISs, A and B. Any communication between hosts in different LISs must be transmitted using the ATM host labeled as the IP router. This ATM host has been configured to belong to both LISs.

FIGURE 18.2.

An ATM network with two logical IP subnet-works.

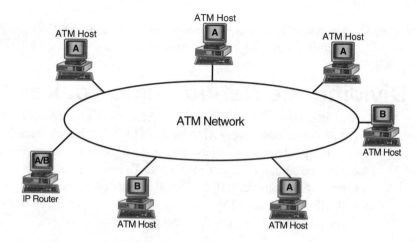

The ATMARP Server

A single ATMARP server must be configured within each LIS. This server resolves all ATMARP requests by IP ATM hosts within the LIS.

The ATMARP server is a passive server. It depends on its clients to initiate the ATMARP registration process. Remember, all ATM hosts that utilize TCP/IP must have a configured ATM request address.

Registering an IP Address with the ATM Server

When the ATM host starts, it connects to the ATMARP server using a point-to-point virtual connection. After the server has been established, the ATMARP server sends an inverse ATMARP (InATMARP) request to determine the configured IP address of the ATM host. The ATM server uses information in the InATMARP reply to build its ATMARP table cache. This cache is used to generate replies to ATMARP requests.

When the ATM server receives the InATMARP reply, the ATM server examines the ATM address and the IP address. If the entry is not found in the ATMARP table cache, the entry is added. If a matching entry is found on both the IP address and the ATM address, the ATM server updates the timestamp on the entry with the new date and time. If the InATMARP reply matches on the IP address but not the ATM address, the packet is discarded because this represents a duplicate IP address on the network. This occurs only when there is also an open virtual circuit with the entry in the current ATMARP table cache.

ATMARP Requests

When an ATM host sends an ATMARP request to the ATM server, the ATM server generates an ATMARP reply based on information in the ATMARP table cache. If no entry is found, a negative ATMARP reply is returned. Sending a negative ATMARP reply indicates to the client that the ATM server received the request but did not have an ATM address mapping for the requested IP address.

When the ATM server receives an ATMARP request, it updates the timeout for the source's entry in the ATMARP table cache. This indicates that the client is still alive. If the source IP address is in the ATMARP request, the ATM server checks to see whether the IP address is registered in the ATMARP table cache. If it is not, the server adds the ATM address, IP address, and timestamp into the ATMARP table. It associates the entry with the virtual circuit used to send the ATMARP request.

When the client receives the ATMARP reply, it adds the ATM and IP address information to its own ATMARP table cache.

Aging of ATMARP Table Entries

On a client system, an ATM host sets a lifetime of 15 minutes on each ATMARP table entry. On the ATMARP server, each table entry is valid for a minimum of 20 minutes. When the timer expires on an ATMARP entry, the table entries are handled differently than in the case of normal ARP aging.

On the ATM server, an InATMARP request is sent on the virtual circuit associated with the entry. If an InATMARP reply is received, the table entry is updated rather than deleted. If the associated virtual circuit is not open, the ATMARP table entry is deleted.

An ATMARP client, however, must prove that the table entry no longer is valid before it can remove the ATMARP table entry. As with the ATMARP server, the table entry is deleted if a virtual circuit is not open. If a virtual circuit is open, the ATMARP client must revalidate the entry before regular traffic can resume. With a permanent virtual circuit, an InATMARP request is sent directly over the virtual circuit. With a switched virtual circuit, an ATMARP request is sent to the ATMARP server. The ATMARP reply is used to update the client's ATMARP table cache.

18

Implementing NetBIOS Services over TCP/IP

 The second half of today's material further investigates implementing NetBIOS services on a TCP/IP network. Several networks and applications make use of NetBIOS services, including the following:

- IBM LAN Server
- Microsoft networks
- SAMBA (a NetBIOS service for UNIX systems)

As discussed on Day 7, NetBIOS name servers can reduce the amount of broadcast traffic on the network related to NetBIOS name resolution. The rest of today's material outlines the configuration of the most widely implemented NetBIOS name server—Microsoft's Windows Internet Name Server, or WINS server.

ATM NETWORKS AND NETBIOS

You must implement either WINS or LMHOSTS files in an ATM network environment. If you do not implement WINS or LMHOSTS, broadcasts must be used to resolve NetBIOS names to IP addresses, and broadcasts are not supported over an ATM network.

Installing the Windows Internet Name Service (WINS)

The *Windows Internet Name Service (WINS)* provides a central repository with which configured NetBIOS clients can register their NetBIOS names. NetBIOS clients also use the WINS server to resolve NetBIOS names to IP addresses using unicasts rather than broadcasts.

The WINS server is a component of Windows NT Server. The following installation steps assume that TCP/IP already is installed. They also assume TCP/IP is configured with a static IP address on the server that will host the WINS service.

The WINS server can be installed in Windows NT Server 4.0 using the following steps:

1. Log in to the Windows NT Server.
2. Select Settings and then Control Panel from the Start menu.
3. Double-click the Network applet in Control Panel.
4. In the Services tab of the Network properties dialog box, select the Add button to add the WINS service.

5. From the list of network services (see Figure 18.3), select the Windows Internet Name Service and click OK.

FIGURE 18.3.

Installing the Windows Internet Name Service.

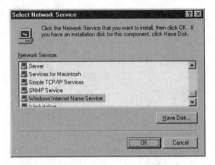

6. After the files for the Windows Internet Name Service are loaded, switch to the Protocols tab of the Network properties dialog box.

7. Select TCP/IP from the list of installed protocols and click the Properties button.

8. Select the WINS tab in the TCP/IP properties dialog box. You must configure your server's IP address as the primary WINS server IP address (see Figure 18.4).

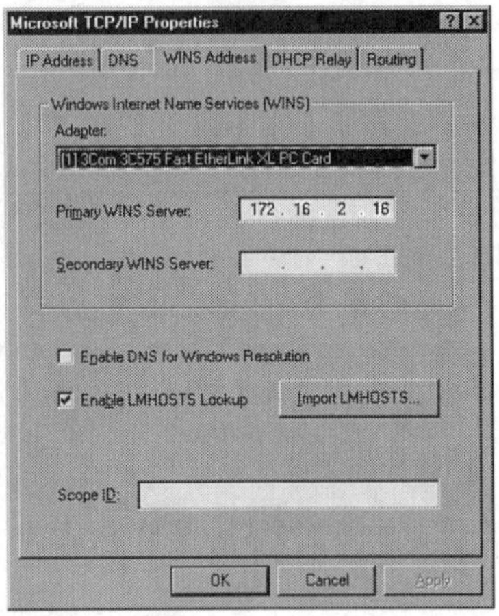

FIGURE 18.4.

Configuring the WINS server parameter for TCP/IP.

9. After you configure the TCP/IP protocol, you must restart the server.

10. When the NT Server restarts, you can configure the Windows Internet Name Service.

> **ISSUES WITH SERVICE PACKS**
>
> If you applied any service packs to your Windows NT Server before the
> Windows Internet Name Service was installed, you need to reapply those
> service packs before you start using the Windows Internet Name Service.
> Several updates have been applied to this service, and they need to be
> reapplied.

Configuring Clients to Reduce NetBIOS-Related Traffic

After the WINS server is configured, the next step is to configure clients to use the
WINS server for NetBIOS-related traffic. This can be accomplished by manually configuring each client or by configuring clients using a DHCP server. Installation and configuration of a DHCP server was discussed in detail on Day 10.

When manually configuring each client, you must enter the IP address of your WINS
server in each client's TCP/IP properties dialog box (refer to Figure 18.4). This can be
performed on all NetBIOS clients. After the WINS server's IP address is configured in
the TCP/IP properties dialog box, the WINS client is configured as an h-node client by
default. As discussed on Day 7, this means the WINS client first queries the WINS server
when resolving NetBIOS names to IP addresses. If they cannot resolve the name using
the WINS server, they will then try a subnetwork broadcast to resolve the NetBIOS
name.

> **CHANGING THE DEFAULT NetBIOS NODE TYPE**
>
> If you are manually configuring TCP/IP, the NetBIOS node type cannot be
> configured using a dialog box in Windows 95 and Windows NT. In this situa-
> tion, you can change this configuration only by editing the Registry directly.
> The value you need to change is the NodeType value in the following
> Registry key:
>
> Hkey_Local_Machine\System\CurrentControlSet\System\Services\NetBT\
> Parameters
>
> Possible settings for NodeType are 0x1 (b-node), 0x2 (p-node), 0x4 (m-node),
> and 0x8 (h-node).

If clients are configured using a DHCP server, the following parameters must be configured within the DHCP scope to ensure that the clients correctly register their NetBIOS
names with the WINS server and utilize the WINS server for NetBIOS name resolution:

- Configure option 44, WINS/NBNS Servers, to indicate the IP address of the WINS/NBNS for the DHCP clients (see Figure 18.5).

FIGURE 18.5.

The WINS/NBNS option for DHCP clients.

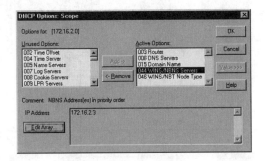

- Configure option 46, WINS/NBT Node Type, to indicate the NetBIOS name-resolution method used by the DHCP clients. The WINS/NBT Node Type is used to configure the NetBIOS resolution order that the NetBIOS client uses when resolving a NetBIOS name to an IP address. This was discussed on Day 7 in the section "NetBIOS Name Resolution."

After the clients are configured, they register their NetBIOS names with the WINS server.

Configuring the WINS Server Environment

Several configuration issues might arise when you implement WINS servers in your network. These issues can include the following:

- Adding static mappings for non-WINS clients
- Configuring WINS proxy agents
- Configuring WINS record timers
- Configuring replication between WINS servers

Adding Static Mappings for Non-WINS Clients

Not all clients on a network can be configured to perform NetBIOS resolution using a WINS server. The network administrator might want to add static mappings in the WINS database for these non-WINS clients. This enables WINS clients to resolve NetBIOS names to IP addresses for these hosts. A network with non-WINS clients is shown in Figure 18.6.

18

FIGURE **18.6.**

*A network consisting
of WINS and non-
WINS clients.*

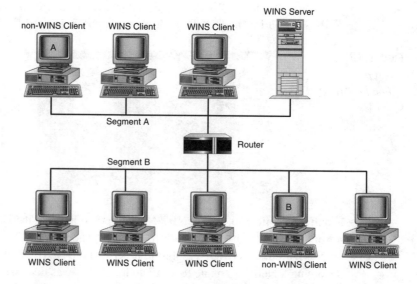

In this sample network, hosts A and B are not configured as WINS clients. This may be
by choice or because a TCP/IP stack does not have a WINS configuration. What issues
arise because these two hosts are not WINS clients? All the hosts on the same segment
A can resolve NetBIOS names for host A to an IP address. This is because the resolution
can be performed using a subnet broadcast. The hosts on segment B, however, cannot
resolve any of the NetBIOS names for host A because the router cannot forward any
NetBIOS resolution packets.

This problem can be corrected by adding static mappings to the WINS database. This can
be accomplished using the WINS Manager utility (see Figure 18.7).

FIGURE **18.7.**

The WINS Manager.

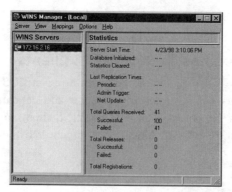

1. After you start the WINS Manager, you can add static mappings by selecting Static Mappings from the Mappings menu.

2. You can add a static mapping by clicking the Add Mapping button.

3. In the ensuing dialog box (see Figure 18.8), you can enter the host's NetBIOS name and the associated IP address.

FIGURE 18.8.

Adding a static mapping.

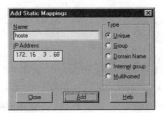

You can add static mappings for Unique, Group, Domain Name, Internet Group, or Multihomed NetBIOS names. These were discussed in detail on Day 7 in the section "NetBIOS Name Registrations."

4. The mappings are now included in the WINS database. WINS clients now can resolve the non-WINS clients' NetBIOS names by querying the WINS database.

Configuring a WINS Proxy Agent

Non-WINS clients only can resolve NetBIOS names using broadcast methods. They cannot resolve NetBIOS names stored in the WINS server database. This generally restricts NetBIOS name resolution to the local network segment.

OTHER RESOLUTION METHODS

Depending on the client, NetBIOS names can be resolved using a configuration file known as LMHOSTS. Microsoft clients use this file to record NetBIOS to IP address mappings for remote NetBIOS hosts. The configuration of the LMHOSTS file was discussed on Day 7 in the section "LMHOSTS." Other resolution methods include DNS and the HOSTS file.

A WINS client can be configured on each network segment as a *WINS proxy agent*. This computer acts as a proxy for non-WINS clients and forwards their NetBIOS name-resolution requests to the WINS server. The WINS proxy agent then broadcasts the result it receives from the WINS server on the local network segment.

In the sample network in Figure 18.7, you would have to configure one of the WINS clients on each network segment to function as a WINS proxy agent. This is accomplished by changing the setting for the value named EnableProxy to 1. The EnableProxy value is located in the following Registry location:

```
Hkey_Local_Machine\System\CurrentControlSet\System\Services\NetBT\
Parameters
```

After this value is set, the WINS proxy agent must be restarted before it can function.

Configuring WINS Record Timers

WINS clients, by default, register their NetBIOS names every time they restart. If a WINS client is not shut down regularly, timers can be configured to tune the name-registration process. These timers determine when a NetBIOS name entry can be removed from the WINS database.

The following timers can be configured for a WINS server:

- *Renewal timer.* This timer specifies how frequently a running client reregisters its NetBIOS name. The default interval on a WINS server is 144 hours, or 6 days. The client actually renews its NetBIOS name at half this interval, or every 72 hours. When the timer expires, this entry is marked as released. This setting can be increased to reduce NetBIOS name-registration traffic.

- *Extinction interval.* This timer specifies the interval between when an entry is marked as released and when it is marked as extinct. The default setting is 144 hours.

- *Extinction timeout.* This timer specifies the interval between when an entry is marked extinct and when the entry is finally removed from the database. The default value for this setting is 144 hours.

- *Verify interval.* This timer specifies the interval after which the WINS server must verify that old names it does not own are still active. The default depends on the extinction interval. The minimum value is 24 days. This is necessary when multiple WINS servers replicate their information between themselves.

To configure these timers, select Configuration from the Server menu in the WINS Manager.

Configuring Replication Between WINS Servers

The final configuration commonly used in a network is replication between multiple WINS servers. These generally are larger-scale networks with thousands of NetBIOS clients (see Figure 18.9).

FIGURE 18.9.

A network implementing WINS replication.

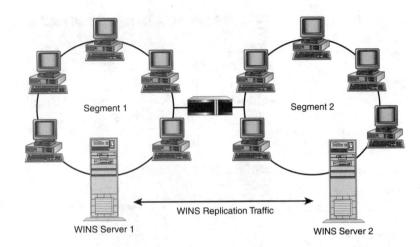

WINS replication must be configured when more than one WINS server is implemented in the network. The WINS replication process makes sure each WINS server contains a total copy of the NetBIOS names registered on the network. The records have an Owner designation that indicates which WINS server accepted the NetBIOS name registration.

WINS servers can perform two different roles during the replication process. They can be pull partners and push partners.

A *pull partner* is a WINS server that requests new database entries from its replication partner. This is configured to occur at regular time intervals. The WINS server requests only WINS records newer than the last record it received from its replication partner. Pull-partner replication often is used across slow WAN links because the replication can be configured to take place during lower network-utilization periods. Slow WAN links are any links less than T1 speed (1.54Mbps).

A *push partner* is a WINS server that notifies its pull partners that a preconfigured number of changes have been registered to the WINS database. This message acts as a trigger for the pull partner to request the updated WINS records. Push partners generally are configured when fast network links exist. They tend to cause more frequent network traffic than pull replication alone.

A WINS replication partner can be configured using the following steps:

1. Select Replication Partners from the Server menu in the WINS Manager.

2. In the Replication Partners dialog box, click the Add button to configure replication to the other WINS server.

3. In the ensuing dialog box, enter the IP address of the WINS server with which you want to replicate (see Figure 18.10).

18

FIGURE 18.10.

Adding a new WINS replication partner.

4. After you add the WINS server, you can configure the replication settings between the newly added replication partner in the Replication Partners dialog box (see Figure 18.11).

FIGURE 18.11.

Configuring replication partner settings.

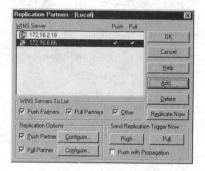

In this figure, the WINS server at 172.16.6.66 is configured as both a push partner and a pull partner with the WINS server (172.16.2.16). To force replication between the WINS servers, click the Replicate Now button.

5. The other WINS server also must have its replication settings adjusted so it can send and receive WINS database changes.

After replication is established, WINS clients can connect to any NetBIOS resources in the enterprise network. The WINS servers each contain the entire enterprise NetBIOS name database.

To configure the replication interval for a pull partner, click the Pull Partner Configure button in the Replication Partners dialog box. In the Pull Partner properties dialog box (see Figure 18.12), you can configure the replication interval and the starting time for the replication process.

Click the Push Partner Configure button to set the push partner configuration. In the Push Partner properties dialog box (see Figure 18.13), you can configure how many updates must occur before the WINS server informs its push partner that it should pull the changes.

FIGURE 18.12.

Configuring the pull partner properties.

FIGURE 18.13.

Configuring the push partner properties.

Applying What You Have Learned

Many networks now are looking to implement ATM as a transport mechanism for network traffic. TCP/IP requires a revised version of the Address Resolution Protocol, known as ATMARP, to work within the nuances of an ATM network. This protocol enables address resolution to take place, even though ATM devices do not have a physical address.

The second topic covered today was the configuration of the most commonly implemented NetBIOS name server—the Windows NT WINS server. Additional configuration of the WINS server was discussed, including installation, static mappings, and replication.

Test Your Knowledge

1. What are some of the reasons that a modified version of the Address Resolution Protocol must be implemented in an ATM network?

2. How does a TCP/IP implementation in an ATM network circumvent the lack of a broadcast mechanism when performing address resolution?

3. How are ATM hosts grouped together for a TCP/IP network?

4. What process is followed to remove an entry whose timer has expired in the ATMARP cache for a client?

5. Describe the issues involved when multiple WINS servers are implemented in a network.

6. How do WINS proxy agents assist in the resolution of NetBIOS names for non-WINS clients?

18

7. When would you have to add static entries to a WINS database?

8. In a worst-case scenario, how much time will pass before a record is removed from the WINS database for a computer that has been permanently removed from the network?

9. What is the difference between a push partner and a pull partner in WINS replication?

Preview of the Next Day

Tomorrow's material discusses configuring TCP/IP on client operating systems. The material covers native TCP/IP stacks shipped with operating systems and third-party stacks such as FTP OnNet Host Suite.

DAY 19

Configuring Network Servers to Use TCP/IP

Today's material examines the three most common network operating systems that implement the TCP/IP protocol. This chapter investigates TCP/IP configuration for the following network operating systems:

- Microsoft Windows NT Server 4.0
- Novell IntranetWare 4.11
- UNIX Servers

> **WHAT ABOUT VERSION 5.0?**
>
> This chapter does not examine Windows NT Server 5.0 or IntranetWare 5.0 because they both are still in the beta stage and probably will not be released within the next year.

Configuring TCP/IP on a Windows NT 4.0 Server

Windows NT Server 4.0 ships with a TCP/IP protocol stack and additional TCP/IP services. The following sections guide you through implementing TCP/IP in a Windows NT environment. They include detailed installation steps and reasons why you might or might not want to include these services.

The Network Applet in Control Panel

All TCP/IP configuration and service installation is performed using the Network Control Panel applet (see Figure 19.1).

FIGURE 19.1.

The Windows NT Server Network Control Panel applet.

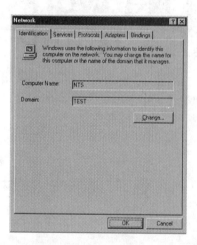

From the Network applet in Control Panel, you can install additional network card adapters, new protocols, and new services. This applet also enables you to configure bindings. *Bindings* enable you to select which protocols are used by which services. They also enable you to prioritize protocol usage by service.

Adding a Network Adapter

Windows NT Server should detect a network adapter during the installation process. If you add an additional network adapter after the installation of NT Server, the following steps should be performed to install the necessary drivers:

1. Log in as the Administrator or as an account with administrator privileges on the target server. To modify the system configuration on a Windows NT Server, you should log in as a member of the Administrators local group.

2. To open Control Panel, select Settings and then Control Panel from the Start menu.

3. Double-click the Network applet in Control Panel.

4. Select the Adapters tab to verify whether a network adapter already has been installed.

5. If your network adapter is not present, click the Add button. Select your adapter from the Select Network Adapter dialog box (see Figure 19.2).

FIGURE 19.2.

The Select Network Adapter dialog box.

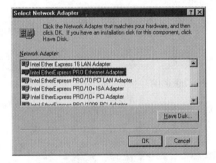

If you do not see your adapter in the list, you need the manufacturer's driver disk to install the necessary Windows NT 4.0 drivers. You then can add the drivers using the Have Disk option.

6. After the driver is loaded, you can verify the device settings by selecting the network adapter and clicking the Properties button (see Figure 19.3).

FIGURE 19.3.

Configuring the resources used by a network adapter.

7. In the resulting dialog box, you can set different properties for the network card (if you aren't sure whether the card works at the suggested settings). The available settings vary depending on the manufacturer of your network adapter.

After the necessary drivers have been installed, you need to restart Windows NT Server.

Adding the TCP/IP Protocol

Both the TCP/IP protocol and the NWLink IPX/SPX protocol are installed by default during the initial installation of Windows NT Server. If the TCP/IP protocol has since been removed or was not installed during the initial installation, you can add the protocol using the following steps:

1. Start Control Panel.

2. Start the Network applet in Control Panel.

3. Switch to the Protocols tab. Verify whether TCP/IP already is installed. If the protocol already exists, you can skip ahead to the next section, "Configuring the TCP/IP Protocol."

4. If TCP/IP is not in the list of installed protocols, click the Add button to install TCP/IP.

5. From the protocol list in the Select Network Protocol dialog box, select TCP/IP Protocol and click the OK button.

6. A dialog box will ask you whether DHCP exists on your network (see Figure 19.4).

FIGURE 19.4.

The DHCP warning message.

If DHCP exists, click the Yes button to configure TCP/IP using DHCP. If DHCP is not implemented, you must select No and then manually configure the TCP/IP properties.

7. You next are prompted for the path from which to copy the necessary configuration file. If you have an Intel-based system, it would be from the \i386 directory of your CD-ROM.

8. You must restart the server to initialize TCP/IP.

MULTIPLE PLATFORM SUPPORT UNDER WINDOWS NT SERVER 4.0

Windows NT Server 4.0 supports four different platforms for installation. The following listing shows the installation directories for the four platforms on the Windows NT Server 4.0 CD-ROM.

Platform	Directory
Alpha	[CD]:\alpha
Intel	[CD]:\i386
Mips	[CD]:\mips
Power PC	[CD]:\ppc

SERVICE PACK WARNING

If you have applied any Windows NT Server service packs, you should reapply the most recent version *before* you restart the system. This prevents you from mixing driver versions. Anytime you install software from the original Windows NT Server distribution machine, you *must* reapply the most recent service pack before restarting. This includes adding new drivers or new services.

Configuring the TCP/IP Protocol

The followingTCP/IP sections outline the configuration of the TCP/IP protocol on a Windows NT Server. The discussion takes place on a tab-by-tab basis in the following order:

- *IP Address.* This section discusses the configuration of IP address, subnet mask, and default gateway information. It also discusses advanced configuration, including multiple gateways, PPTP filtering, and IP packet filtering.
- *DNS.* This section details the issues associated with configuring DNS for the Windows NT Server. This includes defining the DNS domain and DNS server search order.
- *WINS Address.* This section discusses the configuration of NetBIOS name resolution. Additional discussion focuses on issues associated with installing a backup domain controller over a wide area network link when WINS is not implemented.
- *DHCP Relay.* This section details the required configuration when the DHCP relay service is installed. This service enables a DHCP client to obtain an IP address from a remote DHCP server.

19

- *Routing.* This section details the configuration required for Windows NT to function as an IP router.

Configuring the IP Address Tab   The IP Address tab enables you to decide whether to configure TCP/IP manually or using DHCP (see Figure 19.5).

FIGURE 19.5.

Configuring the IP Address tab.

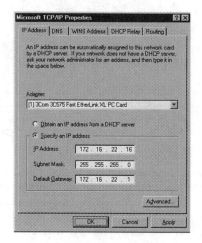

If you choose to configure TCP/IP using DHCP, you should not have to configure any additional information. This assumes you have correctly configured the DHCP server as discussed on Day 10, "Auto Configuration of Hosts Using RARP, BOOTP, and Dynamic Host Configuration Protocol (DHCP)." If you choose to configure manually, you must enter the IP address and the subnet mask. These are the only required fields for a TCP/IP configuration. If you are part of a multiple-segmented network, you need an IP address for your default gateway.

The Advanced button enables you to configure additional information as shown in Figure 19.6.

The following additional information can be configured:

- Multiple IP addresses for a single network interface
- Multiple gateway IP addresses
- PPTP filtering
- TCP/IP filtering

FIGURE 19.6.

The TCP/IP Advanced configuration.

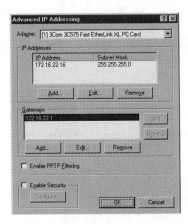

Specific configurations require multiple IP addresses in a single interface. The most common scenario is when a Windows NT Server is configured to host multiple Web sites. Each Web site needs a unique IP address so the Web server knows which home page to display. This is known as configuring a *virtual Web server*.

HTTP 1.1 HOST HEADERS

With the release of Internet Information Server 4.0, Windows NT supports *host headers*. These enable a Web server to host multiple Web sites using the same IP address for all sites. By reading the host header, the Web server can determine the site to which the client is attempting to connect.

When a network has multiple gateways to other networks, you can configure multiple gateways for the NT Server. Any additional gateways are used only if the initial gateway is detected as being dead. The secondary gateways are used only when the primary gateways cannot be reached.

Enabling PPTP filtering is tied to the Point-to-Point Tunneling Protocol discussed on Day 15. This protocol enables tunnels to be established across public networks (such as the Internet). These tunnels provide access to internal networks. This option is equivalent to three filtering options (see Table 19.1).

19

TABLE 19.1. PPTP FILTER OPTIONS.

Incoming Port	Outgoing Port	Protocol ID
1723	Any	
Any	1723	
Any	Any	47*

* Protocol ID 47 indicates the Generic Routing Encapsulation (GRE) protocol, which PPTP uses to encapsulate all traffic over the public network.

The Enable Security option opens the dialog box in Figure 19.7.

FIGURE 19.7.

The TCP/IP Security dialog box.

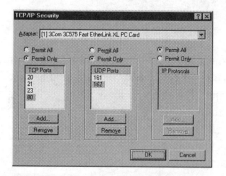

This dialog box enables you to limit which protocols can be accepted by the network interface. The following configurations can be set:

- *TCP Ports.* You can enable the interface to accept all TCP port addresses or to list specific ports on which connections are accepted. The figure shows that only FTP (20 and 21), Telnet (23), and HTTP (80) are accepted.

- *UDP Ports.* You can enable the interface to accept all UDP port addresses or to list specific ports on which connections are accepted. The figure shows that the configuration accepts SNMP requests (161) and SNMP traps (162).

- *Protocol ID.* You can choose which protocols the network interface accepts. These protocol IDs are based on the assigned numbers in STD002.

Configuring the DNS Tab   The DNS tab enables you to configure how Windows NT Server resolves hostnames. This tab can be configured as shown in Figure 19.8.

FIGURE 19.8.

The DNS configura-tion tab.

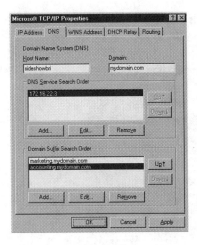

The following information can be configured in the DNS tab:

- *Host Name.* This contains the name by which the NT server will be known on the Internet. This generally matches the NetBIOS computer name configured for the NT Server.

- *Domain.* This parameter sets the Internet domain of which the NT server is a member. The combination of the hostname and the domain name provides the Fully Qualified Domain Name for the NT Server.

- *DNS Service Search Order.* This parameter enables multiple DNS servers to be configured for the NT Server for hostname resolution. The order of the list determines the order in which the DNS servers are queried.

- *Domain Suffix Search Order.* This parameter enables the host to try different Internet domain names as suffixes when you ping a hostname. If you configure the domain suffix search order as shown in Figure 19.8, for example, and you type `ping behometh` at the command prompt, you actually perform the following DNS queries:

  - `behometh`

  - `behometh.mydomain.com`

  - `behometh.marketing.mydomain.com`

  - `behometh.accounting.mydomain.com`

19

Configuring the WINS Address Tab   The WINS Address tab configures NetBIOS name resolution methods for the Windows NT Server (see Figure 19.9).

FIGURE 19.9.

The WINS Address tab.

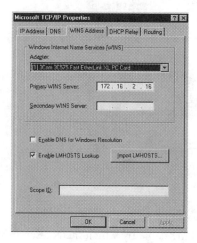

The following options can be configured on this tab:

- *Primary WINS Server.* The WINS server with which the NT Server first communicates for NetBIOS name registrations, name queries, and name releases.

- *Secondary WINS Server.* This WINS server is used for name registrations, name queries, and name releases if the primary WINS server is unavailable.

- *Enable DNS for Name Resolution.* This option enables NetBIOS name resolution to query the configured DNS server if the WINS server or the broadcast methods cannot resolve the NetBIOS name.

- *Enable LMHOSTS Lookup.* This option enables the NT Server to use the LMHOSTS file for NetBIOS name resolution. This file is stored in the `%SystemRoot%\System32\Drivers\Etc` directory.

- *Import LMHOSTS.* This option enables you to import a previously configured LMHOSTS file during the installation of an NT Server computer. This option is especially useful when installing a backup domain controller (BDC) located on a remote subnetwork and WINS is not implemented. This enables an LMHOSTS file to be imported that identifies the primary domain controller (PDC) on the remote subnetwork. Performing this import enables the BDC to successfully connect to the PDC and to synchronize a copy of the domain's account database.

- *Scope ID.* This option enables you to further segment NetBIOS computers into separate work units. The scope ID must match for two computers to communicate with each other using NetBIOS communications. If the scope IDs do not match, NetBIOS communication is impossible.

Configuring the DHCP Relay Tab   The DHCP Relay tab should be configured only when the DHCP Relay Agent service is installed on a Windows NT server. This service enables the DHCP Relay agent to forward DHCP requests to a DHCP server on a remote subnetwork.

The DHCP Relay Agent tab can be configured as shown in Figure 19.10.

FIGURE 19.10.

The DHCP Relay tab.

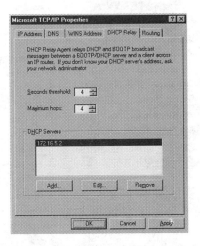

The DHCP Relay Agent tab has the following configuration options:

- *Seconds Threshold.* This parameter sets how long the DHCP Relay agent backs off before it forwards the DHCP packet to its configured DHCP servers.

- *Maximum Hops.* This parameter sets the maximum number of routers a DHCP packet will be forwarded through en route to a DHCP server. This is accomplished by setting a Time-to-Live (TTL) value equivalent to the value in this field. At each router, the TTL decrements by one. If it reaches a value of zero, the DHCP packet is dropped.

- *DHCP Servers.* This parameter contains a list of known DHCP servers to which the DHCP Relay Agent can forward DHCP packets. This prevents the DHCP Relay Agent from forwarding DHCP packets to all segments of the network.

Configuring the Routing Tab   The Routing tab enables a multihomed Windows NT Server to function as a router. By default, Windows NT requires static routing entries to perform routing. The optional RIP for IP service also can be installed. This enables the Windows NT Server to function as a dynamic RIP router.

To enable this option, select the Enable IP Forwarding check box.

19

Configuring Bindings

After TCP/IP has been configured and the NT server has been restarted, you might want to optimize how the network adapter and services interact if multiple protocols are installed.

The Bindings tab enables you to configure the order in which each service interacts with multiple protocols (see Figure 19.11).

FIGURE 19.11.

The Bindings tab.

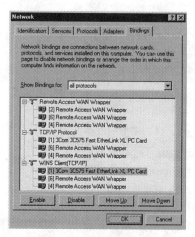

The bindings in Figure 19.11 show that the TCP/IP protocol is bound to both the 3Com PCMCIA card and the two WAN Wrappers used by the remote access protocol. If TCP/IP is not used on the internal network, you can disable the binding to the 3Com card by clicking the Disable button.

Bindings can be viewed in one of the following presentation formats:

- By service
- By adapter
- By protocol

Choosing different presentation formats enables you to configure how each protocol, adapter, and service interacts with one another. You can adjust the binding order to optimize network traffic based on protocol usage.

If you use the TCP/IP protocol only to communicate with other servers, for example, and you do not host any TCP/IP services, you might want to disable the TCP/IP protocol for the Windows NT Server service.

Adding Additional TCP/IP Network Services

Several additional services can be installed on a Windows NT Server after TCP/IP has been configured. These services provide additional TCP/IP functionality. The following services can be installed:

- *DHCP Relay Agent.* This service enables a Windows NT server to forward DHCP requests to a DHCP server on a remote subnetwork. The DHCP servers are configured in the DHCP Relay tab of the TCP/IP properties dialog box. The DHCP Relay Agent cannot be loaded on an actual DHCP server.

- *Microsoft DHCP Server.* This service creates a pool of IP addresses and configuration information that can be leased to clients. If you install this service, you are required to configure a static IP address for the server. The specific configuration of the DHCP server was discussed on Day 10 in the section, "Dynamic Host Configuration Protocol (DHCP)."

- *Microsoft DNS Server.* This service enables Windows NT Server to function as a domain name space server. The Windows NT Server DNS server can function with other DNS servers. Although this service does not require a static IP address, it always is recommended that you configure a static IP address for your DNS server. The specific configuration of a DNS server was discussed on Day 8 in the section, "Configuring a Windows NT DNS Server."

- *Microsoft Internet Information Server.* This service provides three Internet services: Web services, FTP services, and Gopher services. This service differs from most Windows NT services in that Windows NT does not have to be restarted when the service is installed.

- *Microsoft TCP/IP Printing.* This service enables the NT Server to manage TCP/IP printers. It installs a *Line Printer Daemon (LPD)* service on the NT Server that can control *Line Printer Router (LPR)* connected printers.

- *RIP for Internet Protocol.* This service enables Windows NT to function as a dynamic TCP/IP router using the RIP protocol. Multiple adapters must be installed on the Windows NT server or a single adapter must be assigned multiple addresses on different network segments.

- *Simple TCP/IP Services.* This service installs additional TCP/IP services such as Character Generator, Daytime, Discard, Echo, and Quote of the Day. These services were discussed on Day 11 in the section, "Installing the Optional TCP/IP Services in Windows NT."

19

- *SNMP Service.* This service installs the SNMP agent for Windows NT Server so it can participate in an SNMP-managed network. It also installs the counter for the TCP/IP protocol in the Windows NT Performance Monitor so analysis of the TCP/IP protocol suite's performance can be monitored.

- *Windows Internet Information Service.* This service enables Windows NT to function as a NetBIOS name server. This service does not require a static IP address, although one is highly recommended. The configuration of this service was discussed on Day 18 in the section, "Installing the Windows Internet Name Service (WINS)."

All Windows TCP/IP services are added using the Services tab of the Network applet in Control Panel.

Configuring TCP/IP on an IntranetWare 4.11 Server

This configuration information assumes IntranetWare currently is installed and configured correctly (running the default IPX/SPX protocol). This section details the steps involved in performing the following tasks:

- Installing the TCP/IP protocol
- Configuring the NetWare DNS server
- Configuring the NetWare domain SAP/RIP server (DSS)
- Configuring the NetWare DHCP server

All these products are included on the IntranetWare installation CD-ROM.

Installing the TCP/IP Protocol

The TCP/IP protocol can be installed as part of the default installation of IntranetWare. The following installation instructions assume the TCP/IP protocol was not installed during the initial installation of the network operating system:

1. Before you begin the installation, you must stop all services that use the IntranetWare Pkernel by issuing the following command at the system console:
   ```
   unistop
   ```

2. To configure the TCP/IP protocol on the IntranetWare server, you must run the Internetworking Configuration utility by entering the following command at the system console:
   ```
   load inetcfg
   ```

NetWare Loadable Modules

Utilities that are executed on the NetWare system console are called
NetWare Loadable Modules (NLMs). They are loaded using the LOAD command and are unloaded using the UNLOAD command. You can determine
which NLMs are loaded by issuing the MODULES command.

---

3. From the Internetworking Configuration menu, select Protocols. In the ensuing
   menu, select TCP/IP. The TCP/IP Protocol Configuration dialog box opens (see
   Figure 19.12).

FIGURE 19.12.

*Enabling and config-
uring the TCP/IP pro-
tocol.*

This dialog box enables you to configure the following features:

- *IP Packet Forwarding.* This enables IntranetWare to act as a router.
- *RIP.* You can enable or disable the RIP routing protocol.
- *OSPF.* You can enable or disable the OSPF routing protocol.
- *Static Routes.* You can configure static routing information.
- *SNMP Manager.* You can configure the SNMP management system.
- *Filtering Support.* You can enable or disable packet filtering.
- *Expert Configuration Settings.* These configuration settings include broadcast
  forwarding, BootP forwarding, and EGP configuration.

4. After your TCP/IP protocol configuration is set, press Esc and select Yes to update
   the TCP/IP configuration.

5. Press Esc again to return to the Internetworking Configuration menu. From this
   menu, select Bindings to configure which network cards use the TCP/IP protocol.

19

6. Press Insert and select the TCP/IP protocol from the list of configured protocols. Press Enter.

7. Select the desired board name and press Enter to bind TCP/IP to that network card. This opens the TCP/IP configuration dialog box shown in Figure 19.13.

FIGURE 19.13.

Binding TCP/IP to a LAN interface screen.

This dialog box enables you to configure the IP address and subnet mask assigned to the network card. It also provides specific configuration options for the RIP and OSPF protocols. The Expert Options section enables you to configure the frame type and broadcast address.

8. Press Esc to exit the dialog box. Select Yes to update the TCP/IP configuration. A dialog box opens that shows the configured IP address for the interface (see Figure 19.14).

FIGURE 19.14.

Viewing the configured protocols.

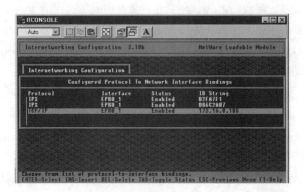

9. Press Esc until you are asked whether you want to exit configuration. Select Yes to complete the TCP/IP configuration.

10. Restart the IntranetWare server by issuing the following set of commands:

```
SERVER:down
SERVER: exit
C:\nwserver>server
```

11. To verify the assigned IP address, you can load the PING NetWare NLM by issuing the following command at the system console:

```
load ping
```

12. Ping the IP address you configured for the IntranetWare server (see Figure 19.15).

FIGURE 19.15.

Using the Ping NLM.

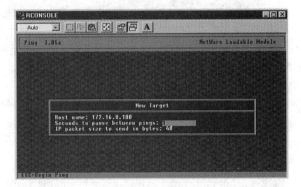

You also can ping other hosts on your segment. At this point, however, you only can use IP addresses because you have not configured a DNS server.

Configuring NetWare/IP

The next step in the TCP/IP configuration process is to configure NetWare/IP. This configures the DNS and DSS servers used by the IntranetWare server.

1. From the IntranetWare server console, enter the following command to load the INSTALL NLM:

```
load install
```

2. The NetWare Server Installation 4.11 NLM provides a menu of options (see Figure 19.16). From the Installation Options menu, select Product Options (Other Optional Installation Items).

19

FIGURE 19.16.

The NetWare Server Installation Options menu.

3. From the Other Installation Items/Products menu, select Install Netware/IP. This starts the transfer of necessary configuration files to the IntranetWare server. The installation program asks whether you want to read the online documentation first. This generally is a good idea; it prepares you for the installation requirements.

4. After reading the documentation of NetWare/IP, you can proceed with the installation.

   Switch to the system console using the Alt+Esc key combination.

5. The installation program prompts you for the hostname you want to assign to the IntranetWare server.

   In this example, the hostname BIGRED was assigned. After the hostname is entered, the initial configuration files are configured.

6. An information screen appears next, stating that you must run the UNICON utility to configure a DNS server, primary DSS (directory SAP/RIP server), or NetWare/IP server.

7. Answer No to configuring the NetWare/IP server at this time. You first need to configure the DNS and DSS server properties.

8. A warning states that you must have NDS installed to access network resources.

9. Select Yes to exit the NetWare/IP Configuration Console.

10. After you exit the NetWare/IP Configuration Console, you automatically are redirected into the UNICON utility. This utility requires that you authenticate into the NetWare directory services.

11. After you authenticate, the UNICON product performs a series of initialization steps. At the end, press Esc to continue.

12. The Installation Status Message displays, as shown in Figure 19.17.

FIGURE 19.17.

The Installation Status Message.

Following the instructions, you should now DOWN the server and EXIT to DOS. After you perform these steps, restart the server by executing the SERVER command.

Configuring DNS and DSS

The UNICON utility enables the initial DNS server for the IntranetWare environment to be configured. This provides all resolution for hostnames in the IntranetWare environment. The following steps configure the DNS server after your server has restarted:

1. From the system console, load the UNICON utility by entering the following command:

   load unicon

2. When prompted, provide the NetWare server name, your username, and your password to authenticate with NetWare directory services. Upon entry, you see the menu in Figure 19.18.

FIGURE 19.18.

The UNICON Main menu.

19

3. To install the DNS server, select the menu options Manage Services, DNS, and Initialize DNS Master Database.

4. In the ensuing dialog box, enter the name of the DNS domain this DNS server will be hosting (see Figure 19.19).

FIGURE 19.19.

Configuring the DNS domain reddom.com.

In this example, the DNS domain name is set to reddom.com.

5. After you configure the DNS domain name, you can configure which subnetworks the DNS will service. If you are on a single network, select No to indicate that there is only a single network segment. If you select Yes, you can configure each network address implemented in your network. The initial network address is obtained from the configured IP address for the IntranetWare server. Each network address is added using the Insert key (see Figure 19.20).

FIGURE 19.20.

Adding an additional subnet for the DNS server.

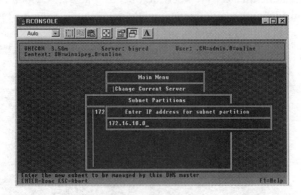

6. After you configure each subnet supported by the DNS server, initialize the DNS database by selecting Yes. A message informs you that your zone and

reverse-lookup zone have been created successfully and that the DNS server has been started (see Figure 19.21).

FIGURE 19.21.

Confirmation that the DNS server has been configured correctly.

Press Esc to continue.

7. You now must configure a DNS subzone necessary for the NetWare/IP domain name. Select Administer DNS, Manage Master Database, Delegate Subzone Authority. Press Insert to add the NetWare/IP domain name. It is common to name the subdomain `nw.parent domain`. In this example, the subzone is `nw.reddom.com`.

8. Select your NetWare server as the host for the new subzone. This zone houses the new domain SAP/RIP server (DSS). DSS is a distributed, replicated Btrieve database of all services and routes within a NetWare/IP domain. It is meant to reduce the broadcasts associated with SAP and RIP by keeping a central repository of this information.

9. Press Esc four times to get back to the Manage Services menu.

10. From the Manage Services menu, select NetWare/IP and then Configure Primary DSS. This takes you to the Primary DSS Configuration dialog box.

11. The following information is entered into the Primary DSS Configuration dialog box (see Figure 19.22):

    - *NetWare/IP Domain.* Enter the name of the DNS subzone you created in step 7.

    - *Primary DSS Host Name.* Enter the fully qualified domain name of the DSS Server (such as `bigred.reddom.com`).

    - *IPX Network Number.* Enter the IPX external network number you are using for your NetWare/IP network.

19

FIGURE 19.22.

*Configuring the DSS
server.*

- *Tunable Parameters.* This enables you to configure parameters such as the
  UDP port to use and synchronize intervals.
- *DSS SAP Filters.* This enables you to use SAP filtering for outbound and
  inbound services.

Press Esc to exit the screen and select Yes to save the changes.

12. After saving the DSS configuration changes, you are reminded that the hostname
    you configured to be the DSS host must be configured as a name server for the
    subzone. You can ignore this reminder, however, because this was accomplished
    when you previously configured DNS.

13. From the NetWare/IP Administration menu, select Configure Netware/IP Server.
    Figure 19.23 shows the NetWare/IP Server Configuration screen that appears.

FIGURE 19.23.

*Configuring the
NetWare/IP domain
and DSS for the
IntranetWare server.*

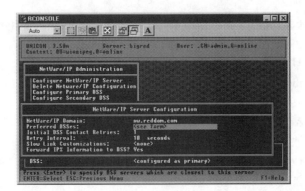

This screen includes the following configuration information:

- *NetWare/IP Domain.* Enter the name of the subzone you created for the DSS. All NetWare/IP servers and clients must belong to the same NetWare/IP domain to use a common NetWare DSS server.
- *Preferred DSSes.* Enter either the hostname or the IP address of the primary DSS server. If using a hostname, make sure it resolves correctly to an IP address through DNS.
- *Initial DSS Contact Retries.* This entry configures how many times the NetWare/IP server retransmits a query to the configured DSS server during startup.
- *Retry Interval.* This entry configures how many seconds the NetWare/IP server waits before transmitting an unacknowledged query.
- *Slow Link Customizations.* This field enables customization to take place when connecting over a slow link.
- *Forward IPX Information to DSS.* This field (if enabled) configures the NetWare/IP server to act as a forwarding gateway between IP and IPX segments.

14. Press Esc until you return to the Main menu. From the Main menu, select Stop/Start Services. The DNS server service should be running. Press Delete to stop the DNS service temporarily.

15. Press Insert and select DNS Server to restart the DNS server.

16. Press Insert and select Domain SAP/RIP Server to start the DSS server. Switch to the system console screen and make sure the message Domain SAP/RIP Server ready to service NetWare/IP Domain: <your domain> appears. If it does not appear, you have a DSS configuration error.

17. Switch back to the UNICON utility and press Insert. From the list of services, select NetWare/IP Server. Again, switch to the system console to make sure the message NetWare/IP Server is initialized and functional appears.

18. Switch back to the UNICON utility and press Esc until you return to the Main menu. Select Quit from the Main menu to exit UNICON.

19. Load Ping and test the configuration of the IntranetWare server again.

Configuring the NetWare DHCP Server

IntranetWare ships with a fully functional DHCP server. Use the following steps to configure the DHCP Server NLM.

19

1. Load the INSTALL NLM by entering the following command at the system console:

   ```
   load install
   ```

2. From the Installation Options menu, select Product Options.

3. From the Other Installation Items/Products menu, select Install NetWare DHCP. This transfers the necessary files from the CD-ROM to the IntranetWare server.

4. From the Installation Options menu, select Install Product.

5. From the list of IntranetWare servers, select the server to which you want to install the DHCP server. Select Yes to start the installation.

6. Shut down and restart the IntranetWare server to make sure the latest NLMs are in use. Make sure to exit all opened NLMs before proceeding.

7. After the IntranetWare server restarts, enter the following command at the system console to start the DHCP server console utility:

   ```
   load dhcpcfg
   ```

   The DHCP server console is shown in Figure 19.24.

FIGURE 19.24.

The DHCP server console screen.

8. From the Configuration menu, select Subnetwork Profile to create a new DHCP scope.

9. Next, you will see a list of configured subnetworks for which you can configure the DHCP scope. Press Enter on the desired network to view the Subnetwork Profile screen (see Figure 19.25).

FIGURE 19.25.

*Configuring the
DHCP scope options.*

10. The following parameters can be configured in the Subnetwork Profile screen:

   - *Frame Type.* Configure the frame type in use for TCP/IP on the network.

   - *Default Router.* Configure the default router IP address configured for all DCHP clients.

   - *Domain Name System Used.* If set to Yes, this enables you to configure the domain name and IP addresses of DNS servers.

   - *Lease Time.* You can set the Total Lease Time, the Renewal Time Percentage, and the Rebinding Time Percentage. The two percentage values are based on a percentage of the total lease time.

   - *NetBIOS Parameters.* If NetBIOS is used on the network, a NetBIOS name server, NetBIOS node type, and NetBIOS scope can be configured for the scope of DHCP addresses.

   - *Automatic IP Address Assignment.* If this option is set to Yes, you can configure the pool of IP addresses from which DHCP allocates addresses. You then can enter a start and an ending IP address for the scope.

   - *NetWare/IP Configuration.* If this option is set to Yes, you can configure the NetWare/IP domain name, the primary DSS, and other NetWare/IP configuration options.

11. Press Esc until you can exit the DHCP Server Console utility.

12. To start the DHCP server, load the DHCP Server NLM by entering the following command at the system console:

```
load dhcpsrvr
```

19

> **DETERMINING LEASED IP ADDRESSES**
>
> Leased IP addresses can be viewed in the DHCP Server Console screen (DHCPCFG). From the Configuration menu, select IP Address Assignment to view the current leases. Details can be viewed by pressing Enter when a DHCP lease is selected.

Configuring TCP/IP on a UNIX Server

As described in Day 1's history lesson of the TCP/IP protocol, UNIX and TCP/IP have evolved together. As a result, the TCP/IP protocol is a standard configuration option in all UNIX systems. This section details the steps to configure TCP/IP on a Berkeley Software Distribution (BSD) version of UNIX.

> **ACQUIRING A BSD VERSION OF UNIX**
>
> You can acquire the freeware version of BSD (called FreeBSD) from the Web site http://www.freebsd.org.

The configuration of TCP/IP is outlined as follows:

- Creating a kernel that contains your network adapter
- Configuring the network adapter
- Reviewing the TCP/IP configuration files
- Configuring the Internet daemon
- Configuring routing
- Testing the TCP/IP configuration

Adding the Network Adapter to Your UNIX Host

Compared to Novell IntranetWare and Windows NT server, the UNIX kernel requires additional configuration for TCP/IP. The UNIX kernel must understand each piece of hardware on the system and how to use it. This can be compared to NetWare's use of LAN drivers and Windows NT's use of device drivers.

To add a new network adapter to the UNIX station, you need to re-create the UNIX kernel. The new device generally contains all the necessary steps for installing the new device.

The actual creation of the new kernel is a series of compilations of C-language programs. The compilation is based on the script stored in the configuration file in the
/usr/sys/conf directory. This configuration file typically uses the same name as the
hostname for the UNIX workstation.

THE CONFIGURATION FILE

When creating a new configuration file, you always should start with the
previous version of the configuration file. This ensures that all previous configuration changes are maintained. If no changes have been made, a basic
configuration file named generic can be used as your starting point.

The following is an example of a typical kernel configuration file.

```
Options            INET

pseudo-device      loop
pseudo-device      ether
pseudo-device      pty

device ix0 at isa? port 0x300 net irq 10 iomem 0xd0000 iosiz 32768 vector
➥ixintr
```

- The INET option is mandatory. It indicates that the kernel supports TCP/IP networking.
- *Pseudo devices* are device drivers that do not have corresponding hardware. In this
  configuration file, pseudo devices are created for the loopback device, Ethernet is
  a low-level networking scheme for ethernet connectivity, and pty enables users to
  connect to the network as if they were connected by a terminal directly attached to
  the UNIX workstation.
- The device statements indicate actual hardware devices installed on the system.
  This device line is the configuration line for an Intel EtherExpress 10.

After the configuration file has been edited, the kernel must be recompiled using the
updated configuration file. In the following, note that the user executes only the first two
steps:

1. cd /etc
2. config [config file]
3. The system creates a new directory in /usr/sys based on the configuration file's
   name. If the configuration file is named beard, for example, the directory is
   /usr/sys/beard.

19

4. The system copies all C-language files necessary for the compilation into the newly created directory.

5. The system calls the program /bin/make. This file reads its own configuration file and begins compiling the code. The output of this compilation is a new kernel named vmunix.

After the compilation is complete, the newly created kernel must be transferred to the root directory. The following steps make sure the previous kernel is not overwritten (just to be safe). These steps assume the hostname is beard.

1. mv /vmunix /vmunix.old

2. cp /usr/sys/beard/vmunix /vmunix

OTHER VERSIONS OF UNIX

Other versions of UNIX provide easier methods of creating the kernel. The System V kernels launch a program that prompts you to enter information about the options you want to include on your system. This program also can be used any time you want to reconfigure your system. When you finish running the program, a new kernel is created. In SCO UNIX, this program is called netconfig. The name varies between flavors of UNIX, but the operation generally is the same.

Configuring the Network Adapter

When the UNIX host is prepared to run TCP/IP, the next step is to configure the TCP/IP information for the network adapter. This is accomplished using the ifconfig utility. The ifconfig utility enables you to assign IP addresses to an interface, to define the subnet mask, to define the broadcast address, and to enable or disable the network interface.

The following is the syntax of the ifconfig command:

ifconfig [interface] [address] netmask [subnet mask] broadcast [broadcast ↪address]

- [interface]. This is the name of the network adapter as named in the kernel. If multiple devices exist on the host, you need to run ifconfig once for each adapter.

- [address]. This is the IP address to be assigned to the network adapter. This can be either a dotted-decimal notation of the address or a hostname to be resolved from the /etc/hosts configuration file.

- `netmask [subnet mask]`. This is the subnet mask to be used with the configured IP address. Make sure to enter the correct subnet mask or communication might not work as expected between other hosts.

- `broadcast [broadcast address]`. The address to which local subnet broadcasts are sent.

For example, if you want to configure the interface ix0 to have the IP address 192.168.20.15 with subnet mask 255.255.255.0 that uses the broadcast address 192.168.20.255, use the following command:

```
ifconfig ix0 192.168.20.15 netmask 255.255.255.0 broadcast 192.168.20.255
```

As previously mentioned, the `ifconfig` command also can enable or disable an interface. The following is the syntax for this:

```
ifconfig interface down|up
```

If you want to enable the interface, execute this command with the UP option. To disable the device, use the DOWN option.

If you want to view the configuration for an IP address, execute the following command:

```
ifconfig interface
```

In this case, you would receive the following screen output:

```
# ifconfig ix0

epro0: flags=63<UP, BROADCAST, NOTRAILERS, RUNNING>
        inet 192.168.20.15 netmask ffffff00 broadcast 192.168.20.255
        ether 08:00:20:19:e3:bc
```

Reviewing the TCP/IP Configuration Files

After you verify that your network adapter is configured correctly, make sure all the TCP/IP configuration files are configured correctly. The following files in the `/etc` directory should be verified:

- *hosts*. This configuration file contains mappings of IP addresses to hostnames. Programs such as ping and ifconfig consult this file for name resolution.

- *ethers*. This configuration file contains mappings of MAC addresses to hostnames. The ARP utility uses this file to load the ARP cache with static entries.

- *networks*. This optional configuration file assigns logical names to network addresses. This can be used by the route command when creating the routing table.

19

- *protocols.* This configuration file is used when a packet arrives on the host. The protocol ID is extracted from the IP header to determine which upper-level protocol this packet should be sent to for further processing.

- *services.* This configuration file determines which service is responding to requests on a specific port number. This configuration file assumes that the server and the client are using the same version of the file.

- *hosts.equiv.* This configuration file contains the list of trusted hosts that can connect to the UNIX server over the network.

- *resolv.conf.* This configuration file configures the DNS properties for the DNS server. This file includes the domain name for the host and the primary and secondary DNS server for the host.

Sample configurations of these files were shown on Day 7 in the section, "TCP/IP Configuration Files." All these files can be edited using an ASCII text editor such as VI.

Configuring the Internet Daemon

After you configure the TCP/IP settings for your UNIX host, you need to configure which services should run on your system. These programs generally are launched as *daemons* that run at all times. Some programs, however, need to be configured to launch on demand.

The *Internet daemon (inetd)* provides the functionality to listen on specific ports for incoming service requests. If a request is received, the Internet daemon launches the appropriate daemon to handle the request. After the request is completed, the Internet daemon shuts down the configured daemon.

This information is based on the entries in the configuration file /etc/inetd.conf. The following is the format of each entry in the inetd.conf file:

```
service-name socket-type protocol wait-status user server-pathname
➥arguments
```

- service-name. This parameter must match an entry in the /etc/services file.
- socket-type. This parameter describes the type of socket used by the service. Possible entries include stream, datagram (dgram), raw, and reliably delivered message (rdm).
- protocol. This is the protocol used by the service. This protocol much match a protocol in the /etc/protocols file.
- wait-status. This field determines how inetd moderates the service. If set to wait, inetd must wait until the server releases the socket before allowing another process

to access the service. If set to no-wait, inetd can allow additional server requests to access the service.

- user. This field contains the user account used by the service to determine the security level of the process. The process executes with the permissions assigned to this user account.

- server-pathname. This is the actual name of the program inetd launches when a request is received. This entry should include the full path to the program. If the word internal appears instead of a program name, inetd services the request itself instead of calling a separate process.

- arguments. This field contains any additional arguments required by the process to launch correctly. As a minimum, this field contains the actual program name.

The only time you should edit the inetd.conf file is when you add an additional service. Most software includes the necessary entries to be added to the inetd.conf file. When modifications are made to the inetd.conf file, the inetd process must be restarted for the changes to take place. The following commands accomplish this:

```
#ps -acx | grep inetd
131 ? IW 0:04 inetd

kill -HUP 131
```

The following is an example of the inetd.conf file from a SUN UNIX box:

```
##ident  "@(#)inetd.conf 1.22    95/07/14 SMI"   /* SVr4.0 1.5   */###
Configuration file for inetd(1M).  See inetd.conf(4).## Syntax for socket-
➥based Internet services:
#  <service_name> <socket_type> <proto> <flags> <user> <server_pathname>
➥<args>
#
# Ftp and telnet are standard Internet services.
#
ftp     stream  tcp    nowait  root    /usr/sbin/tcpd  in.ftpd -d
telnet  stream  tcp    nowait  root    /usr/sbin/tcpd  in.telnetd
#
# identd is to support RFC 1413 authentication / identity lookups
#
ident   stream  tcp    nowait  root    /usr/sbin/in.identd    in.identd
#
# Shell, login, exec, comsat and talk are BSD protocols.
#
shell stream  tcp     nowait  root    /usr/sbin/tcpd  in.rshd
login stream  tcp     nowait  root    /usr/sbin/tcpd  in.rlogind
exec  stream  tcp     nowait  root    /usr/sbin/tcpd  in.rexecd
comsat          dgram  udp     wait    root    /usr/sbin/in.comsat
➥in.comsat
talk    dgram   udp     wait    root    /usr/sbin/tcpd  in.talkd
```

19

```
ntalk   dgram   udp     wait    root    /usr/sbin/in.ntalkd in.ntalkd

# Tftp service is provided primarily for booting.  Most sites run this
# only on machines acting as "boot servers."
#
tftp dgram     udp     wait    root    /usr/sbin/tcpd  in.tftpd -s
➥/tftpboot
#
# Finger, systat and netstat give out user information which may be
# valuable to potential "system crackers."  Many sites choose to disable
# some or all of these services to improve security.
#
finger         stream  tcp     nowait  nobody /usr/sbin/tcpd  in.fingerd
#systat stream  tcp     nowait  root     /usr/bin/ps             ps -ef
netstat        stream  tcp     nowait  root    /usr/bin/netstat
➥netstat -f inet
#
# Time service is used for clock synchronization.
#
time  stream  tcp     nowait  root    internal
time  dgram   udp     wait    root    internal
#
# Echo, discard, daytime, and chargen are used primarily for testing.
#
echo  stream  tcp     nowait  root    internal
echo  dgram   udp     wait    root    internal
discard        stream  tcp     nowait  root    internal
discard        dgram   udp     wait    root    internal
daytime        stream  tcp     nowait  root    internal
daytime        dgram   udp     wait    root    internal
chargen        stream  tcp     nowait  root    internal
chargen        dgram   udp     wait    root    internal
#
```

Services in the inetd.conf file with duplicate entries can respond to requests on both the TCP and UDP protocol.

Configuring Routing

If your network comprises of multiple segments, you need to configure routing for the UNIX host. This can be accomplished using the program command /usr/etc/route to define the routing table.

The syntax of the route command was discussed on Day 9 in the section, "Static Routing." The syntax of the Windows NT route command is not that different from the FreeBSD version.

When configuring routes, you should include the following:

- A route to the local host address. This prevents communication with services on the local computer from being transmitted on the network interface.
- The local network broadcast address.
- A default gateway address. This address is used when a specific route to a destination network is not defined.
- Any specific network routes. If a specific route to a destination network must be defined, it should be configured for the UNIX host.

After the routing table is configured, the `ping` command and the `traceroute` command can be used to make sure routing has been configured correctly. The `ping` command also can be used to make sure that the correct address has been bound to the network interface and that remote hosts can be reached using the routing table's information.

The `traceroute` command can be used to determine whether specific routes are used to reach a remote network. The `traceroute` command indicates each router crossed en route to the destination host.

VIEWING THE ROUTING TABLE

After the routing table has been configured, it can be viewed by issuing the `netstat` command as follows:

`Netstat -r`

19

Applying What You Have Learned

Today's material, although procedural, details the steps involved in implementing TCP/IP in Windows NT Server, IntranetWare, and UNIX environments. Each environment has its own nuances and configuration issues that must be addressed.

Always plan ahead no matter which network you implement. Know the IP addressing scheme used on the network, the logical names you intend to use for the new host, and other TCP/IP configuration information. The installation process is a little easier if you do not have to search for details as they are requested.

Test Your Knowledge

1. How can you tune Windows NT Server to perform better when multiple protocols are installed on the server?

2. How can you implement packet filtering on a Windows NT Server?

3. What NLM is used to start the TCP/IP installation process on an IntranetWare server?

4. What role does a domain SAP/RIP server (DSS) play in an IntranetWare TCP/IP environment?

5. What must be rebuilt on a UNIX server when a new network adapter is installed?

6. Which daemon is used by a UNIX server to launch the correct daemon to handle an Internet request from a remote client?

7. What command enables you to view the routing table on a UNIX server?

Preview of the Next Day

Tomorrow's material examines the configuration of client software. You will learn to configure TCP/IP in both a Windows 95/98 environment and a Windows NT Workstation environment.

In addition to configuring TCP/IP using the software included with these operating systems, you also will look at third-party products that can provide additional TCP/IP functionality.

Tomorrow also includes a brief overview of thin-client technology. Thin clients are a driving force in the effort to reduce the total cost of ownership of a corporate network. A thin client does not execute the program using its processor; it runs the program on a host server.

DAY 20

Configuring Client Software

Today's chapter looks at configuring the TCP/IP protocol for the following client operating systems:

- Windows 9x (This includes Windows 98 and Windows 95.)
- Windows NT Workstation 4.0

In addition to the TCP/IP stacks that ship with these operating systems, you also will examine two of the more common third-party TCP/IP stacks. The two suites discussed are FTP Software's OnNet Host Suite and Trumpet Winsock.

Today's material concludes with an overview of *thin clients*. Thin clients have been proposed as a new measure to reduce the total cost of ownership for a network. This section outlines some of the proposed solutions and guides you through the evolution of networking to the creation of Thin Client technology.

Installing TCP/IP in Windows 98 and Windows 95

The Windows 98 and Windows 95 operating systems are by far the most commonly used today. The following sections detail the steps to install TCP/IP on a Windows 98 or Windows 95 system. The following steps are based on a Windows 98 client. Any differences between the two operating systems is noted during the installation steps. From this point on, these two operating systems are referred to collectively as Windows 9x.

Adding a Network Adapter

When configuring your Windows 9x system to take part in a TCP/IP network, the first step is to install the network adapter in your computer. Windows 9x is a Plug and Play operating system. This means that, if the peripheral you are adding supports the Plug and Play architecture, the operating system should be able to autodetect and autoinstall the correct drivers for your system.

If the card is not autodetected, you must launch the Add New Hardware Wizard to install the necessary drivers. Use the following steps to install a network adapter's drivers:

1. To open Control Panel, select Settings and then Control Panel from the Start menu.

2. Double-click the Add New Hardware applet. This launches the Add New Hardware Wizard (see Figure 20.1).

FIGURE 20.1.

The start of the Add New Hardware Wizard.

3. Close any programs currently running; they might interfere with the installation of the network drivers. After you have closed all programs, click the Next button to proceed with the wizard.

4. The wizard next prepares to detect any Plug and Play devices. If any are found, the installation prompts you for the necessary drivers. Click the Next button to commence the search for Plug and Play devices.

5. If no Plug and Play devices are found, the Add New Hardware Wizard can perform an invasive search for the newly added hardware. It is recommended that you let Windows search for new hardware. Click the Next button to search using the default settings.

6. During the search, you are informed of the progress of the detection. After the detection process is complete, you can click the Details button in the Add New Hardware Wizard to see the detected hardware (see Figure 20.2).

FIGURE 20.2.

Viewing the detected hardware.

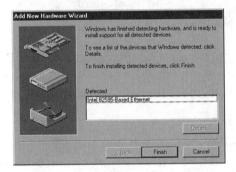

7. Click the Finish button to install the necessary drivers. You need the original Windows 9x media to install the drivers.

8. You must restart the computer for the drivers to be activated.

Adding the TCP/IP Protocol Stack

After your client system restarts, the next step is to add and configure the TCP/IP protocol stack that ships with your operating system. This is where Windows 98 and Windows 95 differ in the implementation of TCP/IP. Windows 95 does not automatically install the TCP/IP protocol, whereas TCP/IP is the only protocol installed under Windows 98. The following steps are required to add the TCP/IP protocol under Windows 95.

1. To open Control Panel, select Settings and then Control Panel from the Start menu.

2. In Control Panel, double-click the Network applet.

3. Click the Add button to add a new protocol.

4. From the Select Network Component Type dialog box, select Protocol and click the Add button. Figure 20.3 shows the Select Network Protocol dialog box.

2(

FIGURE 20.3.

The Select Network Protocol dialog box.

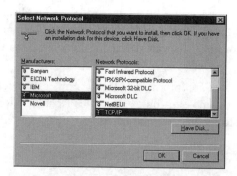

Select Microsoft from the list of manufacturers and select TCP/IP from the list of protocols. After these are selected, click the OK button to transfer the necessary files.

DIFFERENCES BETWEEN WINDOWS 98 AND WINDOWS 95

The dialog box in Figure 20.3 is the Select Network Protocol dialog box in Windows 98. Windows 95 presents the same dialog box, except there are fewer options to install.

---

5. You might be prompted to insert your Windows 9x media for the installation of the drivers. After these drivers and support files are installed, you must restart the computer.

Configuring the TCP/IP Protocol

After you install the TCP/IP protocol, you probably need to make some changes to your TCP/IP configuration. The configuration tasks can include the following:

- Assigning a static IP address or selecting to use a DCHP-assigned address
- Assigning a default gateway
- Configuring DNS parameters
- Configuring whether NetBIOS is used on the network
- Configuring WINS parameters (if running on a network that requires NetBIOS)
- Configuring whether TCP/IP is the default protocol (if multiple protocols exist)
- Selecting which of your installed adapters use TCP/IP

All these options are configured in the TCP/IP properties dialog box. This can be opened using the following steps:

1. Open Control Panel.

2. Double-click the Network applet in Control Panel.

3. Select TCP/IP from the list of installed network components and click the Properties button (see Figure 20.4).

FIGURE 20.4.

The Network dialog box.

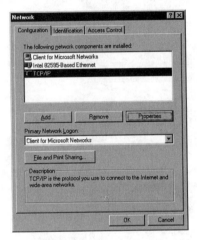

Assigning an IP Address

You can use two different methods to assign TCP/IP information to a Windows 9x client. You can statically assign TCP/IP information, or you can retrieve the client's TCP/IP configuration parameters from a DHCP server.

If you statically assign an IP address to the client, you must also make sure all other parameters are correctly configured. If you use DHCP to assign TCP/IP configuration information to the Windows 9x client, you also should check the other tabs of the TCP/IP dialog box. This is because any settings in the TCP/IP properties dialog box override the DHCP-assigned settings.

Figure 20.5 shows the IP Address tab in the TCP/IP properties dialog box.

You can choose to obtain an IP address automatically, which retrieves the TCP/IP configuration from a DHCP server, or you can configure the IP address manually. This requires you to enter both the IP address and the subnet mask for your network.

20

FIGURE 20.5.

Configuring the IP address for a Windows 9x client.

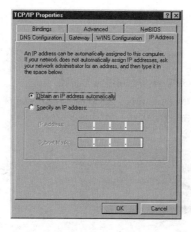

Configuring the Default Gateway

The second step in configuring TCP/IP on a Windows 9x client is to set the default gateway entry (see Figure 20.6).

FIGURE 20.6.

Configuring the default gateway.

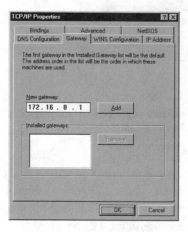

The default gateway is the router to which you want all network traffic destined for remote networks to be sent. This entry is not required in the following scenarios:

- Your Windows 9x client is configured using DHCP, and the DHCP server already provides a default gateway entry.
- Your network is a single-segment network that does not use a default gateway.

- Your network supports router discovery. *Router discovery* uses an extension of the Internet Control Message Protocol (ICMP). This extension enables hosts attached to multicast or broadcast networks to discover the IP addresses of their neighboring routers.

After you manually enter the IP address of the default gateway, click the Add button. This adds the IP address to the list of installed gateways.

Configuring DNS Properties

The DNS Configuration tab of the TCP/IP properties dialog box enables you to configure DNS settings (see Figure 20.7).

FIGURE 20.7.

Setting DNS properties.

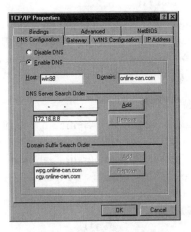

The first major choice in the dialog box is whether to enable DNS resolution on the client. If you enable DNS, the following options can be configured:

- *Host.* The Host field provides the hostname for the Windows 9x client. This usually is set to the computer name assigned during installation. It can, however, be set to a different value if desired.
- *Domain.* The Domain field provides the host's Internet domain. The Fully Qualified Domain Name (FQDN) for the client is a combination of the Host and Domain fields.
- *DNS Server Search Order.* The listing of DNS servers (by IP address) specifies the order in which a client attempts to connect to multiple DNS servers. If a connection is established to a DNS server, no further connection attempts result.

20

- *Domain Suffix Search Order.* This parameter enables the host to try different Internet domain names as suffixes when you ping a hostname. If you configure the Domain Suffix Search order as shown in Figure 20.7, and if you type `ping smallguy` at the command prompt, you actually are performing the following DNS queries:

  - `smallguy`
  - `smallguy.online-can.com`
  - `smallguy.wpg.online-can.com`
  - `smallguy.cgy.online-can.com`

Enabling NetBIOS over TCP/IP

If your network supports running NetBIOS applications over the TCP/IP protocol, you can configure this support for your Windows 9x client in the NetBIOS tab of the TCP/IP properties dialog box. This option automatically is enabled if you are using the Client for Microsoft Networks (because it requires NetBIOS).

Configuring WINS Properties

In a NetBIOS network, you might be required to configure a NetBIOS name server entry. The Windows 9x TCP/IP configuration assumes you are using Microsoft's Windows Internet Name Server (WINS). The WINS configuration tab of the TCP/IP properties dialog box enables you to configure WINS settings (see Figure 20.8).

FIGURE 20.8.

Configuring WINS settings for a Windows 9x client.

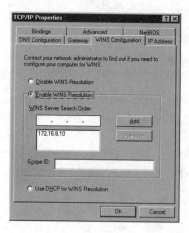

Depending on your network environment, you might want these settings to be provided by a DHCP server. This can be accomplished by selecting Use DHCP for WINS Resolution.

If you choose to configure WINS manually, the following options can be set on the WINS configuration tab:

- *WINS Server Search Order.* The WINS servers to which the client can connect for NetBIOS name registrations, requests, and releases. The Windows 9x client always attempts to connect to multiple WINS servers based on the order displayed here.

- *Scope ID.* Only members within the same NetBIOS scope can connect to one another other using native Windows networking. Scope ID is a case-sensitive field. If you plan to connect to Windows NT class systems, make sure you enter the Scope ID in uppercase letters. If you do not use uppercase, you cannot communicate with Windows NT systems because they always enter the Scope ID in uppercase letters.

CONFIGURING THE NETBIOS NODE TYPE

If you configure your client using DHCP, you also can configure the NetBIOS node type that indicates how a NetBIOS name should be resolved. Valid options include B-Node, P-Node, M-Node, and H-Node. (For more information about these node types, see Day 7, "NetBIOS Name Resolution.")

If your WINS information is configured manually, Windows 9x uses the following defaults:

- If a WINS server is configured, the client functions as an H-Node client.
- If no WINS server is configured, the client functions as a B-Node client.

If you want to change these settings, you must edit the Registry by running the Registry Editor (regedit.exe). You must edit the value NodeType in the following location in Windows 9x:

HKEY_LOCAL_MACHINE\System\CurrentControlSet\Servers\Class\MetTrans\0001

The NodeType value can be configured as B-Node(1), P-Node(2), M-Node(4), or H-Node(8). Set the NodeType data to the numeric equivalent for the desired NodeType setting.

20

Setting TCP/IP as the Default Protocol

If you are running multiple protocols, the Windows 9x operating system enables you to designate one protocol as the default. This setting should be checked if your network connections always are slow but eventually succeed. This can be a sign that connection attempts use an incorrect protocol at first. The default protocol is configured in the Advanced tab of the TCP/IP properties dialog box (see Figure 20.9).

FIGURE 20.9.

Setting TCP/IP as the default protocol stack.

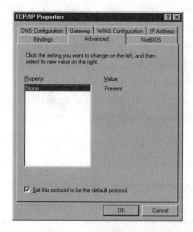

To set TCP/IP as the default protocol, select Set This Protocol to Be the Default Protocol. This deselects the previous default protocol.

Binding TCP/IP to Specific Adapters

Your Windows 9x client may have multiple clients installed. You can configure which clients should have use of the TCP/IP protocol by setting the bindings in the Bindings tab of the TCP/IP properties dialog box (see Figure 20.10).

FIGURE 20.10.

Configuring the TCP/IP bindings.

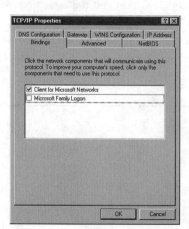

In the figure, TCP/IP is enabled only for transactions using the Client for Microsoft Clients, not the Microsoft Family Login client.

Non-Graphical Configuration

In addition to the configuration settings in the TCP/IP properties dialog box, text files to configure TCP/IP also are available in Windows 9x. These text configuration files include the following:

- HOSTS
- LMHOSTS
- NETWORKS
- Protocols
- Services

All these configuration files are stored in the %WINDIR% directory where you installed Windows 9x. The HOSTS and LMHOSTS files initially are stored with the .SAM extension to indicate that they are sample files. To actually be used, the extension must be removed from the filename.

CASES FOR CONFIGURING THE **LMHOSTS** FILE

The only configuration file modified on a Windows 9x client is the LMHOSTS file (if WINS is not deployed on the network). The LMHOSTS file enables Windows 9x to authenticate with a domain controller not located on the same physical segment of the network. To accomplish this, the following entry must be added to the LMHOSTS file on the client:

```
10.20.30.40    Server    #PRE    #DOM:ourdomain
```

This entry configures the client to use the domain controller named Server at IP address 10.20.30.40 to authenticate the user into the domain named ourdomain.

Installing TCP/IP in Windows NT Workstation 4.0

This section examines configuring TCP/IP on a Windows NT Workstation 4.0 client. The following configuration tasks are outlined in this section:

- Adding a network adapter card
- Adding the TCP/IP protocol

- Configuring the TCP/IP protocol
- Loading additional TCP/IP network services

Adding a Network Adapter Card

Windows NT Workstation requires that a network adapter card exist before the TCP/IP protocol can be installed. This section outlines the steps to install a network adapter after Windows NT Workstation 4.0 has been installed. If the network card is present during the installation process, it should be detected correctly and the appropriate drivers should be installed.

WHAT IF YOU DO NOT HAVE A NETWORK ADAPTER?

If you do not have a network adapter, all is not lost. A special network adapter, the *MS Loopback Adapter*, has been included (see Figure 20.11).

When this adapter is present, it enables TCP/IP to be installed. It is not an actual network card, however, so testing cannot be performed between multiple hosts.

FIGURE 20.11.

Adding the MS Loopback Adapter.

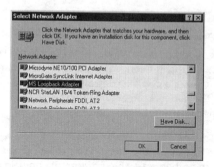

Use the following steps to install a newly added network adapter:

1. Log in either as the Administrator or as an account with administrator privileges on the target workstation.

2. Start Control Panel by selecting Settings and then Control Panel from the Start menu.

3. In Control Panel, double-click the Network applet.

4. Select the Adapters tab to verify whether a network adapter already has been installed (see Figure 20.12).

WHO CAN INSTALL NEW DRIVERS IN WINDOWS NT?

To install a new network adapter or to make any changes to the configuration of the Windows NT Workstation computer, you must be a member of the Windows NT local group Administrators. If you are not a member of this local group, the option to add a new adapter is grayed out, preventing you from adding the new adapter.

FIGURE 20.12.

Viewing the Network Adapters tab of the Network properties dialog box.

5. If your network adapter is not present, click the Add button and select your adapter from the list shown in Figure 20.12. If you do not see your adapter in the list, you need to use the manufacturer's driver disk. You then can add the drivers using the Have Disk option.

6. After the driver is loaded, you can verify the device settings by selecting the Network Adapter and clicking the Properties button (see Figure 20.13).

FIGURE 20.13.

Viewing the resources used by a network adapter.

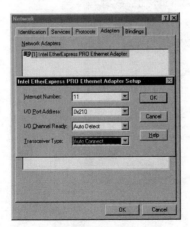

20

7. In this dialog box, you can set different properties for the network card (if you are unsure whether the card works at the suggested settings).

Adding the TCP/IP Protocol

As in Windows NT Server, the TCP/IP protocol is installed by default during the initial installation of Windows NT Workstation. If the protocol has been removed or is not installed during the initial installation, you can use the steps described on Day 19 in the section, "Adding the TCP/IP Protocol."

You likely will use DHCP for your TCP/IP configuration when you configure Windows NT Workstation.

Configuring the TCP/IP Protocol

After you install the TCP/IP protocol on a Windows NT Workstation, you might need to perform some additional steps to configure TCP/IP. These steps can include the following:

- Configuring an IP address (if you are not using DHCP)
- Providing DNS configuration information
- Providing WINS configuration information
- Enabling the Windows NT Workstation to function as a router
- Enabling advanced packet filtering

All this configuration can be performed in the TCP/IP properties dialog box (see Figure 20.14).

FIGURE 20.14.

The Windows NT Workstation TCP/IP properties dialog box.

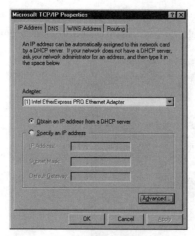

The only difference between the Windows NT Workstation and Windows NT Server TCP/IP properties dialog boxes is the exclusion of the DHCP Relay tab in the NT Workstation version.

Loading Additional TCP/IP Network Services

As in Windows NT Server, additional network services can be added after the TCP/IP protocol is installed in Windows NT Workstation. The following services can be added:

- *Microsoft Peer Web Services.* This stripped-down version of the Microsoft Internet Information Server is optimized for a maximum of 10 connections.
- *Microsoft TCP/IP Printing.* This service enables the NT Workstation to manage TCP/IP printers. This service installs a *Line Printer Daemon (LPD)* service on the NT Workstation. It then can control *Line Printer Router (LPR)* connected printers.
- *Simple TCP/IP Services.* This service installs additional TCP/IP services: Character Generator, Daytime, Discard, Echo, and Quote of the Day. The section "Installing the Optional TCP/IP Services in Windows NT" on Day 11 discussed these services in more detail.
- *SNMP Service.* This service installs the SNMP agent for Windows NT Workstation so it can participate in an SNMP-managed network. It also installs the counter for the TCP/IP protocol into the Windows NT Performance Monitor. This enables analysis of the TCP/IP protocol suite's performance to be monitored.

Using a Third-Party TCP/IP Stack

Several third-party TCP/IP stacks are available for use in Windows NT and Windows 95. Why would you purchase a TCP/IP stack when one is shipped with the operating system? This decision generally is based on the additional client software and functionality offered by these stacks. Additional software that might be included with a third-party stack includes Trivial FTP Client and Server software, NFS Client and Server software, FTP Client and Server software, IBM 3270 or 5250 Terminal Emulation software, and Berkeley R-Utilities.

OnNet Host Suite 4.0

This section details the configuration of OnNet Host Suite 4.0 by FTP Software. A demo version of this software can be downloaded from the FTP Software Web site at http://www.ftp.com.

OnNet Host Suite can either install its own TCP/IP stack or run on top of the Microsoft TCP/IP stack, extending its capabilities.

During the installation of OnNet Host Suite, you can select the components to install on your computer (see Figure 20.15).

FIGURE 20.15.

Choosing OnNet Host Suite components.

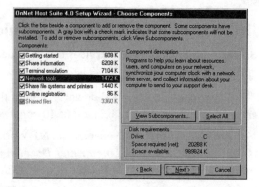

After OnNet Host Suite is installed, it adds an additional program container to the Programs menu containing the following programs:

- *Application Help Files.* This container includes the help files for all OnNet Host Suite applications.
- *Network Tools.* This container includes the following utilities:
    - *IP Trace.* A network packet-monitoring utility that allows for the analysis of incoming and outgoing traffic from your protocol stack.
    - *Network Time.* A time-setting utility that enables you to synchronize your computer's clock with a Network Time Server.
    - *Ping.* A graphical utility that enables you to verify that remote hosts are reachable. This utility also includes a graphical traceroute functionality.
    - *Query.* A graphical utility that enables Finger queries, Whois queries, Quote of the Day requests, Host queries, DNS queries, and NIS queries.
    - *Retrieve.* A utility that can be run on each client system in your network to produce a system report that includes details about the computer such as CPU, memory, disk space, and specific Registry information.
- *Scripting Tools.* Tools that enable you to create scripts to perform network management tasks using a Visual Basic-like language called Open Script.
- *Application Assistant.* A wizard that takes a user's input and launches the appropriate OnNet Host Suite tool to perform the requested task.
- *File Transfer.* An FTP client that enables data to be retrieved from an FTP site. The FTP client is configured to work like the Windows Explorer (see Figure 20.16).

FIGURE 20.16.

The OnNet FTP application.

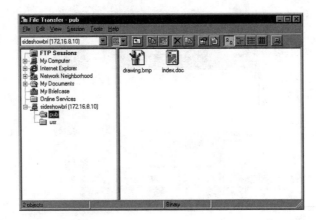

- *FTP Server.* A utility that enables others to connect to your computer with the FTP protocol for the transfer of files.

- *KEYview.* A utility that enables you to view files without using the original software used to create them. It also can perform file conversions.

- *Print Client.* A graphical Line Printer Router (LPR) print client that enables files to be printed to a printer running an Line Printer Daemon (LPD) service.

- *Remote Utilities.* A graphical utility that enables you to execute the RCMD and RCP commands against a remote UNIX host.

- *TN3270-TN5250.* A terminal emulation client that provides access to IBM midrange and mainframe computers that support TN3270, TN3270E, and TN5250 connections through SNA gateways.

- *TNVTPlus.* A terminal emulation client that provides connection to a remote computer using the Telnet protocol, a modem, or a null-modem cable.

Trumpet Winsock

Trumpet Winsock is an alternative TCP/IP protocol stack that can be used in place of the Microsoft TCP/IP stack. It also is commonly used as a dial-in TCP/IP protocol stack.

After you install the necessary software, you must configure which interfaces will use the Trumpet Winsock stack. This can be accomplished in the Trumpet Winsock TCP/IP Manager using the following steps:

1. On the desktop, double-click the Trumpet Winsock icon.

2. In the TCP/IP settings tab of the Trumpet Winsock Manager dialog box, right-click any open space and select Add.

3. A dialog box opens, showing any interfaces the Winsock manager has found (see Figure 20.17).

2

FIGURE 20.17.

Adding a new interface to Trumpet Winsock.

Select the Interface you want to add and click the OK button. You must install the interface using Windows 9x, as described earlier today in the section "Adding a Network Adapter."

4. After the interface is added, you need to configure its TCP/IP parameters (see Figure 20.18).

FIGURE 20.18.

Configuring the TCP/IP interface.

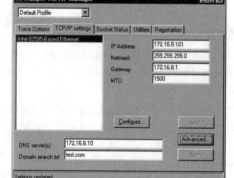

In this figure, the IP address, subnet mask, default gateway, Maximum Transmission Unit (MTU), DNS server, and Domain search list all have been configured for the network interface.

5. You can verify that TCP/IP is initialized by checking the Trace Options tab of the Trumpet TCP/IP Manager (see Figure 20.19).

FIGURE 20.19.

Viewing the Trace Options tab in Trumpet Winsock.

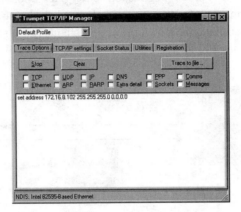

You should see that the address you assigned to your adapter has been initialized using the set address command.

6. As a final test, you can verify that the host is configured correctly using the Utilities tab (see Figure 20.20).

FIGURE 20.20.

Verifying the TCP/IP configuration using the PING utility.

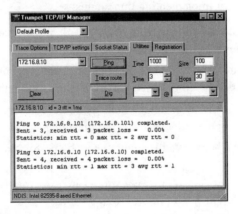

The PING button in the Utilities tab can verify the following addresses:

- The localhost address 127.0.0.1
- The address you assigned to the host
- The address of your default gateway
- The address of a host on a remote network segment

This standard PING test proves that the TCP/IP configuration is correct.

Thin Clients

Thin client technology shifts processing responsibility back to the large, back-end server (similar to the days of the mainframe computer). Instead of having high-powered clients that execute programs utilizing their own processor, clients run sessions hosted on a centralized server (see Figure 20.21).

FIGURE 20.21.

A Thin Client utilizing a Terminal Server.

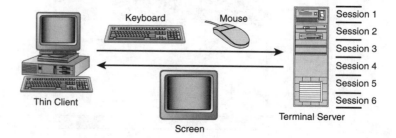

The client sends only keyboard and mouse input to the terminal server. After processing is complete, the terminal server sends updated screen information to the remote client. No other data is transmitted between the client and the server. All processing takes place in memory space and on the processor of the terminal server.

The following are goals of implementing thin clients:

- Reducing the total cost of ownership (TCO) by deploying low-cost and low-maintenance systems to the desktop
- Reducing hardware costs by redeploying older client systems with sufficient resources to function as thin clients, but not enough to function as PC clients
- Reducing support costs by removing configuration requirements from the client systems and moving toward a centrally administered system
- Reducing LAN/WAN bandwidth requirements by performing all processing on the back-end server
- Improving performance over slow WAN links by sending only screen images and mouse/keyboard inputs across the WAN link
- Increasing security by running server-side processes only at the security level of the connecting client

Models in Use

Currently, four different client architecture models provide thin client functionality:

- X-Window systems
- Citrix Winframe/Microsoft Terminal Server

- Java Virtual Machine running on network computers
- Web browsers

X-Window systems enable graphical screen information from remote servers to be displayed locally. This has been utilized in UNIX environments for many years.

Citrix Winframe and *Microsoft Terminal Server* (code named Hydra) use Windows terminal clients that can run Windows and DOS applications from a modified Windows NT server that hosts multiple sessions.

Java Virtual Machine is a newer architecture that enables small JavaScript applets to be launched from a central server and executed on a local device.

Web browsers also can link HTML pages from a central server to a client browser. Using technology such as Active Server Pages, all processing can take place on the remote server, and the generated scripts and data can be transported to the remote client.

The Terminal Server

The Citrix Winframe model introduces the concept of a centralized Terminal Server. This server hosts all the user sessions. To the client, it appears as if he is sitting at the server console working directly at the server. In truth, he is operating in a session established on the Terminal server for the workspace.

Each individual user session has the following characteristics:

- All keyboard and mouse input from the client is received and processed by the terminal session.
- Each user has an independent session that is not affected by other sessions.
- All display output is redirected to the client's video display.
- All passwords and data are transported over an encrypted connection.

The actual technology used to implement Citrix Winframe is made up of two individual protocols:

- Independent Computing Architecture (ICA)
- Thinwire

Independent Computing Architecture (ICA) is the physical line protocol used for communication between the client system and the Citrix server. ICA is a higher-layer protocol that can run on top of any transport protocol. Most frequently, this protocol is TCP.

Thinwire is the data protocol used by Winframe to send the actual screen image to the client station. The Thinwire protocol is encapsulated within an ICA packet for transmission. This protocol provides access to the following client types (see Figure 20.22):

- Local network clients
- Dial-in clients
- Web clients over the Internet
- UNIX clients
- Native Windows clients
- Macintosh clients

FIGURE 20.22.

Multiple client types can connect to Citrix Winframe server.

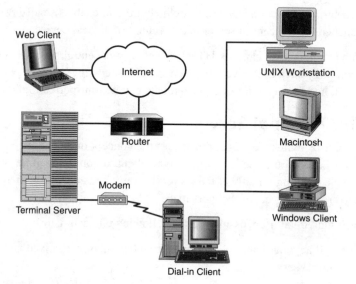

WINDOWS TERMINAL SERVER (AKA HYDRA)

Microsoft has developed a proprietary version of a terminal server called Windows Terminal Server. This product uses a different protocol for transmission of screen, mouse, and keyboard data between the thin client and the terminal server. This protocol is called *Remote Desktop Protocol (RDP)*.

The RDP protocol is based on the International Telecommunication Union's (ITU) T.120 protocol. This is an international, standard multichannel conferencing protocol also used in Microsoft's NetMeeting product. RDP can be optimized for both high-speed LAN connections and low-bandwidth dial-up connections.

Terminal Server also supports third-party products that use the ICA standard. This provides connectivity to UNIX and Macintosh clients.

Applying What You Have Learned

Today's material included the steps for configuring TCP/IP in a Windows 98/95 environment. It also provided an overview of the differences between installing TCP/IP in a Windows NT Workstation environment and yesterday's Windows NT Server environment.

Third-party TCP/IP stacks and utilities can be used to further extend your client's capabilities. FTP OnNet Host Suite and Trumpet Winsock were discussed here, but other alternatives are out there. If you need additional functionality for your clients, you should research third-party options.

This chapter closed with a discussion about thin clients. This technology's usage is growing consistently. The reduced costs combined with the performance gains provided by sending only screen and input data are making this a widely researched networking model.

Test Your Knowledge

1. How can a network adapter be added to a Windows 9x installation if it was not detected by the Plug and Play BIOS?
2. What does the term *total cost of ownership* mean?
3. If you are manually configuring the TCP/IP protocol for a client running on a single-segment LAN, what is the minimum configuration required?
4. If your client's TCP/IP configuration is provided by a DHCP server, which takes precedence: a DHCP configuration setting or a manually entered configuration setting?
5. What does the Domain Suffix Search order provide?
6. What functionality does the SNMP service provide to a Windows NT Workstation client?
7. What is one reason for installing a third-party TCP/IP stack or TCP/IP suite?
8. Describe the four models currently used to deploy thin clients.

Preview of the Next Day

Tomorrow's material examines future trends in the world of TCP/IP. The material first looks at the new version of the IP protocol, called IPv6. The following information is discussed:

- The major changes in IPv6 from IPv4
- The packet format for IPv6
- Security extensions for IPv6
- Methods for migrating from IPv4 to IPv6

The chapter closes with a discussion about one of the newest technologies used in a TCP/IP network—Voice over IP. It outlines how Voice over IP is accomplished and discusses some of the issues involved with this application.

Day **21**

Future Applications of TCP/IP

With the growth of the Internet, the current IP addressing scheme is quickly running out of available addresses. Recognizing this, the IETF has been commissioned to create the next generation of the IP address.

Several published RFCs lay out the needs for the new protocol. This new release of the IP protocol, called *IPv6*, should begin to replace the current IPv4 as the year 2000 rolls out.

Today's material gives you some insight into the design of IPv6. It also discusses the effect this new addressing scheme will have on networks that need to integrate both IPv4 and IPv6.

After examining the changes that will occur with IPv6, today's discussion concludes with some information about implementing Voice over IP, a technology rapidly being deployed.

What Are the Major Changes in IPv6?

IPv6 is being designed as the successor to the current 32-bit addressing scheme, IPv4. Major changes in the next release of IPv6 include the following:

- *Expanded addressing capabilities.* The address size for IPv6 will be 128 bits. This will provide a larger pool of IP addresses for the Internet. Each user will have access to a pool of IP addresses equal to the total number of IP addresses currently available on the Internet today.

- *Simplification of the IP header.* Much of the IPv4 header information has been made optional or dropped entirely. This will result in faster processing of IP header information by receiving hosts.

- *Improved extensibility of the IP header.* The IP header has been formatted to provide more efficient forwarding, more flexibility on the length of option fields, and easier inclusion of new options in the future. This will enable the IP header to change as the protocol evolves over the next few years, without having to redesign the entire header format.

- *Improved flow control.* IP datagrams will be able to request a better quality of service. This will include time-specific delivery of information and the capability to request a minimum bandwidth availability or real-time service.

- *Increased security.* The IP header will include extensions to support authentication of source and destination hosts and better assurance that data will not be corrupted. This also will provide the option of encrypting data as it is transported over the network.

Address Formats Under IPv6

RFC 1884 Hosts using IPv6 will be assigned 128-bit addresses. These addresses will fall into the following address classes:

- Unicast
- Anycast
- Multicast

A *unicast* address is a unique identifier assigned to a single interface.

An *anycast* address is an identifier assigned to multiple interfaces, generally on distinct hosts. When a packet is sent to an anycast address, the packet is delivered to only one of the interfaces associated with the address. This usually is the nearest address based on routing table distance.

Anycast addresses use the same syntax as unicast addresses. They become anycast addresses when assigned to more than one network interface. Hosts assigned anycast addresses must be explicitly configured to know it is an anycast address.

A *multicast* address also is an identifier assigned to multiple interfaces on distinct hosts. A packet delivered to a multicast address is delivered to all the interfaces assigned this multicast address.

Multicast addresses use the syntax shown in Figure 21.1.

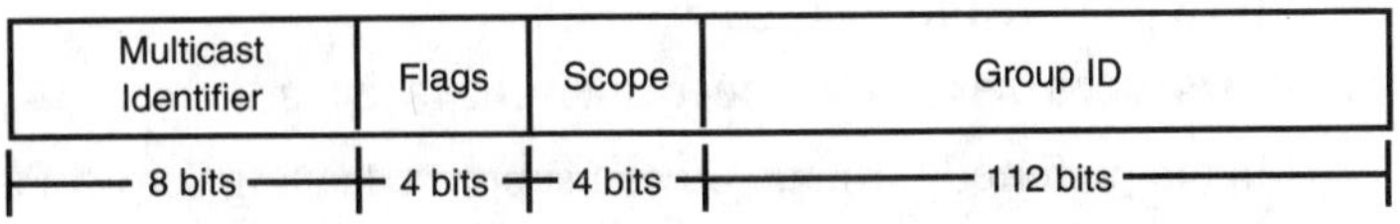

FIGURE 21.1.
Multicast IPv6 address format.

Multicast Identifier	Flags	Scope	Group ID
8 bits	4 bits	4 bits	112 bits

- *Multicast Identifier.* The first eight bits are set to 1. This identifies that the IPv6 address is a multicast address.
- *Flags.* This 4-bit field indicates whether the address is a permanently assigned multicast address (as set by the global Internet numbering authority) or a specially created multicast address. The first three bits are set to 0 and are reserved. The fourth bit is set either to 0 for a permanent multicast address or to 1 for a transient multicast address.
- *Scope.* This 4-bit field sets the address space in which the multicast address is effective. Allowable values are shown in Table 21.1.

TABLE 21.1. ALLOWABLE MULTICAST SCOPE FIELD VALUES.

Value (000X)	Meaning
0	Reserved
1	Node-local scope
2	Link-local scope
5	Site-local scope
8	Organization-local scope
E	Global scope
F	Reserved
3,4,6,7,9,A,B,C,D	Unassigned

21

- *Group ID.* This 112-bit field identifies the group address. This address is effective only within the defined scope.

You might notice that there are no broadcast addresses under IPv6. This is because all functionality handled by broadcast addresses in IPv4 has been replaced by more efficient multicast addresses in IPv6.

Representations of the IPv6 Address

The following three accepted formats can be used to represent IPv6 addresses:

- The preferred format represents the address in eight fields of 16 bits. The 16 bits are represented as a string of four hex digits. The following is an example of an IPv6 preferred format:

  ```
  1079:0005:AB45:5f4C:0010:BA97:0043:34AB
  ```

  In the preferred format, you can suppress leading zeros in any of the eight fields. There must, however, be at least one digit in each of the eight fields. The preceding address also can be represented as the following:

  ```
  1079:5:AB45:5f4C:10:BA97:43:34AB
  ```

- Many assigned IPv6 addresses contain long strings of zeros. A special syntax has been created that represents multiple 16-bit fields of zeros with ::. This can only be used to represent entire 16-bit fields of all zeros. Table 21.2 shows how various IPv6 addresses can be shortened using this syntax.

TABLE 21.2. IPv6 ADDRESS REPRESENTATIONS.

ADDRESS TYPE	ORIGINAL ADDRESS	SHORTER ADDRESS SYNTAX
Unicast	1090:0:0:0:0:876:AABC:1234	1090::876:AABC:1234
Multicast	FF01:0:0:0:0:0:0:67AB	FF01::67AB
Loopback	0:0:0:0:0:0:0:1	::1
Unspecified	0:0:0:0:0:0:0:0	::

- In mixed environments of IPv4 and IPv6, it might be easier to work with an address format of H:H:H:H:H:H:d.d.d.d. The H's are hexadecimal notation for the six high-order fields of the IPv6 address. The d's are the IPv4 format of the address in dotted-decimal format. The following is an example of this address format:

  ```
  0:0:0:0:0:0:10.16.234.15
  FFFF:1234:172.16.4.34
  ```

Special IPv6 Addresses

You should be familiar with the following special unicast IPv6 addresses when you start working with IPv6:

- *0:0:0:0:0:0:0:0.* This *unspecified address* indicates the absence of an assigned IPv6 address. An example of this is a DHCP client that has initialized but has not received an IP address from the DHCP server. This address can only be used in the source address field. It cannot be used as the destination address.

- *0:0:0:0:0:0:0:1.* This *loopback address* is used by an IPv6 host to send IPv6 packets to itself. It can only be used in the destination field of an IPv6 packet. An easy mnemonic (if you worked with IPv4) is that the IPv6 address is 127 zeros 1. The IPv4 loopback address is 127.0.0.1.

- *IPv4-compatible IPv6 addresses.* IPv6 hosts that also will communicate with IPv4 hosts need a special IPv6 unicast address that contains a valid IPv4 address in its lower 32 bits. The first 96 bits are all zeros.

- *IPv4-mapped IPv6 addresses.* This IPv6 address represents nodes that will support only IPv4 and are incapable of working with IPv6 addressing. The format of this address is shown in Figure 21.2.

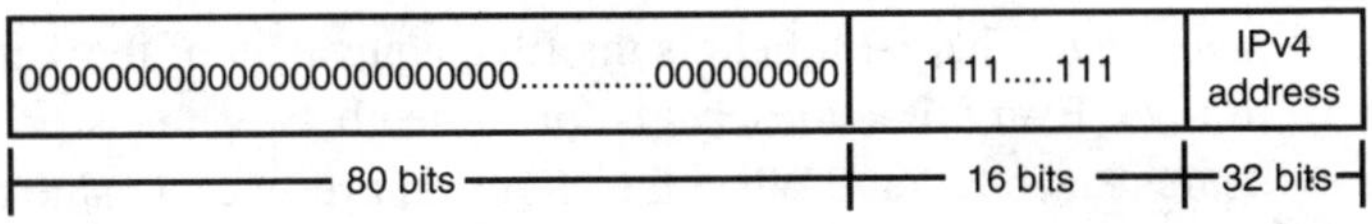

FIGURE 21.2.

IPv4-mapped IPv6 address format.

00000000000000000000000.............000000000	1111.....111	IPv4 address
—————————— 80 bits ——————————	—— 16 bits ——	—32 bits—

The actual IPv6 address is front loaded with 80-0 bits. The next 16 bits are set to a value of 1. The IPv4 address makes up the last 32 bits of the address.

The IPv6 Header Format

The IPv6 header, shown in Figure 21.3, has the following properties:

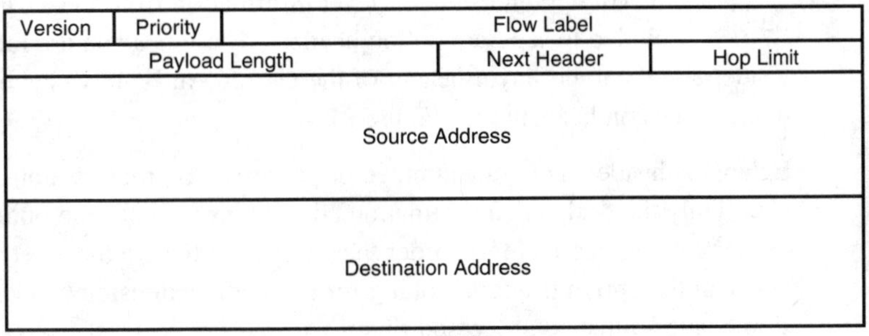

FIGURE 21.3.

The IPv6 header format.

Version	Priority	Flow Label		
Payload Length			Next Header	Hop Limit
Source Address				
Destination Address				

21

- *Version.* This 4-bit field contains the IP version number. It is set to 6.

- *Priority.* This 4-bit field enables a source to prioritize its packets. A lower-priority packet is assigned a value between 0 and 7. Packets at this level give way to packets with a priority level between 7 and 15 if congestion occurs when data is transmitted.

- *Flow Label.* This 24-bit field labels packets from a source host that require special handling by IPv6 routers. Flow options could include real-time service or nonstandard quality of service requirements. If a host or router does not support this functionality, this field's value is set to 0 when a packet originates at that host. If a nonsupporting router is forwarding the packet, the value in this field remains unchanged. This value is ignored entirely if the nonsupporting host is the destination host.

- *Payload Length.* This 16-bit field indicates the length of the remainder of the IP packet. This is the total length of the packet minus the IP header. If this value is set to zero, it indicates a payload longer than 65,536 bytes. This is known as a *Jumbo Payload hop-by-hop option.*

- *Next Header.* This 8-bit field indicates the option header that immediately follows the IP header. The values in this field are the same as the IPv4 protocol field options.

- *Hop Limit.* This 8-bit field is the IPv6 equivalent of the Time-To-Live (TTL) field in IPv4. Every time a packet is forwarded between network segments, this value is decremented by one. When the Hop Limit reaches a value of 0, it is discarded.

- *Source Address.* This 128-bit field contains the source host's IPv6 address.

- *Destination Address.* This 128-bit field contains the destination host's IPv6 address. In IPv6, this destination field might not contain the ultimate destination host address if the Routing header option is included.

IPv6 Extension Headers

RFC 1883 In IPv6, optional Internet-level information from the TCP/IP layered model is included in separate option headers. These headers are located between the IP header and the upper-layer header of the packet. An IPv6 packet can contain zero, one, or many extension headers (see Figure 21.4).

Extension headers are not examined or processed by routers along a packet's delivery path. Only the designated destination address investigates the option headers. Option headers are processed in the order they appear in the IPv6 packet. A receiving host cannot scan the option headers looking for a specific extension header. All preceding extension headers must be processed first.

FIGURE 21.4.

IP option header examples.

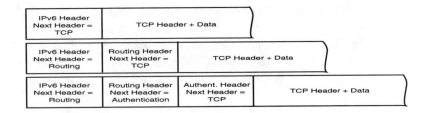

> The Hop-by-Hop option header, discussed in more detail in the following section, is the only exception. Because intermediary hosts can examine the Hop-by-hop option header, it must immediately follow the IP header in the packet. This option header's presence is indicated by a value of 0 in the next header option field of the IP header.

A full implementation of IPv6 contains support for the following extension headers:

- Hop-by-Hop Options
- Routing
- Fragment
- Destination Options
- Authentication
- Encapsulating Security Payload
- No Next Header

Figure 21.5 shows the order in which these extension headers must appear if they are used in the same packet.

FIGURE 21.5.

IPv6 extension header order.

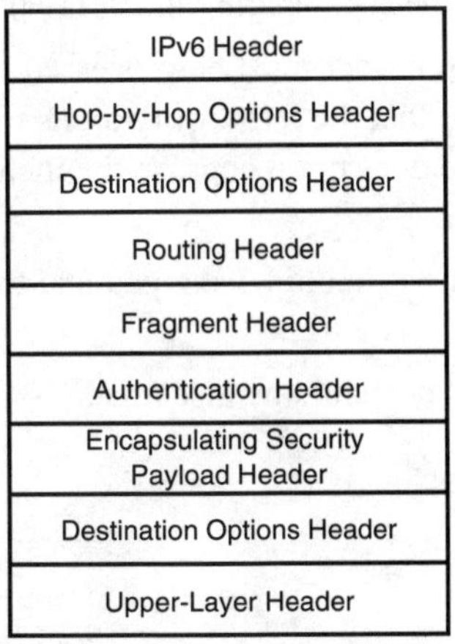

IPv6 Header
Hop-by-Hop Options Header
Destination Options Header
Routing Header
Fragment Header
Authentication Header
Encapsulating Security Payload Header
Destination Options Header
Upper-Layer Header

21

Each extension header should appear no more than once in an IPv6 packet. The only exception is the Destination Options header. A Destination Options header can be located before the routing header. Options in this header are processed by every destination address in the routing header. A destination header also can exist before the Upper-Layer Protocol header. This header can only be processed by the ultimate destination host of the packet.

Hop-by-Hop Options Header

The Hop-by-Hop options header carries information that must be examined by every node a packet crosses along the path to a destination host. The existence of a Hop-by-Hop Options header is indicated by a Next Header value of 0 in the IPv6 header.

The hop-by-hop option also can indicate a jumbo payload. Jumbo payloads are IPv6 packets with payloads longer than 65,536 octets.

The format of the Hop-by-Hop Options header is shown in Figure 21.6.:

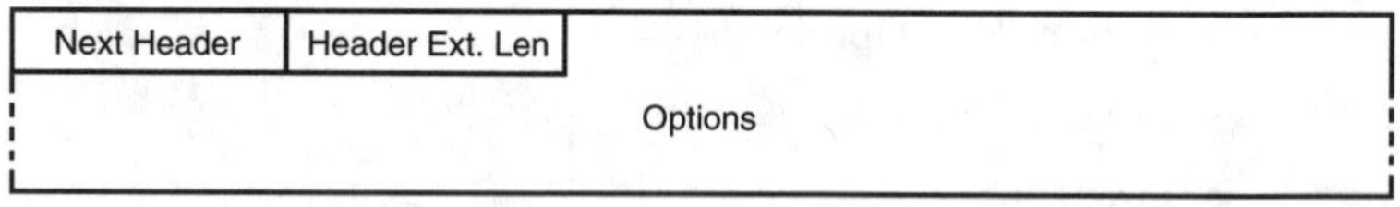

FIGURE 21.6.

The Hop-by-Hop extension header.

Next Header	Header Ext. Len	
	Options	

The Hop-by-Hop Options header contains the following fields:

- *Next Header.* This 8-bit field identifies what type of header immediately follows the Hop-by-Hop header. This field uses the same values as the IPv4 protocol field.
- *Header Extension Length.* This 8-bit field indicates the length of the Hop-by-Hop options field in 8-octet units (not including the first 8 octets).
- *Options.* This variable-length field depends on the number and type of options. These options generally are of the type-length-value (TLV) style (see Figure 21.7).

  Any options in the Hop-by-Hop header must be processed in sequential order. The Option Type field is encoded so that the leftmost two bits indicate what action should be taken if an IPv6 node does not recognize the included option type. The following bit values can be used:

  - *00.* Indicates that this option should be skipped and the next header should be processed.
  - *01.* Indicates that the packet should be discarded.

FIGURE 21.7.

TLV Option field format.

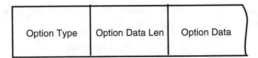

- *10.* Indicates that the packet should be discarded and the source address should be informed using ICMP that the packet was dropped as a result of an unknown option. This is done if the destination is a unicast or multicast address.
- *11.* Sends an ICMP packet to the source host to indicate that an unrecognized option was received. This is sent only if the destination address is a unicast address.

Routing Header

The Routing header is used by an IPv6 source host to list which nodes must be crossed during the transmission of a packet to a destination host. A Routing header is identified in the previous header's Next Header field with a value of 43.

The format of a Type 0 Routing header is shown in Figure 21.8.

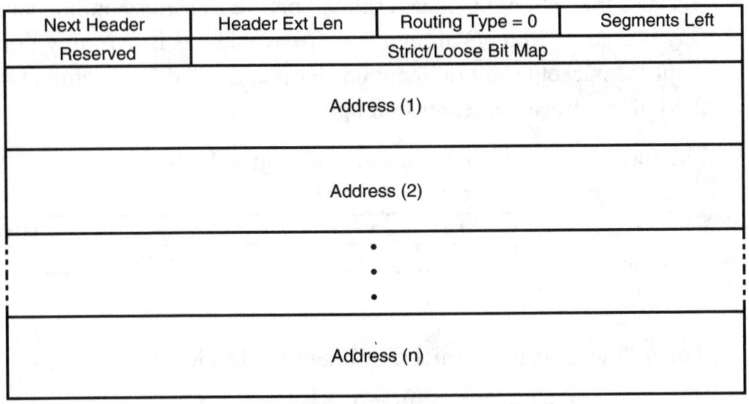

FIGURE 21.8.

Routing option header format.

Next Header	Header Ext Len	Routing Type = 0	Segments Left
Reserved	Strict/Loose Bit Map		
Address (1)			
Address (2)			
• • •			
Address (n)			

The following is the format of a Type 0 Routing header:

- *Next Header.* This 8-bit field identifies what type of header immediately follows the Routing header. This field uses the same values as the IPv4 protocol field.
- *Header Extension Length.* This 8-bit field indicates the length of the Routing header in 8-octet units (not including the first 8 octets). For a Type 0 Routing header, this value equals two times the number of addresses in the header.

21

- *Routing Type.* This 8-bit field identifies the format of the Routing header. This is an example of a Type 0 Routing header.

- *Segments Left.* This 8-bit field indicates how many explicitly listed nodes still need to be visited before reaching the destination host.

- *Reserved.* This 8-bit field is initialized with a value of 0 by the source host and is ignored by the destination host.

- *Strict/Loose Bit Map.* This 24-bit field indicates whether strict or loose routing should be implemented. If strict routing is implemented (using a value of 1), the route must exactly follow the list of addresses. If set to a value of 0, the route must cross the list of addresses, but additional routers also can be crossed along the route.

- *Address[1..n].* This is a vector of 128-bit IPv6 addresses that must be navigated from source host to destination host.

Fragment Header

In IPv6, a key feature is the recognition of the Maximum Transmission Unit (MTU) for the entire path between source and destination hosts. The MTU is the smallest packet size (in octets) required on any of the networks traversed between source and destination.

Because the path MTU is determined before transmission, the source nodes handle all fragmentation. Routers along the delivery path, as is currently done in IPv4, never fragment the packet. The Fragment header is indicated by a value of 44 in the Next Header field of the preceding extension option header.

The format of a Fragment header is shown in Figure 21.9.

FIGURE 21.9.

Fragment header format.

Next Header	Reserved	Fragment Offset	Res	M
Identification				

The following is the format of a Fragment header:

- *Next Header.* This 8-bit field identifies what type of header immediately follows the Fragment header. This field uses the same values as the IPv4 protocol field.

- *Reserved.* This 8-bit field is initialized to zero transmission but is ignored on reception.

- *Fragment Offset.* This 13-bit field is the offset location of the data following this header in 8-octet units. The offset is based on the start of the fragmentable part of the original packet.

- *Res.* This 2-bit field is initialized to zero transmission but is ignored on reception.

- *M.* The more fragments flag is set to 1 if more fragments from the original packet are to follow. It is set to 0 if this is the last fragment of the original packet.

- *Identification.* This unique identifier created by the source host identifies that the fragments together represent an original, unfragmented packet.

The original, unfragmented packet comprises two component parts: the unfragmentable and fragmentable parts. The unfragmentable part consists of the IPv6 header and any extension headers that precede the routing header (including the routing header). This is known as the unfragmentable part of the packet because this information is required in every fragment created. The fragmentable part contains the remaining data within the packet.

Each fragment packet includes the unfragmentable part of the original packet, a fragment header, and a portion of the fragmentable data from the original packet (see Figure 21.10).

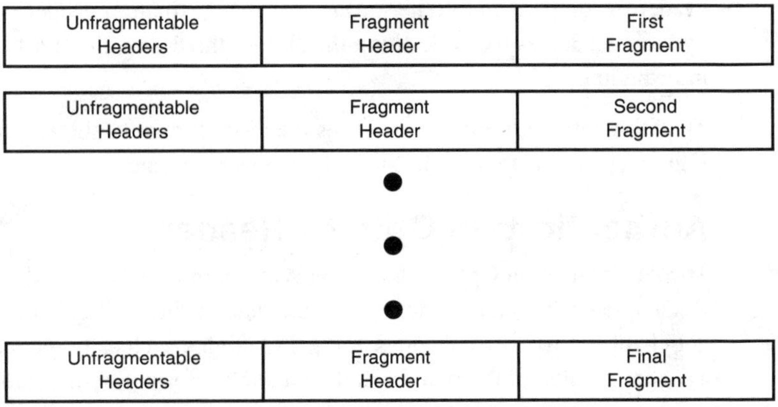

FIGURE 21.10.

Fragmented packet contents.

When the fragment packets are received at the destination host, the reassembly process begins with the identification and offset fields. The payload length of the original fragment is calculated using the following formula:

$$Payload_{original} = Payload_{first} - Frag\ Len_{first} - 8 + (8 * Frag\ Offset_{Last}) + Frag\ Len_{Last}$$

- $Payload_{original}$ is the length of the original packet.

- $Payload_{first}$ is the payload length of the first fragment packet.

- $Frag\ Len_{first}$ is the length of the fragment following the fragment header in the first fragment packet.

21

- Frag Offset$_{Last}$ is the Fragment offset field of the last fragment header. This value is multiplied by 8 to convert the octet value into bytes.
- Frag Len$_{Last}$ is the length of the fragment following the fragment header of the last fragment packet.

This process is similar to the fragmentation process in IPv4. IPv4 uses the Identification field, the More Fragment flag, and the Fragment Offset field to determine how a fragmented packet is reassembled.

In IPv4, the packet is reassembled by collecting all the packets with the same Identification field value. Together, they make up the original packet. They are reassembled based on the offset field values. The offset field indicates the fragment's position in the original packet.

Destination Options Header

The Destination Options header contains information that can be investigated only by the destination host or by intermediate hosts. This depends on the location of the destination header in comparison to other headers. If the destination header is located after a Hop-by-Hop header, every node along the path to the destination host can view this option's information.

The Destination Options header uses the same format as the Hop-by-Hop header (refer to Figure 21.6). It also uses the same TLV option format.

Authentication Options Header

The Authentication Options header provides a mechanism for strong authentication for IP datagrams. This authentication is calculated using all fields in the IP datagram that do not change in transit. This does not include fields such as hop count. These fields are assigned a value of 0 when the authentication information is calculated.

The authentication data is carried in the data of the authentication header so it will work properly without changing the underlying infrastructure of the Internet.

An Authentication header is indicated by a value of 51 in the Next Header field of the preceding extension option. Figure 21.11 shows the format of an Authentication Packet header.

FIGURE 21.11.

Authentication header format.

Next Header	Payload Len	Reserved
Security Parameters Index		
Authentication Data (variable amount of 32-bit words)		

The following is the format of the Authentication header:

- *Next Header.* This 8-bit field identifies the header that follows the Authentication header. This field uses the same values as the IPv4 protocol field.

- *Payload Length.* The length of the Authentication Data field in 32-bit words.

- *Reserved.* This 16-bit field is reserved for future use. It is set to a value of 0 by the source host but is ignored by the destination host.

- *Security Parameters Index.* This 32-bit pseudo-random value identifies the security association for a packet. If the value is set to 0, no security association exists. The security association is unidirectional in nature. The recipient of the packet assigns the SPI value to the security association of that specific sender.

- *Authentication Data.* This variable-length field contains the authentication information for the Security Parameters Index. The destination host uses the destination address and SPI value in the IP authentication header to determine the correct security association for the client. The information in the Authentication Data field and the data packet received are compared to make sure they are consistent.

Encapsulating Security Payload Header

The Encapsulating Security Payload (ESP) header provides integrity and confidentiality to IP datagrams. This is provided by encrypting the data portion of the encapsulating security payload. Depending on the selected level of security, this can include encrypting the entire IP datagram or just the upper-layer data.

The Next Header field of the previous extension option header must point to option 50 for an ESP header. The ESP header is inserted into an IP packet just before a transport-layer protocol header such as TCP or UDP.

ESP can be implemented in two modes. In *tunnel-mode ESP*, the original IP datagram is placed in the encrypted portion of the ESP payload. The entire ESP frame is then placed within an unencrypted IP datagram used to route the datagram from the source host to the destination host. In *transport-mode ESP*, the ESP header is inserted in the IP datagram immediately prior to the transport-layer protocol header. This provides more bandwidth because there are no encrypted headers or options to be decrypted at the destination host.

21

The ESP payload header includes a 32-bit field called the Security Association Identifier (SAI). This field identifies the security association of a datagram. The security association indicates which encryption method should be applied to the data for transport. When the recipient host gets the packet, it strips off the IP header and any optional IP payloads that use clear-text formats. It then uses a combination of the SPI value and the destination address to locate the correct session key for the packet. This key is used to decrypt the ESP payload.

If no key exists at the destination, the encrypted ESP payload must be discarded. This information should be logged to assist in troubleshooting why the packet could not be decrypted.

No Next Header

If the Next Header field in an IPv6 header or extension header contains a value of 59, nothing follows that header. If the Payload field indicates that information exists beyond the end of the header, even though the Next Header value is set to 59, this information is ignored. If the packet is forwarded, the information is passed on unchanged to the next node. It is not truncated.

The Transition from IPv4 to IPv6

 In the next few years, the transition from IPv4 to IPv6 will begin to take place. This section discusses the mechanisms being put in place to make this transition easier.

The Internet will soon enter a transition state, just as it did when ARPAnet switched from NCP to TCP/IP as the standard protocol for transport. The goal of this transition is for IPv6 to be compatible with the large installed based of IPv4. A cold switch is not possible for migration to IPv6.

All mechanisms to help with this transition must be placed in IPv6. This is because the IPv4 packet does not use IPv6 addressing and packet formats.

The following are the proposed mechanisms:

- Installing a dual IP layer that will support both IPv4 and IPv6 for all hosts and routers.
- Including IPv6 over IPv4 tunneling. This method will encapsulate an IPv6 packet within an IPv4 header. This will enable transit over an IPv4 network using IPv4 routing mechanisms.

Using a Dual IP Layer

This is the easier implementation for coexistence of IPv4 and IPv6. Each IPv6 host also would include a complete IPv4 implementation. These nodes would be known as *IPv6/IPv4 nodes*. They would have the capability to send and receive both IPv6 and IPv4 packets. This would enable them to communicate directly with IPv4-only and IPv6-only hosts.

IPv6/IPv4 hosts would require assignment of both IPv4 and IPv6 addresses. These addresses usually would be related to each other, but they also can be totally independent. When IPv4 and IPv6 addresses are related to each other, the IPv6 address would be represented as the IPv4 address prefixed with 96 bits set to 0. The IPv4 address would be the last 32 bits of the IPv6 address (see Figure 21.12).

FIGURE 21.12.

IPv4-compatible address.

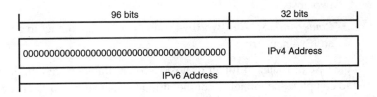

Other issues that must be addressed for IPv6/IPv4 hosts include the following:

- IPv6/IPv4 hosts should be able to acquire their IPv4 addresses from IPv4 configuration methods such as a BOOTP or DHCP server so that these IPv4 configuration methods are leveraged.

- IPv6/IPv4 hosts must treat both the IPv6 address ::1 and the IPv4 compatible address ::127.0.0.1 as loopback addresses. Any packets addressed to either of these addresses should not be put on the network; they should stay local to the node.

- DNS should support A records for IPv4 addresses and AAAA records for IPv6 addresses. IPv6/IPv4 hosts should have DNS resolver libraries that can handle both A and AAAA records.

- If the DNS resolver finds both an A record and an AAAA record for a host, it does not have to return both addresses. It can return the IPv4 address only, the IPv6 address only, or both addresses. The major issue is that the returned address determines whether IPv4 or IPv6 methods are used to communicate with the destination host.

21

IPv6 over IPv4 Tunneling Options

Tunneling IPv6 over IPv4 networks enables IPv6 to be deployed using existing routing infrastructure. The IPv6 packet is encapsulated within IPv4 packets for transmission across the IPv4 network. Tunneling can be implemented in one of the following four configurations:

- *Router-to-router.* IPv6/IPv4 routers connected by an IPv4 infrastructure can create a tunnel that spans the IPv4 network.

- *Host-to-router.* An IPv6/IPv4 host can tunnel IPv6 packets to an intermediary IPv6/IPv4 router that can only be reached over an IPv4 network.

- *Host-to-host.* Two IPv6/IPv4 hosts can create a tunnel that spans an entire IPv4 network between the two hosts. This provides an end-to-end tunnel between the two hosts.

- *Router-to-host.* An IPv6/IPv4 router can form a tunnel to an IPv6/IPv4 host over an IPv4 network.

In the case of router-to-router or host-to-router implementation, the router being connected to complete the tunnel is not the ultimate destination host. This creates a need for *configured tunneling*. The IPv6 packet being transmitted does not have the tunnel endpoint's IPv4 address in its destination address. Based on the ultimate destination address, the source host must have a preconfigured tunnel endpoint to which it sends the encapsulated data. This usually is determined from the source host's routing table.

Another possibility is to configure all tunnels to connect to a common router on an IPv6 backbone. This backbone could include several IPv6/IPv4 routers that have been assigned an IPv4-compatible anycast address (see Figure 21.13).

In this figure, the three border routers all have been assigned the anycast address of ::172.16.2.1. When the IPv6/IPv4 host at ::172.16.4.5 sends an encapsulated IPv6 packet to the anycast address, it is delivered to the nearest border router with the anycast address based on routing distance. Setting the default tunnel to an anycast address provides a high degree of fault tolerance because traffic automatically switches to one of the other border routers if one fails.

In the case of host-to-host or router-to-host tunneling, the ultimate destination host is the endpoint of the tunnel. The IPv4 address of the host can be determined from the IPv4-compatible address in the IPv6 Destination Host field. This requires that an IPv4-compatible address be used. If it is not used, a configured tunneling solution needs to be implemented.

FIGURE 21.13.

Default configured tunnel using an anycast address.

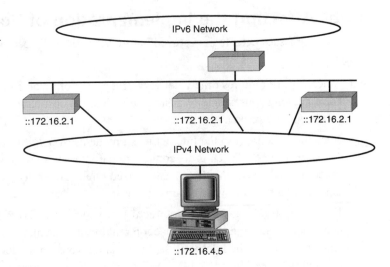

Voice over IP

More and more people are discussing the concept of using the Internet as a backbone for voice conversations—*Voice over IP*. This technology uses the Internet, a packet-switched network, to transport digitized voice data to a destination host. This technology is being researched because of the cost savings for the participants. Instead of having to use long distance phone exchanges, the Internet can be accessed using local phone calls.

The Conversion of the Voice Input

The actual voice input is transported as digitized data. The digitization of voice data falls into one of two categories: voice coders or waveform coders.

Voice coders use speech input to create a signal that resembles the original voice input. The voice coder is configured to use a specific speech model. The created signal is analyzed against the speech model, and a set of parameters is generated. It is this set of parameters that is transmitted to the destination station. The destination station uses these parameters to reconstruct the speech input.

Waveform coders directly encode the waveform generated by analog speech. It does so by sampling the voice input and converting the amplitude of each sample to the nearest value from a finite set of discrete values. An example of this technology is Pulse Code Modulation (PCM).

21

Issues Affecting the Implementation of Voice over IP

The following issues need to be resolved before Voice over IP becomes a day-to-day reality:

- Voice over IP requires timely delivery. If a packet of a voice message is delayed, there are long pauses in the transmission while the destination hosts await delivery of the missing packet.

- Many users connect to the Internet using modems over *Public Switched Telephone Networks (PSTN)*. When users connect to the Internet, they generally are assigned random IP addresses. Without a centralized directory service, it is difficult to ascertain the IP address of your destination host.

- Until recently, Voice over IP required the two connecting hosts to have similar equipment. Each end of the connection requires a modem, the same Voice over IP software (such as the Internet Telephone), and a voice input device such as a microphone (see Figure 21.14).

FIGURE 21.14.

Performing Voice over IP with modems and microphones.

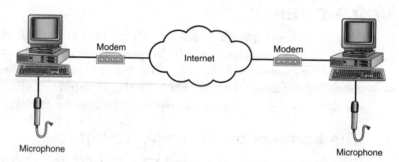

- Voice over IP requires a large amount of bandwidth for timely transport of digitized voice data. The *Resource Reservation Protocol (RSVP)* is being touted as a potential solution to this problem. Routers can request a specific size of bandwidth pipe through the network using the RSVP protocol. This protocol can be used by Voice over IP software to set minimum performance requirements that must be met for transmission to be attempted.

OTHER ISSUES WITH VOICE OVER IP

Lack of bandwidth can be solved in one of two ways. First, you can utilize compression to use less bandwidth. Although less bandwidth is used, this can cause latency problems because of the compression/decompression process. Second, you can add more bandwidth to your network pipes.

The Future of Direction of Voice over IP

The next generation of Voice over IP will enable users to connect to remote users utilizing a regular phone. This functionality is facilitated by the use of phone gateways (see Figure 21.15).

FIGURE 21.15.

Voice over IP utilizing phone gateways.

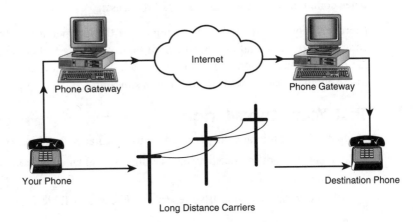

By using phone gateways, this methodology will hide the fact that participants are using the packet-switched technology of the Internet rather than the circuit-switched technology of the PSTN. To users, the phone call will appear to be taking place over the normal long distance carriers.

The Voice over IP (VoIP) forum has been operating as a group in the International Multimedia Teleconferencing Consortium to further the progress of Voice over IP. The following are the main tasks of the VoIP forum:

- Defining and establishing a set of open, consistent guidelines for the implementation of devices that perform voice communications over IP protocol data networks
- Ensuring seamless product interoperability and high quality of service
- Developing a standard for addressing so routers will know how to locate and address remote users

21

Applying What You Have Learned

The IP protocol continues to evolve to meet our ever-changing needs. The migration to IPv6 will lead to an addressing scheme that should provide sufficient address space into the next century. It also will provide more efficient use of the network because it eliminates communication methods such as broadcasts.

More and more applications are starting to use the Internet as a backbone for communication. Today's material discussed one of these emerging technologies, Voice over IP. In the final implementation, the end user probably will be unaware that the Internet is used as the communication network for the transmission.

Test Your Knowledge

1. What fault tolerance is provided by using an anycast address?

2. What is the difference between sending data to an anycast address and sending data to a multicast address?

3. Identify the following IPv6 reserved addresses in Table 21.3:

TABLE 21.3. IDENTIFY THE IPv6 ADDRESS TYPE.

Address	Address Type
0:0:0:0:0:0:0:1	
0:0:0:0:0:FFFF:AC10:0210	
0:0:0:0:0:0:0:0	
0:0:0:0:0:0:C0A8:0344	
FF0E:2322::AD56:0230	

4. How is fragmentation handled differently in IPv6 than it was in IPv4?

5. How is security increased in IPv6?

6. What methods have been proposed to help the conversion of networks from IPv4 to IPv6?

7. What two methods convert voice input into a digital format for transport over the Internet?

8. What issues need to be resolved before Voice over IP is widely implemented?

APPENDIX A

RFC Reference

The following tables of RFCs are based on the maturity level of each RFC. The following levels are included in this Appendix:

- Standard protocols
- Network-specific standard protocols
- Draft standard protocols
- Proposed standard protocols
- Experimental protocols
- Informational protocols
- Historic protocols

Standard Protocols

The Internet Engineering Steering Group (IESG) has established the protocols in Table A.1 as official standard protocols for the Internet. These standard protocols each have been assigned a standard number, and they apply to the entire Internet. Table A.1 shows the current listing of standard protocols.

TABLE A.1. STANDARD PROTOCOL RFCs.

Protocol	Name	Status	RFC	STD *
	Internet Official Protocol Standards	Required	2200	1
	Assigned Numbers	Required	1700	2
	Host Requirements— Communications	Required	1122	3
	Host Requirements— Applications	Required	1123	3
IP	Internet Protocol	Required	791	5
IP	IP Subnet Extension	Required	950	5
IP	IP Broadcast Datagrams	Required	919	5
IP	IP Broadcast Datagrams with Subnets	Required	922	5
ICMP	Internet Control Message Protocol	Required	792	5
IGMP	Internet Group Multicast Protocol	Recommended	1112	5
UDP	User Datagram Protocol	Recommended	768	6
TCP	Transmission Control Protocol	Recommended	793	7
TELNET	Telnet Protocol	Recommended	854,855	8
FTP	File Transfer Protocol	Recommended	959	9
SMTP	Simple Mail Transfer Protocol	Recommended	821	10
SMTP-SIZE	SMTP Service Extensions for Message Size	Recommended	1870	10
SMTP-EXT	SMTP Service Extensions	Recommended	1869	10
MAIL	Format of Electronic Mail Messages	Recommended	822	11
CONTENT	Content Type Header Field	Recommended	1049	11
NTPV2	Network Time Protocol (Version 2)	Recommended	1119	12
DOMAIN	Domain Name System	Recommended	1034,1035	13
DNS-MX	Mail Routing and the Domain System	Recommended	974	14

Protocol	Name	Status	RFC	STD *
SNMP	Simple Network Management Protocol	Recommended	1157	15
SMI	Structure of Management Information	Recommended	1155	16
Concise-MIB	Concise MIB Definitions	Recommended	1212	16
MIB-II	Management Information Base-II	Recommended	1213	17
NETBIOS	NetBIOS Service Protocols	Elective	1001,1002	19
ECHO	Echo Protocol	Recommended	862	20
DISCARD	Discard Protocol	Elective	863	21
CHARGEN	Character Generator Protocol	Elective	864	22
QUOTE	Quote of the Day Protocol	Elective	865	23
USERS	Active Users Protocol	Elective	866	24
DAYTIME	Daytime Protocol	Elective	867	25
TIME	Time Server Protocol	Elective	868	26
TFTP	Trivial File Transfer Protocol	Elective	1350	33
TP-TCP	ISO Transport Service on top of the TCP	Elective	1006	35
ETHER-MIB	Ethernet MIB	Elective	1643	50
PPP	Point-to-Point Protocol (PPP)	Elective	1661	51
PPP-HDLC	PPP in HDLC Framing	Elective	1662	51
IP-SMDS	IP Datagrams over the SMDS Service	Elective	1209	52
POP3	Post Office Protocol, Version 3	Elective	1939	53

Network-Specific Standard Protocols

The Internet Engineering Steering Group (IESG) has established the protocols in Table A.2 as official standard protocols for the Internet. Some network-specific standard protocols have been assigned a standard number but are implemented only on a network-specific basis. Not every TCP/IP installation must implement these protocols. Table A.2 shows the current network-specific standard protocols.

TABLE A.2. NETWORK-SPECIFIC STANDARD PROTOCOL RFCs.

Protocol	Name	Status	RFC	STD
IP-ATM	Classical IP and ARP over ATM	Elective	1577	
IP-FR	Multiprotocol over Frame Relay	Elective	1490	
ATM-ENCAP	Multiprotocol Encapsulation over ATM	Elective	1483	
IP-TR-MC	IP Multicast over Token-Ring LANs	Elective	1469	
IP-FDDI	Transmission of IP and ARP over FDDI Net	Elective	1390	36
IP-X.25	X.25 and ISDN in the Packet Mode	Elective	1356	
ARP	Address Resolution Protocol	Elective	826	37
RARP	Reverse Address Resolution Protocol	Elective	903	38
IP-ARPA	Internet Protocol on ARPANET	Elective	1822	39
IP-WB	Internet Protocol on Wideband Network	Elective	907	40
IP-E	Internet Protocol on Ethernet Networks	Elective	894	41
IP-EE	Internet Protocol on Exp. Ethernet Nets	Elective	895	42
IP-IEEE	Internet Protocol on IEEE 802	Elective	1042	43
IP-DC	Internet Protocol on DC Networks	Elective	891	44
IP-HC	Internet Protocol on Hyperchannel	Elective	1044	45
IP-ARC	Transmitting IP Traffic over ARCNET Nets	Elective	1201	46
IP-SLIP	Transmission of IP over Serial Lines	Elective	1055	47
IP-NETBIOS	Transmission of IP over NETBIOS	Elective	1088	48
IP-IPX	Transmission of 802.2 over IPX Networks	Elective	1132	49
IP-HIPPI	IP over HIPPI	Elective	2067	

Draft Standard Protocols

Draft standard protocols are being considered by the IESG to become standard protocols. Widespread testing is performed on draft standard protocols. Table A.3 shows the current draft standard protocols.

TABLE A.3. DRAFT STANDARD PROTOCOL RFCs.

Protocol	Name	Status	RFC
BOOTP	DHCP Options and BOOTP Extensions	Recommended	2132
DHCP	Dynamic Host Configuration Protocol	Elective	2131
BOOTP	Clarifications and Extensions BOOTP	Elective	1542
DHCP-BOOTP	Interoperation Between DHCP and BOOTP	Elective	1534
MIME-CONF	MIME Conformance Criteria	Elective	2049
MIME-MSG	MIME Msg Header Ext for Non-ASCII	Elective	2047
MIME-MEDIA	MIME Media Types	Elective	2046
MIME	Multipurpose Internet Mail Extensions	Elective	2045
PPP-CHAP	PPP Challenge Handshake Authentication	Elective	1994
PPP-MP	PPP Multilink Protocol	Elective	1990
PPP-LINK	PPP Link Quality Monitoring	Elective	1989
COEX-MIB	Coexistence between SNMPV1 and SNMPV2	Elective	1908
SNMPv2-MIB	MIB for SNMPv2	Elective	1907
TRANS-MIB	Transport Mappings for SNMPv2	Elective	1906
OPS-MIB	Protocol Operations for SNMPv2	Elective	1905
CONF-MIB	Conformance Statements for SNMPv2	Elective	1904
CONV-MIB	Textual Conventions for SNMPv2	Elective	1903
SMIV2	SMI for SNMPv2	Elective	1902
CON-MD5	Content-MD5 Header Field	Elective	1864
OSPF-MIB	OSPF Version 2 MIB	Elective	1850

continues

A

TABLE A.3. CONTINUED

Protocol	Name	Status	RFC
STR-REP	String Representation ...	Elective	1779
X.500syn	X.500 String Representation ...	Elective	1778
X.500lite	X.500 Lightweight ...	Elective	1777
BGP-4-APP	Application of BGP-4	Elective	1772
BGP-4	Border Gateway Protocol 4	Elective	1771
PPP-DNCP	PPP DECnet Phase IV Control Protocol	Elective	1762
RMON-MIB	Remote Network Monitoring MIB	Elective	1757
802.5-MIB	IEEE 802.5 Token Ring MIB	Elective	1748
BGP-4-MIB	BGP-4 MIB	Elective	1657
RIP2-MIB	RIP Version 2 MIB Extension	Elective	1724
RIP2	RIP Version 2-Carrying Additional Info.	Elective	1723
RIP2-APP	RIP Version 2 Protocol App. Statement	Elective	1722
SIP-MIB	SIP Interface Type MIB	Elective	1694
	Def Man Objs Parallel-printer-like	Elective	1660
	Def Man Objs RS-232-like	Elective	1659
	Def Man Objs Character Stream	Elective	1658
SMTP-8BIT	SMTP Service Ext or 8bit-MIME transport	Elective	1652
OSI-NSAP	Guidelines for OSI NSAP Allocation	Elective	1629
OSPF2	Open Shortest Path First Routing V2	Elective	1583
ISO-TS-ECHO	Echo for ISO-8473	Elective	1575
DECNET-MIB	DECNET-MIB	Elective	1559
BRIDGE-MIB	BRIDGE-MIB	Elective	1493
NTPV3	Network Time Protocol (Version 3)	Elective	1305
IP-MTU	Path MTU Discovery	Elective	1191
FINGER	Finger Protocol	Elective	1288
NICNAME	WhoIs Protocol	Elective	954

Proposed Standard Protocols

Proposed standard protocols are in the first stages of consideration to become standard protocols. Several groups are involved with the implementation and testing of these protocols. Table A.4 shows the current proposed standard protocols.

TABLE A.4. PROPOSED STANDARD PROTOCOL RFCs.

Protocol	Name	Status	RFC
IPv6-Jumbo	TCP and UDP over IPv6 Jumbograms	Elective	2147
MAIL-SERV	Mailbox Names for Common Services	Elective	2142
URN-SYNTAX	URN Syntax	Elective	2141
RADIUS	Remote Authentication Dial In Service	Elective	2138
SDNSDU	Secure Domain Name System Dynamic Update	Elective	2137
DNS-UPDATE	Dynamic Updates in the DNS	Elective	2136
DC-MIB	Dial Control MIB using SMIv2	Elective	2128
ISDN-MIB	ISDN MIB using SMIv2	Elective	2127
ITOT	ISO Transport Service on top of TCP	Elective	2126
BAP-BACP	PPP-BAP, PPP-BACP	Elective	2125
VEMMI-URL	VEMMI URL Specification	Elective	2122
ROUT-ALERT	IP Router Alert Option	Elective	2113
MIME-RELAT	MIME Multipart/Related Content-type	Elective	2112
CIDMID-URL	Content-ID and Message-ID URLs	Elective	2111
MHTML	MIME Email Encapsulation	Elective	2110
HTTP-STATE	HTTP State Management Mechanism	Elective	2109
802.3-MIB	802.3 Repeater MIB using SMIv2	Elective	2108
PPP-NBFCP	PPP NetBIOS Frames Control Protocol	Elective	2097
TABLE-MIB	IP Forwarding Table MIB	Elective	2096
IMAPPOPAU	IMAP/POP AUTHorize Extension	Elective	2095

continues

A

TABLE A.4. CONTINUED

Protocol	Name	Status	RFC
RIP-TRIG	Trigger RIP	Elective	2091
IMAP4-LIT	IMAP4 non-synchronizing literals	Elective	2088
IMAP4-QUO	IMAP4 QUOTA Extension	Elective	2087
IMAP4-ACL	IMAP4 ACL Extension	Elective	2086
HMAC-MD5	HMAC-MD5 IP Auth. with Replay Prevention	Elective	2085
RIP2-MD5	RIP-2 MD5 Authentication	Elective	2082
RIPNG-IPV6	RIPng for IPv6	Elective	2080
URI-ATT	URI Attribute Type and Object Class	Elective	2079
GSSAP	Generic Security Service Application	Elective	2078
MIME-MODEL	Model Primary MIME Types	Elective	2077
RMON-MIB	Remote Network Monitoring MIB	Elective	2074
IPV6-UNI	IPv6 Provider-Based Unicast Address	Elective	2073
HTML-INT	HTML Internationalization	Elective	2070
DAA	Digest Access Authentication	Elective	2069
HTTP-1.1	Hypertext Transfer Protocol— HTTP/1.1	Elective	2068
DNS-SEC	Domain Name System Security Extensions	Elective	2065
IMAPV4	Internet Message Access Protocol v4rev1	Elective	2060
URLZ39.50	Uniform Resource Locators for Z39.50	Elective	2056
SNANAU-APP	SNANAU APPC MIB using SMIv2	Elective	2051
PPP-SNACP	PPP SNA Control Protocol	Elective	2043
RTP-MPEG	RTP Payload Format for MPEG1/MPEG2	Elective	2038
ENTITY-MIB	Entity MIB using SMIv2	Elective	2037
RTP-JPEG	RTP Payload Format for JPEG-compressed	Elective	2035

Protocol	Name	Status	RFC
SMTP-ENH	SMTP Enhanced Error Codes	Elective	2034
RTP-H.261	RTP Payload Format for H.261	Elective	2032
RTP-CELLB	RTP Payload Format of Sun's CellB	Elective	2029
SPKM	Simple Public-Key GSS-API Mechanism	Elective	2025
DLSW-MIB	DLSw MIB using SMIv2	Elective	2024
IPV6-PPP	IP Version 6 over PPP	Elective	2023
MULTI-UNI	Multicast over UNI 3.0/3.1 based ATM	Elective	2022
RMON-MIB	RMON MIB using SMIv2	Elective	2021
802.12-MIB	IEEE 802.12 Interface MIB	Elective	2020
IPV6-FDDI	Transmission of IPv6 Packets over FDDI	Elective	2019
TCP-ACK	TCP Selective Acknowledgment Options	Elective	2018
URL-ACC	URL Access-Type	Elective	2017
MIME-PGP	MIME Security with PGP	Elective	2015
MIB-UDP	SNMPv2 MIB for UDP	Elective	2013
MIB-TCP	SNMPv2 MIB for TCP	Elective	2012
MIB-IP	SNMPv2 MIB for IP	Elective	2011
MOBILEIPMIB	Mobile IP MIB Definition using SMIv2	Elective	2006
MOBILEIPAPP	Applicability Statement for IP Mobility	Elective	2005
MINI-IP	Minimal Encapsulation within IP	Elective	2004
IPENCAPIP	IP Encapsulation within IP	Elective	2003
MOBILEIPSUP	IP Mobility Support	Elective	2002
TCPSLOWSRT	TCP Slow Start, Congestion Avoidance...	Elective	2001
BGP-COMM	BGP Communities Attribute	Elective	1997
DNS-NOTIFY	Mech. for Notification of Zone Changes	Elective	1996

continues

TABLE A.4. CONTINUED

Protocol	Name	Status	RFC
DNS-IZT	Incremental Zone Transfer in DNS	Elective	1995
SMTP-ETRN	SMTP Service Extension ETRN	Elective	1985
SNA	Serial Number Arithmetic	Elective	1982
MTU-IPV6	Path MTU Discovery for IP version 6	Elective	1981
PPP-FRAME	PPP in Frame Relay	Elective	1973
IPV6-ETHER	Transmission IPv6 Packets over Ethernet	Elective	1972
IPV6-AUTO	IPv6 Stateless Address Autoconfiguation	Elective	1971
IPV6-ND	Neighbor Discovery for IP Version 6	Elective	1970
PPP-ECP	PPP Encryption Control Protocol	Elective	1968
GSSAPI-KER	Kerberos Version 5 GSS-API Mechanism	Elective	1964
PPP-CCP	PPP Compression Control Protocol	Elective	1962
GSSAPI-SOC	GSS-API Auth for SOCKS Version 5	Elective	1961
LDAP-STR	String Rep. of LDAP Search Filters	Elective	1960
LDAP-URL	LDAP URL Format	Elective	1959
ONE-PASS	One-Time Password System	Elective	1938
TRANS-IPV6	Transition Mechanisms IPv6 Hosts/Routers	Elective	1933
AUTH-SOCKS	Username Authentication for SOCKS V5	Elective	1929
SOCKSV5	SOCKS Protocol Version 5	Elective	1928
WHOIS++M	How to Interact with a Whois++ Mesh	Elective	1914
WHOIS++A	Architecture of Whois++ Index Service	Elective	1913
DSN	Delivery Status Notifications	Elective	1894
EMS-CODE	Enhanced Mail System Status Codes	Elective	1893
MIME-RPT	Multipart/Report	Elective	1892

A

Protocol	Name	Status	RFC
SMTP-DSN	SMTP Delivery Status Notifications	Elective	1891
RTP-AV	RTP Audio/Video Profile	Elective	1890
RTP	Transport Protocol for Real-Time Apps	Elective	1889
DNS-IPV6	DNS Extensions to support IPv6	Elective	1886
ICMPv6	ICMPv6 for IPv6	Elective	1885
IPV6-Addr	IPv6 Addressing Architecture	Elective	1884
IPV6	IPv6 Specification	Elective	1883
HTML	Hypertext Markup Language—2.0	Elective	1866
SMTP-Pipe	SMTP Serv. Ext. for Command Pipelining	Elective	1854
MIME-Sec	MIME Object Security Services	Elective	1848
MIME-Encyp	MIME: Signed and Encrypted	Elective	1847
WHOIS++	Architecture of the WHOIS++ service	Elective	1835
	Binding Protocols for ONC RPC Version 2	Elective	1833
XDR	External Data Representation Standard	Elective	1832
RPC	Remote Procedure Call Protocol V. 2	Elective	1831
	ESP DES-CBC Transform	Ele/Req	1829
	IP Authentication using Keyed MD5	Ele/Req	1828
ESP	IP Encapsulating Security Payload	Ele/Req	1827
IPV6-AH	IP Authentication Header	Ele/Req	1826
	Security Architecture for IP	Ele/Req	1825
RREQ	Requirements for IP Version 4 Routers	Elective	1812
URL	Relative Uniform Resource Locators	Elective	1808
CLDAP	Connectionless LDAP	Elective	1798

continues

TABLE A.4. CONTINUED

Protocol	Name	Status	RFC
OSPF-DC	Ext. OSPF to Support Demand Circuits	Elective	1793
TMUX	Transport Multiplexing Protocol	Elective	1692
TFTP-Opt	TFTP Options	Elective	1784
TFTP-Blk	TFTP Blocksize Option	Elective	1783
TFTP-Ext	TFTP Option Extension	Elective	1782
OSI-Dir	OSI User Friendly Naming ...	Elective	1781
MIME-EDI	MIME Encapsulation of EDI Objects	Elective	1767
Lang-Tag	Tags for Identification of Languages	Elective	1766
XNSCP	PPP XNS IDP Control Protocol	Elective	1764
BVCP	PPP Banyan Vines Control Protocol	Elective	1763
Print-MIB	Printer MIB	Elective	1759
ATM-SIG	ATM Signaling Support for IP over ATM	Elective	1755
IPNG	Recommendation for IP Next Generation	Elective	1752
802.5-SSR	802.5 SSR MIB using SMIv2	Elective	1749
SDLCSMIv2	SNADLC SDLC MIB using SMIv2	Elective	1747
BGP4/IDRP	BGP4/IDRP for IP/OSPF Interaction	Elective	1745
AT-MIB	Appletalk MIB	Elective	1742
MacMIME	MIME Encapsulation of Macintosh files	Elective	1740
URL	Uniform Resource Locators	Elective	1738
POP3-AUTH	POP3 AUTHentication command	Elective	1734
IMAP4-AUTH	IMAP4 Authentication Mechanisms	Elective	1731
RDBMS-MIB	RDMS MIB—using SMIv2	Elective	1697
MODEM-MIB	Modem MIB—using SMIv2	Elective	1696
ATM-MIB	ATM Management Version 8.0 using SMIv2	Elective	1695

A

Protocol	Name	Status	RFC
SNANAU-MIB	SNA NAUs MIB using SMIv2	Elective	1666
PPP-TRANS	PPP Reliable Transmission	Elective	1663
	Postmaster Convention X.400 Operations	Elective	1648
TN3270-En	TN3270 Enhancements	Elective	1647
PPP-BCP	PPP Bridging Control Protocol	Elective	1638
UPS-MIB	UPS Management Information Base	Elective	1628
AAL5-MTU	Default IP MTU for use over ATM AAL5	Elective	1626
PPP-SONET	PPP over SONET/SDH	Elective	1619
PPP-ISDN	PPP over ISDN	Elective	1618
DNS-R-MIB	DNS Resolver MIB Extensions	Elective	1612
DNS-S-MIB	DNS Server MIB Extensions	Elective	1611
FR-MIB	Frame Relay Service MIB	Elective	1604
PPP-X25	PPP in X.25	Elective	1598
OSPF-NSSA	The OSPF NSSA Option	Elective	1587
OSPF-Multi	Multicast Extensions to OSPF	Elective	1584
SONET-MIB	MIB SONET/SDH Interface Type	Elective	1595
RIP-DC	Extensions to RIP to Support Demand Cir.	Elective	1582
	Evolution of the Interfaces Group of MIB-II	Elective	1573
PPP-LCP	PPP LCP Extensions	Elective	1570
X500-MIB	X.500 Directory Monitoring MIB	Elective	1567
MAIL-MIB	Mail Monitoring MIB	Elective	1566
NSM-MIB	Network Services Monitoring MIB	Elective	1565
CIPX	Compressing IPX Headers Over WAM Media	Elective	1553
IPXCP	PPP Internetworking Packet Exchange Control	Elective	1552
SRB-MIB	Source Routing Bridge MIB	Elective	1525
CIDR-STRA	CIDR Address Assignment...	Elective	1519
CIDR-ARCH	CIDR Architecture...	Elective	1518

continues

TABLE A.4. CONTINUED

Protocol	Name	Status	RFC
CIDR-APP	CIDR Applicability Statement	Elective	1517
	802.3 MAU MIB	Elective	1515
HOST-MIB	Host Resources MIB	Elective	1514
	Token Ring Extensions to RMON MIB	Elective	1513
FDDI-MIB	FDDI Management Information Base	Elective	1512
KERBEROS	Kerberos Network Authentication Ser (V5)	Elective	1510
GSSAPI	Generic Security Service API: C-bindings	Elective	1509
DASS	Distributed Authentication Security...	Elective	1507
	X.400 Use of Extended Character Sets	Elective	1502
HARPOON	Rules for Downgrading Messages...	Elective	1496
Mapping	MHS/RFC-822 Message Body Mapping	Elective	1495
Equiv	X.400/MIME Body Equivalences	Elective	1494
IDPR	Inter-Domain Policy Routing Protocol	Elective	1479
IDPR-ARCH	Architecture for IDPR	Elective	1478
PPP/Bridge	MIB Bridge PPP MIB	Elective	1474
PPP/IP MIB	IP Network Control Protocol of PPP MIB	Elective	1473
PPP/SEC MIB	Security Protocols of PPP MIB	Elective	1472
PPP/LCP MIB	Link Control Protocol of PPP MIB	Elective	1471
X25-MIB	Multiprotocol Interconnect on X.25 MIB	Elective	1461
SNMPv2	Introduction to SNMPv2	Elective	1441
PEM-KEY	PEM—Key Certification	Elective	1424
PEM-ALG	PEM—Algorithms, Modes, and Identifiers	Elective	1423
PEM-CKM	PEM—Certificate-Based Key Management	Elective	1422

Protocol	Name	Status	RFC
PEM-ENC	PEM—Message Encryption and Auth	Elective	1421
SNMP-IPX	SNMP over IPX	Elective	1420
SNMP-AT	SNMP over AppleTalk	Elective	1419
SNMP-OSI	SNMP over OSI	Elective	1418
FTP-FTAM	FTP-FTAM Gateway Specification	Elective	1415
IDENT-MIB	Identification MIB	Elective	1414
IDENT	Identification Protocol	Elective	1413
DS3/E3-MIB	DS3/E3 Interface Type	Elective	1407
DS1/E1-MIB	DS1/E1 Interface Type	Elective	1406
BGP-OSPF	BGP OSPF Interaction	Elective	1403
	Route Advertisement In BGP2 And BGP3	Elective	1397
SNMP-X.25	SNMP MIB Extension for X.25 Packet Layer	Elective	1382
SNMP-LAPB	SNMP MIB Extension for X.25 LAPB	Elective	1381
PPP-ATCP	PPP AppleTalk Control Protocol	Elective	1378
PPP-OSINLCP	PPP OSI Network Layer Control Protocol	Elective	1377
SNMP-PARTY	MIB Administration of SNMP	Elective	1353
SNMP-SEC	SNMP Security Protocols	Elective	1352
SNMP-ADMIN	SNMP Administrative Model	Elective	1351
TOS	Type of Service in the Internet	Elective	1349
PPP-IPCP	PPP Control Protocol	Elective	1332
	X.400 1988 to 1984 downgrading	Elective	1328
	Mapping between X.400(1988)	Elective	1327
TCP-EXT	TCP Extensions for High Performance	Elective	1323
FRAME-MIB	Management Information Base for Frame	Elective	1315
NETFAX	File Format for the Exchange of Images	Elective	1314
IARP	Inverse Address Resolution Protocol	Elective	1293

A

continues

TABLE A.4. CONTINUED

Protocol	Name	Status	RFC
FDDI-MIB	FDDI-MIB	Elective	1285
	Encoding Network Addresses	Elective	1277
	Replication and Distributed Operations	Elective	1276
	COSINE and Internet X.500 Schema	Elective	1274
BGP-MIB	Border Gateway Protocol MIB (Version 3)	Elective	1269
ICMP-ROUT	ICMP Router Discovery Messages	Elective	1256
OSI-UDP	OSI TS on UDP	Elective	1240
STD-MIBs	Reassignment of Exp MIBs to Std MIBs	Elective	1239
IPX-IP	Tunneling IPX Traffic through IP Nets	Elective	1234
IS-IS	OSI IS-IS for TCP/IP Dual Environments	Elective	1195
IP-CMPRS	Compressing TCP/IP Headers	Elective	1144
NNTP	Network News Transfer Protocol	Elective	977

The Ele/Req status indicates that the protocol is elective for use with IPv4 but is required for use with IPv6.

Experimental Protocols

Experimental protocols are in the earliest stage of development and are not intended for general use yet. Although they might enter the standards track later, they currently are not intended for operational use unless you are participating in the experiment. Table A.5 lists the current experimental protocols.

TABLE A.5. EXPERIMENTAL PROTOCOL RFCs.

Protocol	Name	Status	RFC
IP-SCSI	Encapsulating IP with the SCSI	Limited Use	2143
X.500-NAME	Managing the X.500 Root Naming Context	Limited Use	2120
TFTP-MULTI	TFTP Multicast Option	Limited Use	2090
IP-Echo	IP Echo Host Service	Limited Use	2075

A

Protocol	Name	Status	RFC
METER-MIB	Traffic Flow Measurement Meter MIB	Limited Use	2064
TFM-ARCH	Traffic Flow Measurement Architecture	Limited Use	2063
DNS-SRV	Location of Services in the DNS	Limited Use	2052
URAS	Uniform Resource Agents	Limited Use	2016
GPS-AR	GPS-based Addressing and Routing	Limited Use	2009
ETFTP	Enhanced Trivial File Transfer Protocol	Limited Use	1986
BGP-RR	BGP Route Reflection	Limited Use	1966
BGP-ASC	Autonomous System Confederations for BGP	Limited Use	1965
SMKD	Scalable Multicast Key Distribution	Limited Use	1949
HTML-TBL	HTML Tables	Limited Use	1942
MIME-VP	Voice Profile for Internet Mail	Limited Use	1911
SNMPV2SM	User-based Security Model for SNMPv2	Limited Use	1910
SNMPV2AI	SNMPv2 Administrative Infrastructure	Limited Use	1909
SNMPV2CB	Introduction to Community-based SNMPv2	Limited Use	1901
	IPv6 Testing Address Allocation	Limited Use	1897
DNS-LOC	Location Information in the DNS	Limited Use	1876
SGML-MT	SGML Media Types	Limited Use	1874
CONT-MT	Access Type Content-ID	Limited Use	1873
UNARP	ARP Extension—UNARP	Limited Use	1868
	Form-based File Upload in HTML	Limited Use	1867
	BGP/IDRP Route Server Alternative	Limited Use	1863
	IP Authentication using Keyed SHA	Limited Use	1852
ESP3DES	ESP Triple DES Transform	Limited Use	1851
	SMTP 521 Reply Code	Limited Use	1846
	SMTP Serv. Ext. for Checkpoint/Restart	Limited Use	1845
	X.500 Mapping X.400 and RFC 822 Addresses	Limited Use	1838
	Tables and Subtrees in the X.500 Directory	Limited Use	1837
	O/R Address hierarchy in X.500	Limited Use	1836
	SMTP Serv. Ext. Large and Binary	Limited Use	1830

continues

TABLE A.5. CONTINUED

Protocol	Name	Status	RFC
ST2	Stream Protocol Version 2 MIME Msgs.	Limited Use	1819
	Content-Disposition Header	Limited Use	1806
	Schema Publishing in X.500 Directory	Limited Use	1804
	X.400-MHS use X.500 to support X.400-MHS Routing	Limited Use	1801
	Class A Subnet Experiment	Limited Use	1797
TCP/IPXMIB	TCP/IPX Connection Mib Specification	Limited Use	1792
	TCP And UDP Over IPX Networks With Fixed Path MTU	Limited Use	1791
ICMP-DM	ICMP Domain Name Messages	Limited Use	1788
CLNP-MULT	Host Group Extensions for CLNP Multicasting	Limited Use	1768
OSPF-OVFL	OSPF Database Overflow	Limited Use	1765
RWP	Remote Write Protocol— Version 1.0	Limited Use	1756
NARP	NBMA Address Resolution Protocol	Limited Use	1735
DNS-DEBUG	Tools for DNS Debugging	Limited Use	1713
DNS-ENCODE	DNS Encoding of Geographical Location	Limited Use	1712
TCP-POS	An Extension to TCP: Partial Order Service	Limited Use	1693
	DNS to Distribute RFC1327 Mail Address Mapping Tables	Limited Use	1664
T/TCP	TCP Extensions for Transactions	Limited Use	1644
MIME-UNI	Using Unicode with MIME	Limited Use	1641
FOOBAR	FTP Operation Over Big Address Records	Limited Use	1639
X500-CHART	Charting Networks in the X.500 Directory	Limited Use	1609
X500-DIR	Representing IP Information in the X.500 Directory	Limited Use	1608
SNMP-DPI	SNMP Distributed Protocol Interface	Limited Use	1592
CLNP-TUBA	Use of ISO CLNP in TUBA Environments	Limited Use	1561

A

Protocol	Name	Status	RFC
REM-PRINT	TPC.INT Subdomain Remote Printing—Technical	Limited Use	1528
EHF-MAIL	Encoding Header Field for Internet Messages	Limited Use	1505
RAP	Internet Route Access Protocol	Limited Use	1476
TP/IX	TP/IX: The Next Internet	Limited Use	1475
X400	Routing Coordination for X.400 Services	Limited Use	1465
DNS	Storing Arbitrary Attributes in DNS	Limited Use	1464
IRCP	Internet Relay Chat Protocol	Limited Use	1459
TOS-LS	Link Security TOS	Limited Use	1455
SIFT/UFT	Sender-Initiated/Unsolicited File Transfer	Limited Use	1440
DIR-ARP	Directed ARP	Limited Use	1433
TEL-SPX	Telnet Authentication: SPX	Limited Use	1412
TEL-KER	Telnet Authentication: Kerberos V4	Limited Use	1411
MAP-MAIL	X.400 Mapping and Mail-11	Limited Use	1405
TRACE-IP	Trace Route Using an IP Option	Limited Use	1393
DNS-IP	Experiment in DNS-Based IP Routing	Limited Use	1383
RMCP	Remote Mail Checking Protocol	Limited Use	1339
TCP-HIPER	TCP Extensions for High Performance	Limited Use	1323
MSP2	Message Send Protocol 2	Limited Use	1312
DSLCP	Dynamically Switched Link Control	Limited Use	1307
	X.500 and Domains	Limited Use	1279
IN-ENCAP	Internet Encapsulation Protocol	Limited Use	1241
CLNS-MIB	CLNS-MIB	Limited Use	1238
CFDP	Coherent File Distribution Protocol	Limited Use	1235
IP-AX.25	IP Encapsulation of AX.25 Frames	Limited Use	1226
ALERTS	Managing Asynchronously Generated Alerts	Limited Use	1224
MPP	Message Posting Protocol	Limited Use	1204
SNMP-BULK	Bulk Table Retrieval with the SNMP	Limited Use	1187
DNS-RR	New DNS RR Definitions	Limited Use	1183

continues

TABLE A.5. CONTINUED

Protocol	Name	Status	RFC
IMAP2	Interactive Mail Access Protocol	Limited Use	1176
NTP-OSI	NTP over OSI Remote Operations	Limited Use	1165
DMF-MAIL	Digest Message Format for Mail	Limited Use	1153
RDP	Reliable Data Protocol	Limited Use	908,1151
TCP-ACO	TCP Alternate Checksum Option	Limited Use	1146
IP-DVMRP	IP Distance Vector Multicast Routing	Limited Use	1075
VMTP	Versatile Message Transaction Protocol	Limited Use	1045
COOKIE-JAR	Authentication Scheme	Limited Use	1004
NETBLT	Bulk Data Transfer Protocol	Limited Use	998
IRTP	Internet Reliable Transaction Protocol	Limited Use	938
LDP	Loader Debugger Protocol	Limited Use	909
RLP	Resource Location Protocol	Limited Use	887
NVP-II	Network Voice Protocol	Limited Use	ISI-memo
PVP	Packet Video Protocol	Limited Use	ISI-memo

Informational Protocols

Informational protocols are developed outside the influence of the IESG. Some are published as RFCs so the Internet community can have easier access to the demos. Some informational protocols are developed by outside organizations or vendors. Table A.6 lists the current informational protocols.

TABLE A.6. INFORMATIONAL PROTOCOL RFCs.

Protocol	Name	Status	RFC
PPP-EXT	PPP Vendor Extensions	No Status	2153
UTF-7	UTF-7	No Status	2152
CAST-128	CAST-128 Encryption Algorithm	No Status	2144
DLSCAP	Data Link Switching Client Access Protocol	No Status	2114
PNG	Portable Network Graphics Version 1.0	No Status	2083

Protocol	Name	Status	RFC
RC5	RC5, RC5-CBC, RC5-CBC-Pad, and RC5-CTS Algorithms	No Status	2040
SNTP	Simple Network Time Protocol v4 for IPv4, IPv6 and OSI	No Status	2030
PGP-MEF	PGP Message Exchange Formats	No Status	1991
PPP-DEFL	PPP Deflate Protocol	No Status	1979
PPP-PRED	PPP Predictor Compression Protocol	No Status	1978
PPP-BSD	PPP BSD Compression Protocol	No Status	1977
PPP-DCE	PPP for Data Compression in DCE	No Status	1976
PPP-MAG	PPP Magnalink Variable Resource Compression	No Status	1975
PPP-STAC	PPP Stac LZS Compression Protocol	No Status	1974
GZIP	GZIP File Format Specification Version 4.3	No Status	1952
DEFLATE	DEFLATE Compressed Data Format Specification V. 1.3	No Status	1951
ZLIB	ZLIB Compressed Data Format Specification V. 3.3	No Status	1950
HTTP-1.0	Hypertext Transfer Protocol—HTTP/1.0	No Status	1945
	text/enriched MIME Content-type	No Status	1896
	Application/CALS-1840 Content-type	No Status	1895
	PPP IPCP Extensions for Name Server Addresses	No Status	1877
SNPP	Simple Network Paging Protocol—Version 2	No Status	1861
	ISO Transport Class 2 Non-use Explicit Flow Control	No Status	1859
	over TCP RFC1006 extension	No Status	
	IP in IP Tunneling	No Status	1853
	PPP Network Control Protocol for LAN Extension	No Status	1841
TESS	The Exponential Security System	No Status	1824
NFSV3	NFS Version 3 Protocol Specification	No Status	1813
	A Format for Bibliographic Records	No Status	1807
	Data Link Switching: Switch-to-Switch Protocol	No Status	1795

continues

TABLE A.6. CONTINUED

Protocol	Name	Status	RFC
BGP-4	Experience with the BGP-4 Protocol	No Status	1773
SDMD	IPv4 Option for Sender Directed MD Delivery	No Status	1770
SNOOP	Snoop Version 2 Packet Capture File Format	No Status	1761
BINHEX	MIME Content Type for BinHex-Encoded Files	No Status	1741
RWHOIS	Referral Whois Protocol	No Status	1714
DNS-NSAP	DNS NSAP Resource Records	No Status	1706
RADIO-PAGE	TPC.INT Subdomain: Radio Paging—Technical Procedures	No Status	1703
GRE-IPv4	Generic Routing Encapsulation over IPv4	No Status	1702
GRE	Generic Routing Encapsulation	No Status	1701
ADSNA-IP	Advanced SNA/IP: A Simple SNA Transport Protocol	No Status	1538
TACACS	Terminal Access Control Protocol	No Status	1492
MD4	MD4 Message Digest Algorithm	No Status	1320
SUN-NFS	Network File System Protocol	No Status	1094
SUN-RPC	Remote Procedure Call Protocol Version 2	No Status	1057
GOPHER	The Internet Gopher Protocol	No Status	1436
LISTSERV	Listserv Distribute Protocol	No Status	1429
	Replication Requirements	No Status	1275
PCMAIL	Pcmail Transport Protocol	No Status	1056
MTP	Multicast Transport Protocol	No Status	1301
BSD Login	BSD Login	No Status	1282
DIXIE	DIXIE Protocol Specification	No Status	1249
IP-X.121	IP to X.121 Address Mapping for DDN	No Status	1236
OSI-HYPER	OSI and LLC1 on HYPERchannel	No Status	1223
HAP2	Host Access Protocol	No Status	1221
SUBNETASGN	On the Assignment of Subnet Numbers	No Status	1219
SNMP-TRAPS	Defining Traps for use with SNMP	No Status	1215
DAS	Directory Assistance Service	No Status	1202
LPDP	Line Printer Daemon Protocol	No Status	1179

Historic Protocols

Historic protocols have been superseded by later revisions during the development process. Table A.7 lists the current historic protocols. It also includes the status each attained as it developed.

TABLE A.7. HISTORIC PROTOCOL RFCs.

Protocol	Name	Status	RFC	STD
IPSO	DoD Security Options for IP	Elective	1108	
SNMPv2	Manager-to-Manager MIB	Elective	1451	
SNMPv2	Party MIB for SNMPv2	Elective	1447	
SNMPv2	Security Protocols for SNMPv2	Elective	1446	
SNMPv2	Administrative Model for SNMPv2	Elective	1445	
RIP	Routing Information Protocol Mapping full 822 to Restricted 822	Elective	1058 1137	34
BGP3	Border Gateway Protocol 3 (BGP-3) Gateway Requirements	Required	1267,1268 1009	4
EGP	Exterior Gateway Protocol	Recommended	904	18
SNMP-MUX	SNMP MUX Protocol and MIB		1227	
OIM-MIB-II	OSI Internet Management: MIB-II		1214	
IMAP3	Interactive Mail Access Protocol Version 3		1203	
SUN-RPC	Remote Procedure Call Protocol Version 1		1050	
802.4-MIP	IEEE 802.4 Token Bus MIB		1230	
CMOT	Common Management Information Services		1189	
	Mail Privacy: Procedures		1113	
	Mail Privacy: Key Management		1114	
	Mail Privacy: Algorithms		1115	
NFILE	A File Access Protocol		1037	
HOSTNAME	HOSTNAME Protocol		953	
SFTP	Simple File Transfer Protocol		913	
SUPDUP	SUPDUP Protocol		734	

continues

TABLE A.7. CONTINUED

Protocol	Name	Status	RFC	STD
BGP	Border Gateway Protocol		1163,1164	
MIB-I	MIB-I		1156	
SGMP	Simple Gateway Monitoring Protocol		1028	
HEMS	High Level Entity Management Protocol		1021	
STATSRV	Statistics Server		996	
POP2	Post Office Protocol, Version 2		937	
RATP	Reliable Asynchronous Transfer Protocol		916	
HFEP	Host—Front End Protocol		929	
THINWIRE	Thinwire Protocol		914	
HMP	Host Monitoring Protocol		869	
GGP	Gateway Gateway Protocol		823	
RTELNET	Remote Telnet Service		818	
CLOCK	DCNET Time Server Protocol		778	
MPM	Internet Message Protocol		759	
NETRJS	Remote Job Service		740	
NETED	Network Standard Text Editor		569	
RJE	Remote Job Entry		407	
XNET	Cross Net Debugger		IEN-158	
NAMESERVER	Host Name Server Protocol		IEN-116	
MUX	Multiplexing Protocol		IEN-90	
GRAPHICS	Graphics Protocol		NIC-24308	

Appendix B

Answers to End of Day Test Your Knowledge Questions

Day 1—The History of the Internet

1. The Internet is based on a packet-switching network. Paul Baran developed the concept of a network that breaks data into datagrams (or packets) that are labeled to include a source and destination address. These packets are forwarded from computer to computer until they reach the intended destination computer.

2. RFCs 854 and 855 and the Internet Standard RFCs that describe the Telnet protocol. In addition, there are several RFCs that describe Telnet options. A listing of specific Telnet Option RFCs can be found in the document STD001.

3. The Internet Engineering Task Force (IETF) is in charge of short- to medium-term research projects within the Internet Society. Each separate project under research is assigned a manager to head the research effort. These managers and the chairman of the IETF make up the Internet Engineering Steering Group (IESG).

4. No. Each RFC is maintained and kept for historical reference (even when it has been designated as obsolete). This allows for comparisons to the updated RFCs to see what has been changed.

5. No. An RFC remains "as is" for its lifetime. If changes need to be applied to an RFC, a new RFC is released and the original's status is changed to obsolete.

6. RFCs can be retrieved using the following methods:

   - Using anonymous FTP and connecting to the following location: `ftp://ds.internic.net/rfc`

   - Requesting an RFC by sending an email message with the message body containing the text `Send RFC####.txt` to `mailserv@ds.internic.net` (in which `####` is the RFC number)

   - Connecting with a Web browser to the following URL: `http://www.isi.edu/rfc-editor/rfc.html`

7. Yes, some RFC numbers do not exist. These are RFC numbers that were assigned for proposed RFCs that never made it to the standards track.

Day 2—Network Types and Open Systems Architecture

1. X.25 networks were developed to run over public switched telephone networks. Due to the unreliability of the lines, extensive error-checking was built into the protocol. Frame relay was developed to run in digital and fiber-optic environments. Due to the reliability of the lines, less error-checking needs to be performed in a frame relay environment. Only a simple cyclic redundant check (CRC) is performed.

2. An ATM network allows Quality of Service (QOS) parameters to be included in any network request. QOS parameters set minimum thresholds that must be met for transmission. These include values for peak bandwidth, average sustained bandwidth, and burst size. If the actual traffic flow does not meet this QOS specification, the cell can be marked as *discard eligible*. Frame relay does not include any QOS parameters.

3. An FDDI network is comprised of a primary and a secondary ring. This provides fault tolerance if the primary ring were to stop functioning. In addition, a computer on an FDDI network can transmit as many frames as it can produce in a preset time interval before letting the token go. Several frames can be circulating the ring at once, which gives an FDDI network an overall edge in speed compared with a token-ring network.

4. Peer-to-peer networks are comprised of hosts that can function as both a client and a server. The clients determine which resources they are willing to "share" with the other users of the network. In a server-based network, at least one host is dedicated to the purpose of sharing resources with the other host on the network. The peer-to-peer model is generally implemented in smaller, decentralized networks. Server-based networks are more common in larger, centralized networks.

5. Quality of Service (QOS) allows a calling host to request that specific performance levels be met for a connection to be established. Parameters include peak bandwidth, average sustained bandwidth, and burst size. If the actual traffic flow does not meet this QOS specification, any ATM switch can discard the cell.

6. B. The Application layer allows programs to access network resources.

7. E. The Presentation layer is responsible for translation of all data.

8. G. The Session layer coordinates service requests and responses between two hosts.

9. D. The Transport layer provides an end-to-end connection between a source and destination host.

10. A. The Network layer determines the best route from a source to a destination host.

11. F. The Transport layer is divided into the Logical Link Control and the Media Access Control layers.

12. C. The Physical layer performs the actual binary transmission of data between networked hosts.

Day 3—The TCP/IP Layer Model and the Core Protocols of the TCP/IP Suite

1. The four layers of the TCP/IP layered model are the Network Interface layer, the Internet layer, the Transport layer, and the Application layer.

2. When a new product is developed, they will fit into one of the layers of a layered model. The new product will need to communicate only with the layers above and below it. This simplifies the development of new products. For example, a new

transport protocol would need to communicate with only the Application layer and the Internet layer in the TCP/IP layered model. It would depend on the Internet layer to communicate with the Network Interface layer.

3. The following comparisons between the layers of the OSI model and the TCP/IP model can be made. The Physical and Data Link layers of the OSI model are comparable to the Network Interface level of the TCP/IP layered model. The Network layer of the OSI model matches the Internet layer of the TCP/IP model. The Transport layer is the same for both the OSI and TCP/IP models. Finally, the Presentation, Session, and Application layers of the OSI model map to the Application layer of the TCP/IP layered model.

4. The Transport layer provides end-to-end communication between hosts. Two protocols exist in the Transport layer. TCP provides guaranteed, connection-oriented communication. UDP provides connectionless, nonguaranteed communication.

5. ARP returns the actual MAC address of the destination host when the destination host exists on the same network segment as the source host.

6. ARP returns the MAC address of the router on the local segment that is used to route traffic destined for the remote destination host.

7. ICMP provides error reporting and control messaging to the TCP/IP protocol suite. Some of the specific functions include

   - Redirecting traffic when a more efficient route to a destination network is found
   - Informing a source host when a datagram's TTL has expired
   - Determining the address of all available routers on a network segment
   - Informing a host to slow down communications when they are saturating a router or network segment
   - Discovering what subnet mask is in use on a network segment

8. IP provides connectionless service. It is left up to the higher layer protocols to implement guaranteed service (if desired).

9. Multicasting is preferred over broadcasting because it limits the number of hosts on a segment that will have to examine the data being transmitted. A broadcast is directed to *every* host on the network segment. This increases network traffic and bandwidth usage. All of the messages sent to a multicast group are sent to an Internet Class D address. Members of the multicast group will know if that address is intended for their group.

Day 4—Internet Protocol (IP) Addresses

1. Convert the following decimal numbers to binary representation:

Decimal	Binary
127	01111111
0	00000000
76	01001100
248	11111000
224	11100000
57	00111001
135.56.204.253	10000111 00111000 11001100 11111101

2. Convert the following binary numbers to decimal format:

Binary	Decimal
11100110	230
00011100	28
01010101	85
11001100	204
11001010 00001100 10100011 11110010	202.12.163.242
00011011 10001001 01111111 10000101	27.137.127.133

3. Identify the address class of the following IP addresses :

IP Address	IP Address Class
131.107.2.8	Class B
127.0.0.1	No Class—reserved for loopback functions
225.34.56.7	Class D
129.33.55.6	Class B
10.2.4.5	Class A
223.223.223.223	Class C

4. The broadcast address for a host with IP address 172.30.45.67 is a Class B address. The default subnet mask for this address would be 255.255.0.0. This indicates that the first two octets represent the network component of the IP address. In this case, the broadcast address would be 172.30.255.255.

B

5. The IP address 204.200.200.15 is a Class C IP address. This means that the first three octets represent the network component of the IP address. The network address would be 201.200.200.0 for this host.

6. The host SUSAN would not be able to communicate with the host KELLY, because based on the subnet mask implemented, SUSAN would believe that KELLY is on the same network segment, when it is actually on a remote network segment.

7. A subnet mask that would allow SUSAN to communicate with KELLY, would be 255.255.255.0. If the ANDing process is then performed on the two IP addresses, they would result in different results, indicating that the two hosts are on different network segments. Other subnet masks that would also work in this case include 255.255.240.0, 255.255.248.0, 255.255.252.0, and 255.255.254.0.

8. The following pools of IP addresses have been reserved by the IANA for use on private, internal networks:

    *   10.0.0.0 through 10.255.255.255

    *   172.16.0.0 through 172.31.255.255

    *   192.168.0.0 through 192.168.255.255

9. IPv6 offers the following benefits over IPv4:

    *   Expanded addressing capabilities

    *   Simplified IP header

    *   Improved extensibility of the IP header

    *   Improved flow control

    *   Increased security

Day 5—Transmission Control Protocol (TCP) and User Datagram Protocol (UDP)

1. TCP provides guaranteed, connection-oriented delivery of data. UDP, on the other hand, provides nonguaranteed, connectionless delivery of data. The use of UDP does not mean that the application does not require that all data is delivered; it simply means that the guarantee of delivery is left to the Application layer programs.

2. TCP provides reliable transport by using acknowledgments. When the destination host receives a series of TCP segments, it acknowledges it has received the segments by requesting the next segment it expects to receive.

B

3. A delayed acknowledgment timer causes an acknowledgment to be sent to the sending host when the timer reaches a value of zero. This allows for acknowledgments to be sent even if two contiguous segments have not been received at the destination host.

4. The TCP three-way handshake establishes a TCP session between two hosts. It is comprised of three steps.

   In the first step, the source host sends a TCP packet containing its current sequence number and with the SYN (synchronize) flag enabled. This indicates that it wants to synchronize sequence numbers with the destination host.

   In the second step, the destination host sends an acknowledgment packet. This acknowledgment has the following properties: It contains the next sequence number expected by the source host, the SYN flag is enabled, and the current sequence number of the destination host is sent to the source host.

   In the final step, the original source host sends an acknowledgment packet containing the next sequence number the destination host expects to use. The completion of this step establishes a full duplex connection between the two hosts.

5. Yes. If the sliding window is configured to be too large, it can result in too many segments being lost during transmission. This results in retransmission timers expiring, which causes the lost segments to be re-sent. The overall effect is excess network traffic due to the resending of data, and delays due to the expiration of retransmission timers.

6. The receiving host adjusts its receive window size to be equal to the sending host's transmit window size.

7. The UDP header contains a 16-bit checksum field that ensures the UDP packet has not been corrupted in transit. The checksum is based on the UDP pseudo header, which contains fields from both the IP header and the UDP header. The Source IP address, Destination IP address, and protocol fields are taken from the IP header, and the Length field is taken from the UDP header.

8. The TCP header's checksum field is based on the fields contained in the TCP pseudo header. The pseudo header is comprised of the Source IP address, Destination IP address, and protocol fields from the IP header and the TCP Length field from the TCP header.

9. The following output shows the port usage when connected to the site `http://www.online-can.com` using the Internet Explorer Web browser:

```
netstat -a

TCP    bkhome:1169          www.online-can.com:80  ESTABLISHED
```

```
TCP      bkhome:1171              www.online-can.com:80   ESTABLISHED

TCP      bkhome:1173              www.online-can.com:80   ESTABLISHED

TCP      bkhome:1174              www.online-can.com:80   ESTABLISHED
```

As you can see, all the connections on the server side are www.online-can.com:80 (or port 80, the HTTP port). My host computer is using random assigned ports. For this connection, I used TCP ports 1169, 1171, 1173, and 1174. All the traffic is using the TCP protocol for this transaction.

Day 6—The Art of Subnet Masking

1. You would require an additional 7 bits from the host portion of the IP address to provide 115 subnets. This would provide you with 126 subnets.

2. The extended network prefix in this subnetwork example would be 255.254.0.0.

3. Using the subnet shortcut table, we see that using a 254 subnet mask, the increment value would be 2. Assuming that zero subnetting is not implemented, the third pool of IP addresses would begin with 6 (2×3). The addresses requested would map as follows:

   Network address   10.6.0.0

   Broadcast address   10.7.255.255

   Beginning address   10.6.0.1

   Ending address   10.7.255.254

4. Using the subnet shortcut table, you would require 4 additional bits to create 14 subnets from this Class B address of 172.30.0.0.

5. The extended network prefix for this example would be 255.255.240.0.

6. The following addresses would be defined for the third subnet in this network (assuming that zero subnetting was not implemented):

   Network address   172.30.48.0

   Broadcast address   172.30.63.255

   Beginning address   172.30.48.1

   Ending address   172.30.63.254

7. Using the subnet shortcut table, you would require 4 bits from the host portion of the address to provide 10 subnets. In this case, you would actually have 14 subnets available for use.

8. This addressing scheme leaves 4 bits to represent the host portion of the address. This provides $2^4-2 = 14$ host per subnet. The two addresses not included are the network address and the broadcast address.

9. Complete the following table of addresses:

Network Address	Beginning Address	Ending Address	Broadcast Address
192.168.23.16	192.168.23.17	192.168.23.30	192.168.23.31
192.168.23.32	192.168.23.33	192.168.23.46	192.168.23.47
192.168.23.48	192.168.23.49	192.168.23.62	192.168.23.63
192.168.23.64	192.168.23.65	192.168.23.78	192.168.23.79
192.168.23.80	192.168.23.81	192.168.23.94	192.168.23.95
192.168.23.96	192.168.23.97	192.168.23.110	192.168.23.111
192.168.23.112	192.168.23.113	192.168.23.126	192.168.23.127
192.168.23.128	192.168.23.129	192.168.23.142	192.168.23.143
192.168.23.144	192.168.23.145	192.168.23.158	192.168.23.159
192.168.23.160	192.168.23.161	192.168.23.174	192.168.23.175
192.168.23.176	192.168.23.177	192.168.23.190	192.168.23.191
192.168.23.192	192.168.23.193	192.168.23.206	192.168.23.207
192.168.23.208	192.168.23.209	192.168.23.222	192.168.23.223
192.168.23.224	192.168.23.225	192.168.23.238	192.168.23.239

10. The following network address and broadcast address would be used for the following host and subnet masks:

172.16.67.16 with subnet mask 255.255.240.0

network = 172.16.64.0 and broadcast = 172.16.79.255

192.168.54.76 with subnet mask 255.255.255.224

network = 192.168.54.64 and broadcast = 192.16.54.79

157.76.2.198 with subnet mask 255.255.255.128

network = 157.76.2.128 and broadcast = 157.76.2.255

11. Assuming that the networks will be assigned their IP addresses based on the lowest addresses being assigned to the leftmost networks, the network address 192.168.30.0/25 could be used for subnetwork #1.

B

12. Keeping this assumption, the following network addresses could be used for sub-network #3, subnetwork #4, and subnetwork #6.

    Subnetwork #3 = 192.168.30.128/27

    Subnetwork #4 = 192.168.30.160/27

    Subnetwork #6 = 192.168.30.224/27

    I have skipped the pool 192.168.30.192/27 and have left it to be divided up between subnetworks 7, 8, 9, and 10.

13. What could be the broadcast addresses for subnetworks 7, 8, 9, and 10?

    Subnetwork #7 = 192.168.30.199

    Subnetwork #8 = 192.168.30.207

    Subnetwork #9 = 192.168.30.215

    Subnetwork #10= 192.168.30.223

14. The first network address in this pool is 198.163.32.0/24 and the final address is 198.163.39.0/24. The difference between these is that the third octet is 7, which rounds up to 8 when we reference the subnet shortcut table. The number of bits required for an increment value of 8 is 5 bits. Therefore, the network address that can be used to aggregate this pool of IP addresses would be

    192.163.32.0/21

15. The missing information for each of the CIDR networks is as follows:

Beginning address:	200.200.64.1
Ending address:	**200.200.67.254**
Subnet mask:	255.255.252.0
Beginning address:	172.32.0.1
Ending address:	172.39.255.254
Subnet mask:	255.248.0.0
Beginning Address:	198.16.0.1
Ending Address:	198.31.255.254
Subnet Mask:	**255.240.0.0**

Day 7—Resolution of IP Addresses and Logical Names

1. Hostname resolution is used to resolve hostname or fully qualified domain names to an IP address. NetBIOS name resolution resolves both a NetBIOS computer name and a NetBIOS service to an IP address. NetBIOS support is not required within a TCP/IP stack unless the network uses NetBIOS services.

2. The top-level domain names that exist on the Internet today include the following: COM, EDU, ORG, NET, GOV, MIL, NUM, and ARPA. In addition, country code top-level domains exist using a two-letter abbreviation for countries. For example, Canada is represented with CA and New Zealand is represented with NZ. Recently, several generic top-level domains have been added as the names available in the COM domain have dwindled. The new generic top-level domains include FIRM, SHOP, WEB, ARTS, REC, INFO, and NOM. These names were added to provide additional expansion room for registering domain names on the Internet.

3. No. The host will not be able to communicate with the destination using the hostname. This is because the HOSTS file is referred to before DNS in a hostname resolution process. The incorrect address would be communicated instead of the correct address that would be obtained from DNS.

4. Yes. As mentioned in the answer to question 3, the HOSTS file is checked before DNS when resolving a hostname to an IP address. If the IP address were correct in the HOSTS file, the destination hostname would be successfully resolved to an IP address.

5. A recursive DNS query requires the responding name server to respond with either the resulting IP address or an error that the hostname could not be resolved. An iterative DNS query, on the other hand, allows the responding name server to provide its best answer when resolving the hostname to an IP address. The best answer may be a reference to another name server that may be able to resolve the hostname to an IP address.

6. You can increase performance on a DNS server by using caching. By increasing the cache parameter for zones, you allow the hostname to IP address resolutions to be cached for longer intervals. This provides a speedier resolution process.

7. The four NetBIOS node types are B-Node (broadcast), P-Node (peer), M-Node (mixed), and H-Node (hybrid). The node types that help to reduce network traffic most are the P-Node and the H-Node. The P-Node will submit NetBIOS name resolution requests only to a NetBIOS name server. No broadcasts are used to resolve NetBIOS names. Likewise, the H-Node will first query a NetBIOS name server to

B

resolve a NetBIOS name to an IP address. The difference is that it will use a broadcast if the NetBIOS name server cannot resolve the NetBIOS name to an IP address. This allows resolution of NetBIOS names for hosts that are not configured to register the NetBIOS names with a NetBIOS name server.

8. The three basic NetBIOS name transactions that occur on a NetBIOS network are name registrations, name discoveries, and name releases.

9. Dynamic DNS provides two features above the feature set of a DNS server. Dynamic DNS allows a host that changes its IP address to register its new hostname/IP address combination with the Dynamic DNS server. Also, Dynamic DNS provides a method for the automatic propagation of zone updates to secondary Dynamic DNS servers. DNS requires that the DNS administrator change the SOA record to accomplish this.

10. The following lines would be required to refer to the shared LMHOSTS file referred to in this question:

```
172.18.56.35      PRIMARY      #PRE

#INCLUDE \\PRIMARY\NETLOGON\LMHOSTS
```

The first line is required so that the IP address for PRIMARY is loaded into the NetBIOS name cache. The second line indicates the location of the shared LMHOSTS file that should be included in the resolution of NetBIOS names to IP addresses.

Day 8—Configuring Domain Name Servers

1. The named.boot file for the Homer computer would be as follows:

```
directory /etc /db

forwarders      192.168.15.1

cache      named.cache

primary          0.0.127.in-addr.arpa          named.local
primary          15.168.192.in-addr.arpa       named.rev
primary          simpsons.com                  named.host
```

2. Create the zone file for simpsons.com that would be stored on HOMER.

```
@                             IN     SOA
➥homer.simpsons.com    mattg.simpsons.com {
                              1998030501      ; serial
```

```
                                            10800               ;refresh
                                            3600                ;retry
                                            604800              ;expire
                                            86400               ;TTL
                                               )

                                  IN     NS
homer.simpsons.com

homer.simpsons.com               IN     A     192.168.15.5
bart.simpsons.com                IN     A     192.168.15.1
lisa.simpsons.com                IN     A     192.168.15.2
marge.simpsons.com               IN     A     192.168.15.4

mail                             IN     CNAME    homer.simpsons.com
bigboy                           IN     CNAME    homer.simpsons.com
gw                               IN     CNAME    bart.simpsons.com
www                              IN     CNAME    lisa.simpsons.com
ftp                              IN     CNAME    lisa.simpsons.com
gopher                           IN     CNAME    marge.simpsons.com
mail2                            IN     CNAME    marge.simpsons.com

simpsons.com                     IN     MX    10    homer.simpsons.com
simpsons.com                     IN     MX    20    marge.simpsons.com
```

3. Configure the reverse lookup zone for this network that would be stored on HOMER.

```
15.168.192.in-addr.arpa.                IN     SOA
➡homer.simpsons.com. mattg.simpsons.com (
                                 1998050301         ; serial
                                 10800              ;refresh
                                 3600               ;retry
                                 604800             ;expire
                                 86400              ;TTL
                                    )

                                 NS
homer.simpsons.com.

1          IN     PTR     bart.simpsons.com.
2          IN     PTR     lisa.simpsons.com.
4          IN     PTR     marge.simpsons.com.
5          IN     PTR     homer.simpsons.com.
```

4. The latest version of the named.cache file can be obtained using anonymous FTP from the following site:

```
ftp://rs.internic.net/domain/named.cache
```

5. The NSLOOKUP command that can be used to determine the mail exchange record for the domain `online-usa.com` is

   `ls -t MX online-usa.com`

6. The NSLOOKUP command that can be used to determine the name server for the `online-can.com` domain is

   `ls -t MX online-can.com`

Day 9—Gateway and Routing Protocols

1. Multicast addresses enable RIP version 2 and OSPF to propagate routing information in a more efficient manner. Rather than using a broadcast address that non-routers would have to inspect, these protocols use a predetermined multicast address that is registered only by the RIP and OSPF routers themselves. RIP version 2 uses the multicast address `224.0.0.9`, and OSPF uses the address `224.0.0.5` for all OSPF routers and `224.0.0.6` for the designated router and the backup designated router.

2. Exterior gateway protocols are used to exchange routing information between other organizations or autonomous systems. Interior gateway protocols are used to exchange routing information between routers that belong to the same autonomous system.

3. The `traceroute` command can be used to determine the route a packet takes to a remote host. The Windows NT implementation of this command is `tracert.exe`.

4. Distance vector protocols are broadcast-based protocols that are commonly used in smaller networks due to their usage of broadcasts to propagate routing information. A distance vector protocol propagates the entire routing table between neighboring routers. A link state protocol floods routing information to all nodes in the network. This routing information will contain only routes to directly attached networks. Even though these routing messages are sent to all routers on the network, their reduced size results in a more efficient exchange of routing information.

5. Common problems faced in a dynamic routing environment include routing loops and the counting to infinity problem. A routing loop exists when a series of routers creates a circular route to a destination network that simply goes around in circles. A counting to infinity problem occurs when an interface fails on a router. Before the router can announce this to the rest of the network, it receives a routing announcement from a neighboring router that it can reach the network on the other side of the dead interface. Rather than removing the route, it increments the hop count from the neighboring router. This leads to the hop count increasing until infinity is reached.

6. Some of the techniques that can be used to prevent routing loops and counting to infinity problems are:

   • The use of hold-downs

   • Implementing split horizons

   • Implementing poison reverse

7. The default gateway address is `203.196.205.1`. This was found in the following routing entry:

```
0.0.0.0              0.0.0.0          203.196.205.1
➡203.196.205.254          2
```

8. The local IP addresses for this router are `172.16.2.8` and `203.196.205.254`. You can find the local IP addresses for a router by determining which addresses are routed to the loopback address of `127.0.0.1`.

9. No. The routing table shows that this is a local IP address. Any requests to this address are redirected to the loopback address `127.0.0.1`.

10. The multicast address shows that all packets destined to a multicast address are routed through the interface with IP address `172.16.2.8`.

11. The metric associated with reaching the network `172.16.4.0` is 2. This means that another router must be crossed after the packet is sent through the router at IP address `172.16.2.1`.

12. The metric associated with reaching the network `172.16.5.0` is 3. This means that two more routers must be crossed after the packet is sent through the router at IP address `172.16.2.1`.

13. The following Windows NT command can be used to add a static route to network `172.16.6.0/24` through the gateway at IP address `172.16.2.1`:

```
route   -p   add   172.16.6.0   mask   255.255.255.0   172.16.2.1
```

Day 11—Remote Command Applications

1. 1. D. Telnet uses TCP port 23.

   2. H. Rlogin uses TCP port 513.

   3. E. Quote of the Day uses TCP or UDP port 17.

   4. F. Daytime uses TCP or UDP port 13.

   5. C. Echo uses TCP or UDP port 7.

   6. B. Discard uses TCP or UDP port 9.

7. A. Character Generator uses TCP or UDP port 19.

8. G. Time uses TCP or UDP port 37.

2. Telnet sends clear text authentication information across the network, which is subject to being intercepted by a network sniffer. rlogin uses entries within the hosts.equiv and .rhosts files to determine which users or hosts can perform rlogin sessions. No actual account and password information is transferred over the network.

3. The syntax of the rlogin command to connect to a host named BART using the username LISA is

```
rlogin bart -l lisa
```

4. A Telnet option negotiation is based on a series of exchanges using the DO, DON'T, WILL, and WON'T functions. When the sending host sends a DO or DON'T request, the receiving host responds with a WILL or WON'T response to indicate whether it will implement the requested option. Likewise, when the sending host sends a WILL or WON'T function suggesting an option that it could implement, the receiving host replies with a DO or DON'T function indicating whether it agrees to the option.

5. The Interpret as Command (IAC) character precedes each command sequence to leave no doubt as to whether a data stream is intended to be a command or simply some data sent to the other host.

6. A network virtual terminal provides a common endpoint at each end of a Telnet communication session that defines what functionality is provided. This provides a minimum environment that must be provided on all Telnet clients and servers. These environments can be enhanced via option negotiation.

7. Telnet client software can be used to connect to various optional TCP/IP services by changing the port that the client software connects to on the server. Telnet can also be used to troubleshoot connectivity problems to SMTP and POP3 mail servers.

8. The following optional TCP/IP services are supported under Windows NT Server: Character Generator, Daytime, Discard, Echo, and Quote of the Day.

Day 12—File Transfer Protocols

1. The FTP protocol uses TCP as its transport protocol, whereas TFTP uses UDP as its transport protocol. When a file is transferred using FTP, two sessions are actually established between the client and the server. The first session is a protocol

interpreter session that is used to transmit FTP commands. The second session is the data transfer process over which data is transported. TFTP does not use sessions, because of the use of UDP as the transport protocol.

2. Anonymous FTP is a common method of granting access to an FTP server to unknown or nonregistered users. Users log in to the FTP server using the account `anonymous` or `ftp` and provide their Internet email address as their password.

3. The Remote Copy Protocol (RCP) depends on the `.rhosts` or `hosts.equiv` file to contain the user account and hostname for allowed connections. No passwords are transmitted across the network unless the user's name does not exist in either file. FTP, on the other hand, sends the account/password information in clear text across the network.

4. Veronica, Jughead, and WAIS searches can be used to search for a file in Gopherspace.

5. The most common method to search for a topic on the Web is to use an Internet search engine such as `www.yahoo.com` or `www.infoseek.com`.

6. The two communication channels used during an FTP session are the Data Transfer Process (DTP) and the Protocol Interpreter (PI). The DTP is used for the actual transmission of data between the client and the server. The PI is used to transmit commands between the client and the server. The FTP server uses TCP port 21 for the PI and TCP port 20 for the DTP. The client uses a random port number over port 1024 for each of the two sessions.

7. The steps involved in the establishment of a Secure Socket Layer (SSL) session are as follows:

   A. The client makes a security request to the server.

   B. The server sends its certificate to the client. This certificate contains the client's public key and the client's cipher preferences.

   C. The client generates a master key.

   D. The client encrypts the master key using the server's public key that it received in step B. The master key of the client can now be decrypted only by the server's private key that is located only on the server.

   E. The client transmits the encrypted master key to the server.

   F. The server decrypts the client's master key using the server's private key.

   G. The server authenticates with the client by returning a message to the client that is encrypted by using the client's master key. This authenticates both sides of the session.

Day 13—Electronic Mail over TCP/IP

1. The steps involved in an SMTP session between an SMTP client and an SMTP server are:

    A. The SMTP client initiates a connection TCP port 25 on the SMTP server. The SMTP server responds with a `220 <Ready>` message.

    B. The SMTP client requests that the SMTP session be established by sending a `HELO` (Hello) command including the Fully Qualified Domain Name (FQDN) of the SMTP client. The SMTP server should respond with a `250 <OK>` message.

    C. The SMTP client informs the SMTP server that is sending the message with the `MAIL FROM:` command. The SMTP server should respond with a `250 <OK>` message.

    D. The SMTP client identifies all the recipients the message is intended for by using the `RCPT TO:` command. A separate `RCPT TO:` command is issued for each recipient of the message. The SMTP server responds to each of the recipients with a `250 <OK>` message.

    E. The SMTP client indicates that it is prepared to transmit the actual email message by issuing the `DATA` command. The actual message is now transmitted to the SMTP server by using 7-bit ASCII characters. If any attachments exist in the message, the attachments must be encoded into a 7-bit stream using BinHex, uuencode, or MIME.

    F. After the message has transmitted successfully, the SMTP client sends a `QUIT` command to terminate the SMTP session. The SMTP server responds with a `221 <Closing>` message to indicate that the session has terminated.

2. The SMTP protocol allows an Internet email client to send Internet email. POP3 or IMAP allows an Internet email client to receive Internet email.

3. A Mail Exchange (MX) record is queried in DNS by an SMTP client to determine the mail exchanger for the domain name it is sending mail to.

4. IMAP mail clients have the following advantages over POP3 mail clients:

    - Initially, IMAP clients are not sent the contents of every mail file, just the header information.

    - IMAP allows messages to be stored in a hierarchical structure on the IMAP server.

- Messages are stored on the IMAP server, which allows the messages to be accessed from multiple IMAP clients and still see the same status information for all messages.
- IMAP servers understand MIME file extensions.
- IMAP supports online, offline, and disconnected access modes. POP3 supports only the online model.

5. The LDAP protocol has been developed by the IETF to standardize access to X.500 and non-X.500 directory systems. This allows for easier integration of foreign email systems.

6. The X.500 name `cn=Crooks, Malcolm; ou=Winnipeg; o=Online Business Systems, c=CA` represents the common name "Malcolm Crooks." Mr. Crooks is located within the Organizational Unit "Winnipeg" within the Organization "Online Business Systems." The organization is located within Canada (CA).

7. Macintosh systems primarily use BinHex for encoding email attachments.

8. The following field headers are used when a MIME attachment exists in an email message:

- MIME-Version
- Content-Type
- Content-Transfer Encoding
- Content-ID
- Content-Description

Day 14—Managing a Network

1. The first category of network management encompasses the management of network resources, including user accounts and security issues. The second category of network management includes the management of the physical devices that form the network.

2. SNMP can also be implemented on AppleTalk, IPX, and OSI networks.

3. The SNMP management system is used to send SNMP requests to SNMP agents. It is also the destination of SNMP trap messages.

4. An SNMP agent responds to SNMP requests and fills in the requested information before sending an SNMP response to the SNMP management system. In addition, an SNMP agent can send an SNMP trap when a preconfigured event takes place, such as a cold boot of a host.

5. The SNMP trap PDU provides the capability for an SNMP agent to alert the SNMP management system when a threshold has been exceeded or a significant event has taken place. This allows for a quicker response to a network device failure.

6. Additional security can be provided by one of two methods. The first method involves changing the community name from the default of PUBLIC (it is easily guessed). The second method involves configuring which SNMP management systems that an SNMP agent will accept SNMP requests from. This limits which SNMP management systems can perform requests on an SNMP agent. It is also a good idea to configure the SNMP agent to send an SNMP trap if a nonconfigured SNMP management system attempts an SNMP request.

7. The three types of community names that can be implemented in an SNMP network are the monitor community, the control community, and the trap community. The monitor community indicates which community name SNMP requests will be responded to. The control community is used to configure which SNMP management systems can perform write functions to an SNMP agent. Finally, the trap community is used to indicate the community's SNMP management system to which all SNMP trap messages are sent.

8. Object identifiers are assigned to objects in the Management Information Base (MIB) in a hierarchical fashion. This hierarchy defines whether the object is a common object or a private enterprise object based on its location in the hierarchy.

9. The major categories within the MIB-II database are System, Interfaces, Address Translation, IP, ICMP, TCP, UDP, EGP, Transmission, and SNMP.

10. The GetBulk PDU provides a more efficient retrieval mechanism for values in a table. Rather than having to send a GetNextRequest for each entry in a table, the GetBulk allows the table to be retrieved in a single request.

Day 15—Dial-Up Networking Using TCP/IP

1. Deficiencies of the SLIP protocol include the inability to automatically assign IP addresses to clients, the inability to use protocols other than IP, the lack of error detection or correction, and the fact that account information is sent as clear text and there is no compressions built into the protocol.

2. PPP can use either Password Authentication Protocol (PAP) or Challenged Handshake Authentication Protocol (CHAP) for authentication. PPP can also choose to not enable authentication at all.

3. SLIP frames data using the END character (decimal 192). The END character is placed at the end of each packet transmitted.

4. Yes. PPP provides the ability to multiplex multiple protocols over a single dial-up session. This functionality is provided by the inclusion of a protocol field in the PPP header.

5. The Remote Access Service (RAS) enables you to configure a dial-up server in Windows NT.

6. The Link Control Protocol is used to establish, configure, and test the data link connection between the dial-in client and the dial-in server. Four phases are involved in the Link Control Protocol: the link establishment phase, the authentication phase, the network-layer protocol phase, and the link termination phase.

7. The three main components of a virtual private network are a tunnel server, a tunnel client, and the tunnel. The tunnel is the logical connection established between the tunnel server and the tunnel client over a public data network. All data transmitted over the tunnel can be encrypted to provide for a secure communications mechanism.

8. The PPTP client uses a random TCP port number over 1024, and the PPTP server listens for connections on TCP port 1723.

9. Dial-in rights are configured in the User Manager for Domains program in Windows NT Server. If the Remote Access Service is installed on Windows NT Workstation, dial-in rights are configured in User Manager. In addition, these rights can also be assigned using the Remote Access Manager program.

Day 16—Firewalls and Security

1. Some of the common security threats faced on a network include
   - The use of clear text passwords for authentication
   - The ease of performing network monitoring
   - The ability to "spoof" network addresses
   - Poor security implementations

2. Network address translation protects an interior network by never exposing the interior-addressing scheme to the exterior network. A proxy server will replace any internal addressing information with its external address when data is transmitted outside of the internal network.

B

3. Some of the rules that can be applied to a password policy include selecting passwords that are not found in a dictionary, forcing passwords to be changed at regular intervals, preventing previous passwords from being reused, and ensuring that passwords are not exchanged among users.

4. The following proxy rules should be established:

Protocol	Interface	Protocol	IP Source	Source Port	IP Destination	Destination Port
POP3	Local	TCP	192.168.5.*	*	10.20.30.40	110
IMAP	Local	TCP	192.168.5.*	*	10.20.30.40	143
SMTP	Local	TCP	192.168.5.*	*	10.20.30.40	25
HTTP	Local	TCP	192.168.5.*	*	*	80
Gopher	Local	TCP	192.168.5.*	*	*	70
Telnet out	Local	TCP	192.168.5.*	*	*	23
Telnet in	External	TCP	172.29.30.31	*	192.168.5.10	23

5. A Ticket Granting Ticket increases security in a Kerberos environment by better encrypting the communication between the Ticket Granting Server and the Kerberos client. All tickets will be requested from the Ticket Granting Server using the session key that was provided with the Ticket Granting Ticket. All replies from the Ticket Granting Server are also encrypted using this session key. The reply contains the session key for communication with the indicated data server.

6. The added advantage of using Kerberos for authentication is that new session keys are created each time communication is established between the user and server. This prevents a network monitoring agent from capturing the session key and using it at a later date. The session key will have expired by that point.

7. The following process can be used by an intruder to spool another host's IP address:

A. The attacking station changes its IP address to that of the client it wants to spoof.

B. The attacking station will now create a source route packet. This packet will indicate the path that an IP packet will take from the server on a return path. The trusted client that is being spoofed will be the last hop in the indicated source route before reaching the server. This makes it appear that the packet originated at the masqueraded workstation.

C. The attacking station will now send a packet destined for the server using the source route packet.

D. Because the packet has been routed through the trusted client, the server accepts the packet because it apparently came from the trusted client.

E. The server returns its response to the trusted client.

F. Because of the source route that was implemented, the trusted client forwards the response to the attacking station.

Day 17—NIS and NFS

1. NFS allows files to be made available to remote clients. Clients have transparent access to the remote file services. The files appear to be stored locally.

2. NIS provides a uniform directory across a UNIX environment. This allows UNIX hosts to share a common NIS directory, rather than maintain their own account/password databases.

3. A portmapper operates on all servers that provide client/server connectivity using Remote Procedure Calls (RPCs). When a client connects to the server to communicate to a server application using RPCs, the portmapper returns the correct port number if the application is running on the server.

4. An RPC function call process follows these steps:

   A. The Client Application issues a normal function call to the Client Stub.

   B. The Client Stub converts the input arguments from the local data representation to a common data representation that can be used between hosts that use different internal data representations (External Data Representation).

   C. The Client Stub calls the Client Runtime (a library of routines that provide functionality to the Client Stub).

   D. The Client Runtime transmits the message containing the encapsulated External Data Representation of the function call across the network to the Server Runtime. The Server Runtime likewise is a library of routines that provide the necessary functionality to the Server Stub.

   E. The Server Runtime issues a call to the Server Stub.

   F. The Server Stub converts the encapsulated arguments from the common data representation to its native data representation.

   G. The Server Stub calls the Server Application and passes the original client inputs for processing.

H. After the processing has completed, the Server Application returns the result set to the Server Stub.

I. The Server Stub converts the result set and any associated arguments to the common data representation for transmission. This is encapsulated within a message that is passed to the Server Runtime.

J. The Server Runtime transmits this message over the network to the Client Runtime.

K. The Client Runtime passes the message to the Client Stub.

L. The Client Stub extracts the result set from the message and converts the message to the local data representation.

M. The Client Stub returns the result set and any accompanying arguments to the calling function.

5. The mount protocol provides NFS with the necessary tools to mount an NFS file system on the underlying operating system.

6. File locking ensures that multiple clients are not able to access a data file simultaneously, unless required by the application. This prevents a file from being corrupted by multiple users attempting to modify the same file simultaneously. The Network Lock Manager (NLM) provides this functionality for NFS.

7. The three configuration issues involved with NIS are

- Configuring which NIS servers will function as master servers and which NIS servers will function as slave servers.

- NIS maps should be configured to allow responses from the NIS server to be optimized for commonly queried fields.

- Clients must be divided into common NIS domains. This establishes which servers will share a common account database.

8. Kerberos authentication offers the strongest protection for data and password transmissions by providing a mechanism that can authenticate both the user and the NFS server. This ensures that a correct client is connecting to the NFS server. It also ensures that the client is connecting to the correct NFS server.

Day 18—IP over ATM and Configuring NetBIOS Name Servers

1. A modified version of ARP must be implemented in an ATM environment, because ATM devices do not have a physical network address. ATMARP resolves an IP address to an ATM address instead.

2. If an ATM host receives an IP broadcast or an IP subnet broadcast for its IP network, the ATM host processes the packet as if it were addressed directly to that host.

3. ATM hosts are grouped into Logical IP Subnets (LIS) to form a logical IP subnetwork. Each host in an IP subnetwork belongs to the same LIS.

4. A client must attempt to prove that the ARP cache table entry is no longer valid before it can remove the ATMARP table entry. If there is no open virtual circuit to the destination, the table entry is deleted. If there is an open virtual circuit, the ATMARP client must revalidate the entry before regular traffic can be resumed. In a permanent virtual circuit, an InATMARP request is sent directly over the virtual circuit. In a switched virtual circuit, an ATMARP request is sent to the ATMARP server. The ATMARP reply is used to update the client's ATMARP table cache.

5. If multiple WINS servers exist in a single network, replication must be configured between the WINS servers to ensure that the entire WINS database is available to all WINS clients for NetBIOS name resolution.

6. A WINS proxy agent forwards NetBIOS name resolution packets to a WINS server on behalf of a non-WINS client. When the WINS server responds to the packet, it broadcasts the response on the network segment so that the non-WINS client can retrieve the data.

7. Static entries must be added to a WINS server for non-WINS NetBIOS clients so that a WINS client can resolve the NetBIOS name for the non-WINS clients to an IP address. This helps to reduce broadcast traffic and enables non-WINS clients on a remote network to be accessed without implementing LMHOSTS.

8. In the worst case scenario, a record will exist in the WINS database for 18 days before being removed entirely from the WINS database after a WINS client has been removed from the network. The first six days encompass the Renewal timer. After six days have elapsed, the WINS record is marked as released. The next six days are the days associated with the Extinction interval. At the completion of these six days, the WINS record is marked as extinct. After the final six days pass, the Extinction timeout elapses and the WINS record is removed from the database.

9. A push partner informs its pull partner that it should pull the changed WINS records when a configured number of changes has been recorded to the WINS database. A pull partner requests all changed records from the WINS database at regularly configured intervals.

B

Day 19—Configuring Network Servers to Use TCP/IP

1. Bindings can be configured on a Windows NT Server to optimize every network services network protocol order. If all the client connections are performed primarily using TCP/IP, for example, TCP/IP can be moved to the top of the binding order for the server service. If most client connections are to another server using IPX/SPX, the workstation service bindings can be configured to have IPX/SPX as the first protocol binding.

2. Packet filtering can be implemented in the Enable Security option in the Advanced option of the IP Address tab in the TCP/IP Protocol Properties. Filters can be configured either by TCP port, UDP port, or IP protocol number. Note that these filters are not implemented at the kernel level and are not as secure as an actual firewall implementation.

3. The `inetcfg` NLM is used to start the TCP/IP installation process on an IntranetWare server. This NLM also enables you to configure TCP/IP on the IntranetWare server.

4. A Domain SAP/RIP Server (DSS) is a distributed Btrieve database that replicates every service and route within a NetWare/IP domain. DSS is used to reduce the number of broadcasts associated with SAP and RIP by storing the same information in this Btrieve database.

5. The UNIX kernel must be rebuilt on a UNIX server when a new network adapter is installed. Depending on the version of UNIX, this could involve a compilation of C language programs. The compilation is based on the script stored in the configuration file stored in the `/usr/sys/conf` directory.

6. A UNIX server that determines which daemon will handle an Internet request from a remote client uses the `inetd` daemon. The `inetd` daemon also determines how the daemon will act when the session is closed.

7. You can use the command `netstat -r` to view the routing table on a UNIX server.

Day 20—Configuring Client Software

1. You can add a network adapter to a Windows 9x installation by launching the Add New Hardware Wizard to install the necessary drivers. The Add New Hardware Wizard can be launched from the Add New Hardware applet in the Control Panel.

2. The phrase "Total Cost of Ownership" refers to all the costs involved with operating a client computer system, including the hardware, maintenance, and support costs related to a client system.

3. If a TCP/IP client is installed on a single segment LAN, it will require an IP address and a subnet mask for a minimum TCP/IP configuration.

4. A manually entered configuration setting takes precedence over a DHCP setting if a manual configuration is set. To prevent this from taking place, you must implement system policies that restrict a user's access to the Network Control Panel applet.

5. The Domain Suffix Search order provides additional Internet domain names that will be appended to a hostname when a hostname is resolved using DNS.

6. The SNMP service allows a Windows NT Workstation to be managed by an SNMP manager. It also allows the Windows NT Workstation to report issues via SNMP traps to an SNMP management system. In addition, the SNMP service installs the TCP/IP objects and counters for the Windows NT Performance Monitor.

7. A third-party TCP/IP stack or suite might be installed if the third-party software provides additional functionality. For example, if you required NFS clients and servers to be implemented, a third-party TCP/IP suite may include this software in its bundle.

8. Thin client models that are currently deployed include X-Window systems, Citrix Winframe/Microsoft Terminal Servers, Java Virtual Machines running on network computers, and Web browsers.

Day 21—Future Applications of TCP/IP

1. You can assign an Anycast address to multiple interfaces that are generally on distinct hosts. When a packet is sent to an Anycast address, the packet is delivered to only one of the interfaces associated with the Anycast address. This is generally the "nearest" address based on routing table distance. If one of the routers goes down, the packet can be sent to another host with the same Anycast address.

2. When data is sent to an Anycast address, it is sent to only one of the interfaces that has the same Anycast address. Data sent to a multicast address is sent to all interfaces that have registered the multicast address.

3. The following IPv6 addresses are:

Address	Address Type
0:0:0:0:0:0:0:1	The loopback address
0:0:0:0:0:FFFF:AC10:0210	An IPv4-mapped IPv6 address
0:0:0:0:0:0:0:0	The unspecified address
0:0:0:0:0:0:C0A8:0344	An IPv4-compatible IPv6 address
FF0E:2322::AD56:0230	A Global Scope Multicast Address

4. Under IPv6, the Maximum Transmission Unit (MTU) for the entire path between source and destination hosts is determined. This allows all fragmentation to be performed by the source node. The packet does not have to be fragmented again as it crosses routers along the delivery path as in IPv4, resulting in a more efficient fragmentation process.

5. Security is increased under IPv6 with the introduction of the Authentication Options header and the Encapsulating Security Payload (ESP) header. The Authentication Options header provides a mechanism for strong authentication of IP datagrams. The ESP header provides integrity and confidentiality to IP datagrams by encrypting the data in the data portion of the ESP header.

6. The following methods have been proposed to help convert from IPv4 to IPv6: Installing a dual IP layer that supports both IPv4 and IPv6 for all hosts and routers, and IPv6 over IPv4 tunneling. This method encapsulates an IPv6 packet within an IPv4 header. This allows transit over an IPv4 network using IPv4 routing mechanisms.

7. You can use voice coders or waveform coders to convert voice input into a digital format for transport over the Internet. Voice coders use the speech input to create a signal that resembles the original voice input. Waveform coders directly encode the waveform generated by analog speech by sampling the voice input and converting the amplitude of each sample to the nearest value from a finite set of discrete values.

8. The issues that need to be resolved before Voice over IP becomes widely implemented include:

   • Voice over IP requires timely delivery.

   • Because most users are assigned random IP addresses when they connect to the Internet, a centralized directory service is required to allow hosts to be found for communication sessions.

   • The need for similar equipment at each end of the connection must be removed.

   • Voice over IP requires a large amount of bandwidth for the timely transport of digitized voice data.

APPENDIX C

Glossary of Terms

10BASE-2 Also known as *thin ethernet*, this wiring standard allows for network segments of up to 185 meters on coaxial cable.

10BASE-5 Also known as *thick ethernet*, this wiring standard allows for network segments up to 500 meters on coaxial cable.

10BASE-T This wiring standard is commonly used with both star and ring networks. The 10-BASE-T wiring standard allows for cable length segments of 100 meters from the central wiring hub.

Abort Output (AO) This allows the running process to continue running until completed. It stops the sending of output to the remote user's terminal screen, however, during a Telnet session.

Abstract Syntax Notation One (ASN.1) The notation used to define each object within the Management Information Base (MIB). ASN.1 describes the name of the object and the syntax used to access the object.

Active Users This service returns a message to the calling system informing it of all the users currently active on the system running the Active Users service. The Active Users service can be called on both TCP and UDP port 11.

Address (A)   An address resource record is used to map a hostname to an IP address.

Address Resolution Protocol (ARP)   This Internet layer protocol provides address resolution between IP addresses and physical MAC addresses on network interfaces.

aliases   email addresses that actually reference a different email mailbox. Aliases are commonly set up to reference a function within an organization (for example, personnel@org.com), rather than a person.

ANDing process   The process of determining whether a source host is located on a local network or on a remote network in the TCP/IP protocol. The process involves comparing the source and destination IP addresses to the source's subnet mask.

anycast address   An IPv6 address that can be assigned to multiple interfaces that are generally on different hosts. Data sent to an anycast address is delivered to the "nearest" interface that is assigned the anycast address.

Application-level firewalls   These firewalls perform an evaluation of data at the application layer before a connection between two hosts is established. Connection states, sequencing information, user passwords, and specific service requests are all monitored.

Archie   A search utility that allows a client to search for specific files stored in anonymous FTP file archives.

Are You There (AYT)   This function enables remote users to determine whether their connection to the Telnet server is still functioning.

area border router   An OSPF router with interfaces that attach to networks belonging to different areas.

ARPA   In 1957, ARPA, the *Advanced Research Projects Agency*, was commissioned to take the United States' lead in science and technology.

ARPAnet   ARPAnet, the *Advanced Research Projects Agency Network*, was the originator of the network that today is known as the Internet.

ASCII   ASCII, the *American Standard Code for Information Interchange*, is an 8-bit character set used to define all alphanumeric characters. It is the most common implementation of text transmissions on computers.

ATM   *Asynchronous Transfer Mode* (ATM) is an advanced method of packet switching that makes use of fixed-length cells of data. Transmission rates on an ATM network reach 155Mbps but could theoretically reach 1.2Gbps. An Asynchronous Transmission Mode backbone was introduced on the Internet in 1996 when NSFNET officially contracted out the Internet backbone to privatized companies.

ATMARP   A revised version of ARP used in an ATM network that resolves an IP address to an ATM address rather than a physical MAC address.

authentication   The validation of a user/password combination to a server's account information database. Different mechanisms can be implemented to validate the user with the server.

authentication server   The server at which users and network services register their private/public key pairs.

authenticator   A Kerberos message that contains the current time and other identifying information about the user establishing the session that is locked using the assigned session key. Authenticators are used to prevent impersonation.

autonomous system   A network that is managed by a single network administrator. This is commonly used to represent your internal network.

autonomous system boundary router   An OSPF router that exchanges routing information with routers from an external autonomous system.

backbone area   A special area in an OSPF network that has been assigned the area ID of 0.0.0.0. The backbone area acts as a routing hub for traffic between areas.

backbone router   An OSPF router that has an interface attached to the backbone area.

backup designated router   A backup router used to exchange routing information within an OSPF area elected in case the designated router fails.

B-Node   A NetBIOS name resolution method that uses broadcast methods to resolve a NetBIOS name to an IP address after the NetBIOS name cache is checked. If this fails, the host attempts to resolve the NetBIOS name to an IP address using the LMHOSTS file, the HOSTS file, and DNS.

BBN   Bolt, Beranak, and Newman (BBN) were contracted by ARPA to build the ARPAnet.

Berkeley Internet Name Daemon (BIND)   A common method of configuring DNS name servers that utilizes a named.boot file to configure the DNS name server.

Berkeley R-Utilities   A set of remote commands that enable remote users to run processes and applications as though they were local users on the systems hosting the remote daemons.

binary   The binary notation system is the underlying method used to represent IP addresses assigned to hosts.

BinHex   A file encoding system initially implemented for Macintosh systems. BinHex converts a binary file into an encrypted text version using hexadecimal characters. BinHex attachments are generally saved with the extension .hqx.

BNC   British Naval Connectors (BNC) are used to connect coaxial cable in a bus topology network.

BOOTP protocol   This protocol is used to automatically configure a host with an IP address. In addition to an IP address, additional options can also be assigned to the client.

Border Gateway Protocol (BGP)   This protocol allows autonomous systems to exchange network reachability information. BGP improves on the EGP protocol by including all autonomous systems that must be crossed in transit to the destination network. This helps to develop a network layout graph and identify routing loops for removal from the routing tables.

boundary layers   A protocol located in one layer of a layered model needs to interact only with protocols located in the layers immediately above or below its layer. This helps the development of new protocols because they have to interface only with their defined boundary layers.

Break (BRK)   This Telnet function is used by many systems to indicate that the Break or Attention key has been invoked.

bridging   The process of transferring data between two segments of a network that share the same logical network address. This occurs at the data link layer of the OSI model.

broadcasting   This transmission method is used to send a message to every host on a network segment. Broadcasting is not an efficient communication mechanism in that all hosts on a network segment must inspect the datagram to determine whether it is intended for them.

bus network   A network topology in which every computer is connected by a single cable segment.

caching-only name server   A DNS name server that does not store any zone data locally. All information is obtained via DNS requests to other DNS name servers. The results are cached and DNS responses are formulated from the cache (if found in the cache).

CAN A campus area network (CAN) uses wide area network (WAN) technologies to join local area networks (LANs) on a university campus.

Canonical Name (CNAME) This resource record is used to provide alias names to a hostname. It is configured in forward-lookup zones.

Challenged Handshake Authentication Protocol (CHAP) An authentication mechanism that uses a three-step process. In the first step, the server sends a challenge string and its hostname to the client. In the second step, the client uses the hostname to determine the shared secret between the client and server. This shared secret is used to encrypt the challenge string. In the final step, the encrypted challenge string is returned to the server. The server performs the same encryption and compares the results. If they match, the client is authenticated.

Character Generator This service returns a list of all 95 printable ASCII characters. It can be called on both TCP and UDP port 19.

Circuit-level firewalls These firewalls act as a referee for connections. Each connection request is monitored to ensure that a correct TCP three-way handshake takes place. If it does not, the connection is dropped. In addition, a session table is established that contains all the current sessions. If any communication sequences do not follow their normal course, the connection is terminated.

Citrix Winframe This thin client methodology allows clients to use sessions on a central terminal server. This server is capable of running DOS, WIN16, and WIN32 applications.

Class A addresses This class of IP address allocates the first 8 bits to the network portion of the IP address and the remaining 24 bits to the host portion of the address.

Class B addresses This class of IP address allocates the first 16 bits to the network portion of an IP address and the remaining 16 bits to the host portion of the address.

Class C addresses This class of IP address allocates the first 24 bits to the network portion of an IP address and the remaining 8 bits to the host portion of the address.

Class D addresses This class of address is used for addressing multicast groups. The first 4 bits are set to 1110, and the remaining 24 bits represent the actual multicast group address.

Classless Inter-Domain Routing (CIDR) An addressing scheme that removes the concept of classes of IP addresses. Each address is simply a combination of network and host portions that do not have a specific number of bits assigned to each part.

community name   A low-level method of security implemented in SNMP. The community name must match the SNMP management system and the SNMP agent for SNMP requests to take place.

Compressed Serial Line Internet Protocol (CSLIP)   A version of the SLIP protocol that allows compression of data over the point-to-point connection.

configured tunneling   A preconfigured tunnel endpoint that an IPv6 packet uses to transmit data to an IPv6 destination address over an IPv4 network. The encapsulated data is delivered to this endpoint where it is unencapsulated and delivered to the IPv6 destination host.

convergence time   The amount of time it takes a network to adjust to a topology change and recalculate all the routing tables for the network.

count to infinity problem   A routing scenario in which each router informs its neighbor that it knows the route to a no-longer-accessible network. Each exchange causes the metric to increase by one until the maximum hop count is reached, at which time the route is discarded.

CSMA/CD   Generally, *carrier-sense multiple access with collision detection* is used with bus topologies. A station listens to the physical network to determine whether another host is currently transmitting data on the network. If a collision occurs, the sending stations must wait a random period of time before attempting to retransmit.

CSU/DSU   A *channel service unit/data service unit* converts network data into digital bipolar signals that are able to traverse a synchronous communications environment.

DARPA   ARPA was renamed the Defense Advanced Research Projects Agency in 1972.

Data Transfer Process (DTP)   The FTP protocol uses the Data Transfer Process for the actual transfer of data between the FTP client and FTP server.

database description packets   Packets sent from the master OSPF router to slave OSPF routers that contain descriptions of the master router's Link State Database (LSDB).

Daytime   This service returns a message that contains the current date and time to the connection system. A connection is established using TCP or UDP port 13.

DCE   A *Data Communications Equipment* device takes input from a DTE (*Data Terminal Equipment*) device and transforms the input signal before sending it across a wide area network. A modem is an example of a DCE device.

DDNS NOTIFY A DDNS message that allows a master name server to inform its configured slave name servers that a DDNS update should take place.

DDNS UPDATE A DDNS message that includes updated information for a hostname participating in the DDNS system.

default route A "catch-all" route used if an explicit route is not defined in the routing table for a destination network.

de-militarized zone A network configuration in which all services available to the outside world are located on their own private network segment rather than in the internal network.

designated router The router used as a central contact point for routing information exchange within an OSPF area.

DHCP Ack The final phase in a DHCP exchange. The DHCP server acknowledges that the DHCP lease has been assigned to the client. Any options requested by the DHCP client are sent at this time.

DHCP Discover The first phase in a DHCP exchange. This message is sent by a DHCP client to indicate that it requires an IP address from a DHCP server.

DHCP Nack This DHCP message is sent from the DHCP server to a DHCP client when the DHCP client has requested an IP address that cannot be used on that segment of the network.

DHCP Offer The second phase in a DHCP exchange. This message, sent by a DHCP server, indicates an IP address that it is willing to assign to the DHCP client.

DHCP relay agent An agent that forwards DHCP broadcast requests to DHCP servers located on remote subnets.

DHCP Request The third phase in a DHCP exchange. This message is sent by the DHCP client to indicate the DHCP offer that it has accepted.

Dijkstra algorithm A routing algorithm used to find the shortest path from a single source node to every other node in the network.

Discard This service discards all information that is sent to it on either TCP or UDP port 9. It is often used to test routing.

distance vector protocols Broadcast-based protocols that primarily use hop counts as the routing metric. These protocols propagate the entire routing table between neighboring routers.

Distinguished Name   The full X.500 name for an object within the X.500 directory services tree. This includes all containers back to the ROOT of the X.500 tree.

distribution list   A single email address that refers to a group of email addresses.

DLCI   DLCIs (*data link connection identifiers*) are used to identify a circuit ID in a frame relay network. DLCIs provide addressing between network segments in a frame relay network.

DNS cache file   A text-based configuration file for a DNS name server that contains the ROOT DNS name servers and their IP addresses.

DNS Manager   The Windows NT utility that provides the ability to configure a DNS name server in Windows NT.

DNS resolvers   The client that performs the query to resolve a hostname to an IP address.

Domain Name Space (DNS)   The hierarchical name database containing the entire name space for the Internet that replaced HOSTS.TXT on the Internet. DNS provides name resolution to every host on the Internet.

Domain SAP/RIP Server (DSS)   A distributed Btrieve database that replicates all the services and routes within a NetWare/IP domain. DSS is used to reduce the number of broadcasts associated with SAP and RIP by storing the same information in a Btrieve database.

DTE   *Data Terminal Equipment* is any device that has the capability to transmit information in a digital format over a communications line. A data terminal is an example of a DTE device.

Dual-ring network   A network topology, consisting of a primary and secondary ring, in which data flows in opposite directions. The secondary ring is used only when a break in the primary ring occurs.

Dynamic DNS   A modified Domain Name Space methodology that allows for the dynamic registration and release of domain name space names.

Dynamic Host Configuration Protocol (DHCP)   This protocol allows a pool of IP addresses (scope) to be created that can be dynamically assigned to configured clients. Each scope can have options configured that will be assigned to DHCP clients.

dynamic packet filter firewalls   These firewalls combine the services of application-level firewalls and packet filter firewalls. The added advantage of this firewall is that security rules can be implemented as the service is running. This allows filters to be created for UDP connections.

dynamic routing   The automatic configuration of all routing paths through the network. This is accomplished by implementing routing protocols that advertise changes to the network topology.

EBCDIC   The *Extended Binary Coded Decimal Interchange Code* is a text representation method used extensively on IBM mainframe and mini computers.

Echo   This service returns as a response any information that is passed to it. Connections are established on either TCP or UDP port 7.

encryption   The protection of transmitted data by "scrambling" the data with a method that can be deciphered only by the intended recipient.

Enhanced B-Node   A Microsoft-specific resolution method that first uses a broadcast to resolve a NetBIOS name to an IP address once the NetBIOS name cache has been checked. If that fails, the LMHOSTS file will be consulted to attempt to resolve the NetBIOS name to an IP address. If the Enable DNS for Windows option is selected, the client will also check the HOSTS file and DNS for name resolution.

Erase Character (EC)   This Telnet function deletes the last character input by the remote user.

Erase Line (EL)   This Telnet function is used to delete the contents of the current "line" of input.

ethernet   This network is based on Carrier-Sense Multiple Access with Collision Detection (CSMA/CD). The development of ethernet allowed for the proliferation of local area networks.

extended network prefix   The combination of the network and subnetwork portions of a subnet mask.

Exterior Gateway Protocol (EGP)   An interdomain reachability protocol that allows autonomous systems to exchange routing reachability information on the Internet.

exterior gateway protocols   Protocols used to exchange routing information between other organizations or autonomous systems.

eXternal Data Representation (XDR)   XDR is used by applications such as NFS and NIS to provide a universal format for text transmission between two hosts. It is used to facilitate text transmissions between two hosts using different internal text representations (such as EBCDIC and ASCII).

FDDI   *Fiber Distributed Data Interface* networks allow for high speed, fiber-optic, local area networks running at speeds of 100Mbps. FDDI uses a dual-ring topology.

file encoding   A method of converting binary data into text data so that SMTP clients can transmit binary attachments.

File Transfer Protocol (FTP)   This protocol is used to transfer data from one host to another computer using TCP as the transport protocol.

Firewall   A host that provides a boundary service between the local area network and the external world. Rules can be implemented at the firewall to determine which specific traffic is allowed to cross this boundary service.

forward-lookup zone   A DNS configuration file containing resource records that generally provide hostname to IP address name resolution.

fragmentation   This process occurs when a packet is too large for the underlying network. The packet is broken into smaller fragments that can be transported on the underlying network.

frame relay   An advanced packet switched network that transmits variable length data using Permanent Virtual Circuits over digital networks. Due to the conditioned lines of a digital network, less error correction is built into frame relay than X.25, which results in faster transmission rates.

full adjacent routers   The term used to indicate two routers that have exchanged link state requests.

Fully Qualified Domain Name (FQDN)   The combination of the hostname and the Internet domain of which it is a member. For example, the hostname www in the domain xyz.org would have a FQDN of www.xyz.org.

Generic Routing Encapsulation (GRE)   This protocol is used by the PPTP protocol to transport all data over a virtual private network.

Gopher   A menu-based system that enables users to navigate through the information stored in "Gopherspace." Gopher was developed at the University of Minnesota.

Gopherspace   The collection of a Gopher servers and their data stores on the Internet.

H-Node   A specialized NetBIOS name resolution method that first queries a NetBIOS name server to resolve a NetBIOS name to an IP address. If this does not work, a local broadcast is sent to attempt to resolve the NetBIOS name to an IP address. If this fails, the host attempts to resolve the NetBIOS name to an IP address using the LMHOSTS file, the HOSTS file, and DNS.

hold-downs   The ignoring of routing messages that indicate a dead link is still reachable for a configured period of time (known as the *hold-down time*).

hostname A logical name that is assigned to an IP address. It does not relate directly to any service.

HOSTS file This locally stored TCP/IP configuration file is used to resolve hostnames to IP addresses.

hosts.equiv This file contains entries for hosts, or specific users on a host, that are trusted to connect remotely to a UNIX host. This file is stored in the /etc directory.

HTTP 1.1 host header Host headers allow a Web server to host multiple Web sites but use only a single IP address for each site. The site being accessed by a client is referenced in the host header.

Hypertext Transfer Protocol (HTTP) A request/response protocol that enables a user to view resources stored on the Web. A client requests a page from a Web server, and the Web server responds with the contents of that Web page.

IAB The *Internet Architecture Board* (IAB) is in charge of strategic planning for the Internet.

IANA The *Internet Assigned Number Authority* (IANA) is in charge of setting the policies of how IP addresses are assigned and is in charge of these assignments.

idempotent A disk operation model that leaves the management and tracking of all operations to the client rather than to the server.

IESG The *Internet Engineering Steering Group* (comprised of the area managers and the chairman of the IETF) determines which RFCs can enter the standards track.

IETF The *Internet Engineering Task Force* is concerned primarily with short- to medium-length projects that resolve technical problems and needs that arise as the Internet develops.

InATMARP A modified version of Reverse ARP (RARP) used in an ATM network. InATMARP resolves an ATM address to an IP address.

increment value The value used to determine the starting address for each pool of addresses in a subnetted network.

Independent Computing Architecture The line protocol used to communicate between the client system and the Citrix server in a Citrix Winframe environment. This line protocol can run over any transport protocol.

interior gateway protocols Protocols that are used to exchange routing information within an autonomous system.

internal router   An OSPF router whose network interfaces are all connected to networks belonging to the same area.

Internet Control Message Protocol (ICMP)   This Internet layer protocol provides an error reporting mechanism and control messages to the TCP/IP protocol suite.

Internet Daemon (inetd)   This service is used to launch the appropriate daemon when an Internet protocol request is received by a UNIX host. The `INETD` daemon reviews the `inet.conf` file to determine which daemon is associated with the requested service.

Internet Group Management Protocol (IGMP)   This protocol is used to define groups of computers that share a common multicast address.

Internet Mail Access Protocol (IMAP)   A newer protocol that allows clients to retrieve email messages from a server. It also allows messages to be stored in a hierarchical structure on the IMAP server.

Internet Protocol (IP)   This Internet layer protocol provides the logical addressing used for hosts in a TCP/IP network. This protocol is also used in determining whether a packet must be routed to a remote network or sent on the local network.

Interrupt Process (IP)   This provides the ability to suspend or interrupt a process running on the Telnet server.

inverse query   A DNS resolution method that resolves a queried IP address to a fully qualified domain name.

IPv6   The next implementation of the Internet Protocol (IP) that expands the address space from a 32-bit address scheme to a 128-bit address scheme. IPv6 also uses a simplified header that allows for easier extensibility of the protocol.

IPv6/IPv4 nodes   Hosts with the capability of sending and receiving IPv6 and IPv4 packets. This allows them to communicate directly with IPv4-only and IPv6-only hosts.

IRSG   The *Internet Research Steering Group* sets the priorities and coordinates all research projects for the IRTF.

IRTF   The *Internet Research Task Force* is in charge of all research activities related to TCP/IP protocols (including any proposed changes to the Internet architecture).

ISDN   *Integrated Services Digital Network* is a digital service that is available in two formats: Basic Rate ISDN and Primary Rate ISDN. Basic Rate ISDN provides two B channels of 64Kbps and one D channel that can provide transmission rates of 16Kbps. Primary Rate ISDN can provide up to 1.544Mbps over 23 B channels and uses a D channel of 64Kbps for signal and link management.

ISO The *International Standards Organization* works to establish global standards for communications and information exchange.

iterative query A DNS name resolution method that returns a definitive answer from the DNS name server to the DNS resolver. This answer can be a referral to a different DNS name server that may be able to resolve the logical name to an IP address, the IP address of the host, or a response that the hostname could not be resolved.

Java Virtual Machine This thin client architecture allows small JavaScript applets to be launched from a central server and executed on a local client device.

Jughead *Jonzy's Universal Gopher Hierarchy Excavation and Display* is an alternative search engine for Gopherspace. The index for a Jughead search includes both top-level and nested menu items.

Jumbo Payload hop-by-hop option An IPv6 packet that has a payload greater than 65,636 bytes. This is indicated by a payload length field that is set to a value of zero.

Kerberos authentication A method of authentication and data encryption that enables users to authenticate with services and to validate themselves to users based on private/public key technology.

kernel proxy firewalls These firewalls are implemented at the kernel level of the underlying operating system. Kernel proxy firewalls increase security because data is not passed up the levels of the network stack if a rule is broken.

LAN *Local area network* computers operate together in a contained area connected with high bandwidth media.

LAT The *Local Address Table* is configured on a firewall to determine the IP addressing scheme implemented on the interior network.

Layer 2 Tunneling Protocol (L2TP) This tunneling protocol is in the draft stage for becoming an RFC. It combines the technology of Microsoft's PPTP protocol and Cisco's Layer two forwarding protocol.

Lightweight Directory Access Protocol (LDAP) A protocol that allows names to be found in a diverse directory services implementation. LDAP offers a standardized method for storing and retrieving names from directory services.

Line Printer Daemon (LPD) This service allows a server to accept print jobs from remote TCP/IP hosts and print them to a local printer.

Line Printer Router (LPR) This service is used to send a print job to a server running the Line Printer Daemon (LPD) or to a TCP/IP printer.

Link Control Protocol (LCP)   A PPP extension used to establish, configure, and test a data link connection.

Link State Advertisement (LSA)   The network advertisements used to build the OSPF link state database. These advertisements include each OSPF interface on a router, the attached networks for the router, and the cost to reach each of the attached networks.

Link State Database (LSDB)   Existing on each router interface in the network, this database contains entries for each network and the outgoing cost assigned to each network interface of a router.

link state protocols   These protocols flood routing information to all nodes in the network. This routing information contains routes to directly attached networks only. Even though these routing messages are sent to every router on the network, their reduced size results in a more efficient exchange of routing information.

Link state request   Requests for Link state advertisements based on the database description packets received from a master or slave router. The link state request contains the entries required to complete its own link state database.

LMHOSTS (LAN Manager Hosts) file   This Microsoft-specific TCP/IP configuration file is used to auto-load NetBIOS names into the NetBIOS name cache, resolve NetBIOS names to IP addresses, and configure important NetBIOS servers on the network.

logical IP subnets (LIS)   Logical IP subnets are used in an ATM environment to group ATM hosts into a closed IP subnetwork. Multiple LISs can exist on the same physical network segment. For traffic to be routed between the LISs, one ATM device must be configured as a member of each LIS.

longest match route   The route in a routing table that most specifically defines the route to the destination network. This is used when variable length subnet masking is implemented.

MAC address   The *Media Access Control* address is the physical address of a network interface card.

Mail Exchanger (MX) records   Mail Exchange records are used to indicate the host that accepts email messages for an Internet domain. Priorities can be configured so that multiple mail exchangers can be configured for a single Internet domain using the preference field.

MAN   A *metropolitan area network* is a distributed computer network joined by telecommunication links that reside in a close geographic area.

Management Information Base (MIB)   A database used to specify the details that a managed device will report to an SNMP management system.

master name server   A DNS name server that transfers its zone information to a secondary name server. Both a primary name server and a secondary name server can function as a master name server.

master servers   NIS servers that maintain the original copy of the NIS database.

MAU   A *Multistation Access Unit* is the connecting mechanism in a ring topology network.

Maximum Receive Unit (MRU)   The maximum length of the data field in a PPP packet. It is the largest size of data stream that can be received by a PPP client/server. The default value is 1,500 bytes.

Maximum Transmission Unit (MTU)   The largest packet size that can be used on a network segment. Routers use the MTU to determine whether a packet must be fragmented during transmission over a network segment.

mesh network   A mesh network connects remote sites over telecommunication links. The defining characteristic of a mesh network is that routers are able to search multiple paths to determine the best route to take at that moment.

metrics   Costs or values assigned to a property of a network link. Metrics are used to determine the lowest cost route to a destination network. Common metrics include hop count, delay, throughput, reliability, and communication costs.

MILNET   The *Military Network* evolved in 1983 when the ARPAnet was split into military and public access networks.

M-Node   A specialized NetBIOS name resolution method that first uses broadcasts to resolve a NetBIOS name to an IP address after checking the NetBIOS name cache. If this fails, a query is sent to the configured NetBIOS name server. If this fails, the host attempts to resolve the NetBIOS name to an IP address using the LMHOSTS file, the HOSTS file, and DNS.

mount protocol   A protocol that provides the NFS protocol with the necessary tools to share a network drive based on the underlying operating system.

mounting   The process that creates a file handle to connect a client to a remote file source so that it appears to be a local resource.

MS loopback adapter   A virtual network card that can be installed on a Windows NT-class computer to allow TCP/IP to be installed on the computer and bound to the loopback adapter.

multicast address   An IP address that is assigned to multiple interfaces on different hosts. Data sent to a multicast address is delivered to *every* interface assigned the multicast address.

multicasting   This transmission method is used to send a single message to a predefined group of computers. All multicast messages are sent using UDP as the transport protocol.

multiplexing ports   A method that allows multiple sessions to be connected to a single port on a host. This is possible because the other end of the connection will always have a unique combination of IP address, port, and protocol.

multipurpose Internet mail extensions (MIME)   A file encoding system that provides a mechanism for translating non-ASCII messages into an ASCII format for transmission over the Internet. Different MIME types are defined that allow each file category to be encoded in a defined manner.

name discovery   The process of resolving a NetBIOS name to an IP address.

name registration   The process of registering a NetBIOS name on a network.

name release   The process of releasing a NetBIOS name from the network.

name server (NS)   The Name Server resource record is used to indicate which hosts contain copies of a domain's zone file.

named daemon   On a UNIX-based DNS name server, this is the daemon (service) that runs which provides the DNS name server services.

Named.boot   A configuration file in BIND-compatible DNS name servers that provides startup information for the named daemon.

NCP   The *Network Control Protocol* (NCP) was the initial protocol used to communicate between hosts on the ARPAnet. The TCP/IP protocol suite replaced this protocol on January 1, 1983.

NETASCII   A TFTP mode used for the transfer of 8-bit ASCII data between a TFTP client and a TFTP server.

NetBIOS Name Server (NBNS)   A centralized server configured to accept NetBIOS registrations and releases from clients. NBNS also resolves queried NetBIOS names to an IP address.

NetBIOS names Logical names assigned to computers, domains, and users in a network, such as Windows NT, that use NetBIOS as an upper-layer protocol.

NetBIOS Node Type A NetBIOS configuration parameter that determines the resolution methods used to resolve a NetBIOS name to an IP address. The NetBIOS Node Type can be configured to be either B-Node, P-Node, M-Node, or H-Node.

Netconfig This program is used by SCO UNIX to update the UNIX kernel when configuration changes are performed to the UNIX host.

NETSTAT This TCP/IP command enables the network administrator to investigate current port usage and port connections.

NetWare Loadable Modules (NLMs) The utilities that are executed on a NetWare system console using the `load name.nlm` command.

network address translation (NAT) An addressing scheme in which the internal network's IP addresses are hidden from the external network. Every internal address is replaced with a common external address when packets are passed through a firewall to the external world.

Network Control Protocol (NCP) Used by a PPP connection to establish and configure different network-layer protocols.

network file system (NFS) A protocol that allows transparent access to remote file services for networked clients.

Network Information System (NIS) A global and centralized information database that allows user account information to be synchronized between hosts in a UNIX environment.

Network Lock Manager (NLM) This service provides file-locking capabilities to the NFS protocol.

network management In the case of SNMP, network management is the management of the physical devices that make up the network infrastructure. This includes routers, bridges, and hubs. This can also refer to the logical management of the network, such as the management of users, groups, disk and printer resources, and network security.

Network News Transfer Protocol (NNTP) This protocol is used to facilitate the reading and posting of documents stored on Internet News servers.

network segment A physical section of the network that is separated from all other areas of the network by a routing device.

network sniffers   These devices (or software applications) capture network traffic and analyze what is being transmitted.

Network Virtual Terminal (NVT)   This provides a common endpoint at each end of a Telnet communication session that defines what functionality is provided. An NVT defines the minimum feature set for a Telnet session.

NETWORKS file   This locally stored TCP/IP configuration file is used to assign logical names to network IP addresses.

NIS domain   A collection of hosts that share the same NIS database for user authentication.

NIS maps   The configuration files that contain the NIS database consisting of keys and values.

Non-Broadcast Multiple Access (NBMA) networks   Networks that do not have the capability of transporting multicasts or broadcasts. An example of this network is an X.25 network.

NSFnet   In 1985, the National Science Foundation created a T1 backbone network that replaced the ARPAnet as the primary network backbone.

NSLOOKUP   A tool commonly used to troubleshoot and verify the configuration of a DNS name server. This tool can be run in either batch mode or interactive mode. Interactive mode allows for multiple DNS queries to be performed at once.

object identifier   The unique hierarchical identifier that defines each object within the Management Information Base (MIB).

octet   A collection of eight bits of information. An IPv4 address consists of four octets of data.Class.

octet mode   A TFTP transfer mode used for transferring binary data between a TFTP client and a TFTP server using raw 8-bit bytes.

one's complement   A mathematical method used to calculate a checksum on both TCP and UDP headers to ensure that the data has not been corrupted in transit from the source host to destination host.

Open Shortest Path First (OSPF)   A link state routing protocol that builds a link state database at each router interface. From this database, the shortest path to each network address is determined.

OSI The *Open Systems Interconnect* reference model is a seven-layer networking model that describes the flow of data from the physical network connection to an end-user network application.

P-Node A NetBIOS name resolution method that queries a NetBIOS name server to resolve NetBIOS names to IP addresses only after the NetBIOS name cache is checked. If this fails, the host attempts to resolve the NetBIOS name to an IP address by using the LMHOSTS file, the HOSTS file, and DNS.

packet filter firewalls A firewall implementation that analyzes traffic at the transport layer of the OSI model. Each incoming/outgoing packet is scrutinized and compared to a set of rules that will either accept or reject the packet.

Packet Internet Groper (PING) The PING utility is commonly used to inspect the TCP/IP configuration of a TCP/IP host or to test the "reachability" of a network host. This utility uses the ICMP protocol to determine "reachability."

packet switched network A network that delivers data by breaking it into smaller packets. These packets are routed from the source to the destination host on an individual basis. Each packet may take a different route through the network but is reassembled at the destination host.

PAD A *Packet Assembler/Disassembler* breaks large blocks of data into packets for transmission over an X.25 network. At the destination network, the PAD reassembles the packets.

passwd file This file is used for determining valid login accounts on a UNIX system.

Password Authentication Protocol (PAP) An authentication mechanism that uses a two-step process. In the first step, clients transmit their account/password combination. In the second step, the server compares the account/password combination to its secret database and either accepts or rejects the connection attempt.

peer-to-peer network A LAN configuration where all the participants function as both clients and servers.

phone gateways A next-generation voice over IP solution that enables a person to dial directly into a phone gateway using a normal phone, and use the Internet as a backbone network to connect to another phone in a remote location.

Point-to-Point Protocol (PPP) A standardized protocol that has been developed to solve the problems of encapsulating the IP protocol over point-to-point links. PPP allows the automatic assignment of IP addresses to remote clients, the ability to transport multiple protocols over the same link, the ability to negotiate options between the client and server, and automatic error detection.

Point-to-Point Tunneling Protocol (PPTP)   A Microsoft-specific protocol that allows IP, NetBEUI, or IPX to be encapsulated within an IP header for transmission across an intermediary network.

Pointer (PTR)   This resource record is found in reverse lookup files. These records relate an IP address to a specific hostname.

poison reverse   When a router learns about a network on a specific interface, it will send out advertisements on that interface that the network is unreachable. If the network is up, the receiving routers will maintain their current routing information. If the network is down, the routes will be dropped, because the infinity value has already been reached.

portmapper   A service that determines whether a requested application is running on a specific server. This service returns the correct port number that the application is accepting connections on to the calling client.

ports   A host can provide access to multiple applications. When a client connects to the host for a specific application, a port is used to provide access to that specific application. Well-known ports are assigned port addresses between 0 and 1023.

Post Office Protocol 3 (POP3)   A protocol used by email clients to retrieve email messages from a server using TCP as the transport protocol.

primary name server   The DNS name server in which the actual zone configuration files are stored. All updates to the zone data files should be performed on this name server.

protocol   A method of packaging information as it is transferred between two networked hosts.

Protocol Data Unit (PDU)   The actual definitions of the SNMP message formats. The following PDUs are supported in SNMPv2: GetRequest, GetNextRequest, GetBulk, SetRequest, GetResponse, and Trap.

PROTOCOL file   This locally stored TCP/IP configuration file contains the protocol ID numbers that have been configured for the standard TCP/IP protocols.

Protocol Interpreter (PI)   The FTP protocol uses the Protocol Interpreter to transfer FTP commands between the FTP client and FTP server.

proxy services   Services that act on behalf of a client performing requests to the external world. The client issues the request to the proxy service and the proxy service performs the request. When a response is received, the proxy service returns the result set to the calling client.

pseudo header   A pseudo header is a header that is comprised of fields from more than a single header in a data stream. In TCP and UDP, the pseudo header is comprised of fields from the TCP/UDP header and fields from the IP header.

PSTN   Public Switched Telephone Networks are circuit-switched networks that can be used for data traffic as a wide area networking solution as well as for voice data.

Quote of the Day   This service returns a quotation from a central file of quotations by connecting to it on TCP or UDP port 17.

reassembly   The reassembly process occurs when the fragmented packets reach the destination network. The fragmented packets are reassembled into their original packet based on the fragment IDs.

recursive query   A DNS name resolution method that returns either the answer to the DNS query or an error stating that the name could not be resolved.

Remote Access Service (RAS)   The Windows NT service that is used to configure the Windows NT PPP server and SLIP/PPP client software.

Remote Copy Protocol (RCP)   This utility enables you to copy directories and their contents to and from a remote host. The RCP utility is part of the Berkeley R-Utilities suite.

Remote Desktop Protocol   A protocol based on the ITU T.120 protocol. It allows Microsoft terminal servers to send optimized transmissions to remote clients, which includes the transmission of the screen, mouse, and keyboard data between the terminal server and the thin client.

Remote Procedure Call (RPC)   A procedure executed on a remote system at the security level of the calling user.

RESOLV.CONF file   This TCP/IP configuration file is used to store the DNS configuration information for a UNIX host. This file is located on a DNS resolver.

resource records   The records that are stored in a DNS name server configuration file. Resource records can include Address (A), Pointer (PTR), Mail Exchange (MX), and Canonical Name (CNAME) records.

Resource Reservation Protocol (RSVP)   A protocol that is able to request a specific amount of bandwidth from the source host to the destination host. This provides the minimum bandwidth pipe required for the transmission of Voice over IP.

retransmission timers   These timers are used during a TCP connection to determine a resend time if an acknowledgment is not received in a timely manner from the destination host.

Reverse Address Resolution Protocol (RARP)   This protocol is used by a terminal to receive an IP address from an RARP server. The client will broadcast its MAC address, and the RARP server will send a preconfigured IP address to the client.

reverse lookup file   This DNS name server configuration file provides IP address to hostname resolution.

rexec   The rexec (Remote Execute) command allows for remote execution of programs to take place. Unlike rlogin and rsh, the rexec command does not use the HOSTS.EQUIV or .RHOSTS files for determining trusted hosts.

RFCs   *Request for Comments* are the documents that define the TCP/IP protocol suite.

.rhosts   This file allows specific accounts to be named for a remote host. It contains entries for hosts and users that can gain access to the local system.

ring network   A network topology where all computers are connected in a circle. Data travels around the circle in a single direction using a method known as *token passing*.

rlogin   This command enables a user to remotely log in to another system on the network.

root domain   The starting point of the name space for the Internet.

route aggregation   The use of a single route into an enterprise network that can be used to contain the address space of several networks. This is used to reduce the size of Internet backbone routing tables.

router discovery   An extension of the Internet Control Message Protocol (ICMP) that enables hosts attached to multicast or broadcast networks to discover the IP addresses of their neighboring routers.

routing   The process of moving a packet of information from one physical network segment to another physical network segment. This takes place at the Network layer of the OSI model.

Routing Information Protocol (RIP)   A distance vector routing protocol that uses hop count as its routing metric. The hop count is measured as the number of routers that must be navigated from source to destination network. All routing information is exchanged using broadcasts directed to UDP port 520.

Routing Information Protocol (RIP) version 2   An enhancement to the original RIP protocol that includes subnet masks in router announcements, authentication included in routing packets, the use of multicasts instead of broadcasts, and route tags to distinguish internal routes from external routes.

routing loops   The situation that occurs when a series of routers create a circular route to a destination network that simply goes around in circles without ever arriving at the destination network.

routing protocols   Protocols that exchange routing information to build routing tables for a network. After all the known routes are gathered, the routing protocol determines the best route to each destination network.

rsh   The remote shell utility enables you to execute a single command on a remote host without logging in to the remote host.

ruptime   This command displays a list of all machines on the network. It includes statistics on their status, the time they have been "up," the number of active users, and their current load.

rwho   This command displays a list of users on the network.

scope   A pool of IP addresses that can be leased from a DHCP server.

second-level domains   These domains are located below the top-level domains. These names are registered with InterNIC.

secondary name server   A DNS name server that obtains its zone configuration files from another DNS name server known as its *master name server*. A secondary name server is used to provide redundancy in a DNS environment.

Secure Socket Layer (SSL)   A layer implemented between the TCP/IP transport layer and the application layer that encrypts all transmissions between a client and a server.

Serial Line Internet Protocol (SLIP)   A packet framing protocol, SLIP is used for transporting data over a point-to-point connection using a serial line. SLIP defines a specific sequence of characters that frame each IP packet.

Server-based network   A LAN configuration in which all data is stored on centralized server locations.

SERVICES file   This locally stored TCP/IP configuration file is used to assign text names to well-known TCP/IP port addresses. This is used for both TCP and UDP ports.

session key   A separate key that is generated by the authentication server for a specific connection session between a client and a server. This key expires at the completion of the session.

shortest path first (SPF) tree   This tree contains the shortest path through the network for each network and each router. Each router in the network will maintain their own unique shortest path first tree.

Simple Mail Transfer Protocol (SMTP)   This protocol provides mail transfer between two hosts using TCP as the transport protocol.

Simple Network Management Protocol (SNMP)   An application-level protocol that allows for management of network devices including routers, hub, and switches.

slave name servers   An alternate name for secondary name servers. This highlights that the secondary name server receives its zone information from a configured DNS master name server.

Slave servers   NIS servers that maintain a duplicated copy of the master database. It is maintained using the propagation process.

SNMP agent   This component of SNMP exists on managed devices. The SNMP agent responds to queries by filling in the request values and sends SNMP traps to the SNMP management system.

SNMP-enabled   A network device with an SNMP agent built in that responds to SNMP requests.

SNMP management System   This component of SNMP is used to issue queries against SNMP agents to determine the status of an SNMP agent.

SNMP proxy agent   An SNMP agent that functions on behalf of another network device. All SNMP requests are sent to the SNMP proxy agent. The proxy agent then queries the network device by using alternative methods to fulfill the SNMP response.

SNMP trap   A communication in an SNMP system sent from the SNMP agent to the SNMP manager. This occurs when a preconfigured event takes place that the SNMP management system wants to be notified about.

SNMPUTIL   A Windows NT Resource Kit utility that allows queries to be performed against an SNMP agent.

socket   A socket provides an endpoint for a communication session. It is comprised of an IP address, a transport protocol, and a port address.

split horizons   The prevention of sending routing information back in the direction from which it is received. Under split horizons, routes that originated from a specific neighboring router are never sent back to that neighboring router.

star network   A network topology in which each computer is connected to a central hub by a cable segment.

Start of Authority (SOA) The prime configuration resource record for a domain, the SOA provides configuration parameters that describe how primary and secondary name servers interact. It also contains configuration information about how long a DNS name server will cache resolved hostname to IP address resolutions.

static routing The manual configuration of all routing paths through an internetwork. Generally, this is implemented only in smaller networks.

static WINS mappings These mappings are added to a WINS server for non-WINS clients that are not able to register their NetBIOS names with the WINS server.

Structure of Management Information (SMI) A standardized framework for defining the information that can be managed by an SNMP manager. SMI provides a basic format for all managed objects.

sub-domains These domains exist below the second-level domains. These names are registered with the second-level domain below which they exist.

subnet mask A subnet mask determines the dividing point between the network and host portions of an IP address.

supernetting Another term used to represent Classless Inter-Domain Routing (CIDR).

Synchronize (SYNCH) This Telnet function provides a method for remote users to ensure they are able to regain control of the Telnet session in the case of a runaway process.

T1 service A digital line service that provides transmission rates of up to 1.544Mbps. It can carry both voice and data transmissions.

T3 service A digital line service that provides transmissions of up to 45Mbps. It can carry both voice and data transmissions.

TCP A transport-level protocol that provides guaranteed, connection-oriented delivery of data.

TCP/IP A suite of protocols that allows connectivity between heterogeneous environments.

TCP sliding windows A method of providing improved transmissions in a TCP session. Multiple TCP segments can be sent that require only a single acknowledgment from the receiving host.

Telnet   A protocol that provides a bidirectional communication session between two hosts. Telnet uses the TCP protocol to ensure the reliable delivery of information between the two hosts.

Terminal Server   The central server in the Citrix Winframe/Microsoft Terminal Server implementation of thin clients. The terminal server hosts all remote users' client sessions.

thin client   A technology that allows a client to connect to a central server and per-form all of its processing on the remote server. The only information transmitted to the client is the screen output from the central server. The client transmits only keyboard and mouse input to the central server.

Thinwire   The data protocol used by Citrix Winframe to send the actual screen image from the Terminal server to the client station.

ticket   A Kerberos message that contains a copy of the session key and an identifier for the user that wants to communicate with a service. This message is locked by using the service's public key.

Ticket Granting Server (TGS)   A server in a Kerberos environment that grants tick-ets that can increase security. All future tickets are requested from the TGS using the Ticket Granting Ticket. Each reply is encrypted using the session key for the TGS and client. The session key for the requested server is encrypted by the TGS session key.

Ticket Granting Ticket (TGT)   A ticket granted that establishes a session between the client and the ticket granting server.

Time   This service returns the number of seconds that have elapsed since midnight, January 1, 1900, on a connection to TCP or UDP port 37.

time-to-live (TTL)   This option is used to set a maximum lifetime on a datagram. Each time a datagram crosses a router, the datagram's TTL is decremented by at least one. When the TTL reaches a value of zero, the datagram is dropped from the network.

top-level domains   The first level of domain names below the root domain in the domain name space. Top-level domains are broken into types of business and country codes.

total cost of ownership (TCO)   This term refers to the total cost involved with pur-chasing, operating, and maintaining your organization's computers and computing resources.

traceroute   A command used to determine the route to an external network. This com-mand shows each router that is crossed en route to the destination network.

Transmission Control Protocol (TCP) This transport layer protocol provides connection-oriented, reliable delivery of data on a network. The use of TCP requires that a session be established between the source and destination hosts.

Trivial File Transfer Protocol (TFTP) This protocol allows the transfer of files between two hosts using the UDP protocol. The client will connect to UDP port 69 on the TFTP server.

tunneling A network transfer method that allows a routable protocol to transfer the frames of another protocol to a destination network by encapsulating those frames. The frames are decapsulated at the receiving end.

unicast address A unique IP address that is assigned to a single interface.

uniform resource locator (URL) The combination of the protocol, fully qualified domain name, and content that you want to view in a Web browser. For example, `http://www.online-can.com/default.asp` is comprised of the protocol `http`, the fully qualified domain name `www.online-can.com`, and the content to be viewed `default.asp`.

Also, the text description that defines the location of an HTML document on the Internet. This includes the protocol, the server, the directory and the document that is going to be located. For example, the URL `http://www.online-can.com/training/index.htm` describes that the transfer protocol in use will be `http`, the server is `www.online-can.com`, the directory on the server is `/training`, and the file that is being located is `index.htm`.

User Datagram Protocol (UDP) This transport layer protocol provides connection-less, nonguaranteed delivery of data on a network. Applications that use UDP as their transport protocol must provide their own acknowledgment mechanism to provide reliable delivery.

UTP *Unshielded twisted pair* wiring is a cable where the interior wires are twisted around each other a minimum number of twists per foot. This cabling standard does not have any insulation or shielding.

UUEncode UNIX-to-UNIX Encoding is a file encoding system that converts binary data into a series of 7-bit ASCII characters for the transmission of binary data using SMTP. uuencoded files are usually stored with the extension `.uu` or `.uue`.

variable length subnet masking (VLSM) This method of allocating subnet masks allows for different subnet masks to be implemented in the same network. This requires that the routing protocols transmit the subnet mask in their routing information.

Veronica   The *Very Easy Rodent-Oriented Net-wide Index to Computerized Archives* is used to search Gopherspace. Queries are performed against an index that maintains all top-level menus found in Gopherspace.

virtual circuit   A method that allows communication between two defined endpoints to take place through any number of intermediate nodes on a mesh network.

virtual private network (VPN)   The completed link between a tunneling client and a tunneling server. Logically, a VPN appears to be a single hop between the client and the server, even though multiple routers may be crossed in transit.

virtual Web server   This term refers to a Web server that hosts multiple Web sites that appear to be unique Web servers. Each Web site within the Web server is known as a *virtual Web server*. To the external user, virtual Web servers appear to be independent Web servers.

voice codecs   A method of digitizing voice data that converts speech input into a signal that resembles the original voice input. The created signal is analyzed against a speech model and a set of parameters is generated. These parameters are what are transferred to the destination station.

Voice over IP   The use of the Internet as a transport medium for digitized voice data.

Voice over IP (VoIP) Forum   A working group in the International Multimedia Teleconferencing Consortium to further the progress of the Voice over IP development.

WAIS   A *wide area information server* is capable of performing searches on the actual text in documents stored on the server.

WAN   A *wide area network* is a computer network that uses telecommunication links to join computers over a vast geographic area.

waveform codecs   A method of digitizing voice data by sampling the voice input and converting the amplitude of each sample to the nearest value from a finite set of discrete values.

WINS (Windows Internet Name Service)   The Microsoft NetBIOS name server that ships with Windows NT Server. This product functions as a central repository from which NetBIOS clients can register, resolve, and release NetBIOS names.

WINS Lookup   A Windows NT-specific DNS resource record that provides the ability to look up IP addresses of hosts that register their NetBIOS names with a WINS server.

WINS Manager   The Windows NT Server administration utility used to manage a WINS server.

WINS proxy agent   A NetBIOS host that forwards NetBIOS requests from a non-WINS client to a WINS server for resolution. Once the request is resolved, the WINS proxy agent broadcasts the resolution to the local network segment.

WINS pull partner   A WINS server that requests new database entries from its replication partner at regularly scheduled intervals.

WINS push partner   A WINS server that is configured to send notification to its replication partner when a preconfigured number of changes have been applied to its WINS database. This notification acts as a trigger for the replication partner to pull the changes across to its database.

WINS Reverse Lookup (WINS-R)   A Windows NT–specific DNS resource record that provides a method for a DNS name server to look up IP addresses dynamically from a configured WINS server and provide hostname resolution.

World Wide Web (WWW)   The collection of HTML Web servers that are located on the Internet.

X.25   X.25 defines the electrical connection between a terminal and the network, the transmission protocol, and the implementation of virtual circuits between network users. Together, these definitions create a synchronous, full-duplex terminal to network connection. The X.25 protocol has error correcting built in due to its initial implementation on public data networks.

X.500 directory service   A directory standard that defines the different objects and object classes that can be implemented in a directory services tree.

X Window   This thin client system allows graphical screen information from a remote server to be displayed locally. It is commonly used in UNIX environments.

zero subnetting   This is an option available on routers that support the transmission of both the network address and the subnet mask when routing tables are created. The use of zero subnetting allows for a subnet mask of all zeros to be implemented.

zone transfer   The process of transferring DNS zone information from a master name server to a slave name server.

C

INDEX

Symbols

A